ecpr PRESS

Immigration, Integration and Mobility

New Agendas in Migration Studies
Essays 1998–2014

Adrian Favell

ecpr PRESS

© Adrian Favell 2014

First published by the ECPR Press in 2014

© Cover image courtesy of Xessma

The ECPR Press is the publishing imprint of the European Consortium for Political Research (ECPR), a scholarly association, which supports and encourages the training, research and cross-national co-operation of political scientists in institutions throughout Europe and beyond.

ECPR Press
Harbour House
Hythe Quay
Colchester
CO2 8JF
United Kingdom

Typeset by Lapiz

Printed and bound by Lightning Source

British Library Cataloguing in Publication Data

A catalogue record for this book is available from the British Library

ISBN: 978-1-907-301-72-8
PDF ISBN: 978-1-910-259-47-4
EPUB ISBN: 978-1-910-259-46-7
KINDLE ISBN: 978-1-910-259-48-1

www.ecpr.eu/ecprpress

ECPR – Essays

Series Editors:
Dario Castiglione (University of Exeter)
Peter Kennealy (European University Institute)
Alexandra Segerberg (Stockholm University)

Other books available in this series

Choice, Rules and Collective Action: The Ostroms on the Study of Institutions and Governance (ISBN: 9781910259139) Elinor Ostrom (Author), Vincent Ostrom (Author), Paul Dragos Aligica (Editor) and Filippo Sabetti (Editor)

Croce, Gramsci, Bobbio and the Italian Political Tradition (ISBN: 9781907301995) Richard Bellamy

From Deliberation to Demonstration: Political Rallies in France, 1868–1939 (ISBN: 9781907301469) Paula Cossart

Hans Kelsen and the Case for Democracy (ISBN: 9781907301247) Sandrine Baume

Is Democracy a Lost Cause? Paradoxes of an Imperfect Invention (ISBN: 9781907301247) Alfio Mastropaolo

Just Democracy (ISBN: 9781907301148) Philippe Van Parijs

Learning about Politics in Time and Space (ISBN: 9781907301476) Richard Rose

Maestri of Political Science (ISBN: 9781907301193) Donatella Campus, Gianfranco Pasquino and Martin Bull

Masters of Political Science (ISBN: 9780955820335) Donatella Campus and Gianfranco Pasquino

The Modern State Subverted (ISBN: 9781907301636) Giuseppe Di Palma

On Parties, Party Systems and Democracy: Selected Writings of Peter Mair (ISBN: 9781907301780) Peter Mair (Author) Ingrid Van Biezen (Editor)

Varieties of Political Experience (ISBN: 9781907301759) Gianfranco Poggi

ECPR Classics:

Beyond the Nation State (ISBN: 9780955248870) Ernst Haas

Citizens, Elections, Parties: Approaches to the Comparative Study of the Processes of Development (ISBN: 9780955248887) Stein Rokkan

Comparative Politics: The Problem of Equivalence (ISBN: 9781907301414) Jan Van Deth

Democracy Political Finance and State Funding for Parties (ISBN: 9780955248801) Jack Lively

Electoral Change: Responses to Evolving Social and Attitudinal Structures in Western Countries (ISBN: 9780955820311) Mark Franklin,Thomas Mackie and Henry Valen

Elite and Specialized Interviewing (ISBN: 9780954796679)
Lewis Anthony Dexter

Identity, Competition and Electoral Availability: The Stabilisation of European Electorates 1885–1985 (ISBN: 9780955248832) Peter Mair and Stefano Bartolini

Individualism (ISBN: 9780954796662) Steven Lukes

Modern Social Policies in Britain and Sweden: From Relief to Income Maintenance (ISBN: 9781907301001) Hugh Heclo

Parties and Party Systems: A Framework for Analysis (ISBN: 9780954796617) Giovanni Sartori

Party Identification and Beyond: Representations of Voting and Party Competition (ISBN: 9780955820342) Ian Budge, Ivor Crewe, and Dennis Farlie

People, States and Fear: An Agenda for International Security Studies in the Post-Cold War Era (ISBN: 9780955248818) Barry Buzan

Political Elites (ISBN: 9780954796600) Geraint Parry

Seats, Votes and the Spatial Organization of Elections (ISBN: 9781907301353) Graham Gudgin and Peter Taylor

State Formation, Parties and Democracy (ISBN: 9781907301179) Hans Daalder

The State Tradition in Western Europe: A Study of an Idea and Institution (ISBN: 9780955820359) Kenneth Dyson

System and Process in International Politics (ISBN: 9780954796624) Mortan Kaplan

Territory and Power in the UK (ISBN: 9780955248863) James Bulpitt

Please visit www.ecpr.eu/ecprpress for up-to-date information about new publications.

Contents

List of Tables

Preface

The ideas and arguments in this book date back to the day in February 1989 when a death threat was pronounced on the British Commonwealth writer Salman Rushdie while I was working at a multi-ethnic inner city school in France; editing was nearing completion the day that European election results announced huge successes for the United Kingdom Independence Party and the French National Front in May 2014. Between these dates and events, questions concerning Islam, multiculturalism, new migrations and free movement in an integrating Europe, have fallen and risen on the political agenda. But throughout there has been precious little clear conceptual or theoretical understanding in public debates – and also much academic scholarship – about the deep problems involved in our routine understandings of these subjects. Much public discussion is stuck with inappropriate conceptions of migration, integration and diversity, as well as naive sociologies of how economy and society in a regional and global society now work. To hear some politicians in Europe talk, it is as if we are still living through a late nineteenth century period of nation-state building, anchored in romantic, homogeneous, ethnic conceptions of nationhood and citizenship. Yet many of these same conceptions are reproduced unquestioned by academic scholarship, in a sub-field of social science that has burgeoned dramatically over the past twenty-five years while often gaining little depth.

I have always tried to position my work at the edges of the field of ethnic and racial studies or migration studies: as a problematiser of paradigms, or conceptual trouble maker for those engaged in the honourable, but sometimes wrongheaded business of 'normal science' in this field – whether qualitative or quantitative. The essays collected in this book thus represent both my fascination and frustration with the massive growth of the field of migration studies, and our notions of immigration, integration and mobility as dominant concerns of our times. I still believe that re-examining these notions and the research that has been structured by them, can key us into some of the most puzzling paradoxes of the modern nation-state, regional integration and globalisation. But as the feeble impact on everyday political debate of so much research shows, migration studies has been able to boom without necessarily accumulating wisdom. As I argue insistently in this book, the international migration studies we have inherited is a necessarily interdisciplinary field. Yet it is squeezed and debilitated by disciplinary divisions caused by reductive research assessment and impact factor pressures; even free of these, there is still precious little talk across disciplines or understanding across national political contexts.

Another migration studies is nevertheless possible. The essays in *Immigration, Integration and Mobility* seek to explore the fluid possibilities of a field which is uniquely well positioned to chart the landscape of a social science beyond container nation-state-societies; in which interdisciplinarity and multiple methods can be used to engineer a non-methodologically nationalist social science incorporating methods and conceptions, not only from sociology and political science, but just as much from geography and anthropology, as well as economics and demography. The search for policy relevant research also calls for engagement with normative political theory and ethics, which again may question the normal relations of knowledge between the state and social science. At the same time, we have to migrate with our methods and our minds to get out of nation-centred local perspectives, as much as the routine fallacies of disciplinary codes: learning how to be aware of commonalities as well as distinctions across countries, and how to juxtapose but not collapse regions of the world, as we search for the necessary comparative models of explanation and understanding.

It is easy to forget that migration studies as a field was very little developed when – after my year of teaching young *maghrèbin* students in a French *collège* – I was doing my PhD work at the European University Institute, Florence in the early 1990s. In Western Europe, research on immigration or ethnicity was mostly bounded by very national political concerns in local political contexts with little attempt at productive comparison. Debates in Britain, for example, were dominated by a 'race relations' paradigm, peculiar to its national politics, which had been ascendant since the 1960s. Migration was believed to have stopped in the 1970s; the narrative stressed the difficult emergence of a multi-racial society cast in the colours and cultures specific to Britain's immigrant populations; and other European experiences with immigration were seen as backwards. Stepping outside of this frame, and influenced decisively by the ambitions of American comparative historical sociology and comparative politics, my earliest work thus sought to operationalise a better comparison between the political philosophies underpinning immigration and the idea of citizenship in two central European cases, Britain and France. It sought, in other words, to develop an analytical language, both explanatory and normative, to detox discussions from these ideological distortions and pervasive *langues de bois* (wooden languages).

The essays in this book reflect this starting point and where it led me, roaming recklessly across disciplines and national borders over the years. Developing on from the initial comparison of two classic immigration nations, it deals in turn with the return of 'integration' as the central conceptual logic of contemporary immigration in European nation-states; the rise of dramatic and diverse 'new migrations' across all of Europe from the 1990s onwards; the conceptual adaptations needed with the diversification of high-end to middling skilled and professional migration in a global context; and the metamorphosis of migration in Europe as European integration created new kinds of meaning and potentialities for new mobilities in the continent. Accordingly, the essays reflect four central concerns, partly paralleled by the four-part division of the book, which also shadow the chronological development of my post-PhD thinking from 1998 to 2014. They are bookended by my two most systematic programmatic recent statements about the field of study.

A first central concern is the interlacing of normative and explanatory issues in the study of immigration politics. In particular, I develop a distinctively European counterpoint to the liberal political theory developed by Will Kymlicka and others about North American issues, also insisting upon difficult methodological issues of interpretation and contextualisation often avoided by philosophers. The second insists upon the problem itself of comparison, across nation-state-societies whose ideological narratives and self-perceptions can never be entirely flattened into straight institutional comparison of law and policies, as so much research does. Straight comparisons are flawed by issues of power and asymmetry across cases, which requires sensitivity to interpretative comparatism (in the literary studies sense), as well as some emphasis on how knowledge and categories concerning migrants, culture, race and ethnicity have been internally constructed by policy intellectuals and academics differently in different countries. A third concern, then, is with category change, particularly as rising awareness of the effects of globalisation and the post-industrial shift lead to a new emphasis on (i.e.) 'transnationalism', 'mobilities' and 'super-diversity' in migration research, pointing to the expiry of exclusively nation-centred models of citizenship, integration, territory and container-like borders. Linked to this also are concerns with understanding the complex continuum of international migrations and mobilities between traditional low-skilled labour migration and atypical highly-skilled and middling migrations. Fourthly and finally, all these essays display my concern with issues of empirical and normative operationalisation. I was raised as a philosopher and theorist, but I can never escape my deep dissatisfaction with both the 'clean hands' abstractness of political philosophy (even when applied), as much as the sweeping exaggerations of most macro-level 'global' social theory. Part of this is my solid rejection of post-humanist (post-modern) trends in critical theory. Migration studies, indeed, as a distinctively agent- (or) human- centred field of research, is uniquely well equipped – via its grounded narratives of the lives and experiences of real migrants – to temper the excesses of the armchair theorists and go well beyond generalisations based only on seminar room debate, discourse analysis or sweeping macro-structural data.

Structure of the volume

The structure of this volume is built on four distinct parts in which two essays are chosen to represent and, as far as possible, exhaustively cover my views on each of these respective areas. The parts are introduced and concluded by two of my most broad and encompassing views of the field. The essays have been thoroughly revised and updated, along with a systematically compiled bibliography and references that reflect the full range of migration studies and my reading during the past twenty-five years.

The introductory essay, *Immigration, migration and free movement in the making of Europe* (2008) represents my most encompassing synthetic view of the question of migration in Europe. With a historical sweep, it identifies the normality of migration and mobility in the history of Europe – that is, against the myth of nationalist immobility – and points out how migration in the post-1990 period has dramatically diversified in terms of classic non-European immigrations, new intra-European migrations (i.e. East-West movements), and new forms of internal European mobility linked to European integration.

Part One, Applied Political Philosophy: The Problem of Multicultural Citizenship, develops and extends the arguments of my PhD and first book (Favell 1998a/2001). I have selected two pieces which best illustrate the *problématique* of applying political philosophy to the empirical and comparative institutional analysis of immigration policies/citizenship in Western Europe. The first, *Multicultural citizenship in theory and practice: applied political philosophy in empirical analyses* (1998), is a systematic exploration of the weaknesses of existing 'applied' political philosophy on these subjects, and a presentation of institutionalist tools that can be used to do a normative political analysis of citizenship and integration in France and Britain less distorted by North American concerns. The second, *Multicultural race relations in Britain: problems of interpretation and explanation* (1998), is concerned with how a classic distinction in the philosophy of social science – of explanation versus interpretation – could be applied to better understanding the socially conservative, classic liberal compromise of British 'race relations' based on ethnic diversity and religious tolerance.

Part Two, The Question of Integration, reflects how, post-*Philosophies of Integration*, I developed a broader comparative view of the resurgent question of 'integration': the central conceptualisation adopted by European nation-states to discuss how they have responded to the challenges of immigration in the post-war period. Part of this, was the necessary discussion of how dominant European conceptions relate – albeit asymmetrically – to American debates on assimilation, which still largely structure scientific and policy related studies of immigrant trajectories in the USA. The first, *Assimilation/Integration* (2005), is a short, encyclopaedia-type essay on the complicated relation of concepts in this field. The second, *Integration policy and integration research in Europe: a review and critique* (2001), is a long and systematic discussion – drawing on a Bourdieusian-style sociology of knowledge – of how integration research and integration policy has been shaped differently by normative and scientific research in distinct European contexts. It provides a model for the sophisticated version of comparatism I argue is necessary to get beyond both the methodological nationalism of most nation-centred policy research, as well as the distorting flattening produced by quantitative-only comparisons that take no heed of interpretative differences across countries.

In Part Three, Highly Skilled Migration and Social Mobility, I move into an agenda responding to the ascendency in the 1990s and early 2000s of large-scale macro debates on globalisation, and the associated popularity of concepts such as 'transnationalism' and 'mobilities'. Migration scholars often enthusiastically underlined the suggestion that the old nation-state was in decline, with international migrations the vanguard of new, non-spatial social formations, across borders, if not across the planet. While sympathetic to this search, my work in this area has always sought to question and delimit the extent of successful transnationalism or mobilities beyond the nation-state, often using a research strategy that focuses empirically on the most likely candidates for transnational lifestyles: high flying mobile 'elites'. Empirical research, such as my second solo-authored book (Favell 2008a), indeed often reveals the fragile stability of such transnational forms of life, versus the ever present pressures of nation-centred social integration, for different categories of migrants and movers in Europe. The first essay, *The human face of global mobility: a research agenda* (2006), presents an agenda developed with Miriam Feldblum and Michael Peter Smith, from the research project based at UCLA and the later book on *The Human Face of Global Mobility* (2006). We make a programmatic case for the closer look at so-called 'elites', and the delineation of distinct forms of middling migration, barriers to highly skilled international migration, and the extension of varied forms such as the migration of students, nurses, service-sector engineers, and free-moving professionals. In the second, *Social mobility and spatial mobility* (2011) – the first extension of my work in *Eurostars and Eurocities* presented here – I develop with my long-time European research partner, Ettore Recchi, a mixed quantitative/qualitative strategy for exploring how new forms of spatial mobility in the continent might be related to classic concerns of social mobility and change in Europe.

Part Four, New Migration and Mobilities in Europe, reflects further an agenda proposing systematic empirical sociological strategies for studying the bottom-up impact of European integration on migration and mobility in the continent. With Guiraudon and others, I have argued elsewhere (Favell and Guiraudon 2009) that a true sociology of Europeanisation must be clearly distinguished from the top-down legal/institutional/policy conceptions of Europeanisation dominated by political scientists. In the first essay here, *The new face of East-West migration in Europe* (2008), I offer a comparative framework for research on the new East-West migration in Europe after the enlargements of 2004/2008, a topic which has moved to the centre of the political agenda about the future of Europe. This agenda is shot through with misconceptions about 'immigration', 'neo-liberalism' and 'free movement' which I seek to diagnose in the second piece, *The fourth freedom: theories of migration and mobilities in "neo-liberal" Europe* (2014). I come back once again to Britain – which has been the most open economy to migration in Europe during the 1990s and 2000s – as a central crucible for the future of immigrant and free movement driven diversity and growth in the future.

As a conclusion, I return to the concluding essay from Brettell and Hollifield's (2007) handbook for the field. I point out the problematic cross-Atlantic and global asymmetries which dog this effort, the missing interdisciplinary dialogues, as well as the pervasive problem of methodological nationalism in the field. Seeking to 'reboot' the field, I argue for how migration studies may be able to develop a genuinely post-disciplinary, global agenda by focusing more on atypical forms of migration and mobility that indicate the limitations of the traditional nation-centred immigration paradigm.

Re-editing a series of past essays, there is an inevitable feeling of autobiography and introspection. As I have joked in keynote talks a couple of times, I feel that revisiting my old essays is a bit like embarking on a Greatest Hits tour as an ageing new wave band from the 1980s. I have, however, over the years been frequently asked when I would come back to my past contributions and reflect upon their relation to emerging and evolving debates that I have, perhaps, in part, influenced. I hope and trust that the intent and substance of these ten essays are still relevant, and that my updates, additions and new connections are pertinent. I *am* sure, though, that more reflection on the problems and possibilities of the field is still sorely needed.

I continue to owe great thanks to all the numerous colleagues and friends over the years who have helped my work. While repeating the specific thanks mentioned in my previous publications and in the footnotes here throughout, I would particularly like to thank the editors of this series Dario Castiglione and Alexandra Segerberg for the opportunity to publish in the ECPR series. I have also made the references as comprehensive as possible to indicate my full range of intellectual debts and influences, something that becomes obvious scrolling down the (very long) list. The book was compiled and edited while I was the 2014 Alliance Programme Visiting Professor of Sociology at Columbia University, New York; for this, my thanks to programme director, Alessia Lefébure, Department chair, Yinon Cohen, and Victoria de Grazia, Chris Hill and Emmanuelle Saada, at the Blinken European Institute. Also, *un grand merci* to all my colleagues at the Centre d'études européennes (CEE) and the Department of Sociology, Sciences Po, Paris, for their continued support and encouragement for my work.

Adrian Favell
November 2014

Chapter One

Introduction – Immigration, Migration and Free Movement in the Making of Europe

Europe historically has been made, unmade, and remade through the movements of peoples.[1] Despite the present day view of Europeans as a rather sedentary and socially immobile population – particularly when compared to the highly mobile spatial and social patterns of North Americans – contemporary Europe has essentially emerged out of a crucible of local, regional, and international population movements over the centuries.

In this introductory chapter, I consider the crucial impact of migration in Europe on European identity, by building a bridge between historical analyses of the phenomenon and emerging patterns that are shaping Europe as a distinctive new regional space of migration and mobility. My aim is to point out how migration is making and remaking Europe, less at the level of 'identity' in people's heads – in fact, if anything, most migrations are contributing to the growth of anti-European sentiment – but more in a territorial and (especially) structural economic sense. This is less easy to see if a purely cultural view is taken of the question of Europe. After sketching the role of population movements in the making and unmaking of Europe historically, I explore in depth the three kinds of migration/mobility that are most salient to the continent today and its structural transformation: first, the ongoing, traditional 'ethnic' immigration of non-Europeans into European nation-states; second, the small, but symbolically important emergence of new intra-European 'elite' migrations, engaged by European citizens enjoying the fruits of their European Union (EU) free movement rights; and third, the politically ambiguous flows of East-West migrants – which fall somewhere between the other two forms – that have been connected to the EU enlargement processes formalised in 2004 and 2007. The distinctiveness of Europe as a world region – hence in this sense, its economic and territorial identity – can best be grasped by briefly comparing it again to the United States of America (USA) as a similar, but differently structured regional migration space, a theme I turn to in my conclusion.

---

1.   Originally published in Jeffrey Checkel and Peter Katzenstein (eds) *European Identity*, Cambridge University Press (2008), 167–89. Republished with permission. Translated as 'Immigration, migration et libre circulation dans la construction de l'Europe', *Politique Européenne*, no.31 (2010), 33–64. It is also the text of my inaugural lecture as Professor of European and International Studies at Aarhus University, Denmark in November 2008. With thanks to the editors and contributors of this volume, in particular Thomas Risse, for useful comments and criticisms in its development, and to Nauja Kleist and Jan Ifversen for their invitation to lecture on this subject.

Population movements in the making and unmaking of Europe

It is not uncommon to picture European nationals as somehow innately predisposed to not move. Europe is typically seen as a patchwork of 'thick' inherited cultures – divided up by proudly preserved languages and social practices – that map out a continent of stubbornly rooted peoples with strong national and local identities, not much affected by the efforts of European institutions – or globalisation – to get them to think differently. It is also seen as a continent largely hostile to new immigrants, struggling to integrate even the small numbers of ethnically and racially distinct minorities that do manage to get in.

The USA, as is so often the case, is often referred to in order to underline this contrast. If the EU can be thought of for a moment as a kind of federal United States of Europe, the numbers are stark. While around 12 per cent of Americans are foreign born (Batalova and Lowell 2006), less than one in fifty Europeans live outside his/her state of national birth; and even intra-regional migration *within* European nation-states is lower than cross-state migration in the USA, at 22 per cent compared to 33 per cent (European Foundation for the Improvement of Living and Working Conditions 2006). European society is thus seen as the product of historically rooted cultures; America unequivocally has been built on immigration and the melting pot of newcomers. Despite fluctuating political resistance to new immigration, the base numbers and percentages moving to the USA are still bigger than anywhere in Europe, as is the sheer size of recent immigrant-origin populations over two or three generations – which in some states such as California now exceed 50 per cent. The attractiveness of the USA for new generations of the internationally ambitious and talented is still unanswered by Europe as a global economic force: two-thirds of tertiary-educated migrants from developing countries choose America as their destination, with dramatically beneficial consequences for the American economy (Peri 2005). It appears, in short, that Americans are willing to move and accept movers; Europeans are not.

A short pause for thought on this assumption will quickly reveal its historical ineptitude (*see also* Recchi 2006). America, after all, was largely populated by Europeans who moved and moved again: over sea, and then over great stretches of land. Thought of less shortsightedly, Europe is and always has been a continent of migratory flux. Early modern Europe – the kind of Europe celebrated by nationalists everywhere in terms of culturally rooted folklore (Hobsbawm 1983; Anderson 1991) – in fact was already a patchwork of circular, seasonal, and career mobility well before industrialisation. These revolutions then changed everything: sweeping peasants off the land, ripping apart rural communities, packing expansive cities full of new social classes, and creating economic channels of mobility that linked all of Europe, and eventually the world, in a new system of empire and capital (Hobsbawm 1987; Bade 2000; Moch 2003). On the ground, this meant continual flows of migration. By the late nineteenth century, unprecedented numbers were also moving across national borders as worker populations, and across seas as new world migrants and settlers (Hatton and Williamson 1998). Europeans went everywhere.

Why this is forgotten in the image of a sedentary Europe today is, of course, that the wars of the twentieth century stopped much of this migration. Nation-states finally reigned supreme as the dominant form of global social organisation: cementing the institutionalised role of state-centred power as explosive population containers, using military service, citizenship, and welfare rights in the name of national identity, to build political distinctions between insiders and outsiders and fix people spatially (Mann 1993; Torpey 2000). This, then, became the familiar, legitimate political topography of the modern world, leaving numerous ethnic groups on the wrong side of territorial borders or in despised social locations, the stateless residual populations of a now thoroughly nationalised Europe. This left one disaster – the Jewish holocaust – which scarred the continent forever, and an ugly aftermath of war that brutally shifted yet more populations, East and West. Europeans were once again moved, in search of a stable political solution that might for once and for all settle the ethnic and ideological frontiers of the so-called 'shatter zone' in Central and East Europe (Brubaker 1995; Mazower 1998; Mann 2005). Europe gave up its empires, and the Iron Curtain created a new, nearly impermeable material and psychological barrier, freezing East-West mobility and literally severing the latitudinal land movements and interactions that had, in *longue durée* geographical terms, been the greatest civilising resource of the continent (Diamond 1997).

In the West, generous welfare state structures in the postwar period – a kind of liberal democratic form of socialised nationalism prevalent throughout the continent up to 1970 (Mazower 1998) – cemented national populations in place like never before. The shrunken West European powers eventually re-emerged economically, but they did so by now servicing their migrant worker needs, first via a new wave of migrants from the peripheral South to North (from Italy, Spain, Portugal and Yugoslavia), then – as these movements too dried up – via a large, hitherto unprecedented immigration from former colonies and dependencies outside Europe (especially Turkey, North and Central Africa, the West Indies, South Asia, and Indonesia). This, of course, brought an even more explosive mix of race and cultural diversity into the fractious continent (Castles and Miller 2009).

A historical ground map to European population movements – breathless as this sketch is – is necessary for any discussion about the place of migration today in the making of a European identity. It is not an easy map to capture (King 2002). Conventional post-colonial and guest worker immigration was supposed to have ended in the 1970s, leaving only limited channels of family reunification and asylum as entry points for migration. Immigrant populations were supposed to have settled and integrated as nationals and citizens, turning more or less culturally homogenous national societies into reluctantly multicultural ones.

The 1980s, and especially 1990s, have changed all this again (Baumgartl and Favell 1995; Triandafyllidou and Gropas 2012). A wave of 'new migrations' has mixed up the continent once more (Koser and Lutz 1998). A globalising economy has liberalised post-industrial societies, leading to a new dual service economy driven largely by a demand for cheap foreign labour (Piore 1979; Sassen 2001). Global transportation systems have facilitated movement to Europe from increasingly diversified and unpredictable sources (Held *et al.* 1999). European working classes, as in America, no longer wish to take on 3D (dirty, dangerous and dull) tasks that might be left to more motivated and cheaper foreigners. Migration here, as elsewhere, has also dramatically feminised, as women from developing countries have become the carers and domestic workers of the highly developed (Phizacklea 1998; Kofman *et al.* 2000). Asylum, which once functioned as a more symbolic gesture to enable small numbers of political refugees to escape to the West, has turned into an uncontrollable torrent as Europe has picked up the human pieces of numerous regional and global wars; asylum also has become effectively a channel of labour migration. Europe was supposed to become a fortress; by the early 2000s the reverse was happening (Favell and Hansen 2002).

Added to these new forms of immigration, novel *intra*-EU migrations have also become a feature of the European migrant tapestry (Tarrius 1992, 2000). The European Union was built on the four freedoms, including the free movement of persons. Long-standing EU15 member states (i.e. those older members prior to the Eastern enlargements) have enjoyed these rights for decades now (Romero 1991). The numbers of West Europeans on the move have by no means been large, but they are highly symbolic. For every one who moves to work and settle freely in a neighbouring member state of the EU, many more are moving temporarily as students, shoppers, commuters, and eventually retirees. Add to this the ever changing geographical definition of the EU with successive enlargements reuniting Europe, and the potential for a new kind of migration in Europe – 'free movement' – looks set to unmake and remake again the settled patchwork of national societies that had, more or less successfully, used the EU to rescue the European nation-state in the postwar period (Milward 2005). The most visible intra-EU free movers now are, of course, after 2004 and 2007, the socially and spatially dynamic mobile populations of new Eastern and Central Europe, grabbing access to a European space that is now all theirs again. But, arguably, free movers will, due to the concentric logic of an externalising, 'neighbourhood'-building EU, in future be coming from Ukraine, Turkey, and Morocco as well, even if these bordering states never become members.

These combined phenomena leave a confusing setting for evaluating the impact of population movements on European identity. As I will show, by untangling the impact of these various new migrations on the making and unmaking of Europe, it can be seen that Europe is struggling to maintain distinctions among three distinctive groups, but moving towards a new solution. Here, I will sketch the outlines of this likely future, before going on to explore this scenario in more depth in the rest of the chapter.

A first kind of migration – traditional, poor, 'ethnic,' extra-European immigrants from Africa and Asia – insofar as they can be distinguished as such – is being processed, with a great deal of social and political conflict, in line with the established methods for dealing with postwar, post-colonial, and guest worker migrants. These immigrants continue to be framed as the legitimate concern of national societies, not just the EU; recent years have seen the return of nationalist integration policies across all of Europe, alongside a growing instrumental role they play in fuelling the symbolic closure of anti-EU and anti-globalisation politics.

However, in Europe as elsewhere, this often ugly politics of immigration does not square with the economics of migration. Nostalgia for contained, culturally secure, citizenship and nation-based societies sits badly with a globalised dual labour market within service sector-driven economies run by multinationals, which demand an almost endless reserve army of flexible foreign labour.

The experiences of a second group of migrants, at the other end of the social scale – West European movers I call 'Eurostars' – tell a different story about Europe today. Unsurprisingly, they reflect a Europe at its most enthusiastically cosmopolitan and post-national. Yet, even with all formal barriers to migration down, they encounter limitations and resistance to their movement that suggest the resilience of national ethnicities in even the most structurally global and multinational of locations – London and Amsterdam being my examples.

A third group of migrants – the new East European movers – are the most ambiguous of all. Are they cadet Eurostars, as the theory of European integration predicts they will become one day? Or are they still more like traditional 'ethnic' immigrants, and likely to be treated this way? I argue that both are true. They are making a new European space of movement and fulfilling a new idea of European citizenship; but they are also being shuffled into economic roles in the West European economies assigned in the postwar period to traditional non-European immigrants. Herein lies the punch line. A kind of European fortress may yet be built on the back of this ambiguous spread and opening of Europe to the East. A tempting racial logic is at stake for Europeans today. Opening to populations from the East may enable the more effective closing of Europe to the South, filling the structural need for which Western Europe had historically to turn to colonial and developing country immigrants from more distant societies and cultures. Racial and cultural distinctions might be used to achieve what concrete, electronic surveillance, and barbed wire cannot.

The three migrations in Europe

I will now explore in greater detail each of the three migrations identified above: traditional non-European 'ethnic' immigrants; West European Eurostars; and the new East-West post-Enlargement movers. It is essential to distinguish them analytically before showing how the new migration scenario is blurring many of these supposedly clear distinctions.

Traditional non-European 'ethnic' (im)migrants

New forms of migration and mobility have changed the context of population movements in Europe, but the dominant story about immigration today in Europe is still, mostly, the ongoing classic post-colonial and guest worker scenario. Unquestionably, European economies still generate a strong demand for migrant workers, alongside an alluring image that generates a supply – alluring enough to offset the often highly costly and uncertain calculations that lie behind migrants' decisions to move from Africa or Asia. Where the story has most changed is in the increasingly diverse source origins of ongoing immigration: now from a range of countries with little or no colonial connection to the destination countries. Previous generations of post-colonial immigrants could at least count on a symbolic connection to the metropolitan destinations, together often with having been socialised to some extent in the language and culture of the country. Nowadays sources and destinations are equally scattered, a factor that increases the tensions that emerge politically around the migration in the receiving society (Vertovec 2007). For example, the reception context of British West Indian migrants in the 1960s differs dramatically from the Sri Lankis or Kurds arriving in Denmark today. National integration systems thus find it that much harder to deal with the new migrations.

In addition, channels of migration today are much more 'bottom-up' than in the days of relatively planned post-colonial and guest worker recruitment migration. Some of the most remarkable migration systems that have emerged have been very specific in their internal self-organisation: Senegalese street vendors in Italy (Riccio 2001), Cape Verdean domestic workers in Italy and Spain (Andall 1998), Chinese migrants in Britain and France (Benton and Pieke 1998), Middle Easterners in Scandinavia (Diken 1998), and so on. For the main part, though, the largest groups of migrants – from Turkey and Morocco – are rather predictable and continuous migration systems built on long histories and easy connections with a range of countries (for some sources: Kastoryano 1993; Bousetta 2000; Lesthaege 2000; Phalet *et al.* 2000).

As everyone knows, these various immigrations have visibly put black, brown, and yellow faces in white Europe, including in some of the least likely places. Issues of multiculturalism or inter-ethnic conflict that were most familiar to former colonial powers like Britain and France are now raised in every country in Western Europe, including the South, and increasingly in East and Central Europe too. As a majority of these new immigrants hail from predominantly Muslim countries, the Islamic dimension of this immigration – whether practicing religious affiliation or merely the parent culture – has become the defining issue of twenty-first-century European identity most associated with immigration today (Byrnes and Katzenstein 2006).

This is of course an issue imprisoned in broader geo-political struggles linked to the 'war against terror,' and at the mercy of reductive, inflammatory visions of the so-called 'clash of civilizations' (Huntington 1996). It is now difficult to see past the rhetoric to assess qualitatively how different these new migrations and the multicultural problems are from those of the 'old' immigration of the 1950s and 1960s. In fact, the trajectory of these visible, so-called 'ethnic' immigrants in European society is a quite familiar one. At a macro-level, they have been a key structural feature of all postwar European societies. What impacted first the large post-colonial and guest worker countries has had similar effects in asylum-receiving countries in Northern, and later in Southern Europe. Each nation-state has faced similar 'multicultural questions,' albeit with different timings and political saliency (Kastoryano 1998a; Joppke and Lukes 1999). Europe as a whole has become a continent of immigration, and (with more difficulty) a continent of Islam; but the political and social processes raised by these questions have everywhere been dealt with as predominantly national ones, now raging at the core of domestic national politics everywhere, from Britain to Denmark, and The Netherlands to Spain.

Immigration, then, is certainly a European question; but the politics of immigration are still dominantly national in locus. Cooperation at the European level has had its effects, particularly on border control and entry policies; but the EU has little effect on the policies or processes of immigrant settlement. The basic problems for these non-European immigrants – 'Third Country Nationals' as they are known in EU jargon – is one of attaining formal national citizenship and recognised national membership: they are not European citizens, even when they have permanent residency. Naturalisation into their adopted host state provides the one sure route to becoming a European, but successful naturalisation is inevitably a nationalising process (Hansen 1998). The effect on European identity of these new immigrations is, in this sense, negative: it helps to preserve the nation-centred status quo. Whatever transnational, even pan-European social forms migrants might develop – Islam, for example, has taken specific 'Euro' forms in the visions of young leaders like Tariq Ramadan – the socialisation pressures faced by Muslim immigrants are overwhelmingly national. Nearly every European nation-state has formulated in recent years a policy on 'integration' of immigrants that reflects mainly nation-building concerns about imparting national culture and values to newcomers, and very little of the kinds of post-national responses to immigration that would be the consequence of a through Europeanisation of the issues involved (Favell 2003b). The most encouraging message all such immigrants get from their host societies is: 'integrate – or else...'. I explore these issues in greater depth in Chapter Five.

Immigration is thus dominantly a national issue everywhere because of the integration question – even progressive, inclusionary movements are always framed in terms of inclusion into *national* identities: finding your place in 'multi-ethnic' Britain, or 'republican' France, or the 'tolerant, pluralist' The Netherlands and so on. As recent debates in all these countries reveal, immigration issues and the vulnerable populations who embody them are consistently projected by both pro- and anti-immigration politicians and media into grand national debates about citizenship, national culture, language acquisition, and absorption in national welfare and labour market systems. Ongoing 'ethnic' immigration in fact has become one of the primary ways in which nation-building continues its classic operations in Europe today, despite other Europeanising and globalisation processes. If by the making of Europe or a European identity it is meant something over and above the nation-state – something post-national, cosmopolitan, a European 'society' and so on – then 'Europe' is simply not very relevant to most traditional immigration policy questions (Favell 2006).

Moreover, the anti-immigrant reactions seen across Europe in the toughening of politics on immigration and integration are also a crucial pillar in the anti-EU backlash. They are again a distinct part of the un-making of European identity (in a post-national sense), although, as Holmes (2000) points out, these politics themselves have Europeanised nationalists and nativists in support of their own, different vision of Europe – a Europe of nation-states. Populations remain, on the whole, hostile to migrations of all kinds. Progressive immigration policies – on citizenship rights and so on – have generally only been advanced politically in Europe by depoliticising the issues into legal and technical arenas, and typically during periods of low saliency of immigration politics (Guiraudon 1998). In terms of Fligstein's (2008) analysis about how and why people might feel 'European,' immigration in fact is one of the issues leading nationals of member states to feel much *less* European – including the immigrants themselves, who have no option, if they wish to be included in their host society, but to comply with the integrating/ nationalising pressures attached to citizenship and membership acquisition. The effects of immigration, in fact, suggest an opposite dynamic to the standard Europeanisation hypotheses: more mobility and more interaction is leading to a less integrated Europe, the opposite of Karl Deutsch's famous transactionalist argument (Deutsch 1957).

A different view about the aggregate effects of new immigration might be taken if we were to view the question in structural, economic terms, rather than the cultural ones reflected in political debates and discussions on identity. Far from the maelstrom of rhetorical national politics, policy makers in the EU certainly have been talking about coordinating or formulating immigration policies at the EU level; indeed, the only EU policy field where there is rapid integration today is in security-based externalisation efforts on immigration and border control. This is more a question of nations efficiently devolving control mechanisms to more effective agency than anything supra-national as such; but it has certainly Europeanised police forces and other state agencies in ways they would have not expected. There seems to be a huge effort in redirecting the internal European integration project to external border construction and policy – particularly to the South. In this sense, immigration does appear to be helping in the (negative) construction of Europe – as the 'fortress' hoped for by alarmed national populations.

Economics, though, may yet defeat this particular vision of Europe. The numbers of extra-EU immigrants are still rising, despite the efforts to control and limit them. This migration does still seem to be fulfilling a structural demand for migrants, driven by the demographic demand of declining childbirth and ageing populations, and the economic restructuring of European national welfare state economies into a global service economy. No European nation-state can escape the changing structure of labour markets, and their rescaling at a wider European level, as they become organised everywhere around highly polarised, service industry driven, global cities. Every European economy is witnessing a division of labour and widening of inequalities between the primary sectors of middle and upper class employment, and lower-grade working class jobs that native nationals are less and less willing to fill: notably cleaners, domestic workers, restaurant and shop workers, taxi drivers, construction and agricultural workers, and so on. There is national level resistance to this process, as well as variation across the 'varieties of European capitalism' (Esping-Andersen 1999) – Britain is much more polarised and hence open to migrants than, say, Denmark – but these structural economic effects *are* impacting all.

These processes are thus integrating Europe under a new economic rationale. On their convergent economic trajectories, European economies are coming to look more and more like North America in their structural demand for migration to fill the demands of the secondary labour market: this will mean high levels of tacit migration, social and economic marginalisation for immigrants, and policies at the border that 'talk the talk' of control but are porous and liberalising in their effects – what is referred to in the American context as 'smoke and mirrors'-style border control policies (Massey *et al.* 2002). Viewed this way, immigration *is* still building a new Europe, in a structural sense – although host populations don't much like politically the apparently neoliberal Europe that is being built by these processes (*see also* Chapter Nine in this volume).

Eurostars and Eurocities

What happens when you remove race, class, ethnicity, inequality, borders, barriers, and cultural disadvantage from 'immigration'? Answer: you get 'free movers'. Nationals of European member states are also European citizens, amongst whose basic rights are those that ensure their unfettered ability to move, shop, work, live, and settle wherever they want abroad in Europe. Globally speaking, the EU is a unique space in this sense: there is no other such extensive kind of politically constructed post-national space anywhere else on the planet. On paper at least, free moving European citizens don't need visas; they don't need to worry about citizenship or integration; they often don't even need residency to live and work where they choose – they can come and go in a free European space. European free movement laws – which date back to the original Treaty of Rome in 1957 – undid the nationalising logic of nation-states as population containers just as the postwar settlement and the completion of European welfare states was cementing this national system firmly in place.

In theory, then, European free movement could be an avenue for building a very different kind of Europe. Yet, numbers of such migrants have historically been small: still, today, less than one in fifty Europeans live outside their country of origin, and numbers have not grown appreciably with any of the major steps towards European integration. The interest in this small population in comparison to traditional immigrants is precisely as an unexpected limit case: they reveal exactly what other types of immigrants have to face to achieve anything like level playing field conditions with national citizens.

The 'Eurostars', as I call them (Favell 2008a), are at the heart of the EU Commission's efforts to build Europe through dynamic mobility policies; the current talk is not of moving coal miners and factory workers from the South to the North – as it was when Freedom of Movement of Persons was established as one of the basic provisions of the Treaty of Rome in 1957. The talk at the heart of the much touted 2000 Lisbon agenda – imagining a successful, more competitive Europe – is, rather, the movement of professionals, the skilled and the educated: the circulation of talent in a knowledge economy, with its beneficial side effect the building of European identity – the kinds of cross-border interactions discussed by Fligstein (2008). This movement is likely to be a predominantly urban hub phenomenon – hence the emergence of 'Eurocities,' a network of cosmopolitan places driving the new European economy: familiar big cities such as London, Amsterdam, Brussels, Milan, Munich, Berlin, Barcelona, Vienna, and so on, that enjoy semi-detached identities from the national societies in which they are situated.

Unquestionably, London has benefited the most from these trends since the 1990s. Offshore from the continent, a global hub and gateway for all of Europe, London has been *the* European destination of free movement *par excellence*, an urban economy that has in the last ten to fifteen years creamed off the brightest and best of a whole generation of French, German, Italian, and Spanish movers (and others), frustrated with stagnant economies or parochial career hierarchies back home. What began as a large, but rather invisible migration of West Europeans has laid a path now for a new generation of young, talented, and educated Poles, Hungarians, Romanians, and others heading in the same direction – not least because other countries (such as France and Germany, most notably) have unwisely kept doors shut for these very same triple A migrants from new accession countries. European mobility of this kind is also promoted as the model for future post-enlargement migrations. At very least, mobile East European EU citizens taking their new European chances as 'free movers' – no longer 'immigrants' – largely exceed the paltry numbers of West Europeans who moved with these same rights during the previous three to four decades.

For sure, those movers found pioneering the life of Eurostars are the most likely to both feel and make a post-national/cosmopolitan European identity. As the PIONEUR survey documents in some detail (Recchi and Favell 2009), they embody in flesh and blood – albeit in small numbers – that of which the philosophers and cosmopolitan social theorists of Europe have long been dreaming. This much is no surprise. In Fligstein's terms, these people undoubtedly are the prototypical Europeans; although, as PIONEUR shows, they find little difficulty in combining their new European identity with identities rooted in both their nation of origin and nation of residence (Rother and Nebe 2009).

But are they really making or changing Europe in a macro-structural sense? The irony is, of course, still patent: break down all barriers, create all kinds of incentive structures, paint a Europe without frontiers and only opportunities, and still you only get low, statistically insignificant levels of movement. Typically, the assumption here is that this is because Europeans don't like to move; that they are inherently rooted to where they were born by culture and language. But this culturalist view of Europe is unsustainable given its longer and dramatic migration history and the fact that English has provided a common second language that can be used interchangeably by Europeans in most professional circles or multinational corporations located in the major cities. But whatever the reason for immobility, European cross-border movement is a perilously slow and marginal way of making Europe. So much for philosophy and economic theory. This exceptional 'most likely case' scenario is, however, revealing of the stark limitations of any post-national Europeanised space under even the best possible theoretical conditions.

So being European for these 'free movers' is certainly a banal fact in terms of identity survey questions; yes, there are forms of new Europeanised life, highly Europeanised spaces in cities, and slowly growing numbers of 'new Europeans' in these terms out there. But more importantly, even with the low numbers, when the lives, experiences and trajectories of these would-be cosmopolitans are studied ethnographically, the movers can be seen to face surprising local and national barriers blocking their aspirations in even the most ostensibly cosmopolitan of locations.

After London, another vastly popular hub of European mobility is Amsterdam. The Netherlands is often rated the number one open global economy in the world, and Amsterdam is seen as the liberal capital of Europe, widely seen as the most open and tolerant urban culture on the continent. It is a very popular destination with Irish, British, German, and Southern European migrants. Yet even here, EU movers often find themselves excluded on an informal level in their chosen place of residence by locally specific, highly ethnicised processes of exclusion. These centre in Amsterdam, as in other Eurocities, on the competitive struggle for highly sought after prizes of settlement – high quality urban lifestyles – in the most desirable locations of global cities. The Dutch are open, tolerant, cosmopolitan, for sure, but they simply do not make it easy for foreigners to settle on an everyday level, ensuring that even the closest European neighbours have minimal access to the internal secrets of a national culture reserved to native speakers. This culture structures the confusing rules and regulations that police organisational life, access to the best housing, and attainment of the elusive quality of life that native Amsterdammers spend years strategising to attain. Despite its appeal and the very high numbers of foreigners who move there, very few stay, turnover is high, and The Netherlands has one of the smallest foreign resident populations in the continent. It takes elite capital, and the adoption of a disconnected 'expat' life in the city, to surmount these barriers – a stratification which ensures that European mobility cannot be massified downwards to the middle classes, or effect a bigger structural change on the Europe of nation states. It will remain an exclusive property of elites, if at all, and European spatial mobility opportunities will not lead to dramatic new social mobility or the emergence of a more widespread cosmopolitan sensibility (as the theorists dream) (*see also* Recchi 2009). In Chapter Seven, these questions are explored in both quantitative and qualitative terms in greater detail.

It is a fair retort to suggest that expecting Europeans to build Europe by moving and resettling abroad long term is setting the bar too high in some respects. Yet, these same Europeans consistently (in Eurobarometer surveys) rate their rights of free movement as the most important benefit of EU membership – ahead of the economy and security –and around a third claim to be ready to move abroad if the opportunity and demand arose (European Year of Worker's Mobility 2006). Of those surveyed, 37 per cent think they would be willing to move to another country that offered better conditions, 53 per cent think the 'freedom to travel and work in the EU' is the most important single benefit of membership – ahead of the Euro (44 per cent) and peace (36 per cent) – and 57 per cent have travelled internationally within the EU in the last two years. Yet, less than 4 per cent have ever lived and worked abroad. Perhaps other forms of more transient/temporary mobility in Europe will be more significant: businessmen, students, retirees, shoppers, cross-border traders, commuters, and so on. Again, the broader terms of Fligstein's search (2008) for the Europeans establishes the evidence, such as it can be shown through the limited available attitudinal sources of the Eurobarometer surveys. Maybe the experience of any cross-border mobility, even the most short-term, may have big Europeanising effects. However, if mobility consists primarily of holidaying with co-nationals on a beach in the Costa del Sol, or going on the rampage as a hooligan at a European football championship, European identity will not be the result. Thus far the evidence is ambiguous, even for the most likely beneficiaries such as Erasmus students or retirement migrants. Most of the evidence on these other forms of mobility suggest that experience of these benefits of the EU is not particularly destructive or transformative of national cultures or identities (as PIONEUR also underlines; *see also* King *et al.* 2000; King and Ruiz-Gelices 2003), and that when Europeans go home, they go home to their primary national identities. Eurostars, on the other hand, are trying to explicitly live a post-national life; most of them find that it is a rather difficult proposition in the EU today.

East-West movers

Setting up the contrast between these two types of migrants in Europe – 'ethnic' immigrants and 'elite' professional movers – unfortunately emphasises what has become a clichéd view of the polarised mobility opportunities alleged to index the winners and losers of globalisation and regional integration processes (i.e. Bauman 1998). The image, in fact, is far from empirically accurate (on this, *see* Smith and Favell 2006, and the discussion in Chapter Six). 'Ethnic' immigrants often contain a fair number of middle-class and highly qualified movers, who often use their relatively privileged home-grown social and economic capital to engineer what becomes a social move downward into higher paying, but lower level work in the West. It is a universal fact of migration that it is *not* the poorest and least capable of migrating that move, but those with some degree of human capital or networks-based social capital (Hammar *et al.* 1997). Among the intra-European migrants, as I detail in *Eurostars and Eurocities*, there is much evidence that free movement rights in Europe have been most effectively mobilised by a new generation of 'social spiralists' – upwardly mobile, ambitious, provincial, working-class and lower middle-class migrants, often from the South, often women, using international migration in Europe as an escape from career and lifestyle frustrations at home.

The caricature of 'ethnic' immigrants and 'elite' movers is even less applicable to the new form of migration that has in the last few years grown to become the most important visible proof of a changing Europe: post-Enlargement migration. This migration is dated post 2004 and 2007, the dates of the two major enlargements to the East, although in truth the migration was already well established, both informally and semi-formally, before these dates, and encompasses countries not even now among the twenty-eight official members of the EU. EU A8 movers (those which joined in 2004), new accession country citizens (2007 and after), and by extension migrants from all candidate, possibly candidate, associate, and neighbouring countries may fall under this logic – because of the territorial, 'concentric' effects of integrating markets on a regional scale across these borders through the European neighbourhood policies (Rogers 2000; Favell and Hansen 2002). The question, though, is whether post-Enlargement 'immigrants' are following the classic 'ethnic' trajectory, or whether they are, rather, 'free movers' destined to become the full and free European citizens of the future? Which scenario best applies?

Demographic and economic theory is highly hopeful here. The newly freed 'free movers' are seen as the avatars of an all-triumphant theory of European integration, which predicts a win-win-win outcome for Europe from these new movements (ECAS 2005, 2006): the migrants win through satisfying their ambitions and mobility goals; the receiving society wins from creaming off their talent and enthusiasm; and the sending society will benefit from the positive development dynamics initiated by the movement of talented individuals who circulate money and networks within the new Europe, and who will bring back their talents at some point to the newly integrated Eastern economy – where all the best opportunities will be located in future. In short, movement theoretically promotes European integration, efficient economic dynamics, and a circulation of talent and capital flowing back into development. True to this theory, more spatial/social mobility is seen among East European movers. This generation of new Europeans *are* ambitious, dynamic movers ready to get what's theirs from the West, while benefiting from ease of mobility back and forth from West to East. Well over half a million citizens from the A8 accession countries of 2004, for example, took the chance to move into Britain's boom economy since 2004. In this, at least, they are unequivocally making Europe – regardless of how they or others might express their feelings in Eurobarometers or identity terms. This movement marks arguably the biggest social change in Europe in half a century: the definitive end of the Cold War, and a European social experiment that will leave neither West or East unchanged.

But, at the same time, a negative political scenario continues to react to these migrants as 'immigrants' rather than 'free movers.' Identity can be mobilised negatively on this issue if migrants are seen by domestic populations as threats rather than benevolent economic complements to domestic economies. On this point, the evidence is equivocal. A pragmatic reaction has on the whole received many of these migrants. Over Romanians in Milan and Bilbao, Poles in Berlin and London, Russians and Yugoslavs in Paris or Amsterdam, overt politics has certainly not reacted anything like as violently as it has against the (somewhat) more visible North African or African populations in the same places. For sure, Polish plumbers and the 'invasion' of Roma have grabbed headlines in France and Britain; France remains mostly closed to new accession members, and Britain shut its doors to Romanians and Bulgarians. But, overall, the reaction has been slow and measured, more in tune with the growing realisation that these new faces are part of a rather permanent looking East-West economic system that might have even deeper consequences than the limited settlement of new 'ethnic' immigrants.

This reaction can apply even when these migrants are white, Christian, skilled and in high demand – and it can happen equally to the Romanian farm worker in Italy, the Polish shop owner in Germany, or the highly skilled Hungarian office worker in England (*see* the ethnographies collected in Favell and Elrick 2008). The ambiguity of their presence is sharpened by the fact it is not so clear that the old traditional nation-building integration response is so applicable here. Older immigrant populations might resent that East Europeans can come and go, taking the same jobs, but facing none of the integratory pressures that are put on traditional immigrants to demonstrate that they 'belong' in their West European host countries. There is still room for these migrants to be enveloped in the traditional nation-building processes of exclusion/inclusion, but for the main part they are establishing patterns of circular, temporary, and non-residential mobility in the new European space (Wallace and Stola 2001; Morawska 2002). Locals react with horror when they see the wives and children of Polish workers cluttering up state school and medical facilities. They understand quite well that the solution is to make sure that low cost airlines are plentiful, mobility easy, and economic conditions back home promising enough to ensure it is a temporary residence. West European nations, if they stay open and porous enough, might just get this migration/development equation right with Poland, although more permanent brain- and brawn-drain is an ongoing threat for the new Balkan member states.

An evaluation of the future of this new European migration system, then, needs to stress both dimensions of the Europe it is building. Yes, the integrating Europe of mobility promised by demographers and economists is happening. But the system they are moving into is more often than not a system based on a dual labour market in which East Europeans will take the secondary, temporary, flexible roles based on their exploitability in terms of cost and human capital premium. Europe thus comes to resemble the USA-Mexico model: where East-West movers do the 3D jobs or hit glass ceilings, and where underlying 'ethnic' distinctions between East and West are unlikely to disappear. In a sense, this mode of inclusion continues the iniquitous longer-standing historical relationship between East and West (Zielonka 2006; Case 2009; Böröcz 2010). Eastern Europeans will get to move, and they will learn the hard way that the West only wants them to do jobs that Westerners no longer want. The danger, in short, is they will become a new Victorian service class for a West European aristocracy of university-educated working mums and 'creative class' professionals, who need someone to help them lead their dream lives. I take a closer look at these issues in Chapter Eight of this volume.

The concentric, externalising logic of regional integration is meanwhile pushing the EU to begin negotiations out across the Eastern borders, micro-managing border scenarios with new neighbours to encourage trade and mobility while controlling unwanted security and policing implications. The idea, again, is that free movement of all kinds can be governed; and that when it is governed well, it is a win-win for both sides. This feature of European integration puts it far ahead of other steps towards regional economic integration around the world. Via bilateral external accords and neighbourhood polices, the regional integration project in Europe stretches far east to the Urals, extends South to the Atlas mountains, and laps up against the borders of the Dead Sea. It can be expected that population movements of all kinds will increase within this concentric European space, and that those moving within this space will claim new rights as *de facto* European free movers rather than non-European immigrants (*see* Chapter Nine in this volume).

Conclusion: Migration and comparative regional integration processes

Migration of all kinds is making Europe in new ways, but the new migration system engendered by successive EU enlargements and other externalising efforts will prove the most momentous. In these terms, it is true the founding fathers would perhaps not believe the European regional integration process that they put in motion. As the logic of enlarging has triumphed over deepening, a functional new regional European space is being built, squaring the demography/economy/securitisation question – although the borders of that space certainly do not end at the borders of EU28. When political integration of the EU hit the rocks, all the growth energy of the EU was turned into the activities of governing the porous borders of a new regional space, hence opening mobility and the four freedoms (in at least a partial way) to a notional EU45 or EU55 through the extension of the European market beyond all previous ideas of Europe.

The key question of course will be: Where lie the borders of this 'space' and 'system'? Who is in/out? What, in other words, will be the relationship of the newly fluid East European 'free movers' – both new and potential members – to those post-colonial, 'non'-European 'immigrants' who have filled the secondary economic roles for Europe in the past?

One way of answering this question is to go back to the USA-Europe comparison and lay out the emergent European regional space against the North American one (*see also* Chapter Eight in this volume). Viewed this way, it becomes instructive to compare the expanding, explicitly political logic of European regional integration with the politically ungoverned and socially disastrous scenario that the USA now faces with Central America. Where Europe is increasingly turning to the East for its migrant labour sources, the USA relies massively on Latino migration from the South to fill the same roles. And as the recent politics of immigration in the USA testify, the Mexico-USA immigration scenario (and by extension the relationship with all of Central America) is now tragically hamstrung between the irreconcilable paradoxes of the national container 'migration state' (Hollifield 2004), unable to take effective political steps towards a post-national regional integration in the European mould, while structurally dependent on cross-border mobility (Massey *et al.* 2002). America desperately needs a rational economic solution; but its politics will not allow it.

The USA remains an economy and society driven by immigration. The American economy more than ever is based on its porous borders. The Californian agricultural economy would collapse without it; Texas is much the same. What do Los Angelenos do when there is a hole in their roof, a problem with the garden sprinkler, or a fence that needs patrolling at night? They phone up Carlos, a recently naturalised Mexican-American, who has in fact been living in the city for twenty-five years. He then phones up some 'guys' he knows, and you stop asking questions. Or if you need some help getting the house clean or the baby monitored, your neighbour's home help, Susana, always has a 'sister' or 'cousin' willing to come by, for cash in hand. The middle and upper class can get back to work making money franchising cable comedy shows, or get busy with their yoga class after dropping the kids off at school. This is how the city works, how everyone makes money and creates time for themselves. Nowadays it's exactly how New York, Chicago, Atlanta and Houston work too, and it's getting to be that way in Dalton, Georgia, Las Vegas, Nevada, or even (even) Des Moines, Iowa. European middle classes in London, Paris, or Rome have learnt the same economic logic; and the home helps they are turning to, and becoming increasingly dependent on, are increasingly East European in origin.

Politically, though, the two continents are divergent. Nativism is on the rise in the USA, usually based on spurious cultural and linguistic arguments that are woefully outdated in their views of the population dynamics of major urban centres (Huntington 2004). Congress has recently failed in several attempts to pass legislation to regularise undocumented migration and to square the economic demand for workers with the push for more political control. Only border control and internal security has tightened. But as a satirical movie from 2004 made clear, *A Day Without a Mexican* is the day the miracle American economy grinds to a halt. The scenario was actualised in the massive one-day Mexican protests in Los Angeles and elsewhere in the spring of 2006. America has tried to look east to fill its voracious immigrant demand – one can argue that the USA is so soft on immigration from Korea, Japan, China, and Vietnam precisely for this reason – but it still needs Carlos and his irregular crew. White supremacists in the USA have had their day, thanks to demographics. Even the Bush presidency understood that a Republican with no Asian or Latino voters is a Republican out of office. Nativists will always want to build fences to the sky, and they may still feel empowered and legitimated to take their rifles out as minutemen to patrol the Arizona desert. A symbolic politics of deportation has also taken a strong hold under the Obama presidency (De Genova 2010). But as is shown by the trucks pouring northwards across that border, while American capital and tourism pours South, the US economy does not and will not ever end at El Paso or Tijuana – and arguably a lot more of the Central and South American continent than US citizens would like to admit is indisputably, North America (*see also* Pastor 2001). But, as ever, this reality is driven by economic facts way in advance of any political understanding, as ongoing, contradictory struggles about immigration policy in the USA illustrate. It awaits a political leadership able to grasp it.

Europe faces similar issues with immigration, but politically and economically it is choosing a different path. In the twentieth century, Europe's greatest weakness in relation to the USA was that its borders were ambiguous and its internal politics and economics fractious – to the tune of millions dead. Discounting its tiny and practically empty neighbour, Canada, the USA took a lead as the major container nation-state in the world because it had seas on either side and vast deserts to the South. It was a nation-state like no other, and it pursued a policy of essentially open doors to immigration – and a flattening of barriers to all internal migration – that fuelled its growth and power to a scale that dwarfed all its rivals. Europe, too, eventually opened its societies to immigration and intra-regional migration, and now it seeks to manage a migration scenario that is close to being as dynamic and unruly as the one that dominates North American debates. London, *the* boomtown of European mobility, in fact shadowed the mythical immigrant city of New York in terms of immigrant-led population growth in the period 2000–2005. But there is one major difference between the continents. The USA has to look South for its sources of cheap labour. Europe, on the other hand, can look East; and this is what it has been increasingly doing.

But where does this leave Europe's own South? Put another way, this is the ethnic question of European identity again: the crucial issue of whether or not Moroccans and Turks – by far the largest immigrant populations in Europe, and the closest 'ethnic' neighbours – are also mobile Europeans by the logic of regional integration. The politics currently do not look good: Europe may choose to heed nativism and treat its Moroccans and Turks in the same dismal fashion in which the USA treats its Central American 'alien' workforce. Yet, by a purely economic/concentric logic of regional integration, their mobility should come to resemble less and less the traditional nationalising/ integrating immigrant trajectory, and more that of new and potential East European members. Other contiguous populations to the South and East might also make this claim – although the space of the European neighbourhood, as any space, has to end somewhere. Physical borders matter; to some extent you can build walls and patrol seas. The USA is trying this again on its Southern border, although as tens of thousands of have discovered at great human cost, it does not stop migration. But other mechanisms can make migration a lot more unpleasant. What if Europe could remove its reliance on ethnic workers in the lower, secondary slots in the economy; if demand itself could be removed by a racial and ethnocentric logic? For the time being, this seems the underlying logic determinate in defining who can be a 'free mover' and who cannot. The strong suspicion is that the eastward expansion of Europe is being built with a racial logic, seeking to open borders to the East while closing them to the South. This is politically functional, economically attractive, and a dynamic solution in the short term.

European enlargement and externalising agreements have made it possible for Europe to look East. These same policies are being used to more effectively border and police borders in the South – reinforcing borders and, through neighbourhood policies, enticing Southern states in Africa and the Middle East financially and politically in order to implement more effective means of remote control. The payoff for a Europe, which is uneasy primarily about a neighbouring Islamic South rather than a less familiar Balkan East, is clear. Poles, Romanians and Ukrainians are white and Christian; Turks, Moroccans, Senegalese, or Somalians are not. But there is a sting in the tail of this logic: it will not solve the longer term demography question. East Europeans have similarly low birth rates to their West European neighbours. The tension here between a porous East and a bordered South is thus likely to be a central defining feature of the ongoing regional integration being built after Enlargement. As always with the study of population movements, this dramatic macro-process can be most effectively viewed and humanly grasped through the micro-level experiences of the various migrants enacting these processes in Europe at the ground level, a task to which I return in several of the chapters in this volume.

Part One

Applied Political Philosophy:
The Problem of Multicultural Citizenship

Chapter Two

Multicultural Citizenship in Theory and Practice: Applied Political Philosophy in Empirical Analyses

There has been strong interest in political philosophy in recent decades, but the discipline remains plagued by doubt about whether its reflections can really be applied to politics and policy making in the real world.[1] As any empirical political scientist will readily point out, there is an enormous gulf between 'ideal' foundational philosophical reflections on rights, liberty, equality or justice, and the murky institutional and technocratic practice of 'actual existing liberalism': the complex world of policy dilemmas, legal technicalities and party politics, of tragic choices, trade-offs and dirty hands.

As I argue in this chapter, this problem runs through even some of the most 'applied' reflections in contemporary political philosophy. Here, taking one area of applied normative political theory – the problem of 'multicultural citizenship' – I illustrate why mainstream liberal philosophy, in particular the liberal-communitarian debate centred on the work of Will Kymlicka and others, does not always contribute a great deal to understanding questions of multicultural citizenship in practice. In contrast to the justice-based questions explored by post-Rawlsian 'philosophy and public affairs', I will argue that the questions normative political theory should be asking are the ones that follow most naturally from the comparative *empirical* study of liberal democratic forms and practices. This kind of approach leads to an exploration of the normative logic embedded and legible in actual existing liberal institutions. I thus make a rather different 'normative political analysis' and critique

1. Previously unpublished in English (the article was serially rejected by a string of eminent political philosophy journals!). Appeared translated in Dutch as 'Multicultureel burgerschap in theorie en pratijk: empirische analyses in de toegepaste politieke filosofie', in *Krisis: Tijdschrift voor Filosofie*, nr.72, herfst (1998), 67–85. Both this chapter and the following draw heavily on Adrian Favell (1998a/2001) *Philosophies of Integration: Immigration and the Idea of Citizenship in France and Britain*. London: Palgrave, which started life as a PhD (1995) at the European University Institute, Florence. This work was eventually much better received by comparative historical sociologists, particularly in the USA, than by the Anglo-American normative political philosophers to whom it was initially most addressed. I would like to acknowledge, however, the enormously supportive engagement of Will Kymlicka with this work, as well as the strong influence of my original supervisors, Steven Lukes and Alessandro Pizzorno, and my examiners, Jean Leca, Bhikhu Parekh and Christian Joppke. Some of the arguments were also developed in collaboration with Tariq Modood (a project which eventually led to Modood *et al.* 2006), and before this while holding a Hoover Fellowship alongside Wayne Norman, with Philippe van Parijs at Louvain-la-Neuve. My thanks to all these scholars. Thanks also to Ben Crum, Andreas Føllesdal and Ido de Haan in relation to the argument here; also to two Oxford PhDs, Romain Garbaye and Varun Oberoi, with whom I was subsequently delighted to be involved.

of the institutional responses found in two societies central to the West European experience with multicultural citizenship, Britain and France. The intention of this preliminary work is to sketch out a methodology for the practice of applied political philosophy alternate to those familiar from the rarefied seminar rooms of contemporary political theory.

Liberals and communitarians: The limits of a philosophical research programme

After the publication of John Rawls's seminal work *A Theory of Justice* (1971), there was a veritable re-birth of analytical political theory in Anglo-American political science, which quickly took on increasingly applied dimensions, particularly centred on the journal *Philosophy and Public Affairs*. One of the central strands was the liberal-communitarian debate, which arose out of various critiques of Rawls's astringent Kantian individualism by Michael Sandel (1982), Michael Walzer (1983), Joseph Raz (1986), Will Kymlicka (1989), Iris Marion Young (1990) and Charles Taylor (1992) (*see* Gutmann 1994). Essentially, the terms of this debate enabled the formulation of complex public policy and jurisprudential dilemmas in the form of a seductive philosophical binary opposition and paradox, most forcefully emphasised in the work of Kymlicka: how to reconcile the defence of the rights, liberties and equality of individual citizens in a constitutional polity, with a recognition of the value of community-based identities, and the provision of special group rights or concessions to minorities? Another version of this formulation, most associated with Walzer, is the reconciliation of universally-granted equal membership and entitlements in a society, with the fact that membership and citizenship must be based on some kind of boundary closure and exclusion of outsiders. From the mid-1980s onwards, these terms of debate became the dominant transatlantic framework for the theoretical discussion of 'multicultural citizenship' as the philosophical response to growing dilemmas of diversity and immigration in public life (other key references include Mulhall and Swift 1992; Kymlicka 1995; Parekh 2000; Barry 2000; *see also* Favell and Modood 2003).

With the rising prevalence of all kinds of 'ethnic dilemmas' (Glazer 1983) in Europe and North America – the problems of immigration, minorities or ethnic and racial conflict – the philosophical question of reconciling cultural or value pluralism with political unity has undoubtedly grown politically in importance and circulation during these years. Although at first the two sides of the debate drew lines of opposition between individualist, rights-based liberals, and communitarian or identity-based liberals, the opposition gave way increasingly to a search for theoretical solutions, often versions of civic republicanism or constitutional patriotism, drawing in other figures such as Jürgen Habermas (1992), David Miller (1995), Chantal Mouffe (2000) and Seyla Benhabib (2001). Most broadly speaking, 'citizenship' was the central buzzword and focus for these concerns, hooking up the theoretical debate with the current political debates about citizenship rights and duties, membership and nationality laws in many Western liberal democratic states and supra-national arenas (*see* especially Kymlicka and Norman 1994). In terms of the core reference of contemporary political philosophy – Rawls's ongoing defence and development of *A Theory of Justice* – the new liberal-communitarian debate even inspired a notable shift in his central concerns towards the problems of cultural pluralism and diversity. Beginning in 1985 and culminating in his second book *Political Liberalism* (1993), Rawls reformulated his work in terms of a search for an 'overlapping consensus' – a strictly political, constitutional framework detached from a substantive liberal morality – that could provide an acceptable frame of reference and identification for all kinds of cultural and religious groups within a properly tolerant liberal polity.

The Rawlsian framework has remained the most natural philosophical idiom for these debates – for liberal sympathisers and their more radical critics alike – because of the sharp, line-drawing dilemmas it poses. The search for overlapping consensus immediately poses the question of where its limits lie. Should a tolerant society tolerate the intolerant: those who do not consciously accept and adhere to the constitutional framework on offer? It is not difficult to recognise in this formulation, the heart of classic political dilemmas with immigrant diversity, particularly those which have long gripped politics in countries like The Netherlands, Denmark and France.[2] Where does the liberal state draw the line on group practices that appear to infringe the constitutional rights and liberties of the individual? These theoretical conundrums are the perfect idiom for the kind of set piece 'hard cases' beloved of philosophy and theory seminars. Should the public education system force Amish children to go to school? Should the state allow indigenous North American groups to impose exit restrictions on their younger members? Should the Western state tolerate certain culturally 'sacred' practices towards women and children – wearing veils, female circumcision, polygamy, etc. – that it would not tolerate for white Westerners, for example, in relation to Islam in Western Europe? These classic dilemmas are all important questions, but I wish to here raise an issue about the extent it is useful or representative to formulate complex political and institutional questions of policy and jurisprudence, solely in terms of the initial philosophical paradox. Such formulation presupposes of course that philosophical reflection alone might lead to a philosophical solution, and hence have some use in enlightening or even dissolving the real live cases at hand in contemporary law or politics.

In effect, the original liberal-communitarian debate, and the more applied works that it has engendered, amounted to an intellectual 'research programme' of the kind discussed by the philosophy of science. Around a fixed, widely shared core of philosophical method and goals – the intuitive Rawlsian method of generating abstract foundational principles from seminar room discussion – thought within this frame has gone on to apply itself to an ever wider range of cases. What is most characteristic of its applied versions is the eclectic and almost casual way case-study material is introduced to illustrate foundational positions. The very different applied questions mentioned above – that involve rather different types of racial,

---

2. The philosophical terms of this debate were played out again in the debates about the Danish cartoon affair debated by Modood and others in 2006; much of Christian Joppke's prolific output of the 2000s has focused insistently on these stylised 'hot button' issues, i.e. Joppke (2014).

ethnic or religious groups, in very different national or institutional contexts – are all identified as expressing the same essential core opposition and paradox of liberal-communitarian theory, and hence processed through this frame. Yet this is a frame whose terms and reasoning delimit and restrict what can be seen through it, as much it enables and enlightens. It is at this point, to again borrow language from the philosophy of science, that the research programme may become a 'degenerate' one.

This can be illustrated by briefly looking at the kinds of things enabled and delimited by what was perhaps the most widely-read practical philosopher at the heart of the liberal-communitarian debate: Kymlicka, particularly his *Multicultural Citizenship* (1995). Despite being an applied work dominated by distinctly Canadian political concerns (Uberoi 2007), it is work deeply attached to the thought that the problems of multicultural citizenship can be encapsulated in a single 'reasonable' philosophical position that helps 'solve' the practical dilemmas to which it refers. Despite the Canadian starting point, there are no formal geographical boundaries to the scope of the philosophical frameworks on offer: they are intended to apply to liberal pluralism wherever it exists and is practised. Accordingly, it was work which rapidly became cited across Europe and further afield as a model of how liberalism might reconcile its ethnic and multicultural dilemmas.

What such work does provide is an intelligently reflective ethical background for more practical legal-based discussions of hard cases in practice: arguments for the Herculean-style supreme court judgements that ideally should take place over constitutional type questions, but which inevitably will be compromised by contextual and contingent political influences. Yet there are problems with the accumulative choice and use of illustrative case material in both works, particularly as they reach outside of the North American legal culture in which the arguments work best. Kymlicka adheres to the philosopher's presumption that sufficiently subtle clarification and reflective, common-sense arguments about the examples cited will be enough to fit disparate examples from across the Western world into the same philosophical problematic. This magpie-like approach to appropriating illustrative material as 'hard cases', characteristic of political philosophy seminars, however, pays little attention to the preliminary problems of empirical interpretation or comparative method, which any comparative explanatory study of the same subject would be duty bound to consider.[3]

Kymlicka builds his defence around a recognisable justice-based foundation, influenced also by Dworkin's notion of an 'egalitarian plateau' (*see also* Kymlicka 1989), which draws the line on both the degree of external protection of group rights by the state, and the tolerance of limitations put on members of groups by their own communities. On top of this, he draws a central interpretative distinction between the claims of national minorities and those of ethnic immigrant groups that hinges on a core philosophical assumption about the importance of a secure national-cultural upbringing as the source of liberal 'autonomy'. The former groups thus have a strong

---

3. Kymlicka (2010) himself explores the question of the relation of normative theory to empirical evidence, discussing also my critique of his work. Particularly important in his later work has been the attempt with Banting (2006) to collect data on the relation of multiculturalism to welfare state solidarity (i.e. the politics of recognition and the politics of redistribution), as a counter to the conservative claims by authors such as Putnam (2007) that diversity damages social cohesion.

claim to group rights and self-government, whereas the latter can only claim them to assist integration into their new national home and identity. These bold distinctions indeed help clarify the stakes in national cases where both groups are present and competing for minority rights and entitlements, most obviously in contemporary Canada. But equally, they fail in cases where such distinctions are not the centre of the political or legal dilemmas. Notably, the question of post-slavery Blacks in the USA – the classic 'American dilemma' – does not fit, a group that was neither an indigenous national minority nor a voluntary immigrant group. By a similar token, the criteria do not capture the complex stakes involved with the integration of post-colonial immigrants and guest workers in traditional (non-immigrant built) European nation-states, particularly as Europe evolves into a new kind of transnational political and social entity (*see also* Kastoryano 1998a; Jacobs 2000; Modood *et al.* 2006).

For example, what in Britain is called multiculturalism (for example, the provision of *halal* meat in hospitals, or allowing Sikhs to carry daggers in public), Kymlicka would call 'polyethnicity' (Kymlicka 1995). British 'polyethnicity', however, is a legacy of empire; most migrants came from states that had been incorporated into the British Empire in ways not dissimilar to the incorporations of 'nations' in Canada and the USA. These states contributed to Britain's economic development and to its superpower status; some migrants were ex-servicemen, with many others having relatives who had risked or given their lives for Britain. For the West Indians, England was the 'mother country'; for the children of the Raj, the Queen was the head of the British Commonwealth and the migrants were subjects of the Crown, transposing their village kinship networks to the metropolitan centre of the Empire. They moved mostly to Britain to meet its demand for cheap labour. The post-colonial relationship with Empire thus created specific kinds of ties, which in turn legitimated specific multicultural claims of recognition; these cannot be captured by Kymlicka's thinner notion of 'polyethnicity' in which immigrant groups have lesser claims than national minorities.

Another controversial application of Kymlicka's work was debating the limits of minority rights representation for territorial minorities in East and Central Europe in the light of his original theory (Kymlicka 2000). Kymlicka's ideas on nationhood push us dangerously towards ethno-cultural secession if taken seriously in this context, but his crisp formulation does show why there is and has to be a stand off between the drive for improved cultural rights and representation for minorities and the need to build (or re-build) inclusive federal citizenship regimes that can include all within the nation. The toughness of these dilemmas has often led hard-line liberal individualists to denounce all culture sensitive arguments as condoning the slippery slope to 'tribal' identity politics and the undermining of liberal values.[4]

The emphasis in the liberal-communitarian debate, in Kymlicka and others, on reducing all 'ethnic dilemmas' across North America and Western Europe to

---

4. A vituperative attack on the emergent 'liberal culturalist' consensus in the 1990s – and the work of Kymlicka in particular – was Brian Barry's *Culture and Equality* (2000). Barry picked up and discussed several points of my critique here, but from a much more negative anti-multicultural stance.

problems of 'multicultural citizenship', was an effect of the theoretical approach that had significant consequences as it has become the dominant frame of wider public debate. There was a general tendency across Western liberal states to discuss issues raised by immigration and integration as predominantly problems about the limits of *cultural* pluralism, which the theorists abetted. One consequence of highlighting only this core liberal-communitarian question, was to stereotype and over-problematise the cultural 'difference' of a minority group in relation to 'Western' culture, and hence exaggerate the threat of 'cultural fundamentalism'. This became the typical reaction to the growing issue of Muslims in Western Europe. It created the perception that the integration of Muslim groups or individuals is all a question of accommodating (or refusing) 'their' cultural diversity and the value pluralism this entails. Thinking only along this dimension, however, casts a blind eye to the fact that such integration problems might be more a question of socio-economic inequality, majority population insecurity and discrimination, or symptomatic of wider problems of social integration and national unity.

To avoid these conceptual restrictions – and illustrate how real multicultural dilemmas and responses involve much more than the abstract liberal-communitarian frame can capture – a different 'case-study' led approach is required. Whatever 'philosophies' exist *historically* in liberal democracies, they must have taken shape as actual existing institutions that might, in incipient form at least, be found in actual existing liberal democracies (a point inspired by Walzer 1987). What, then, if we turned the question around, and instead tried to 'read' the institutional solutions to certain multicultural dilemmas found by two liberal democratic states – in this case, Britain and France – as examples of liberal thinking *in practice*, rather than starting from philosophical first principles?[5] Would this not teach us something about the achievements and limitations of applied liberal political thought that ideal philosophical formulation might not reveal?

Two liberal democracies and their 'ethnic dilemmas': An empirical enquiry

Although radical theorists may wish to dispute their progressive credentials, in terms of comparative politics Britain and France can both lay claim to being among the most established, liberal democratic states, with political and social institutions that have been at the forefront historically of establishing enlightenment values in the Western world. Yet ask a political philosopher to apply his or her justice-based theory of multicultural citizenship to the institutions these two countries have created in the post-war period for dealing with immigration and cultural pluralism, and they are likely to conclude that these institutions do not match up to the ideal philosophical standards prescribed.

---

5. It might be argued in fact that in his later work Kymlicka did indeed shift to a more historical and institutional approach, arguing in (2007) for a reading of the political origins and practices of liberal multiculturalism in certain countries and international rights standards that might have worldwide application. Although philosophers have barely glanced at work by sociologists on this subject, Rex (1985) also offers a relevant social theoretical starting point for the approach here.

Why is this? After all, it is possible to make a plausible 'rational reconstruction' of the distinct national 'institutional solutions' that have been developed in these respective countries. In this way, each can be read as a relatively coherent version of philosophical liberalism in practice: 'public theories' of moral social integration formed under the constraints and conditions of liberal democratic politics, existing institutional forms and the specificities of the problems they faced. Read like this, these public theories can be seen to be normative in intent, and dependent on an underlying normative rationale for their operation, their successes and, over time, their deficiencies and failures. Such a public theory, or 'public philosophy' (Favell 1998a) as I prefer to call it, is a loose interpretative frame that can be read from the central public discourse, political documents and formulations surrounding key legislative or political events in the historical emergence of an overall institutional solution. In crude terms, France developed public policies that embody a revamped version of its traditional individualistic republicanism: an idea of assimilation into the open, 'universal' and meritocratic French political culture, that is adapted to the specific problems associated with turning North African and African immigrants of mainly Islamic origin into competent individual French *citoyens* (*see also* Favell 1997). Britain, meanwhile, built its post-colonial institutions on a predominantly paternalistic liberal logic of race relations management, coupled with a decentralised philosophy of multiculturalism: combining race-based anti-discrimination laws with social policies that aim to integrate groups by allowing them to organise around cultural and religious goals at local levels (*see also* the following chapter).

Whatever their internal logic and applied credentials as theories of moral social integration, it seems certain that both the philosophy of republican *intégration* in France, and that of multicultural race relations in Britain, would fail any test of 'overlapping consensus' as conceived in Rawlsian style work. Constitutionally and in substantive political terms, neither country recognises the concessions or assistance offered to immigrant groups as fundamental or minority *rights*. Moreover, those special provisions that are available have been made specifically in terms of the two countries' post-colonial obligations and are limited to certain well-defined target groups: they are thus *partial* and not *generalisable* in their justification. Thirdly, these institutions can be seen to be founded predominantly on an underlying rationale of historical *expediency* and concern for *social order*, not justice-based criteria. Such institutions would fail any justice-derived principles that based their rationale – as all applied philosophers in the Rawlsian vein do – on being principles that could be accepted with conscious, reasonable and impartial agreement by all notional parties involved: the high principled 'constructivist' Kantian starting point which rejects utilitarian justifications. Paternalist and partial reasons, and reasons based on expedient trade-offs are, in particular, ruled out by these terms. Rawls adhered to these 'tests' because he believed that the stability of a 'good' society depends on the existence of such consensually accepted principles, which provide the social glue across other moral and cultural differences. It is this that makes possible the achievement of a moral social order – the moral overlapping consensus beyond the 'mere' instrumental *modus vivendi*. In explanatory terms, this will strike historical social scientists as questionable: an obviously functionalist claim about the principles said to be agreed on in the ideal liberal order: that the ideals themselves that cause (pull) a genuinely liberal society's institutions to work. What is the explanatory realism of this claim? If it does apply to contemporary societies – as Rawls certainly thought it did – it must be that the ideal principles could be shown to exist *empirically* as ideas with causal explanatory power, and that they do in fact at some level independently *explain* (i.e. net of other explanations) the existence and success of actual liberal democratic institutional forms, as opposed to other forms of political organisation.

Applied political philosophy in a Rawlsian vein is, in effect, left to make sense of this tacit explanatory claim. The problem shows up very clearly in Kymlicka's work. Despite avoiding many of the complex thought experiments that sustain the full Rawlsian model, Kymlicka is still led to argue that it is the justice and principled foundations of minority rights institutions *not* their political expediency or historical tradition that ensure and sustain their success in practice. This is not only a normative claim. It smuggles in with it a rather implausible historical and explanatory claim about how just institutions do in fact work in the real world. The problem, as Kymlicka recognised at the end of *Multicultural Citizenship*, is going on to demonstrate *why* it is the normative ideals expressed in the philosophical justification and *not* expediency or tradition, that create the norms of good citizenship behaviour in actual liberal democratic societies. To explain, as he put it, how multicultural citizenship solves the 'the mystery of the ties that bind'. Yet the British and French cases indicate that such institutions have in reality established themselves by incorporating a logic of expediency, trade-off and non-generalisability that would be ruled out of court by his standards. The justice-based approach in other words imposes a lens that makes it impossible to understand how and why these two actual existing liberal democracies work in their own terms.

Turning to the case studies at hand, we need therefore to make an analysis of the normative logic in the British and French institutions, which is able to account for their normative achievements, even if they do not match up to the ideal conditions of overlapping consensus. This sort of approach might be framed in terms of two other classics of modern political theory. There is, firstly, a Tocquevillian question. If we look to the cases to see how and by which rationale these institutions actually work, what kind of evidence do they produce about the conditions and institutional forms of social and political association most essential to rooting and sustaining liberal democratic practices? Secondly, there is a Madisonian question. With a much less idealistic conception in mind about how citizens and political actors in fact are, what kind of artificial institutional devices have been implemented in these cases, to ensure progressive outcomes and avoid a breakdown of the political system and society?[6] Both of these questions are normative in nature, but both can also be used to explore the way Britain and France have faced up to the challenge of resecuring moral and social integration in the face of immigration and growing cultural pluralism.

---

6. *See also* Favell (1998c), which links the Tocquevillian point to Bellah *et al.* (1985) or Putnam (1993), and the revival of civic culture arguments. The Madisonian point, meanwhile, has been pursued by analytical political theorists interested in institutional design, such as Elster *et al.* (1998).

In theoretical terms, in other words, applied normative theory thus needs to rediscover institutions in its account of the justification of actual existing liberal democratic forms (a point also made by Bellah *et al.* 1991). What will be found, is that there is a whole range of normative achievements that can be attributed to the rational and coherent *organisation* of institutional arrangements. That is, it is not only the existence of agreed-on principles that may justify a political or social institution; but also its manner of structural organisation. As explored by theorists such as North (1990), and developed by March and Olsen (1989) and Powell and DiMaggio (1991) under the banner of 'new institutionalism', thinking about the organisational basis of liberal democratic politics focuses on the role of structural institutional factors in explaining how it works. It also involves thinking about how institutions emerge and evolve over time. Institutions, on the one hand, can be thought of as the formal institutions of politics, law and constitution, and the rules by which different parts of the state and polity relate to one another. But beyond this, institutional analysis considers the emergence of social norms, and the linguistic and symbolic process of establishing the classifications and meanings with which a political system builds a frame for approaching public problems. It is these kinds of normative achievements that we can look for in the institutions of multicultural citizenship that have emerged in Britain and France in the post-war period.

Institutions as conceptual frames and narratives

If we look at the two empirical cases this way, what is most striking about the two cases are the differences in the language, terms and concepts by which Britain and France identify what is at stake in the public problem of immigration and integration. This concerns the way in which the public philosophies codify and classify their 'ethnic dilemmas'. The social 'reality' these represent is, firstly, carved up in a variety of ways, according to the distinct ethnic/racial/cultural/national differences and identities that immigrant groups are seen to embody. Secondly, the philosophies identify what the essential mechanisms of integration are in different ways, 'narrating' an ideal-typical story in relation to a distinct national history and political culture. This is a key element of the institutional picture, because the objects, processes and causality of integration are by no means self-evident, and are in fact constructed by the public philosophy as it seeks to justify its distinct national approach.[7]

Both countries in fact adapted their colonial classificatory devices of management to the new post-colonial situation. The first step for Britain was institutionalising through new nationality laws key distinctions between 'commonwealth' immigrants and others. Identifying these immigrants as a special 'responsibility', this in part enabled the doors to be so effectively closed to others at such an early stage (Favell 1998a, Ch.4; *see also* Dummett and Nicol 1990;

---

7. In recent work, Schinkel has developed this line of approach with a more ostensibly critical theory of public philosophies of integration; *see* Schinkel (2013).

Hansen 2000; Bleich 2003). The select group that got in, were unproblematically seen as legal residents and full British citizens, without further conditions. This was not a problem identity-wise because of the gap that already existed between the legal category of 'British' nationality/citizenship and the multiple idea of 'national' identity, given the existence of distinct national identities within Britain (i.e. English, Scottish, Welsh etc.). Nor was it a problem substantively, given the emptiness of the citizenship category and the weakness of its political meaning in fundamental or formal rights terms. Ethnic minorities were essentially accepted in Britain on condition of being good subjects of the Crown, rather than full citizens in the classic philosophical sense of the word. Within the frame of strictly controlled external distinctions, a progressive-minded set of distinctions could then be created to manage internal relations through public law: the 'race relations' classifications, which broadly identified the ethnic immigrants according to an artificial generic category of 'race' (basically Black/Asian), but allowed for further evolution to adapt to new cases ('racial' became 'ethnic', allowing for other cultural groups to gain legal coverage). This symbolic logic of extending recognition to the select range of post-commonwealth groups is at the heart of the evolving philosophy of multiculturalism. Although progressive minded, it is a select logic, that does not admit other cases that fall outside of Britain's special post-colonial responsibilities; nor does it foresee potential problems with the break-up of British nationality, the fragmenting of artificial racial groupings themselves, or new migrations bringing on the phenomenon of 'super-diversity' (Favell 1998a, Ch.6; Vertovec 2007).

France is an excellent counterpoint to Britain in all these classificatory measures, because officially it sought to exclude all racial or ethnic type classifications from its public philosophy. Despite a similar post-colonial starting point, the French political consensus that emerged as the 'new republican synthesis' on immigration and integration policy in the 1980s, adhered vehemently to the thought that 'French' is a universally open category, linked to a specifically *political* identity and form of social membership, not any specific ethnic characteristics (Favell 1998a, Ch.2; Schnapper 1991; Todd 1994). This idea has always enjoyed wide acceptance, despite being frequently contested by the political extremes on the spectrum, either for excluding a culturally-specific ethno-national definition of France or a truly multicultural one. Given that 'natural' ethno-cultural criteria are ruled out, the drawing of boundaries between French/non-French – and hence official naturalisation procedures – becomes the key policy issue. With the problematisation of this at the heart of political conflict, France thus saw in the decades since all kinds of further conditions on attaining full nationality: in order, it is always said, to guarantee successful *intégration*. The ideal category of French *citoyen* thus increasingly has become moralised in its terms and conditions. Full *citoyenneté* is predicated on proofs of political participation, cognitive adhesion to French republican values, and the public display of the moral virtues of citizenship. In other words, one has to *deserve* to be French. What has been kept strictly out of the picture is the thought that integration could pass through the identification with any kind of ethnic or cultural groupings that are not in some way regulated as official associations by the central state. The French for this reason typically always look with dismay at the British practices of 'communitarian' ethnic and racial and classification. Officially, the counting of ethnic and racial minorities is not permissible in France: all population statistics have been done by nationality origin, with *immigrés* and *étrangers* set in binary opposition to the category of French citizen (*see* fuller discussion in Simon 2005). *Minorités* meanwhile are also not officially possible in a liberal state that is still conceived to be based on the collective will of all free and equal *individual* citizens. These restrictions can be a problem if in public perceptions people habitually identify ethnic or racial traits with the category of *étrangers* or *immigrés*; but they also impose a strict official meritocracy and colour-blindness in public life. As ever, the key process is the transformation of the outsider *immigré* into model *citoyen*: a journey that passes through an ideal, and heavily stylised, public institutional formation in the rules and identity of the political system.

In both countries, these systematic methods of categorising policy responses to immigration and integration were established by 'naturalising' the terms and concepts used to fit with the wider narrative of the nation. The narrative component of the public philosophy thus built a wider acceptance of the mainstream liberal goals and efforts, by linking the new policies on immigration and integration with national tradition on the one hand, and national destiny on the other. Britain and France differ in some important respects on these questions.

Britain is curious in that the logic of the justification for race relations was essentially based on a forward thinking, *avant-garde*, yet a thoroughly expedient calculation. Adopting a repertoire of control and management techniques that certainly had distant roots in both colonial rule and the classic political management of the Union, the overt justification was in fact based on a kind of medium-term vision: that British public order and national stability would best be secured by an early resolution of the ethnic minorities' status and acceptance of those already there. It was, in other words, an example of utilitarian consequentialist reasoning, put together by a white paternalist elite. It was not notably pushed from below by ethnic minority mobilisation; nor did it mirror progressive social attitudes, being well in advance of public opinion. The logic was conservative, with a nervous eye on majority population reaction and any break-up of the two party domination of mainstream politics. In many ways, before the break-up of this compromise with the impact of new migrations after the 1990s, the solution synthesised the best of classic British conservatism and liberal progressive thought.[8] However, a medium-term solution is not necessarily a long-term one. The reasoning has also been self-effacing in many ways. In the 1990s, it was indeed possible to look back at the successes of multicultural race relations and claim that the logic was in fact the fulfilment of a process of incremental social incorporation, along the lines of the classic theories of T.H. Marshall (1950), seeing the progressive expansion of legal and political rights through to the full social rights of the welfare state. This rights-based logic in fact masks the much longer historical antecedents of

---

8. In *Philosophies of Integration* (1998a/2001), Ch.4, I discuss this in relation to the classic liberal inheritance of Locke, Hume, and Mill, and in connection with contemporary theorists such as Joseph Raz (1986), John Dunn (1990), and John Gray (1993).

the conflict management technique and political organisation, justified by more utilitarian means (Barry 1965). Crucially, it also masks the dangers that have so far been avoided by keeping immigration issues strictly separate from other minority issues within the fragile British Union. Above all, Britain's public philosophy is an island-bounded, strictly national solution.

French social architects, meanwhile, went out of their way to root the solution put together under very contingent and politically-driven pressures in the 1980s on the long term 'classic' French tradition. There was an effort across the board to picture the new republican synthesis as simply the reproduction of traditional French practices of nation building at the end of the 19th century, where Italians, Polish and other working-class immigrants were integrated into full French citizenship, along with all the disparate regional identities of *l'Hexagone*. The inappropriateness of these myths to post-war, post-colonial immigration in a globalising, post-industrial society were systematically airbrushed out of the picture. The teleology of the French integration story, still anchored today, is always conceived as a smooth unbroken tradition, working through to the present and a fully integrated 'universalist' future. It is untroubled by the breaks for Vichy, racialised immigration politics after World War Two or the trauma of colonial war in Algeria (Shepard 2006). Similarly, the very different competing French traditions of nativist ethno-cultural identity, and the place of the Catholic church were left out of the picture. Even the recent fact that, prior to the 1980s, immigration questions were dealt with by a pragmatic, devolved focus on welfare and dissipating class conflict (closer to Britain's approach), was lost in the new teleological vision. Despite coinciding with the 1989 *bicentennaire*, *la République du centre* pronounced by intellectuals at the end of the 1980s, and which has reigned since, was in fact a recent and rather contingent invention. The French Republican model is a brave and extraordinarily particular one, which has always given little thought to how France is being changed by its place in Europe, and the growing effects of sub-state regionalisation.

Institutional spheres and arenas

The organisational basis of liberal democratic politics can be considered not only in terms of its language and categorisation, but also in terms of its formal structural properties. Again, this may open up the thought that justice-based criteria of conscious reasoned agreement is not the only source of normative legitimacy or justification in a liberal political system. Trade-offs and institutional compromises are an inevitable, yet still potentially virtuous, part of this picture; problems may also be dealt with by separating them into different *spheres* of jurisdiction (Walzer 1983). There is also the question of the distinct *levels* of institutional organisation (Elster 1992). Competing arenas at the local or supra-state level – which counter-balance the rationale pursued by the central state – may also be an essential part of the political system's overall approach to practical problems.

The institutional structures and separations that cut across the conceptual frameworks thus play an integral role in the normative logic and goals of both public philosophies. Again, these are structures that have faced new challenges in recent years. The establishment philosophies though are still clear in their outline. In Britain, integration is assured for those minorities recognised within the philosophy, through a strict separation of the spheres of exterior immigration control and internal race relations management. Immigration control is strictly disassociated from the anti-discrimination criteria of race relations, and successive Home Secretaries have always refused to allow the two spheres to be connected, as they would be if immigration procedures and agencies were brought under the coverage of the anti-discrimination laws. Moreover, re-thinking immigration policy in terms of more universalistic naturalisation procedures – let alone rights-based or economic criteria – has been consistently refused, despite a net emigration from Britain and a very strong brain-drain to the USA and mainland Europe. The controls are focused on upholding the original Commonwealth-based categories and the special status of those already there: with the widely accepted belief – shared in the main by British ethnic minorities themselves – that integration and the progressive evolution of public opinion is dependent on a strict doors-closed policy. Race relations and multiculturalism work on an entirely different logic. The role of anti-discrimination law is regulatory, shaping change through its evolutionary and symbolic logic, rather than in pursuing interventory social change. The law does not enforce 'constitutional' rights: cases are brought as private law challenges to named companies or organisations, expanding the range of the legislation when they become test cases that open new coverage within its provisions. In public life, the emphasis has been on the bi-partisan depoliticisation of race and ethnicity issues in mainstream politics. Integration is not conceived to pass through the mainstream representation of minority interests, or a full range of special civil and political rights (as in the USA). Nor is the fulfilment of integration seen to be the transformation of the newcomer into a full public political category of citizen (the idea of citizenship remains a weak, non-politicised one in Britain). Integration, rather, is seen to pass through representation at local levels, especially voluntary involvement in 'civic' spheres such as local education, religion and homeland-oriented cultural associations. The ideas here about achieving a moral social order represent the influence of classic, anti-Statist English pluralism, and a prudent, *laissez-faire* idea of managing cultural and class differences.

France, again, officially does largely the opposite. Immigration laws and subsequent processes of integration are seen to be closely bound up through the naturalisation procedures, and the fact nationality law spells out the terms and conditions of citizenship in the French nation. Integration is thus centrally seen to pass through the formal public political sphere of open conscious adherence to public law, and full political participation as a political individual in the state. Classically, the two pillars of membership in the political community are symbolised as *la code et la carte*: the system of civil law, and the national identity card. There is a strict dividing of the public and private spheres: cultural pluralism, as represented by religious diversity is allowed, even welcomed, but only on the condition that it does not infringe on the public sphere. The great enemy is political pluralism: the existence of organised groups representing factional 'interest groups' using the public sphere for their own interests not that of *la République*. A meso-level of heavily 'organised' state-regulated associations is designed to mediate the two spheres, and assure that the citizenship identity of political participation is not dissipated in the interests of narrow ethnic sections or groupings. The state thus retains a high level of control over cultural politics regulating these questions, and in particular centralises the regulation of the spheres of education and religion. An independent judiciary offers no special provisions for ethnic or cultural groups. However, a well-developed range of constitutional rights-based provisions protect equality and enforce anti-discrimination as essential to good republican principles and maintaining universal human rights.

The normative logic of these two distinct systems has been best revealed by how they deal with ethnic dilemmas in practice. As an illustration, we might turn to two well-known 'hard cases' beloved of political philosophy seminars, that have often been cited as illustrating classic liberal-communitarian dilemmas: the Rushdie affair (when a well-known British Asian writer faced a death threat from Muslims worldwide over the publication of an allegedly blasphemous book) and the *affaire du foulard* (when three Muslim girls were barred from school in France for wearing their traditional religious head-scarves in class). Read in context, what was significant was how these two cases reflected the complex institutional stakes involved in multicultural issues in the two countries, and the way the two political systems worked through the crises in distinctive ways. On the other hand, neither case can be viewed as making much sense in the ideal terms of multicultural citizenship put forward by applied political philosophers, although both cases appear in Kymlicka and others' discussions (for example, Spinner-Halev 1994; Parekh 2000).[9]

Kymlicka, for example, mentions the Rushdie case as one that raises the 'classic' problem of the need to draw a constitutional line against the internal restriction of individuals within a minority group by other members of that group. This, however, would be a rather restrictive way of characterising the normative issues at stake in the case. The question of free speech versus the protection of community values was part of the picture, but this was mainly a preoccupation of intellectual debate which only partially captured the central political and institutional issues. Rather, the case revealed fault-lines in the existing institutional framework for dealing with ethnic dilemmas in Britain. Firstly, it showed up the lack of protection against religious discrimination for Muslims within a framework designed to recognise only generic 'racial' groups (the fictional 'Asian' sub-category) (*see also* Modood 1992, 1994). Second, there was the lack of legal mechanisms for dealing with a blasphemy case of this kind, because of there being no institutionalised distinction between public and private spheres in a case raising an issue of public morality over a work of art. The real normative substance of the case was thus a struggle about how and in what terms the conflict was to be publicly conceptualised for

---

9. The analysis I make of these dilemmas here and in Favell (1998) is broadly similar to the contextual reading developed in Parekh (2000), who was one of the external examiners of the original PhD (1995). My original idea for the thesis, in turn, was hugely inspired by first reading Parekh and Bhabha's (1989) discussion in *Marxism Today* as an undergraduate, as well as their early encouragement to pursue the PhD. I also discussed the PhD at an early stage with John Dunn, Gerald Cohen, and Brian Barry, and prior to this I was strongly influenced by Tim O'Hagan who introduced me to political philosophy at the University of East Anglia.

political responses. It was for this reason that the case became a focus for various challenges by certain groups to the existing institutional compromise. Seen in this way, it had very little do with the constitutional individual versus group rights issue. One might argue (as Kymlicka seems to suggest) that this only goes to prove that Britain thereby needs a formal minority rights structure to deal with this sort of problem; but this is an external perspective that would overlook all that is positive in the existing framework. Moreover, this proposition would in practice entail scrapping the complex arrangements that currently exist. Political actors involved on all sides – politicians, religious and cultural representatives, the race relations lobby – were in fact at pains after the Rushdie case to re-establish the merits of the existing mechanisms for managing ethnic diversity.

The *'affaire du foulard'*, meanwhile, would seem to be a perfect example for discussing the question: 'what are the limits of toleration?' or 'should there be a group right to wear religious symbols?'. These philosophical formulations were indeed present in the public debate – in the shape of the philosophical republican hard line on *laïcité* in the public sphere on the one hand, and *droit à la différence* type rhetoric on the other hand – but there was a great deal more at stake than abstract philosophical principles. It was, firstly, a case which at its most substantive raised questions about *who* in a centralised state such as France should have the institutional power to decide, and *which* rationale it should use (should it be the politicians, or the media, or the supreme *Conseil d'État* fixing the principles in advance; or should it be devolved to a local case by case pragmatism?). Secondly, it questioned who the girls in fact were for the purposes of political decision making and the wider goals of *intégration* (were they culturally embedded Muslims, disadvantaged immigrants, oppressed women, or potentially autonomous future *citoyens*, etc.?). And thirdly, with intellectuals playing such an important role in the public debate, it asked which type of theories were most important in answering the questions it raised (should philosophical, political, sociological or anthropological arguments count most in deciding?). In short, the case cannot be reconstructed as a one paragraph 'hard case' that can be reduced to quick 'moral' judgement according to abstract principles. Indeed, if philosophers wish to take seriously the idea of doing empirically-based contextual work, they will be forced to recognise that there are even good *philosophical* reasons why such abstract formulation of multicultural questions might be wrong. The *practice* of addressing 'ethnic dilemmas', unlike its justice-based theoretical formulation, entails more pragmatist considerations about *how* desirable ends can be achieved, as well as a recognition of the epistemological issues raised by the conceptualisation of public problems.

Political processes and dynamics

As is suggested by the analysis of the active responses that a particular 'hard case' causes them to produce, the institutional approach is distinctive because it includes institutional and political *dynamics* in the normative picture. The Rawlsian approach of uncovering the normative 'basic structure' of liberal institutions, tends to produce a static and fixed picture of how liberal democratic systems ought to be. For this reason, it underestimates the question of political *achievement*: it is often a remarkable fact that any progressive provisions for ethnic minorities have been institutionalised at all given the difficulty of pursuing legislation in open liberal democracies. After all, we know that many right-wing, mainstream, even left-wing politicians would never adopt – even after reasonable reflection, or under ideal communication conditions – the enlightened positions of ideal philosophers proposed by an overlapping consensus. In other words, the turbulent crucible of democratic conflict and compromise is a necessary part of the normative legitimacy of any new institutions. The history of immigration politics in Britain and France here demonstrate the same thing: that despite conservative reluctance to embrace progressive measures, and the new provisions created falling far short of what an ideal justice-based position would prescribe, each country nevertheless has developed over a period of years a recognisably liberal national approach to its immigration and integration dilemmas that was able to command bi-partisan adhesion and a broad social consensus. In both cases, the key element pushing this was the presence of socially destabilising extreme right-wing figures fracturing the conservative vote: Enoch Powell in Britain in the 1960s and 1970s; Le Pen in France in the 1980s and 1990s. The solutions that emerged are thus normative because they are examples of a liberal democratic political system addressing deep social problems and finding solutions: what might be considered a process of progressive 'social learning'.

Beyond the realm of 'ideal theory', it ought to be possible therefore to develop terms of evaluation and critique from a fully contextual position close to existing practices (Walzer 1987).[10] The really key question in evaluating existing liberal political institutions should be in the question of their 'institutional performance' *over time* (North 1990). A well-balanced, virtuous institutional arrangement can function well at the moment in time it is brought together. There is much to be said for the thought that the solutions produced in France and Britain were the best that might be expected given the difficult political and social conditions under which they were produced. Over time, there has also been a good deal of struggle to produce new responses to new problems as they arise. But in time, through an inability to evolve innovatively enough, and adapt in the face of new questions or unforeseen policy challenges, even the most ideal starting arrangement can begin to show *effets pervers*: what might be read as 'pathologies' or institutional 'inertia'. Such problems are an inevitable part of the disjunction between the political 'puzzling' process that brought new institutions and legislation together, and the business-as-usual functioning of this framework over the years. In institutionalist terms, they can be analysed in terms of the 'path dependency' of institutional forms (Pierson 2004). Path dependency need not be an indication of the inertia of tradition or unresponsive, mystificatory ideologies or habits. Rather, even in a normatively progressive arrangement, there will be a problem with the fact that

---

10. Michael Walzer's notion of interpretation and social criticism, developing on from his 'spheres of justice' approach is here a crucial influence on my method, as is the model of analysis on local justice developed by Jon Elster (1992). Re-winding, my sceptical and pragmatist mode of thinking in political philosophy was also decisively shaped by reading the work of John Dunn (1979, 1990).

the political and institutional forces that brought it together were invested in the original arrangements, not any potential adaptations or mutations that might be forced by change. Hence, there will be reluctance or inability for political actors to reinvest in a new arrangement with uncertain costs and benefits.

What in effect such an institutionalist path dependency analysis is charting and comparing is the *rationality* of the respective institutional solutions over time: how well the original political settlement continues to map onto the 'truth' and 'reality' of new social situations. There are three dimensions to what might be called the 'epistemological effectiveness' of a policy framework over time. It depends, firstly, on the *coherency* in practice of the framework set up: how well the elements of the framework fit together when applied, both across different institutional arenas and other public policy domains. Problems may follow if the public policy identifies the objects of policy in incoherent ways: calling them 'Blacks' in anti-discrimination law, and 'Asians' in census collection, and 'Muslims' in public political debates. Such incoherencies can only be maintained by creating sharp institutional boundaries: between 'ethnic' issues and 'poverty' issues for example. However, the constraining work of artificial institutional boundaries has costs and can become strained if not secured by tenable justifications and concrete achievements over time. The second dimension is the *representativeness* of the policy framework. 'Facts' and 'events' exist outside of the narrower political 'reality' it constructs: for example, the true numbers and origins of newcomers, or political developments taking place internationally. Faults in the representativeness of the policy construction can be diagnosed when an institutional structure has problems fitting the categories it imposes on the facts it seeks to shape. An example is 'race' legislation which tries to reduce other types of discrimination such as religious prejudice or xenophobia to the same existing categories for legislative purposes. Thirdly, there is the question of *commitment* incurred by the establishment of a policy framework. If they are established and agreed to, the very use of abstract principles in policy justification – for example equality or liberty – can have substantial feedback effects on society. These may be both in the positive effect of universalisation and abstraction, when social and political behaviour is held up to a principled standard. Or they may be, in some cases, the kinds of problems caused when morally limited individuals fail to match up to the ideals set for them. If citizens are meant to be rational, publicly spirited, politically informed, and ethically pure, then the public philosophy of integration will falter in practice if they are not in fact like that. One should think of there being stakes involved in the ordinary language use of certain words. Language contains within its meaning its own rules and prescriptions about its successful application to cases.[11]

---

11. Just as it is clearly necessary to Rawlsian assumptions about the explanatory power of principles of justice, and while immensely seductive, the classically *functionalist* logic of this version of new institutionalism I operationalise here is also clear (as was first pointed out to me by Neil Fligstein). The suppressed presence of basically Parsonian arguments in much contemporary institutionalism and (also) constructivism in political science troubled me more in later work; we critique it in Favell and Guiraudon (2009), following Barry (1971). *See also* pp.159–160 in this volume.

Evaluating the British and French frameworks for multicultural citizenship in these terms leads to a variety of contextual normative questions. What have been the benefits of the frameworks, and what have been their failures or ongoing sore-spots? Which conditions have changed that render the original solution less appropriate? What potential elements or questions of policy were not represented in the public theory? Which elements did not fit the classification and place they were given?

The basic British framework of multicultural race relations, for all its conservative/liberal paradoxes, deserves some of its reputation as an *avant-garde* and enlightened European philosophy of integration. Its anti-discrimination laws, however peculiarly they are grounded, have rarely been matched by many European countries. Moreover, the framework embodied the virtues of the legendary piecemeal and evolutionary logic of the British political system, enabling a distinctive British multiculturalism to flourish and gain wide acceptance by both the public and the political mainstream. Where ethnic minorities were visible and concentrated, then a genuinely multicultural society emerged. While the system worked, Britain was able to congratulate itself (as it often did, *see* the following chapter) on its depoliticisation of race and ethnic issues, and the exclusion of an extreme right from domestic politics: in stark contrast to many other Western European states, where the sustained rise of new right anti-immigration parties has been more marked.

This rosy picture, however, must be set against the failings of the British liberal solution in the years since immigration and diversity got politicised in the 2000s. The specific post-colonial definitions of ethnic minorities and the harshness of immigration control made these barriers and distinctions impermeable and unadaptable to new kinds of migration and the super-diversity it heralded. Britain has thus always had a poor refugee and asylum record, precisely because universalist rights-based considerations do not enter the political justifications made regarding the claims of these groups. The status, rights and welfare of resident non-nationals not able to get British citizenship is precarious and over-looked. Increasingly, too, new migrations were made up of mobile European populations, particularly from Eastern Europe, who sat very awkwardly in the integrationist multiculturalism reigning in Britain (*see* Chapter Eight on issues concerning new East-West migration). Meanwhile, the practice of multiculturalism increasingly came into conflict with the intentions of the race relations mechanism. There was a declining emphasis on addressing poverty and welfare in the integration process, and a great deal more emphasis on national cultural issues and socialisation. Woefully neglected over the years, there was the constant threat of inner city rioting for those not bought off by the large range of cultural concessions made at the expense of genuine positive discrimination. The protection and recognition of racial categories have only ever been problematically extended to Muslim groups, who also happen to be the section of the Asian population most susceptible to poverty and inner city conditions (Modood *et al.* 1997). The conjunction of these factors lay behind the emergence of Muslims in Britain in as a militant group, for which the Rushdie affair was an epicentre (*see* the following chapter). Riots and radicalisation of this population followed. The lack of political representation remains a sore point, with ethnic minorities still heavily dependent on paternalist white benefactors in parliament. There is the suspicion that racist attitudes – although not politically expressed – are still strong and prevalent in the provinces. And, although no direct attack was made on the multicultural race relations during the 1980s, the destruction of local political powers and the autonomy of education from central control during that period also destroyed much of the pluralist backdrop on which local management of ethnic tensions was predicated.

The really spectacular emergent problems for Britain, however, have concerned Europe and the cohesiveness of the 'United Kingdom'. These are two areas that have always been separated from the question of integrating ethnic minorities, but which increasingly coincided within a European context, in which national sovereignty is in decline. British legislation, wholly devised for a post-colonial, island-bound nation state with a pre-modern constitution, has been completely out of line with European legislation on citizenship, or the rights of migrants and non-nationals. Its welfare provisions are poor and declining, and Britain has maintained its hostility to European cooperation on immigration policy – such as the Schengen agreement – which it did not sign. Within this unfriendly context, there has always been the chance that the idiosyncratic medium-term solution to the problems of immigration/integration, contrived by a very different independent Britain in the 1960s and 1970s, would fall apart as surely as the Union might, if Britain is forced by external circumstances to relinquish its *ancien régime* methods of managing peripheries and minorities.

The virtues of the French institutional solution do indeed lie in its missionary philosophical drive. The concern of the central state with positively promoting political identity and integration has enabled high levels of achievement in formal indicators of integration: education, public representation, and cognitive adherence to French values, language and ideology. Welfare levels and standards of public provision continue to be better than Britain, except where devolution of finances has worked to the exclusion of poorer *banlieues* from wealthy urban concentrations. The open fight in the political sphere against the ideas of the *Front national* have aligned a majority of the population around a progressive, inclusive vision of French public life: the extraordinary racial diversity of Paris being a testimony to this. The role of the courts in upholding human rights and non-discriminatory equality – hence balancing the dangers of populist democratic politics – has generally been progressive.

On the minus side, there has been the persistence of systematic blindspots, verging on self-delusion, in the gap between the ideal 'model' of official public rhetoric and the social realities of integration. This continues to be an open political sore-spot and source of capital to the extreme right. It manifested itself in the unnecessary obsession with reform of nationality laws, and the refusal to officially countenance the palpable existence of ethnically organised and culturally distinct minority groups within the French polity, who have diverse yet still legitimate collective political interests. In public discussion and perceptions, even third generation French nationals of African origin are often still referred to as *étrangers* and *immigrés*. This binary logic of exclusion runs through the public/private distinction. The most problematic symptom has been the place of Islam in France, that has at times been an almost hysterical source of fear to those intent on defending the public/private separation of the Republican system (Bowen 2007). State schooling has been the epicentre of these problems – hence the rupture and political crisis of the original *affaire du foulard* and its ongoing recycling – and the official public attitude towards Islam has had only the effect of encouraging its most militant minority elements. Moreover, the decline of the powers of the state to control all matters from the centre – and the fact that economic and juridical devolution was forced during the 1980s to regions and cities – has meant the heavy-handed centralised control on cultural politics rang increasingly hollow with local administrative and financial adaptations. There appears to be a need for the official political rhetoric to recognise that integration primarily takes place at local social levels, and can by no means be exhaustively represented in terms of the rules on nationality, formal citizenship and participation in the public sphere (Garbaye 2005).

Again, European political integration provides an acid test of the viability of the distinct nationalist philosophy that has been built in France. France is better integrated with European constitutional structures than Britain, but it nevertheless faces the same problems over the treatment of non-national residents (who are more or less non-persons from the point of view of French citizenship theory) and relinquishing border control: the Schengen agreement was signed, but initially not implemented; later, the French kept up accession barriers to migrants from the new enlargement countries. As the ongoing crises of French politics demonstrate, the realities of globalisation and internationalisation have hit hard the French national myths of cultural particularity, and its uneasy combination of universalism and *distinction nationale*.

Conclusion

What can be concluded from the British and French experience is that immigration and cultural pluralism in a liberal democratic system is not a problem in itself. Rather, it becomes a problem when it emerges as a symbolic focus of wider political dynamics, conflict and change attached to wider issues and political currents. As these examples suggest, the most difficult issue at stake in a liberal democracy's ethnic dilemmas, is how to deal with the reaction and behaviour of the majority population on whom the continued functioning of these institutions depends. I would suggest that this question about the moral and social integration of society *as a whole*, is a far deeper and more significant problem than the kind of questions that the liberal-communitarian debate leads us into: such as specifying the limits of cultural pluralism, or whether certain Islamic practices are compatible with Western values. It is a question to which I will return to in Chapter Five of this volume.

It is in this sense that the policy challenge of immigration and ethnic diversity has become such a litmus test of liberal pluralist democracy generally in recent years. As I have suggested throughout, responses to this challenge need to be sought, not from a disengaged philosophical reflection, but by comparing the practices and experiences of liberal democracies that have faced such problems, and for better or worse found institutional solutions for dealing with them.

Chapter Three

Multicultural Race Relations in Britain: Problems of Interpretation and Explanation

It is widely accepted both in Britain and on the continent that Britain is, politically speaking, a special case in Europe.[1] Such political exceptionalism has become a familiar and self-serving British strategy in Europe over the years, and the field of immigration and integration policies is no exception. Yet Britain clearly is a difficult case for the systematic *comparative* politics of immigration and citizenship that I and others sought to develop in the 1990s (*see* Joppke 1998a): that is, a field of research able to connect disparate national cases in Western Europe and North America in terms of macro-processes of social change and the transformation of the nation-state, and locate each in relation to common dynamics of political debate and policy evolution. As already suggested in Chapter Two, Britain's peculiar institutional formula of race relations and multiculturalism fits awkwardly with other cases across the Western world, in particular emerging institutions at the European level. Its post-colonial history, and the problems faced by its distinct and now established ethnic minorities, are not the same as those of newer migrants and refugees across Europe. The relative lack of salience of race or xenophobia in mainstream politics in Britain, until recent years at least, ran against the rising tide of ethnic dilemmas in liberal democratic societies elsewhere. How then might we go about fitting Britain into a wider comparative scheme and make sense of its peculiarities and apparent divergence from other cases?

The lack of any genuinely comparative dimension was always the most important deficiency in the copious home-grown British literature on immigration, race relations and ethnic minorities. Indigenous conservative, liberal, and radical commentaries resembled each other at least in the lack of any serious effort to translate the peculiar language and logic of the British institutional solution of multicultural race relations into terms that might read Britain as but one in a group of other West European case-studies

---

1. Originally published in Christian Joppke (ed.) *Challenge to the Nation State: Immigration in Western Europe and the United States*, Oxford: Oxford University Press (1998), pp.310–349. Republished with permission. This collection was, in my view, the best single handbook of essays on the new comparative immigration studies of the 1990s, but it languished for years as an over-priced hardback. Happily now the chapters are available online as part of OUP's e-scholarship. The article was written with the support of a Leverhulme Fellowship, and the kind invitation of Pascal Perrineau enabling me to be based at CEVIPOF, Sciences Po, Paris in 1996–7.

(*see also* Favell 2001b).[2] This in part may be because the often-told story of the emergence of British race relations legislation appeared to take place so much earlier than the rest of Europe. In response to the dangerous heating up of racial issues as long ago as the 1960s, the mainstream British political parties appeared to have fashioned by the mid-1970s a durable compromise of tight immigration control and self-styled 'progressive' legislation that pre-empted the emergence of the kinds of racial and ethnic conflict seen across Europe later. Within this framework an apparently benign but peculiarly esoteric form of British multiculturalism evolved up to the 2000s, which was often taken to be wholly particular: a translation of British colonial practices, which took the specificities of Commonwealth immigration and its island status and tailored them to British legal and parliamentary structures. These particularities restricted British commentators to relate Britain to Europe only in terms which underlined its distinctiveness or originality. Some set it up as a more advanced 'model' that might offer instruction to policy-makers on the continent (Forbes and Mead 1992). Others used their critique of British institutions as the starting-point for an exposure of the racism and exclusion similarly inherent in other European countries (Miles 1993; Solomos and Wrench 1993). All of these works wrongly assumed that the esoteric language of the British sociology of race and ethnicity – a lexicon profoundly structured by the institutions that it grew up around – could be meaningfully transposed to other European cases without any loss in understanding.

New opportunities for locating the British case in relation to European ones, however, were opened by the North-American-led growth in study of immigration and citizenship in Europe. Following Rogers Brubaker's work – itself deeply influenced by the pioneering vision of Aristide Zolberg (1989) – and especially Brubaker's *Citizenship and Nationhood in France and Germany* (1992), there was an explosion in explicitly comparative attempts by political scientists and sociologists to fit other cases into a similar general theoretical frame that would draw on mainstream theoretical debates in the social sciences (Ireland 1991, 1994; Brubaker 1992, 1989; Freeman 1992, 1995; Hollifield 1992; Messina *et al.* 1992; Soysal 1993, 1994; Cornelius *et al.* 1994; Baldwin-Edwards and Schain 1994; Geddes 1995, 2000; Favell 1998a; Guiraudon 1998, 2000; Feldblum 1999; Joppke 1999). Brubaker's work suggests there might be mileage in looking to see if a similar account of deeply held historical ideas about citizenship and nationhood in Britain might explain the tendencies and development of recent internal British politics and policies on immigration and ethnic minority

---

2. The respective 'standard' accounts were at the time: the new right critique of Honeyford (1988); the orthodox liberal reading of e.g. Hiro (1991) or Layton-Henry (1992); and the radical critique inspired by the new field of 'cultural studies', e.g. Centre for Contemporary Cultural Studies (1982) or Gilroy (1987). The majority of the literature thus offered either the technical and descriptive policy-orientated approach characteristic of writers associated with the government quango the Commission for Racial Equality, the influential non-governmental organisation the Runnymede Trust, and the designated ESRC Centre for Research in Ethnic Relations at Warwick University; or it offered the thoroughly disenchanted vision of endemic 'institutionalised racism' in Britain, exposed by radical academics who combined post-Marxist and post-modern theorising with openly polemical anti-racist activism. There were, however, notable exceptions to this division of labour, works which I cite in the course of this chapter.

integration. However, the immediate problem of this kind of approach is that it seems to only re-emphasise nationally bounded and nation-state sustaining views of the politics of immigration and citizenship over other accounts that emphasise the convergence of European practices and the breaking down of nation-state control over policy-making on the subject. This is an issue that needs to be sorted out by distinguishing between the influence of apparently fixed national political cultural 'legacies' on the politics of the present, and the more mundane dynamics of contemporary party-political interaction and policy development within an evolving political context. In theoretical terms, this is a debate between a historical institutionalist approach and a version of new institutionalism that attempts to downplay the determining force of national tradition, and show rather how such ideas are continually reworked and transformed by political actors for self-interested reasons at contingent points in time. I shall argue that the latter, more *contingent* type of explanation offers a better view of the dynamics of national politics in this field, a theoretical frame which may open the way to a fully comparative perspective of Britain in relation to other European cases.

The superficial peculiarity of the British case still presents an initial barrier to this kind of comparative framework. To get to questions of comparative *explanation* – and illustrate the relevance of new institutionalism to this field of study – it is thus necessary first to do a good deal of preliminary *interpretative* work to make sense of some of the distinctive peculiarities of the British case. My strategy in this chapter therefore is to foreground the dual methodological need for interpretation and explanation in comparative work, by raising problems at the interpretative level in the first half that I shall fully answer at the explanatory level in the second.[3] In the first half, I take two distinctive and puzzling features of the contemporary British case – issues concerning the place of Muslims in Britain, and British behaviour towards policy developments at the European level – and indicate the pitfalls connected with getting the interpretation of these phenomena right. Only then do I move to the explanatory level in which Britain is fitted into a wider theoretical scheme of immigration and citizenship politics in Europe. In the latter half of the chapter, I thus first discuss the theoretical issues thrown up by applying the theoretical terms of Brubaker and his critics to the British case. I then go on to use this perspective in order to retell the familiar British story of the invention and evolution of multicultural race relations in more general and comparative terms.

Interpreting a peculiar case 1: Muslims and multiculturalism in Britain

One of the hottest issues thrown up by multiculturalism in Britain has been the growing significance of political and social issues involving Muslims. Since the mid-1980s, issues involving Muslims in Western liberal democracies came to prominence right

---

3.   Whereas Chapter Two takes its starting point in political philosophy, here my starting point is the philosophy of social science, influenced above all by the teaching of the UEA philosopher, Martin Hollis. On the classic terms of the discussion about intepretation (or understanding) and explanation *see* his seminal text Hollis (1994), as well as its application to international relations in Hollis and Smith (1990). Behind this also lies the key influence of Quentin Skinner (*see* Tully 1989).

across Europe. This 'discovery' of Islam among otherwise integrated ethnic groups – often now full citizens of their host countries – and their apparently militant Islamic tendencies in some cases, raised a great deal of general political and academic debate (Rex and Drury 1994; Gerholm and Lithman 1998). In this emergent agenda, Britain provided much of the more spectacular case material: the Rushdie affair in 1989, in which a death threat was pronounced on the author of a blasphemous novel; the subsequent controversial creation of a parallel 'Muslim parliament' by a radical group financed by Iran; Muslim rioting in 1995 and 2001 in Bradford, a Northern city with a large Asian population; and growing troubles with radical fundamentalist groups in universities. All this was widely apparent well before 9/11, or the discussions incited by the incendiary work of Samuel Huntingdon (1996).

Such examples are still often cited to show that there is something culturally specific about Islam that makes it inherently a problem for Western society, and which would explain Muslims' behaviour (Hansen 2011; Joppke 2014). They are also read more generally as generic dilemmas of 'cultural pluralism' that can be found everywhere in Western liberal democracy. These problems are often framed as 'philosophical' dilemmas: in terms of the limits of tolerance or as the threat to the political unity – the universal rights and duties – of citizenship, that certain distinctive elements of Muslim 'culture' are typically seen to threaten (*see* Gellner 1992; Lukes 1993).

Many of the attempts by outside observers to cast these questions into fully fledged academic comparative studies have been crude and have failed to pay attention both then and now to the peculiarities of the distinct institutional framework within which British Muslims have operated *politically*, and which thereby explains their behaviour in perfectly comprehensible, self-interested terms. In the 1990s, a number of the more strongly critical studies initially came from French writers anxious to use the British case as a negative looking-glass for the virtues of republican citizenship in France, and a tough anti-Islamic line in French politics. This is a kind of typological approach in which Britain represents the archetypal 'multicultural' society. Integration is pictured to take place through a so-called 'communautarisme' in which distinct, racially classified ethnic groups are allowed political concessions to their communal forms. Over time, this has been said to lead to a growing wave of ethnic politics and cultural intolerance, urban ghettos and politically marginalised minorities, a generally racially divided apartheid in society, and an expedient, unprincipled flexibility about the rights and duties of citizens in politics (Schnapper 1992; Kepel 1994; Todd 1994). In these type of discussions, Britain and America are usually meaninglessly lumped together as the 'modèle anglo-saxon' (a classic francophone intellectual stereotype). Weaker versions of this critique would rather see Britain as one in a series of 'multicultural' countries which generally display certain pathological 'paradoxes of multiculturalism', others being Sweden, The Netherlands, Canada, and Australia, for example (Alund and Schierup 1991; Lapeyronnie 1993; Joppke 1996). Such studies often derived their root insights from neo-conservative worries about multiculturalism in the USA – rough-house urban ethnic politics, shrill campus debates about political correctness, the threat of 'balkanisation' and the disintegration of American citizenship (e.g. Schlesinger 1992). Suitably focused on a select part of the evidence available, the British case would then yield many examples of ethnic politics and conflict rampant at local levels (e.g. the 'loony left' politics of the 1980s), and the apparent disregard shown in separatist claims raised by Muslim communities (in Bradford and elsewhere) of the liberal principles of the British education and legal systems. These were also arguments that were made much of by new right critics of British race relations, such as the controversial school headmaster Ray Honeyford (1988).[4] The uncovering of many radical networks and plots after 9/11, through to Britain's own terrorist attacks in 2005, was seen to bolster this line of argument.

Without doubt, such studies did put their finger on some of the more problematic consequences of British multicultural race relations, but they were far from providing a complete or sensitive comparative picture. The alarmist concern with the threat of Islam, and the search for fundamental millenarian 'cultural' conflicts, masked the fact that the behaviour of a minority of militant British Muslims has always been predominantly an exception to the way multiculturalism has generally functioned in Britain.[5] Concentrating on this group thereby gives a false picture of the essence of the British institutional framework. What we find rather is that the particular issues associated with Muslims in Britain have to be set in the context of several decades of generally successful functioning of these institutions, a framework designed to deal with dilemmas associated with race relations and multiculturalism and lay a path towards integration. In this context, it has to be noted that typically ethnic minority issues are mostly localised away from mainstream politics in Britain and, before the rise of quite different issues linked to new migrations and super-diversity (Koser and Lutz 1998; Vertovec 2007), they were much less politically salient in Britain compared to elsewhere in Europe (measured in social attitudes or the emergence of powerful right-wing or nationalist movements) (*see* Baumgartl and Favell 1995). This leads to the conclusion that the narrow emergence of Muslims as a focal issue in Britain has more to do with the structuring institutional conditions specific to British political and social circumstances than any wider millenarian geopolitical tide.

The emergence of British Muslims as a distinct political group and voice should thus be traced, not so much to the rise of global Islam and certainly not to the 'clash of civilisations', but to certain peculiarities of the British institutional framework of multicultural race relations.[6] Three reasons stand out. To begin with, British race relations legislation has been a framework which does not provide minority rights as such, but rather allows – via the incremental extension of anti-discrimination claims to different groups through individual test cases – recognition to groups

---

4. For more sensitive discussions of the issues involved, *see* Poulter (1990), or CRE (1990).

5. Later studies have emerged which have offered more balanced accounts contrasting the radical minority of Islamist activists with more moderate Islamic political representation in Britain and elsewhere. *See* Klausen (2005), Saggar (2009), Bowen (2009), Laurence (2012), Joppke and Torpey (2013).

6. I owe great thanks to Tariq Modood (1992, 1994), who influenced much of my thinking on this subject. We subsequently collaborated to develop an agenda for studying multiculturalism and religious dilemmas in Europe, a group project which was published as Modood, Triandafyllidou *et al.* (2006). *See also* the excellent collection by Modood and Werbner (1997).

able to identify themselves as a publicly identified 'racial' group. This works as a kind of symbolic 'safety-valve' that offers a channel for ethnic minority claims and frustrations that would otherwise boil over into public demonstrations. Beyond the obvious allowances for 'Blacks' or 'Asians', the framework thus allowed for certain 'visible' groups such as Sikhs and Jews to gain recognition, but crucially not Muslims, who were classified as a non-racial religious group. Although the Commission for Racial Equality (CRE) identified this as a problem, the situation was difficult to change because the maintenance and coherence of the whole 'race relations' framework always depended on the legal recognition – spelt out in the famous *Mandla* v. *Dowell Lee* case about Sikhs – that ethnic groups be seen to have a 'racial flavour'.[7] In other words, this block to anti-discrimination provisions for Muslim interests represented the limits of the adaptive properties that the self-styled 'evolutionary' race relations legal framework depended on for securing successful integration.

Secondly, despite this, the framework elsewhere at the same time encouraged the promotion of specifically cultural issues. Such issues are often channelled by offering representation for ethnic minority interests through specifically religious and ecumenical groups that are provided finances and concessions for building mosques and 'spreading the word', courted by local politicians, and strongly involved as 'religious' representatives in local civic affairs (Rex 1991; Lewis 1994; Joly 1995). An example in the 1990s was the Inner Cities Religious Council, a forum funded by the Department of Environment which liaised closely with the UK Action Committee on Islamic Affairs on questions of education, health, housing, and social services. A motive was created and encouraged for 'Asian' groups to fight for distinction from the generic category of 'Black' in order to better pursue their political interests (Gilroy 1990; Modood 1992). One of the consequences of this split in ethnic minority interests was the sidelining in social policy of inner-city issues about poverty and welfare in favour of cultural interests concerning education and language provision. This shift was reflected most notably in the controversial changes in focus of successive versions of the eventual Swann Report of 1985, *Education for All*, the report of a special commission set up to reflect on education provisions for Britain's ethnic minorities. After several resignations and attacks by Tory ministers and the press, the radically worded inner-city poverty concerns of the interim Rampton Report were abandoned in favour of a more conservative, consensual position that represented the balance of power held by Asian members of the committee (Swann 1985; Verma 1989; Modgil *et al.* 1986).

However, thirdly, there have always been serious divisions within the Asian community along race, class, and urban lines. While middle-class Hindi or Tamil groups have prospered and thrived in Britain – and often escaped entirely the damaging effects of racial prejudice and barriers to advancement – Pakistani or Bangladeshi groups have often not been so fortunate (Modood *et al.* 1997). They come from poorer rural backgrounds, have had greater problems with language and cultural adaptation, and – most crucially – have endured the same

---

7.   *Mandla* v. *Dowell Lee* (1983) HL 2 AC 548; *see* Bourne and Whitmore (1993) or CRE (1994).

kinds of inner-city concentration and deprivations that West Indian blacks have faced: high unemployment and low achievement (Samad 1992; *The Economist* 1995). Although religious identity provided a focus for frustrations, the cultural concessions won by religious representation were at the expense of more targeted, interventionist social policies for these inner-city problems.

The intersection of three factors thus pushed the creation of a distinct Muslim group: a group fuelled by grievances about institutional non-recognition and a poor, disfranchised social status, and encouraged by the promotion of religious and cultural forums as the place to raise these issues. The 'problems' specifically associated with Muslims in Britain are therefore the *side-effects* of an institutional structure that can be said to have had beneficial effects *overall* for ethnic minorities globally conceived (and the idea of a multicultural Britain generally). The reason Islam became a salient point of local political conflict in Britain – e.g. the riots and political militancy in Bradford – is because the general framework of multicultural race relations provided a structure of opportunities for such groups to use cultural issues to solder collective action in this way (Saggar 1991). It is incorrect then to use the specific example of Muslims in Britain as fuel for crude rhetorical or normative conclusions about 'multicultural politics' generally conceived, as do Hansen (2011) and Joppke (2014): that multiculturalism is therefore wrong and always leads to such so-called disintegrative, balkanised effects. 'Multiculturalism' in fact should be avoided as the frame of comparison for Britain in relation to other national cases, because it simply does not mean the same thing in different countries.[8] Sensitivity to the rules of comparative research should underline the fact that the differences between national cases lie in the different ways they illustrate the institutionalising of ethnic dilemmas into politically tractable terms: the way they are constructed and focused as issues of public policy (Gusfield 1981; Majone 1989). Across different national cases, we will find distinct constitutional frameworks for minority issues, differing legal mechanisms and categories for dealing with discrimination or protection, and different political forums as the sites for bringing problems into the open. Within these institutional frameworks, we will also find ethnic minorities behaving as we would expect any political actors: in a rational, self-interested fashion, tailoring their interests to the structural opportunities on offer.

The Rushdie case of spring 1989 was the mainspring of the emergence of Muslim politics in Britain. As such, it has also been the perfect source of many poorly contextualised false interpretations that failed to respect these comparative rules. The basic political and legal issue at stake was overlaid with a *fin de siècle* 'clash of civilisations' plot line, which orientalised the genuine anger and offence taken by Muslims – and their right to protest and affirm certain beliefs – into a series of grand

---

8. The academic attack on multiculturalism dovetailed with a concerted challenge to the term and fall from fashion in politics across European states, which often led commentators to then argue that multiculturalism was disappearing as a creed and practice (Joppke and Morawska 2003; Joppke 2004). The discrediting of the policy term however does nothing to change the fact that European nations are and remain as *a matter of fact* highly multicultural, leading to issues of diversity and recognition that naturally require pragmatic 'multicultural' solutions (Uberoi and Modood 2013).

ethical dilemmas about free speech, the limits of toleration and cultural flexibility, and the starting-line requirements of citizenship in the public sphere.[9] None of these frames for the issues involved were typical of the way ethnic dilemmas have been usually dealt with by the institutions of race relations and multiculturalism in Britain. Cultural and anthropological East-West 'differences' were suddenly claimed to be the source of an impasse that reversed overnight the fairly benign and well institutionalised way Islam had established itself in Britain, free of the excesses of fundamentalism. Superficial links were made with the threat of fundamentalism in France, where the issues were very different because of the troubled French relations with its former colonies and the closeness of their political struggles.

This way of picturing the issues at stake thus actually denatured the specific form that the problem took in terms of Britain's institutions, and what might be learned about British multicultural race relations from the episode.[10] What should have been noted was the way the case revealed the lack of institutional recourse for Muslim groups to pursue a claim of discrimination through legal institutional channels, which was enough to mobilise even the most moderate groups to articulate their frustration angrily out in the streets. The lack of any clear legal distinctions between the public and private sphere on the question of a writer's right to blaspheme or ridicule – and hence the crude way in which questions of public morality get decided in populist moral majority terms – revealed weaknesses in the British legal system, grounded in a common law that offers no formal constitutional protection to minority groups. The only available legal grounds for the Muslims was an inappropriate and archaic anti-blasphemy law protecting Christian texts that had last been used to prosecute a homosexual magazine in the 1970s. Moreover, the lack of institutional channels available for mainstream Muslim groups highlighted the over-representation in the media given to radical groups, particularly the 'Muslim parliament' group led by Kalim Siddiqui, a media-wise ex-journalist. Their prominence quickly died away, when starved of the oxygen of publicity given to them by paranoid Western fears about the imminent Islamic insurrection.

Muslim groups' behaviour should again, therefore, be explained as typical political action structured by the British institutional context, showing how much the issue was a dilemma about institutional recognition and representation. Perhaps at its widest it questioned the viability of the British idea of subjecthood and loyalty to the crown, when a minority has no constitutional guarantees or rights with which to voice its claims. The Muslims' cardinal sin was to question the sovereignty of British law, and apparently listen to the voice of a foreign leader. It is interesting, however, that, despite the media and public outcry, the behaviour of mainstream politicians most involved in the issue on both the left

---

9. Such as in the well-publicised 'Counterblast' pamphlet by Fay Weldon (1989); *see also* press and other articles collected in Appignanesi and Maitland (1989). For a French perspective of this kind, *see* Kepel on 'Les versets britanniques' (1994).

10. Much more sensitive interpretations of the affair can be found in various writings by Parekh (1989, 1990a), and Parekh and Bhabha (1989). *See also* Asad (1990) and Mendus (1990). For important Muslim perspectives on the affair, *see* Akhtar (1989) and Ahsan and Kidwai (1991).

and right actually followed more closely the contours of the political institutional dilemma. They were listening no doubt to the underlying, longer-term political pressures involved in representing constituencies with significant Muslim populations, and the need to uphold the dominant institutional framework of race relations. Condemning the Ayatollah on the grounds of international law, they nevertheless were at pains to sympathise with the Muslim communities, reaffirm religious toleration and the multi-denominational idea of British multiculturalism, and generally sought to defuse and play down the issue rather than use it for political capital.

However, the well-publicised and somewhat hysterical intellectual interpretation of these events did certainly have a wider effect, and contributed to the growing tension felt between 'Islam and the West', significantly setting back the integration of Muslim immigrants in Western Europe. With 9/11 and its aftermath, the hostile climate got much worse, something which undoubtedly contributed to a growing Islamophobia in Europe (Helbling 2012). It is an interpretation which reinforces the thought that such ethnic dilemmas are somehow different from other political dilemmas: in virtue of 'exotic' cultural differences or some property of the minority themselves. This in turn made the political problem harder to see through or diagnose.

Interpreting a peculiar case 2: British Europhobia

> When you travel in Europe you are not protected by the Race Relations Act. Travel in Europe can often be a traumatic experience for Britain's ethnic minorities – even when they have British passports. You could be hassled by an immigration officer, the police or racists in the country you are visiting. Unfortunately there's not a lot that can be done to help you from here [. . .] (Commission for Racial Equality (CRE)/BBC Radio One, *Race Through the 90s*, 1994)

Our enquiry can be broadened by considering another of the curiosities of the British case: its negative behaviour over the years in the face of European efforts to harmonise European anti-discriminatory measures and immigration policies, and the push to create citizenship rights or guarantees for minorities and non-nationals within the framework of the European political system. For example, these were the reasons given by the right-wing Conservative former Home Secretary Michael Howard in 1995, for his rejection of new plans to harmonise anti-racist anti-discrimination laws at a European level:

> Many of the proposed measures are unnecessary and others would be counter-productive. The UK already has effective legislation. It would mean changing our laws in a very significant way for reasons that do not have much to do with the circumstances we encounter in Britain. We have a longer history of laws affecting race relations than almost any other country in the EU, more comprehensive legislation than any other country and better race relations than almost any other country. (*The Financial Times*, 25–6 November 1995)

Stirring words indeed, as are those quoted from the CRE publication above, advising young members of ethnic minorities about the hazards of travel in Europe. Right or left, they share the same conviction: a deep Europhobia, justified by the proud, almost whiggish belief in the progressive superiority of British anti-discrimination provisions and multicultural tolerance. What is remarkable about them is their similarity: how the Home Office and the left-wing race relations lobby in Britain would always put forward the same arguments for why the government must not dilute or weaken the familiar structure of race-based legislation, in order to harmonise with European efforts to reframe positive legislation in egalitarian or rights-based terms. At the time, it was lobby groups on behalf of new migrants and refugees and the Jewish community who reacted against Howard's statement, not the mainstream CRE.[11] Indeed, prominent radical anti-racist activists went so far as to set up a rival organisation in Brussels, the Standing Conference on Racial Equality in Europe (SCORE), to campaign *against* the main organisation pushing for measures at the European level, the Forum for Migrants (*see also* Kastoryano 1998b). When New Labour came to power in 1997, they upheld the race relations lobby's prejudice about the superiority of British legislation. Indeed, the new Labour government immediately underlined its support for the existing institutional status quo, by asserting the sovereignty of British border and immigration control. This, of course, continued through into the later Conservative-Liberal government. In short, there has always seemed to be a curious consensus across the board on the content of Howard's argument, then as much as now. Nobody, it seems, wants to start dismantling parts of this framework. There is hardly any space on the political agenda in Britain for challenging or questioning this consensus. Why is this? What is going on here?

The standard sort of explanation offered by British commentators might attempt to account for this in ideological terms. British resistance to European co-operation is the fault of certain residual insular ideas across the political spectrum that are historically anti-European and which only a more pronounced public shift towards a pro-European position could change: the self-serving British 'exceptionalism' again (Miles 1993). Yet this does not explain the fact that the resistance to change is on all sides justified in 'progressive' terms, in defence of the open, inclusive idea of British multiculturalism and self-sufficiency in terms of immigration against what it sees as a downgrading effect that Europe would have (similar to Scandinavian worries about welfare and workers' rights). A similar weakness afflicts what was one of the most common litanies among British race relations writers: that it was just another example of the Tories 'playing the race card' again.[12] In fact, for many years, it was difficult to argue – particularly when viewed in comparative terms – that any real political capital was made of populist

---

11. The Commission for Racial Equality was in fact replaced by the Equality and Human Rights Commission in 2004, and the Race Relations Act was superceded by a new Equality Act in 2010.

12. This is a rather lazy, 'taken for granted' explanation used by radical and liberal commentators on British race relations alike: e.g. in Gilroy (1987) or Layton-Henry (1992).

racist or anti-ethnic feelings in elections since 1979. Nor, prior to the emergence of the UK Independence Party (UKIP) – driven by a very different set of anti-European concerns – was it even easy to argue that it was a latent issue waiting to be tapped (*see* Saggar 1996). The Conservative Party officially spared no effort in portraying itself in politically correct terms on racial and ethnic issues, while feeling far less inclined to curb open outbursts of anti-European xenophobia. The anti-race relations right made a lot of noise in the Thatcherite 1980s without effecting any significant policy changes. None of this goes to deny the prevalent existence of prejudiced and racist views among the British public at large, but it is surely an enormously significant fact that, beyond a very small right-wing extreme, no significant political use was made of racist or anti-ethnic arguments in open political debate. This is something that cannot be said about France, Belgium, Germany, or Italy in the 1980s and 90s, or even countries widely recognised to be more open and accommodating than Britain, such as The Netherlands or Denmark (Baumgartl and Favell 1995). What explains this strange coalition that held back the left from seriously challenging draconian immigration laws or pushing for more extensive Euro-legislation (indeed which finds the most vocal activists sounding like good 'one nation' patriots), and the Conservative Party from using racial and ethnic tension for easy political capital?

What we find is that, under the perpetual everyday conflict of rhetoric that sees both sides permanently seeking to distance themselves and compete over the issues, there has been a strong and broad underlying consensus across the mainstream left and right on the basic ideas, concepts, and terms of the institutional structure that was put in place in Britain to deal with its particular ethnic dilemmas.[13] An open, inclusive idea of integration and the implementation of anti-discrimination commitments was accepted by all sides as dependent on overtly strict immigration and nationality controls. These are said to have both created stable and relatively fixed ethnic minority groupings with the time and geographical concentration to establish themselves, and forestalled the threat of a hostile majority population reaction. The strategy was to allow integration to happen through civil and social processes, not through the channel of full political representation. This strategy had several key components: to keep the issues out of mainstream politics; to

---

13. My argument here is spelt out in greater length in my reading of Britain in Favell (1998a/2001). *Philosophies of Integration* was essentially based on a close textual analysis of key official public documents in which the terms and language of the British settlement on 'multicultural race relations' was defined and developed. Crucially, it was also the need to make sense of Britain in *comparison* with another national philosophy that enabled this kind of reading. Among the principal documents I used were: Rose *et al.* (1969); jurisprudence of the Race Relations Act 1976; Scarman (1981); Swann (1985); reports by the CRE (e.g., CRE 1985); Commission on Citizenship (1990); and Commission on Urban Priority Areas (1985, 1990). Among indigenous British commentators, it is necessary to be highly selective. I found most helpful the kind of readings put forward by Parekh (e.g. 1990b); the work of Rex (e.g., 1985, 1991, 1996); Dummett and Nicol (1990); Modood (1992); Saggar (1991); Spencer (1994); and in France various writings by Lapeyronnie (1993) and Crowley (i.e. 1993, 1995). My approach was then in turn echoed in work by Joppke (1999), Hansen (2000), Bleich (2003), Garbaye (2005), Uberoi (2007), Statham (1999), Thomas (2011), and Maxwell (2012).

regulate problems paternalistically through a limited race relations framework that allowed incremental symbolic recognition to publicly defined groups; to localise the representation of ethnic minority interests in religious and cultural groups; and to keep the issues well away from substantive questions about constitutional minority rights, citizenship, or welfare (*see also* Chapter Two in this volume). It was thus, despite the forward-looking rhetoric of 'equal opportunities' and 'multiculturalism' (which after attacks on this term, gave way to a more diffuse commitment to a 'multi-ethnic Britain'), an institutional structure built on profoundly conservative political ideas of nationalist subjecthood, common law, *laissez-faire*, and a traditional 'corporation and guilds'-based localised pluralism.

Remarkably, this basic arrangement survived the enormous fundamental changes of the Thatcher decade, in which nearly every other institutional bedrock of the post-war political consensus was dismantled. Yet it was where the framework struggled to adapt to new circumstances, or saw new emerging groups unhappy with the place the framework allows them, that the major problems in British race and ethnic relations have always surfaced. After the failure of the Parekh report (Commission on the Future of Multi-Ethnic Britain 2000) to push for a more radical post-national vision of 'multi-ethnic Britain', the Labour Party embraced increasingly more nationalist rhetoric about integration into cultural values, and talk – if not practice – of multicultural policy was toned down. A bigger break with the consensus emerged however over issues of new migration, particularly the very large scale intra-EU migrations coming to Britain from the 2000s onwards. Yet in many way, this 'anti-immigration' current, so strong in the UKIP's campaigning, has not altered the longer term settlement over race relations and post-colonial minorities. Indeed, there have been prominent Asian and Afro-Caribbean members of UKIP articulating their own anti-European grievances.

If read in a certain way, the underlying institutional structure of British multicultural race relations is by no means as *ad hoc* or unprincipled as it is often claimed. In many ways, its underlying 'philosophy' was already mirrored in the widely discussed all-party reflection *Encouraging Citizenship* (Commission on Citizenship 1990), the report of an official commission of academics and public servants which spelt out the post-Thatcher consensus on the conditions and sources of British social ties and civility.[14] Although this report cited Marshall (1950) as an inspiration, it defended a profoundly un-Marshallian idea of citizenship: given that it did not contain a substantial idea of welfare rights or the exercise of political rights and participation in the public sphere as advancing the cause of social integration (although it did endorse private local voluntary and communal activism). These ideas, however, express a coherent, if idiosyncratic, philosophy: the rather communitarian combination of traditional English pluralism and cultural and religious toleration, best stated in the writings of several well-known 'English' – albeit some by adoption – philosophers (Raz 1986; Dahrendorf 1988; Dunn 1990; Gray 1993; Selbourne 1994; Nicholls 1994). That is, it

---

14. See as a general statement of the post-Thatcher concerns, John Keane's interview with Ralf Dahrendorf (Keane 1990). For a critical view of these developments, *see* Crouch (1992), Phillips (1993, Ch. 4).

is possible to make much more sense of the peculiarities of the British case than either foreign observers or Britain's own writers on ethnic and racial studies, by reading its home-grown idea of multicultural race relations as a curiously anachronistic version of classic conservative English liberalism: a political philosophy, in other words, in the tradition of Hobbes, Locke, and Mill.

If our question is one of understanding the distinctive shape of the institutional structure and the rationale that sustained the political consensus which underlay it, these guiding ideas should be our interpretative key. A sensitivity to such internal peculiarities is certainly the first step to understanding another country's politics and policies in a comparative manner. However, the accent on national peculiarities still appears to put a barrier between inter-case comparison. Given this, a wider question must be asked: how can the interpretative understanding thus far reached of the respective political and institutional dimensions of the British case, be set in more general theoretical terms that enable a comparative explanation of it in relation to other European cases?

Explaining British and European immigration politics

Thus far, my account of two distinctive peculiarities of the British case has concentrated solely on getting the interpretation of certain visible elements of the case-study right. I have put the emphasis on specifying the interaction of the recognisably political behaviour of actors and groups with the nationally specific institutional structure that the British framework of multicultural race relations represents. This naturally raises the explanatory question of how such an institutional structure for dealing with the new public policy problems of immigration and integration got there in the first place. Such a question is indeed the obvious way of broadening out our perspective on the British case into a fully comparative one, and can be posed as a general theoretical one: how and when a given set of political conditions and balance of political forces is able to respond to new social needs and circumstances with the innovative creation of new institutions.[15]

The most obvious suggestion would be to answer this question in the manner of Brubaker's (1992) widely acclaimed comparison of France and Germany, which accounted for contemporary politics of immigration in these two countries in relation to their distinct notions of civic versus ethnic nationality going back to the 19th century. That is, by reading the institutional 'philosophy' I have identified behind British multicultural race relations the expression of a deep historical 'legacy': a national 'political culture' of citizenship that can explain the emergence and evolution of the politics of immigration in Britain. It is here, however, that certain important distinctions need to be made between the historical 'cultural

---

15. This starting point was, in effect, the theoretical starting point of many other contributions to this field. Besides the work of Brubaker and Soysal which I discuss below, *see also* especially Guiraudon (1998), whose approach closely paralleled mine, and numerous essays by Freeman (e.g. 1992, 1995). Peter Hall's general model (1993) was the most influential institutionalist attempt to formulate an answer in general terms; for an application of the approach to the politics of immigration in the USA, *see* Schuck (1992).

idioms' based form of new institutionalism practiced by Brubaker, and a version of new institutionalism based on charting the dynamics of more contemporary political forces, which I first proposed in *Philosophies of Integration* (Favell 1998a).[16] An interpretation of present-day politics in terms of a reworking of classical ideas from British political philosophy is not yet an explanation of any kind. To make this step would be to claim that these culturally rooted ideas directly *cause* institutions and political behaviour within these institutions to take the shape they do. The historical effort of Brubaker's work about France and Germany is to reconstruct the emergence of this political culture during the nation-building of the nineteenth century in order to explain the politics of the present. Yet there is a deep problem with the turn to political cultural explanations (*see also* Favell 1998c). Given his argument that the same nation-building is going on in post-colonial France that went on during the Third Republic, Brubaker's conclusion unsurprisingly was that the effectiveness of distinctly French nation-state nationalism was undiminished. His work thereby underlined and reinforced many of the Third Republic myths that were assiduously reconstructed in 1980s France to justify a new nationalist republican version of citizenship, in the face of new currents of multicultural pluralism, regional devolution, and supranational co-operation.[17] In other words, a political cultural argument about nation-building ('we have always done things differently here') is a perfect way of bolstering nationalism as a political option. It is the perfect self-serving 'neo-nationalist' strategy to mask the political and institutional room for manœuvre that is always there – particularly the new dimensions opened up by European cooperation – in vague, obfuscating talk of national identities or cultural idioms (*see also* Feldblum 1998). It also suggests that fundamental institutional change is less possible than it really is: as evidenced by Brubaker's poor judgement about reform to the 'sacred' idea of *jus solis* in France, which did in fact come in 1993 (a critique pursued by Weil 1996). All of which leaves open the possibility that Brubaker might have been right about the resistance of the nation-state form, but was wrong in identifying the causes as deep cultural or historical reasons rather than more contingent recent political factors.

The historical, political culture-based study of the origin of key political concepts and ideas may then be essential to the interpretative background of the subject (the palette of ideas that exist as reference points in political debates and justifications), but it is insufficient on its own for explanatory questions raised about the political dynamics involved in the emergence and evolution of new institutions. It is not enough, for example, to claim that British race relations institutions simply translated the traditional cultural pluralism of colonial practice

---

16. For the distinction between the form of new institutionalism I defend and other forms of new institutionalism, see the comprehensive literature survey by Hall and Taylor (1996). Mine is closest to what they call 'rational choice institutionalism', most clearly exposed by North (1990) and Pierson (2004). Other uses of the 'historical institutionalism', closer to Brubaker, include Steinmo *et al.* (1992) and Putnam (1993).

17. See especially the highly influential official reports on the subject: Commission de la Nationalité (1988), Haut Conseil à l'Intégration (1993), as well as the surrounding academic literature cited by influential figures such as Schnapper, Todd and Kepel.

into home territory (a point also made by Bleich 2005). This tells us nothing about the timing of their introduction, or the conditions that were required for it to come about: the balance of political forces, the entrepreneurship that was needed, the bargaining or trade-offs that took place, or indeed how ideas were used to solder political agreement at a particular point in time (Hall 1989, 1993; Majone 1989, 1996; Goldstein and Keohane 1993). Nor, more importantly, does it offer a great deal of insight into why those institutions encountered difficulties over time, what new political forces developed within the tracks it provided, and the changes or breakdowns that may take place because of new conditions or external factors.[18] It misses crucially the key dimension of social change that occurred: how Britain became a multicultural and multiracial society profoundly transformed from the one that once ruled over an empire. 'Political cultural' exceptionalism is therefore never an excuse: British behaviour towards Europe is governed primarily by mundane local political reasons, not by any impossible cultural or geographical barriers or the weight of history.

In close succession to the breakthrough marked by Brubaker, an alternative kind of theory for explaining the emergence of new citizenship institutions was put forward by Soysal. She posited an emerging common European framework for dealing with immigration and citizenship questions: a 'post-national' institutional framework of citizenship policies and notions of societal membership in the context of global developments, which, she argued, was shifting the emphasis of national politics away from neo-nationalist barrier-building, and working to break down national cultural particularities in practice (Soysal 1993, 1994). The European question of harmonising legal and political provisions has indeed offered a test site of new institution-building in progress, which may reveal the mechanisms by which new institutions and policy frameworks are able to emerge, as well as indicate the factors or conditions which might be needed for an intransigent member state such as Britain to change its behaviour over new proposals.

Soysal's argument for the convergence of national policies of immigration and integration in a single supranational framework of post-national membership was always gratefully echoed by the arguments of leading policy groups pushing for this at the European level. It was, she argued, being pulled by a rational policy convergence and coordination among the elite civil servants and policy makers who had to respond directly to the problems of new migration, refugees, and the status of non-nationals; and pushed from below by the success of ethnic groups and other lobby groups tailoring their actions to the given institutional structures, first at national levels and then increasingly at the emerging international ones, such as the European courts and European social policy funding. In short, the emergence of new institutions is here created by a mix of lobbying and activist partisanship, which responds rationally to objective needs and circumstances. And the language in which this process is argued for is the set of ideas associated with

---

18. My account is informed by theoretical ideas and terms of analysis in the work of North (1990) ('institutional performance; 'path dependency') and Hirschman (1991) ('pathologies'; *'effets pervers'*).

'new citizenship' predominantly focused on the idea of formal legal guarantees. In practical terms this was translated into the starting-line project for Euro-citizenship and the attempt to get minority guarantees into a revised version of the Treaty on European Union, first discussed at the Intergovernmental Conference of 1996–7. Other proposals sought to extend the developing immigration co-operation within the European Union's 'third pillar' of justice and home affairs on the back of the Schengen Agreement signed in the mid-1980s (Hix 1995).

Here then is a powerful alternate 'new institutionalism' to contrast with one grounded in historical 'cultural idioms' and 'political culture'. The example of Britain, however, poses an anomaly for Soysal's perspective; as, on the face of it, does Brubaker's France. Although in the 1990s there was widespread evidence of emergent 'new citizenship' talk, and no shortage of 'behind-closed-doors' contact between responsible national civil servants and policy makers at the European level, there have always been plenty of counter-currents in the mainstream 'open' politics (e.g. public democratic debate and electoral behaviour) in these two countries and others to suggest that national forms of dealing with the problems were predominantly resistant and particular to the nations concerned. This is evidenced as much by the political potency of xenophobia or right-wing nationalist parties as by the open hostility of countries such as France and Britain over the years to many European proposals, consistently rejected on 'progressive' grounds – in defence of the benefits of their 'particular' national philosophies of integration. The nationally bounded models of citizenship and integration that sustain the distinct institutions that France and Britain developed to deal with their dilemmas of immigration and ethnic conflict, remained far stronger unifying frames of reference for the issues and political perception of the public – what might be called 'policy paradigms' (Hall 1993) – than the vague promise of a new European conception of citizenship or identity.

Soysal was right to build arguments with a mechanistic political institutional theory that seeks to downplay the longer-term historical, political culture-based explanations that Brubaker used. However, her arguments were difficult to sustain empirically, at least for the French and British cases. The weakness in her theory does, however, reveal what is needed for the mechanisms to work: the critical element in establishing new institutions is the political dynamic which pushes policy making out of the behind-closed-doors technocratic circles into a wider public democratic sphere.[19] In effect, this involves the political recognition of the issue as a distinct public problem and the creation of a whole new niche or policy focus. In the case of immigration, this would entail creating a new policy language of categories into which these groups can be fitted, and conceptual ideals that spell out the goals of the integration process. There will indeed be much conflict and confusion politically and socially until this is achieved; the search is given urgency by the extreme reactions against the immigrants who are identified as

---

19. A model, adopted from Schattschneider (1961), that was revived by Baumgartner (1989). Schain (1988) and Guiraudon (1998) also made use of this model.

causing the confusion. The expansion of the issue out of technocratic circles into wider democratic ones is thus a potentially dangerous process. In creating an open political issue out of the status and accommodation of immigrants–foreigners and so on, it opens up a large political space for reaction and xenophobia, and opportunities for populist politicians. Yet it is this opening up and heating up of the issue that provides the crucible for innovative ideas. My position is thus different to the ostensibly similar approach proposed by Guiraudon (1997). Her case-studies find that the opening of the issue to the public democratic forum is in fact dangerous, and that advances in the building of new institutions can be made only by keeping the policy process behind closed doors or in the elite legal arena. As we will see, the British case in the 1960s and 1970s contradicts this, with growing fears over the democratic deficit in European institutions suggesting that the public democratic forum can only be ignored at peril.

Retelling the history of multicultural race relations in Britain

With these thoughts in place, it may now finally be possible to give a full account of the British case – tracing the emergence and evolution of its distinctive institutions (the path of institutional change) and diagnosing where it currently stands as regards Europe – in genuinely translatable comparative terms. In doing so, I hope also to vindicate a particular form of new institutionalism. The following provides a dynamic historical supplement to the more static systems-based vision of the British case in the previous chapter.

In Britain new policy institutions did indeed emerge out of period in the late 1960s and early 1970s in which the issue of immigrants and the place of ethnic minorities in Britain became a heated, salient issue of party-political debate and conflict. And an open, socially inclusive conceptual frame of 'integration' – qualified by a set of inflexible, complex, institutional trade-offs – did become the one around which the mainstream parties found a consensual focus. However, the actual mechanisms by which this took place demonstrate a very un-whiggish sort of story, very different from the classic kind of Marshallian explanation for the emergence of the British welfare state: the happy evolutionary tale in which left-wing partisanship and campaigning from below achieved the incremental, expansive creation of new sets of legal, political, and social rights, and the transcending of class conflict in a nationally unifying idea of citizenship (Marshall 1950; Rose *et al.* 1969).

It was indeed a paternalist liberal lobby – led by Roy Jenkins in a brief spell as Home Secretary in the mid-1960s – that put forward the ideas that were to found the new British race relations institutions. These were inspired rhetorically by American civil rights language, but were transformed beyond recognition for the British institutional frame-work of common law and localised pluralism (for more detail, *see* Hansen 2000). But the power of the ideas themselves and the objective needs they responded to – violence in the streets and the growing intolerance of the white indigenous population – would have been insufficient to pull through any kind of reforms had it not been for the political dimension behind their development. Firstly, their very possibility was conditional on the Wilson government of 1964 – and all successive Labour leaderships – immediately going back on its internationalist commitments and accepting that strict immigration restriction was an unavoidable necessity. Secondly, Jenkins' ideas were going nowhere until the dramatic intercession of Enoch Powell, a prominent right-wing Conservative, with his infamous 'rivers of blood' speech (April 1968), which thrust the political question of integration into the centre of British political life at the end of the 1960s. Powell's speech threatened to split the right over the issue of English nationalism and the stability of the British 'Union'.

It was thus the aligning of the main body of the Conservative Party with the need for a new institutional framework – focused on an idea of national integration able to incorporate the new ethnic minorities 'here to stay' – that proved the key. The threat of continued majority population reaction against these groups, and the destabilising of the national political order, pushed the Conservative Party to join Labour in seeking to depoliticise the issue and take it off the mainstream political agenda (*see* Katznelson 1973: 123–51; Freeman 1979; Banton 1985; Messina 1989). Cast in the right way, reformist ideas on race relations and a multicultural Britain could be found to ring true with traditionally conservative principles about managing public order and devolving citizenship to localised, communitarian representation: something that has historically been the dominant practice of the elite English centre towards the various national peripheries of the 'United Kingdom'. The path of integration for the designated post-colonial immigrants – within strictly closed doors to further immigration or British nationality – was thus chosen as the best consensual point between left and right views on the subject, expressing a loose core of traditional British liberal ideas that all could agree on. The triumph of the 'liberal hour', then, was not down to any public ideological swing to 'progressive' ideas; but rather the outcome of a contingent political situation and wider political pressures on the 'Union' that favoured consensus across the mainstream political spectrum on creating a new open and inclusive framework around an idea of multicultural, multinational Britain. For the main part, this consensus held remarkably firm until the 2000s, and provided a stable structure within which a new idea of Britain as a multicultural society was able to evolve.

The left–right political dynamics of this story – incorporating the key role of 'ideas' in consensual policy framework building – suggests a more general explanatory model of policy-making in immigration politics might equally be found to apply to other cases, such as France. It might be hypothesised conditionally that for new institutions to emerge, it hinges on the opening up of reformist ideas and policy formulations to the forces of public democratic debate and party political positioning. *If*, under pressure from extreme figures articulating 'exclusive' ideas of the nation, the issues become centralised in the open political mainstream and debated in publicly recognised terms across the political spectrum, and *if* the right finds an instrumental need to identify with the nationally inclusive frame being offered, *then* new institutions are able to emerge. What is of course characteristic of the framework of integration converged on in Britain – and other 'experienced' immigration societies such as France – is that it is a strictly bounded 'national' solution. This is typical of the post-colonial or the guestworker situation, where immigration is delimited by a special national 'responsibility' for strictly defined groups of immigrants, and where integration is predicated on tight border control and closed doors to new immigrants. Moreover, we have here the reason why national integration (or assimilation) policies *appear* deceptively to be one more instance of classical nineteenth-century nation-building, despite the paradoxical fact that the new immigration simultaneously undermines the fixed classical notions of nationhood and boundaries based on distinct cultures or peoples.

This also provides a clue as to why problems associated with new migrations emerge: new mobilities, refugees, resident non-nationals, super-diversity and so on, call for rather different institutional responses from those contained in the idea of integration for post-colonial immigrants or guestworkers. They call less for social and political assimilation into the host country culture than a devolution of responsibilities for rights and protection to agencies other than the traditional nation-state: whether local, federal, or supranational. Under these conditions, issues such as freedom of movement, welfare benefits, work rights, and legal protection for 'non-members' – the kinds of things proposed in extending European citizenship to third-country nationals – become more important than access to the full symbolic status of membership in the 'British' or 'French' nation. And, in an era of political deregulation and rolling back the state, it should come as no surprise that the state has lost powers over the rights, benefits, and freedoms it used to control and redistribute. Yet, to a greater or lesser degree, all of the Western European countries with immigrants of the original kind tried to create a nationally bounded, nation-state-focused solution of integration along the older British and French paths. I explore this problem with the notion of national integration in greater depth in Chapter Five.

Conclusion

In this chapter, I have sought to break with the dominant indigenous and foreign interpretations of multicultural race relations in Britain, and instead locate the British case fully within the new emerging field studying the comparative politics of immigration and citizenship in Western Europe. As I have emphasised throughout, fitting Britain into the scheme raises complex theoretical problems of interpretation and explanation. It is precisely the awkwardness of fitting Britain into any European and North American comparisons that makes it an interesting and important case. Such an approach offers a new way of reading British multicultural race relations and unlocks the paradox of why such a self-styled 'progressive' and advanced legislative framework ran into such problems under the very changed conditions of the 'new migrations' from the 2000s onwards, a theme I will return to in Chapters Eight and Nine.

Most of the growing problems with British multiculturalism and immigration politics – associated with the European question and the increasingly undesirable side-effects of its particular off-shore relationship to the EU – come from the fact that Britain committed itself to the curious idea of building a self-sufficient 'multiculturalism in one nation'. This is a brand of multiculturalism that is not in any way internationalist, as the idea of multiculturalism is generally understood to be. In the end, this made the British institutional solution to its ethnic dilemmas an unstable one in an increasingly regionalised and globalised European context. In the final analysis, the functioning of British multicultural race relations and immigration policies have come to depend on the shaky idea of British national unity. As the Union creaks and crumbles, 'British' Blacks and Asians have rightly grown nervous that they, like the Poles and Romanians who arrived in the 2000s, might find themselves excluded from a re-emerging *English* nationalism. Their diasporic tendencies might get used against them, to delegitimise the place that they have found through integration into a multicultural Britain. Everyone remembers Thatcherite minister Norman Tebbit's famous cricket 'test', when he suggested that West Indian or Asian claims to be British could be assessed by asking who they supported in Test matches. Many people have thought that the success of 'multi-ethnic Britain' proved Tebbit wrong. Yet some of the success of racial and ethnic politics in Britain until the 2000s has proven an illusion, as the old institutional settlement – unable to adapt to new needs and conditions – began to look like one with no answers to the evolving challenges of new migration in Europe.

Part Two

The Question of Integration

Chapter Four

Assimilation/Integration

Assimilation and integration are the two leading concepts referring to the process of settlement, interaction with the host society, and social change that follows immigration.[1] Both are strongly contested terms politically, with shifting meanings, yet they have enjoyed a comeback in public policy debate and scholarly work in recent years. In this chapter, I offer a dictionary style definition and summary of the basic literature before going on in the following chapter to do a reflexive analysis and critique of the field of comparative integration research in a European context.

As sociological concepts, assimilation and integration have their roots in a Durkheimian style functionalist sociology: in which society is imagined as a complex, 'organic' bounded whole, made up of differentiated parts, but held together by shared abstract values and dominant mainstream norms of behaviour. Assimilation and integration are, thus, abstract, performative concepts pointing towards the unifying cohesion that functionalist theories posit is necessary for any society to achieve – via the socialisation of its members – in order for it to be said to work properly. Applied to research, the concepts were popularised by the Chicago school of urban sociology in the early twentieth century, before becoming familiar terms in public policy debates about the consequences of immigration and the challenge of diversity in hitherto (seemingly) unified societies. Both terms also promote a slippery metaphorical link between the social processes they describe and mathematical and/or biological theories that describe processes in the natural world using the same terms. Although applicable to any country of immigration, they are concepts that have been most developed, along rather distinct lines, in the USA and Western Europe.

Assimilation in the USA

Assimilation is the more commonly used term in the USA. It is one pole in the debate over the degree to which new immigrants can and should strive to resemble average American middle class (and above) norms and behaviour as the path to successful settlement in the society. The most original or root important theoretical formulation of how assimilation works in American society is the work of Gordon (1964). He distinguished between various dimensions of assimilation in American society, identifying the need for structural assimilation – into the labour and housing markets, as well as language and education – as the most

---

1. Originally published in Matthew Gibney and Randall Hansen (eds) (2005) *Immigration and Asylum: From 1900 to the Present*, Santa Barbara, CA: Clio, pp.19–23. Republished with permission.

important element in immigrant success, ahead of racial, cultural or moral (value) assimilation. Although a neutral typology, his framework is often equated (wrongly) with the conservative argument that new immigrants must conform to the norms and values of the dominant white majority in order to be accepted.

The idea of successful immigrant assimilation is clearly still today a vibrant part of the myth of the 'American dream'. Yet assimilationist assumptions about how America works as a society have led to numerous critiques, proposing a more differentialist or multiculturalist view of society. In these, various minority or subordinate groups are viewed as able to assert their own cultural autonomy or distinctiveness from the white mainstream as a means to get ahead in American society. This became an important position in the multiculturalist debates that have raged in the USA since the success of the civil rights movement in the 1960s and 1970s.

However, the term has enjoyed a comeback in recent years in response to heightened concern about the separatism latent in multiculturalist positions. It has been recognised that some set of shared norms and values are a likely precondition for the success of a genuinely pluralist nation of immigrants. Scholars have also sought to rehabilitate the term in the light of the clearly diverse (or 'segmented') success rates (or social mobility, see Gans 1992) of new immigrants from around the world since US immigration policy reforms in the 1960s. Arguing that the concept need not be equated with the discredited white majority bias of earlier uses, Alba and Nee (1997; 2003) have laid out an impressive research program documenting the continued importance of historically established patterns of assimilation to middle class residential, educational and occupational trajectories as the crucial precondition for the success of new immigrants in American society. Coming from a more multiculturalist position, Portes and associates (i.e. Portes and Zhou 1993; Portes and Rumbaut 2001) have also used the term prominently to signal how less successful new migrant groups with less 'white' racial or cultural origins often follow a path of 'downward assimilation' to resemble the social profile of inner city African American populations. A key part of this story has been an economic context in which the more stable industrial employment that immigrants used to seek has been replaced by far more precarious and badly paid opportunities in the new service industries.

All of these theories continue to adhere to an essentially functionalist vision of American society, in which immigrant success or failure is charted against a set of taken-for-granted, mainstream American (white) middle- or upper-class norms, bounded by the notion of America society as a wholly self-contained unit of social processes. There is thus little or no space here for a more transnational perspective on the social ties and networks of immigrants, in which their complicated lives embody social structures that can span two or more continents, economically, culturally and politically. Moreover, the mainstream into which they are said to merge is never clearly defined, despite the fact that any majority of the population is likely to be riven by cultural, regional, political and value differences. Beyond this, the assimilationist picture also renders invisible what is distinctly national about the characteristics of the American population. In the USA, folk ideology sees the mainstream culture rather blindly as a multi-national, universal one, whereas in fact assimilation entails the complete re-nationalisation of diverse immigrants into a new, nationally-specific American culture, which is far from universal in its attitudes about patriotism and cultural identity (Waldinger and FitzGerald 2004). Nationalisation, in other words, also entails differentiation from other nationalities, i.e. from 'foreigners'. Hyphenated US identities (Italian-American, Danish-American, and so on) have rarely preserved any more than an ersatz element of the original homeland national culture in the face of the extraordinarily coercive power of the host society to absorb and transform newcomers into 'Americans', particularly by the third generation (what is referred to as 'straight-line assimilation'). And, although in practice the new immigrant American identity has been open to all who embrace the American dream, there is still a lingering sense of exclusion hanging over the possibly 'un-American' tendencies of more recent immigrants (Huntington 2004): for example, Islamic middle Easterners, whose culture and values – like the 'communists' before them – are seen now to be questionably compatible; or the vast population of Spanish speaking Mexicans and other Latinos, who seem able to create a semi-autonomous, bilingual society of their own in the big cities of the American South-West, which is located in a space of flows and transactions that stretches out South across the US border. These problems are shared by the rare examples of assimilationist studies in Europe – most notably in France (Tribalat *et al.* 1996), which I discuss in more detail in the next chapter – in which immigrants' cultural and social features are evaluated in relation to average French norms, generalised from so-called *français de souche* (French citizens born of French origin families) said to embody the universalist aspirations of French society. Such claims appear absurd when they are made about culturally specific, smaller European nations; it is only the sheer scale of the USA that enables it to be so blind to its own nation-building ideology.

Integration in Europe

The term, integration, however, is by far the more popular concept in a European context, including France. In recent years it has been invoked prominently in public policy debates, and high level policy formulations in Britain, France, The Netherlands, Germany, Italy, Denmark, Sweden, Austria and elsewhere (*see* detailed discussion in the following chapter). In policy debates, it generally refers to a 'middle way' between coercive conformism to national norms and values, on the one hand, and the threat of separatism, seen as latent in the excessive preservation of non-European cultures, on the other. In the USA, the term integration was mainly used as a goal in the black civil rights movement, in opposition to the segregation of schools and public services. Scientifically speaking, there are no satisfactory core definitions, despite the growing number of national and cross-national projects. Banton (2001) refers to integration as a 'treacherous metaphor', which alludes to a two-way accommodation of host and immigrant groups, but offers no clear criteria for operationalisation and measurement. Crucially, this is because there is no clear measurement of how integrated (or 'organic') modern societies are to begin to with.

The key historical background to ideas of integration in Europe is the consciously close relation between these ideas and the long-standing narratives of nation-building and national identity that form the bedrock of European national politics. Each European nation has tended to narrate its history as a process of territorial and political integration of regional minorities and social classes, a process now seen to be played out with the new immigrants of the post-war period. A crucial part of this integration story has been the accession to citizenship of these new members, something that can be seen in terms of progressive legal, political and social rights. This classic position evokes again the work of T. H. Marshall (1950), and signals to the centrality of the building and preservation of the national welfare state as an essential part of this story. Residual concerns about the cultural and religious differences of immigrants remain, but in each national case the debate centres on how historical notions of the nation can be adapted to include new, culturally distinct immigrants, and conversely which things these immigrants must change or adapt in their behaviour to become integrated in the nation.

Debates in Europe have come to be increasingly focused around issues involved in integrating Muslim immigrants. These have often centred on issues such as schooling, the recognition and funding of churches, the toleration of certain practices, or the position of women, but there has often been a lively debate in many countries about whether cultural or socio-economic issues should be uppermost in immigrant reception policy. One or two nations that opted initially for more culturally-based differentialist or multicultural policies – such as The Netherlands or Sweden – have in recent years rejected multiculturalism and reverted to a more socio-economic conception of integration (Fermin 1999; Brubaker 2001; Joppke and Morawska 2003). This usually includes a component of language learning, and a presupposition that immigrants need to develop a knowledge and know-how of the host society as a precondition of success in education or the labour market. Far right parties, hostile to new immigration, often point to indicators of integration failure – such as immigrant unemployment, social tensions, or clashes over non-European practices – as an argument against immigration or in favour of repatriation. New issues have also arisen in connection with the integration of a growing number of asylum seekers in Europe, who have often not been able to follow the standard channel of integration through the labour market.

Integration is often used as an all-encompassing frame for a variety of other terms that pinpoint dimensions of the settlement process. Some writers prefer to write about acculturation, adaptation, inclusion, incorporation or other terms: all are euphemisms for the same general process. Integration is useful as a term in that it goes beyond merely political issues, such as citizenship or participation, to encompass more difficult to specify social processes and moral problems. It also indicates that change is likely on both sides, and presupposes no necessary assimilation to the dominant culture or norms. However, it is still strongly criticised by those coming from a more anti-racist or conflict-theory vision of society, who tend to believe that discrimination is inevitable in all majority-minority relations, and that integration is thus a mask for specific relations of domination. What is clear is that like assimilation, integration presupposes the bounded nation-state-society as the exclusive context for immigrant settlement processes. It upholds a nation-centred view of European societies, which is hard to reconcile with the growing European, regional and global interdependence of European societies, and the emerging transnational social organisation of some migrants. Such migrants indeed often use links to their homeland and diasporic cultures as a buffer to integration pressures.

Some scholars have also sought to distinguish different patterns of social and/or political incorporation within the notion of integration. They point to different kinds of conscious strategies followed by immigrants in relation to the host society: either assimilation, differentialism, segregation or marginalisation (i.e. Berry 1997; Esser 1999). Again these are essentially bounded, functionalist visions of how immigrants might interact with host societies, which overestimate how coherent, closed and integrated Western societies are.

It seems likely that the use of the term integration will grow in future years. As immigration rises in political salience, ruling governments are forced to reformulate policies in terms of integration in order to balance the rights of migrants with the popular pressure to close doors to new migrants. Although this leads to a recognition of the permanence of immigrant settlement, and a reformulation of ideas of national culture, it also presupposes a form of national closure and exclusion to some migrants who are seen as not belonging to the society. It also represents a form of rearguard action by agents of the nation-state, seeking to preserve the fiction of bounded nation-state-societies in an increasingly porous, interdependent world. The concept of assimilation has a more shaky future. Its use depends on the implicit blindness of American perspectives on immigration to the particularistic nation-building processes that they – like nations elsewhere – project onto immigration issues in the name of a well-functioning society. In future, America scholars will need to look at their own society in more comparative ways, which will reveal how similar its debates about assimilation are to debates in smaller European countries about integration and national identity.

The frontier for research in this field, therefore, lies in developing detailed comparative, cross-national studies that are able to explore how different dimensions of integration have affected different national origin migrants in different countries. The research also needs to encompass transnational phenomena and challenge the nation-building fictions that continue to portray the context of immigrant integration as a closed society, with coherent norms and values that the immigrant must learn in a one-way fashion as a pre-condition of socio-economic success. One way of breaking with this view is to take global/international cities or regions as the unit of comparison into which immigrants integrate (i.e. Waldinger 2001). Such studies are now beginning to emerge tentatively in Europe, although as we will see large barriers remain due to the very different means each nation has of generating statistics and survey data about the migrant populations across the continent.

Chapter Five

Integration Policy and Integration Research in Europe: A Review and Critique

Preface: The problem of policy research

The following chapter originated with an invitation from the Carnegie Endowment to write a comparative report on integration strategies in Europe.[1] The report was presented at a transatlantic conference on immigration and citizenship questions,

---

1. Full length original version of report prepared for the Carnegie Endowment for International Peace 'Comparative Citizenship Project' and originally published in T. Alexander Aleinikoff and Doug Klusmeyer (eds), *Citizenship Today: Global Perspectives and Practices*, Washington, DC: Brookings Institution/Carnegie Endowment for International Peace (2001), pp.349–399. A shortened version appeared as 'Integration nations: the nation-state and research on immigrants in Western Europe' (2003), which was also anthologised in collections by Bommes and Morawska (2005) and Martiniello and Rath (2010). The title was wrongly 'corrected' in this last edition adding 'and'; the title is meant to evoke the style of phrases like 'Gay nation' or 'Prozac nation'. A slightly different shortened version appeared as 'Multicultural nation-building: 'Integration' as public philosophy and research paradigm in Western Europe' (2001c). Research for this work took place during my time as a TMR Research Fellow at the University of Utrecht (European Research Centre on Migration and Ethnic Relations (ERCOMER), with thanks to directors Malcolm Cross, Han Entzinger and Louk Haagendoorn, and written while working at the Sussex Centre for Migration Research, University of Sussex, led by Russell King and Richard Black. Attentive readers will spot the obvious Bourdieusian influences at work. Every young sociologist must go through a Bourdieusian phase – this was the height of mine. Basic keys to this way of thinking can be found in Bourdieu (1984; 1986); the discussion of methodology in Bourdieu and Wacquant (1992); and Bourdieu and Wacquant (1999), their entertaining polemic on the 'imperialist' diffusion of Anglo-American approaches to race and multiculturalism. My argument may also be read in the light of James C. Scott (2008) – although I discovered his work only much later. The original argument owed most to many informal conversations with friends and colleagues on the subject, and their own views of the academic research field. In particular, I would like to acknowledge long discussions with Karen Phalet, Virginie Guiraudon, Cristiano Codagnone, Patrick Simon, Michael Bommes, Dirk Jacobs, Hassan Bousetta, Marco Martiniello, and Ruba Salih, Bruno Riccio and others at the Sussex Centre for Migration Research, that helped me piece together different parts of the argument presented here. The revised version benefited greatly from discussions with colleagues at the original Carnegie meeting in Lisbon in June 1999; a meeting of 'hard-core' survey-based social mobility and stratification scholars at the European Science Foundation/European Consortium for Sociological Research conference in Sept 1999 at Obernai on 'Migration and ethnic relations in Europe', organised by Hartmut Esser; and, in the same week, a much more qualitative, anthropological conference of the ESRC Transnational Communities programme, organised at the University of Sussex. I am also grateful for an invitation to discuss the work in progress at the Ethnobarometer conference at Castel Gandolfo, Rome, in June 1999, and to Michèle Lamont, Will Kymlicka, Rainer Bauböck, Pnina Werbner, Thomas Faist, Stephen Castles, Yngve Lithman, Tariq Modood and the editors of the original volume, for their suggestions and/or early sight of new or unpublished research.

featuring a number of leading experts on the subject. Faced with this invitation to get involved in 'policy relevant research', I found myself initially stuck – rather self-consciously – in front of an immediate problem. This was not, I think, to do with my knowledge of the subject – although the report was never going to contain the kind of massive scale primary research and data that would be needed to make an even remotely adequate study of this kind. Rather, it was in the 'straightforward' request to simply sit down and synthesise 'what we know' as scholars, for the benefit of an (unspecified) audience of 'policy makers'. My self-consciousness about the awkwardness of this role – and the reflexivity it imposed on me – may try the patience of readers who have no problems with this apparently straightforward exchange of information.

There is, however, nothing straightforward about the exchange of information between academics and a given policy community. The production of knowledge for an audience of academic scholars is deeply different to that for an audience of policy makers. Taken as ideal-types of intellectual work, in the ordinary run of things two kinds of intellectual work are possible here. To illustrate this, I will present a couple of fake scenarios, which might be imagined in my (then) home country, England. The story is set at the time of New Labour, supposedly a good era for 'high impact' policy relevant research.

A rising star scholar (40-ish), well-connected and working as a senior lecturer at a good university, is one day faced with a momentous career choice. The distinguished policy think tank, the Institute for Public Policy Research (IPPR), which has the ear of Prime Minister Blair and is networked up to the eyeballs with the New Labour London literati, offers to commission him to write a report about integration policies in Britain, in the light of other ongoing research and policy across Europe. In a belated recognition of the predictions of one or two other home-grown scholars, and quite a few European and North American observers – although, interestingly, not Britain's own race and ethnic studies establishment – British multicultural race relations policies have been exposed to be conceptually wanting, and are on the verge of collapsing in a resurgence of racism and anti-immigration feeling, linked particularly with identity anxieties over the EU, and the break up of the UK's constitution. There is little in existing policy thinking and institutional channels to answer the challenge of Islam, globalisation, dual nationality/citizenship, transnationalism, new migrations, super-diversity, etc. He is faced with the urgent imperative to condense his many thoughts on these questions into a glossy fifty page report, that will offer decisive recommendations and arguments: with the right packaging, carefully selective data, perfect political timing, and in the form of nationally patriotic top-down formulae, that can offer the politicians an escape route from the disaster in the making for Britain's mainstream liberal consensus. In doing so – in mixing pure academic discourse with the very different logic of governmental, bureaucratic and media-friendly argument – he will lose credibility among his scholarly peers, and ultimately compromise his own deepest convictions about the truth of the subject, with a fudged policy report that in fact leaves the status quo barely shaken – although it is a resounding political success. The report, however, will launch a brilliant career in government policy circles, as well as a long-desired breakthrough into column writing for the intelligent press, and – naturally – several invitations to dine with Tony and Cherie at Peter Mandelson's beautiful new house in Ladbrooke Grove.

That is the first choice he faces. The second choice is to turn down the IPPR, and instead concentrate on finishing his longstanding commissioned book for Oxford University Press, which, due to a fortunate coincidence of academic fashions – the Europeanisation of academic concerns, a high profile ESRC (the British Economic and Social Research Council) project on transnationalism, an emerging cross-disciplinary recognition of the importance of issues about Islam and the West, citizenship, multiculturalism, and so on – contains within its pages the current academic key to international fame in the social sciences; answering, as it does, several of the most widely debated conundrums about globalisation, the future of the nation state, and the secret of democratic social integration in a multicultural society. In writing it, and the well-placed spin-off articles in all the best Anglo-American international journals, he will have to cut out some of the really interesting but difficult theoretical bits, concentrating on a streamlined scientific style of argumentation and maximum current academic impact. However, this publishing boon will be the perfect research output for the upcoming research assessment exercise (later called REF) that will push his department up to five star 'world class' level, secure him promotion, and free him from most of his irksome undergraduate teaching responsibilities. Given this potential, Oxbridge will instead immediately step in and snap up the (now) young professor with a national bargaining-breaking salary offer, and the best sociology job in the country: the Lady Thatcher Chair in Theoretical Sociology (motto: 'There is no society...'). His academic authority will now be established for life, and he will look forward to a fantastic series of guest lectureships in Japan and the USA, along with all the vintage port and cheese at high table. However, by his own admission, he will have foregone the chance of real social power in the wider social circles of British political and media; and when a former colleague takes on the IPPR work to great success, he will have no consolation but to write long and bitter reviews of his colleague's 'superficial' later works in the pages of the Times Literary Supplement.

My point here is that that these two choices represent not only different styles of work, but two very different social systems with different rewards. Genuine quality and impact in either may exclude success in the other: it is foolish to pretend they are the same thing. Put another way, establishing one's authority for one may in fact diminish one's authority for the other. Scholarly work, and the very maintenance of prestige in the academic field requires an autonomy that is proportionately diluted by the 'heteronomy' of seeking contemporary political and social impact. But saving the world – or at least improving it a little – through political engagement in one's work, is not going to produce a Hegelian masterpiece. This is the dilemma of policy research: whatever is produced is bound up with basic questions of establishing authority – i.e. social power – in a particular field, within which the material conditions of production, and the dictates of a particular form of work and audience (the 'habitus' of that 'field'), will determine in large part the intellectual content of the work. It is then impossible to avoid the distortion that follows any co-option into a different discursive logic – and approach to truth – than the straight scientific. And, of course, 'pure' academic work is itself sociological determined by strategic decisions about situating it within the academic field, with its disciplinary borders, its multi-disciplinary conflicts and confusions, and the pressure of the publishing industry and wider social fashions. In all honesty, we are always condemned to writing with an uncomfortable instrumental self-consciousness.

Yet look at the sub-field of migration and ethnic studies, and innumerable examples of work can be found that are trying – rather un-self-consciously – to play both games at once: spread out in an uneven line between politics and scholarship, neither fish nor fowl. Autonomy is not easy: academics are so caught up in chasing after public or private money to fund research, fly the world and write reports, buying liberty from the hard labour of the classroom; they are also sorely tempted by the glittering media/politics/policy opportunities of the information age. And yet at the same time, by definition, the reality of these material conditions of production have to be erased from what they say or do: when they speak as 'experts', they bank on the illusion of neutrality and scholarly authority, feeding ideas and arguments back into the black hole of the 'policy process'. Given this role, it is very easy to go on and self-indulgently write as if they are in fact policy making or legislating, having offered a normative, clean hands prognosis of the world's ills – a view from nowhere – that is not in the slightest bit corrupted by the grittier practical knowledge of politicians and bureaucrats: of how to implement ideas in policy, deal with public opinion, second guess perverse effects. At this level, it is a cosy relationship: practitioners are in no way committed to take heed of what academics say, but the inclusion of the latter offers a veneer of well-argued legitimacy, that can always be easily overlooked.

One can envisage here a perfect compromise, in which the local (by this I mean 'national') intellectual borders of the recognised public intellectual's work preserve a sharp political or media relevance, whilst the public notoriety also reinforces prestige among the national academic elite. Traditionally, some such interpenetration of the academic, publishing and public political fields has reigned on the left bank of the Seine in Paris; feature articles in *Le Monde* or *Esprit* become transferable capital that can scale the hierarchy of the Collège de France, École des Hautes Études or Sciences Po, secure wider book sales and court invitations from the government. To a human geographer it would come as no surprise: the people who populate the fields of media, policy and academia live in the same apartment blocks in Saint Germain-des-Prés, and send their children to the same elite prep schools around the Panthéon. But as my London/Oxbridge scenario suggests above, however, the elite circles cannot everywhere be assumed to coincide, or be bounded by such local national structures of influence. Even the horizons of social power for French academics are changing: the stifling national frustrations of the old game and the competition for a steadily declining intellectual prestige in France, finally being rejected by a new generation of internationally-educated, English-speaking French scholars. Due to the ongoing (if partial) differentiation of the various social systems in which they live, academics need not only exclusively play in a nationally bound field of elite social power. Like certain other elites – though not others – they can lay claim to social power in international circles, that perhaps enable them to forget entirely the otherwise universal truism that knowing one's local national politicians or newspaper editors is of utmost social significance. European networks, among others, are just one example of transnational rewards that have offered a way out of the national for certain academics, lawyers, bureaucrats, even police; although, significantly, this avenue will not necessarily appeal to the barristers, journalists and party politicians who usually run the country. Within this context, the nature of social scientific work will change.

All these preliminary worries might seem to make it impossible to even write a report, but to my mind, the great luxury of writing for Carnegie was the relative mental freedom it offered from the academic and public political pressures outlined above. It had no specific national or supra-national political reference; and also no direct academic publishing credit or constraints. The absence of the rules that these secondary career struggles impose, might have offered some genuine intellectual space in which to get to the bottom of the problem of policy research in this field of study. The work I present, then, is a survey of the state-of-the-art in research on integration in Europe, caught as it is between public policy concerns and scientific scholarly endeavour. While indeed surveying 'what we know' about the subject, I also aim throughout to show how these academic constructions of integration issues and problems – and the deeper theoretical questions they reflect – are bound up with the similar 'common sense' policy formulations on the subject currently found in the policy thinking of most European nation-states and their public officials. The crucial point will be that the interpenetration of these two fields of interest has caused research on the subject to not adequately reflect significant changes in the patterns of migration and immigrant settlement in Europe; moreover, that this problem continues to form a formidable barrier to the production of meaningful cross-national comparative research on the subject. I will also return to these reflexive concerns in my concluding chapter.

Despite the quantity of research on post-war immigration in Europe, then, there are still no fully satisfactory examples of cross-national comparative research on the integration of immigrants, which are able to span the very different experiences and national conceptualisations of such complex processes of social change in these countries. In asking why this is, I assess what has been achieved in national and international research, and explore ways in which better research might be developed. Drawing on my research and experience in four Western European countries – Britain, France, The Netherlands and Belgium – with additional reference to Germany, Austria and Scandinavia, I offer a review of the state-of-the-art in European integration research, which focuses on the initial explosion of work in the 1990s and early 2000s, but will selectively bring the overview up to date. My aim is not to simply synthesise studies of 'integration strategies' in these different countries – with a view to pinpointing 'best practices', etc. – as a conventional policy report might do – although I do discuss those recent studies which have done just this. Rather, I seek to problematise the relationship between academic knowledge and policy constructions in this field, to show how nearly all current thinking on integration (and associated terms such as assimilation, incorporation and inclusion) in Europe is bound up with a reproduction of nation-state and nation-society centred reasoning. Such forms of reasoning – trapped in the bounded conventions of 'normal science' in this field – increasingly fail to represent the evolving relationship between new migrants or ethnic minorities and their host 'societies'.[2]

To break with these restrictions, we need to conceive of doing research which reduces the nation-state and/or nation-society to one among several potential structuring variables explaining the actions of immigrants and minorities and their interaction with existing European populations. After looking at the deep theoretical features of thinking on integration, and the way in which a cross-national and transatlantic research agenda has developed on the subject, I show how the (sometimes hidden) framing of the integration 'paradigm' can be seen equally in commissioned research on immigration politics and policy in Europe, as in current national survey and census-based studies on the behaviour, identities and social mobility of immigrant populations. I also consider the challenge of transnationalism in thinking about integration. Throughout, the general argument of the text is supported by a detailed literature review and discussion in the footnotes. As suggested in the preface, the study also attempts to put into practice a thoroughly reflexive approach to sociological work in this area, which pays close attention to the political and social contextual factors and the material conditions of production which have caused certain types of research and policy intervention to be made.

Integration in theory and practice

There is no shortage of comparative and national research on integration policies in Western Europe and the most straightforward kind of overview to write would be one which tried to synthesise the various findings, in order to perhaps produce a checklist of policies in different countries and an evaluation of their relative effectiveness. However, any such attempt will quickly encounter the fact that the issues of immigration and integration are formulated in very distinct, and context-specific ways across Europe. It is my suggestion then that we might learn as much if not more about the range of integration strategies and policy thinking in Europe, by examining in each case why this work has been produced, and under what conditions particular framings of the question have become dominant.

---

2. My argument and analysis, which was first written and presented in 1999, has obvious connections and affinities to the slightly later article(s) by Wimmer and Glick Schiller (2002) on 'methodological nationalism'. Only Bommes (1998) had seriously explored the 'sociology' of comparative immigration research before this; *see* Boswell and D'Amato (2012). Subsequently, there has been a wide range of reflection by scholars such as Lavenex (2005), Geddes (2005) and Boswell (2009); *see also* the collection by Bommes and Morawska (2005). and Scholten *et al.* (2014). Recently, work by Schinkel (2013) in a more critical theory heavy mode has made a similar reflexive critique of Dutch integration research and policy.

What we have as the unreflective starting point, then, is the image of several distinct, bounded nation-states in Europe, each individually facing more or less similar questions about the 'integration' of different ethnic minorities and immigrants, who have arrived heterogeneously as a result of post-war labour immigration, asylum seeking, and new forms of migration and mobilities (Castles and Miller 2009). At different stages of this long migration-settlement process, what each is then faced with implementing is a series of provisions, policies and social interventions which together might be seen to add up to an 'integration policy'. These may indicatively include the following (*see* similar checklists of policies, rights or incorporation regimes in Kymlicka 1995, 37–38; Soysal 1994, 79–82; Vertovec 1997, 61–62):

- □ basic legal and social protection
- □ formal naturalisation and citizenship (or residence-based) rights
- □ anti-discrimination laws
- □ equal opportunities positive action
- □ corporatist and associational structures for immigrant or ethnic organisations
- □ redistribution of targeted socio-economic funds for minorities in deprived areas
- □ policy on public housing
- □ policy on law and order
- □ agreements with foreign countries about military service
- □ multicultural education policy
- □ special sections within political parties
- □ policies and laws on tolerating cultural practices
- □ cultural funding for ethnic associations or religious organisations
- □ language and cultural courses in host society's culture

What should be asked first is how and why this disparate range of state policies, laws, local initiatives and societal dispositions – which could in theory be implemented by all kinds of agencies and at all kinds of levels – comes to be thought of and described as a single nation-state's overall strategy or policy of 'integration'. But who or what is integrating whom and with what? This is by no means such an obvious question to answer: unless we simply take, as far too many social scientists still do, *the state* and *a society* as the unproblematic, unchallenged backdrops to these debates and processes. For sure, when political actors and policy intellectuals talk about 'integration', they are inevitably thinking about integration into one, single, indivisible (national) 'state', and one, simple, unitary (national) 'society'. But it is precisely the assumptions behind this term that we should be examining. Political language is performative: actors are always trying to *create* the phenomenon of which they are speaking.

So what assumptions does the concept 'integration' contain? One or two points are immediately clear. To talk of integration is to envisage a policy that is distinct from immigration policy – border control, rights of entry and abode, etc. – *per se*. It accepts some idea of permanent settlement, and is dealing with, and trying to distinguish, a later stage in a coherent societal process: the consequences of immigration. It is also a term which partly builds its success on swallowing up other similar, but more precise, partial or politically unfashionable terms for the same kind of process: terms such as assimilation, absorption, acculturation, accommodation, incorporation, inclusion, participation, cohesion, enfranchisement, toleration, etc. And, as I will argue throughout, integration policies and provisions are interventions, with a few exceptions, taken to be almost exclusively the province of nation-state, or more local agencies of the state. The institutions of the EU for example – which has got involved in so many other substantive areas of policy in Europe, and which of course builds its own dynamics around a different use of the same term – is excluded from most of the kinds of integration intervention listed above (*see* Favell 2006).

In most Western European countries by the end of the 1980s, a dominant discourse on 'integration' had emerged as the overarching framework for the various types of policies and practices towards immigrants and minorities being experimented with by actors and agencies in all sectors of society.[3] This emergence as the widest possible conceptual consensus invariably followed a period in which 'older' assimilationist ideas vied with the post-1960s inheritance of ideas about cultural difference and the anti-racist struggle, and in which integration became a comfortable, 'sensible' position for the centre trying to distinguish itself from xenophobic nationalism on the one hand, and radical anti-system discourses on the other. On one level, the success of an ordinary language term like this can be said to be superficial, as Banton (2001) argued, in response to my original report. He argued that it needed to be purged from scientific sociological studies; and indeed it is possible to see it just as jargon that gets picked up as a kind of default language, when other types of argument become unfashionable or distorted by political usage. However, to dismiss it this way, is to foreclose analysis of how and why and particular terms get picked to discuss and frame policies, and what the consequences are of this conception. Integration in recent years has appeared

---

3. Britain has essentially worked within an 'integration' framework since Roy Jenkins' famous speech of 1966 (quoted and discussed in Favell, 1998a, pp. 104ff). For reasons of political distinction, many anti-racist commentators rejected the term from the 1970s onwards, and the term is still sometimes seen by some as having a vaguely 'incorrect' air about it. It remains, however, widely used in political discussions, and indeed enjoyed a strong academic and policy comeback in the 2000s as the Labour Party shifted towards a more explicitly national frame for immigration policies. *See* for example how the terminology was adopted in one of the Oxford research centre COMPAS's early reports (Castles *et al.* 2002). French policy intellectuals constructed a conceptual consensus on 'intégration' in the mid to late 1990s, charting it as a consensus term, although it is still sometimes used interchangeably with 'assimilation' or 'insertion'. The Dutch similarly converged on it in the 1990s, as a reaction against excessive cultural differentialism in their original 'pillars-based' approach. Belgians, meanwhile, on both sides of the country, refer to the term as the natural goal of social policies, although they may differ in the details of its application, according to which of the French or 'Anglo' influences is uppermost. Elsewhere, in Germany, Austria, Scandinavia, Switzerland, Italy or Spain, the word has been widely used in the same self-evident way. *See also* similar discussions in the work of Schinkel (2013).

quite impervious to these same problems: even among academics it has been rarely problematised or examined, when it is used as a conceptual shorthand. Its effectiveness seems to lie in the fact that it best fits the undefined 'conceptual space' gestured to when academics talk about the (counter-factual) goal of successful inter-ethnic relations or a less dysfunctional multi-cultural or multi-racial society. For sure, this must have much to do with its built-in vagueness, and its abstract-yet-positive sounding quality. It suggests a comfortingly technical view of the engineering of modern society, heading in a teleological direction towards a self-evidently progressive outcome. In this respect, its polar opposite is so obviously bad, as to almost force us to accept 'integration' as a necessity. 'Disintegration' is one of the most chilling descriptive terms to use about society – as it is for persons – evoking a disaster striking at an almost molecular level (an imperative that is not felt with quite the same force for 'incohesion', 'disenfranchisement' or 'intolerance', for example). Crucially, too, in relation to terms like 'assimilation', 'integration' sounds like a complex, two way or multiple process, to evoke change that is mutual and organic in some way.

'Integration' also works well as a popular public concept, because of its allusion to more longstanding theories and ideas about the nature of modern society. One area where the sociological thinking of the twentieth century has had a very deep effect on the self-consciousness of how Western society thinks about itself as a collectivity (with collective *agency*), is in the almost essential link that 'society' and 'societal integration' are taken to have. The discipline of sociology as a mode of reflection about the world, is indeed constituted from the construction of society – as a unified, functioning whole – as its overall *object* of enquiry. This link, and hence the *raison d'être* of the discipline, is driven by a fear of the 'logical' alternative: the Hobbesian sub-consciousness of a societal breakdown, and the war of all against all.[4] As was made clear in the previous chapter, the inheritance of Durkheimian-style functionalism can here be pointed out, filtered in the USA through the systematising work of Talcott Parsons, as the core representative American social theorist of the century. Even where conflict is seen to be a fundamental part of Western society, it is accepted as an almost logical truism that underlying this there has to be some degree of 'integration', or else [...] Behind social competition and the organic division of labour, class, social distinction, etc., the thinking goes, there has, in other words, to be some degree or kind of 'value integration' somewhere – probably at least on a normative moral level as Parsons imagined it – but practically speaking embedded at least in some political, economic or legal structures common to all. The alternative is 'anomie' and dysfunctional social forms. These symptoms of breakdown, of societal failure, then become the prime empirical material of

4.   It is, of course, significant that the nightmare scenario of the sociological 'sub-conscious' should be the anarchic, individualistic one (this reflects the dominantly Americanised nature of our thinking about society without integration), rather than other states of nature, whether dystopian (the Freudian primordialism behind civilisation), or utopian (the Lockean spontaneous community; the Rousseauian and Marxist sense of man in nature before alienation, for example).

sociologists, who are thus ultimately driven by a reconstructive urge to provide the 'useful' knowledge with which these fundamental 'social problems' can be answered (in policy).[5]

The other key thing about the list of measures seen to be part of 'integration policy', is that they are all things that a *state* can in fact 'do'. Although for the time being it is rare to come across a specifically designated 'Ministry of Integration', the policy field has emerged over the years as a *differentiated* area of government, often crossing the competences of different departments. Integration is thus not only an ideal goal for society; it is also something a government sets out to achieve. This assumption is crucial to the nation-state centred conceptualisation of social processes that will be found at the core of practical ordinary language usages of the term. Such a use precludes the idea that society might achieve an integrated state of affairs without the state's intervention.

Sociologically speaking, we can, of course, conceive of integration taking place without the structure-imposing involvement of the state. Immigrants can be 'integrated' into the local labour market as employees or service providers, or they can be 'integrated' into complex inter-community relations at, say, city or district level. Looked at from a bottom-up perspective – i.e. where the integration of society as a whole is not assumed as the end goal of interaction between ethnically diverse groups – multicultural relations can be seen to take all kinds of organised and semi-organised forms. These may not at all be encompassed by the top-down, organised structures typical of state thinking on the subject, such as policy frameworks, official channels of participation, or legally circumscribed rights, restrictions and entitlements. Multiculturalism as a *descriptive* state-of-affairs, in this sense, could be the product of something that never had anything to do with the 'multicultural' policies or institutions of the state: one reason why the 'end' of multiculturalism declared by some analysts is vastly over-stated (i.e. Joppke and Morawska 2003). The point is – as historical theorists of the state would remind us with their vivid terminology – the state has always constituted itself in the way it imposes formal structures and institutionalises social relations via a systematic 'embracing', 'caging' and/or 'penetrating' of society (Scott 1998; Torpey 2000). This logic of incorporation – of making society 'legible' by scientific or technical means – has invariably in recent history taken a dominant form of collective social power (to borrow the terms of Mann 1993) that seeks to encompass, contain and bind together the state's domination of society, and all the varied market

---

5. On this understanding of functionalism, *see* especially Alexander (1987). It may not be as fashionable as it once was in the 1960s, but older sociological discussions on integration theories versus conflict/power theories of society are still the essential intellectual backdrop for these discussions. A good selection of debates about Parsons and the Hobbesian dilemma, including contributions by Lockwood, Rex and Giddens, can be found in Worsley (1970); *see also* Haferkamp and Smelser (1992) and Alexander's discussion of Rex. Only German sociology on migration and integration has reflected these absolutely fundamental questions of social theory: for example, the work of Münch (2001) and Bommes (*see* Boswell and D'Amato 2012). Without such reflection, a lot of discussions of 'integration' are hopelessly superficial in nature. My own understanding of the question owes most to the teaching of Pizzorno (i.e. 1991).

or community relations inside it. This form is the modern nation-state. And, as soon as we begin to think of integration as a collective societal goal which can be achieved through the systematic intervention of collective political agency, we inevitably begin to invoke the nation-state in the production of a different, caged and bounded version, of multicultural social relations.

Through some such logic, the common sense public theory – that integration is, at some level, a precondition of any society – converges with the other most pervasive mainstream public theory of our times: that of legal/political constitutionalism.[6] Crucially, they are both hierarchical visions: state-centred and bounded, in which society is able to act upon itself through the agency of government and policy making. The idea that society might function without such methods of intervention – without integration of some kind – is not easily broached; just as it is not easy to imagine political life without a state. To do so, would be to counterpoise integration, not with conflict and disintegration, but with something much harder to grasp: the disengagement and the decoupling of distinct social systems within or across societies, that are somehow able to coexist, but which do not necessarily conflict because they do not always interact. For obvious reasons to do with their role in the maintenance and reproduction of the state, and the state-society relation they depend on, this is not the kind of thing a politician or supreme court judge is ever likely to start talking about.

It is perhaps not surprising that state actors have to speak positively about the possibility and goal of societal integration, but it is interesting to note how academics in the 1980s and 1990s also adopted the same kind of discourse and underlying logic, with a similar 'state-centric' (re-)constructive attitude towards fundamental social thought, re-imagining 'social unity' or 'cohesion' out of diversity and conflict. Reading some of these multicultural theorists, as I argued in Chapter Two, we need constant reminding that these philosophers and social theorists are not speaking from the same social location as the politicians, judges and bureaucrats who actually make decisions and implement policies. Given their officially autonomous status in liberal democracy as free-thinking intellectuals, there is no reason on the face of it why they should have to worry about getting involved in heteronomous, pseudo-policy prescriptions about the building of a better society, instead, say, of engaging in a critique of the fundamental blindspots

---

6.   Of which the most influential public theory is that of Rawls (1971; 1993), and followers: see Mulhall and Swift (1992), and Kymlicka (1989; 1995), and my discussion in Chapter Two, for the essentials of how this way of thinking is applied to questions of integration/citizenship. The great German inheritor of the critical theoretical tradition, Habermas, of course, also converged with the Rawlsian normative paradigm: see Habermas (1995); Rawls (1995). His constitutional patriotism is the epitome of the kind of left-liberal collapsing of social theory and sociology into normative political philosophy, which has been characteristic of so much recent reflection on the subject. Symptoms of the normative urge for usefulness that drives most studies are the fact that many of the most significant commentators actually come from a philosophical background (i.e. Kymlicka, Bauböck, Modood), and that in the current climate, many of the most authoritative empirical commentators, such as Castles, invariably frame their work in normative terms and concerns about citizenship or democracy (i.e. Castles and Davidson 1999). See my discussion of the transatlantic field of multicultural citizenship in Favell (1999).

and self-delusions of those who actually do have this power. After all, in terms of orthodox social theory, whether Marxist – which has enjoyed such a comeback since the post 2008 economic crisis – Foucauldian, Lacanian and so on, the academic's vocation is automatically seen as critical: to refuse hegemony, denounce power, create the conditions for emancipation. Those in the field of ethnic, racial and migration studies (*see*, for example, Winant 2001; De Genova 2010; Schinkel and van Houdt 2010; Castles 2011) show how the world system is built on colonialism and racial exploitation; how the political economy of Western Europe generates exploitative immigration to the continent; how race relations policies mask internal colonialism; how multicultural citizenship subordinates and tames difference with the governmentality of bureaucratic state logic. But even radicals, because of professional pressures, are involved in chasing after ethnic relations policy consultancies, writing minority rights constitutions for obscure African states, compiling OECD reports on world migration, or offering advice about the Balkans to politicians on CNN, and so on. Over the years, one by one, prominent academic voices have been incorporated into the wider, state-sponsored production of 'practical' applied knowledge. Those that are less successful in the 'real' world of politics and policy making, meanwhile, continue to ally their critical stance with activist identity politics and social movements campaigning (and the urban-lifestyle 'alternative' publishing market that thrives on it), a co-option which can also be destructive of academic autonomy and authority.[7] The institutionalisation

---

7.   The development of British ethnic and racial studies is here a case in point. Earlier studies were inspired by one of two things. The first came out of an activist anti-racist tradition, mediated through a critical Marxist or Marxist-Weberian sociological perspective. It began as a critical current, which over time increasingly became co-opted into official policy circles and semi-autonomous research institutes, keen to use academic work in the development of British race relations, creating in the process a 'canon' of policy-relevant sociological research. The influence of John Rex (i.e. Rex and Moore 1967; Rex 1970) was paramount, and the evolution of the field can indeed be traced through the numerous people who followed his work (or, indeed, worked with him), only to then build their own distinctive positions through criticism and rejection of it (Robert Miles, Robert Moore, Sally Tomlinson, John Stone, Malcolm Cross, John Solomos, John Wrench, Harry Goulbourne, Tariq Modood, Steven Vertovec). Other influential early constructions of the empirical subject were the work of Michael Banton, director of the first officially funded research centre at Bristol, which afterwards moved to Aston, then Warwick (Banton 1955; 1967), the Institute of Race Relations' seminal report *Colour and Citizenship* (Rose *et al.*, 1969), and the anthropological collection of studies on different ethnic groups in Britain, *Between Two Cultures* (Watson 1977). Reading some of these studies as historical milestones, it is striking how the construction of data and concepts about migration and settlement of post-war immigrants to Britain in the early period resembles much of the work in more recent years after the new post-1990 migrations in Europe. Solomos and Back (1996) is a useful guide to the evolution of British work on race and racism from this point on, offering an intelligent defence of why British work evolved in this way, as well as an internal guide to a field which became symptomatically limited to British-centric notions and debates. A second current of work, which almost had a separate but much more international life to it, was that based on Marxist political economy, epitomised by Castles and Kosack's (1973) unsurpassed early comparative study of migrant workers in Europe. Although a major breakthrough in the formulation of international questions, the work had probably more impact outside of Britain and outside the sub-field of race relations, and was an approach left behind to some extent by its authors at a later stage (although Castles has returned emphatically to his Marxist roots in his post 2008 writings). The cultural turn of the early 1980s, revealed

of this academic field produced a genuinely constructive turn towards the object of social thought – a multi-racial or multi-cultural society – and the practical problems it can been seen to have. Academics reconceived their role as offering a counterfactual meta-discourse on policy making for the good society, and this was mirrored in the more inclusive and supportive attitude of the state towards including ideas from these origins in the policy process. Intellectuals themselves have thus increasingly engaged with imagining a progressive (future) reality, rather than unmasking the corruption and lies of the present, with a performative discourse about integration which seeks to theorise social possibility rather than offering a denunciatory counter-discourse (about power, domination, exploitation, etc.). Such a role is also a self-styled interpretative role, reconstructing history as a movement towards something better, in which a progressive intellectual position in aligned with progressive political currents in the society.[8]

'new racism', and gave rise to a new generation of critical works using cultural studies approaches which attacked the canon above, but did not break out of its British-centric limitations. Central to this were the Centre for Contemporary Cultural Studies (1982), Paul Gilroy (1987), and, above all, Stuart Hall (i.e. Hall 1995). The rise of cultural studies – alongside the new and highly politicised gender and identity-based studies of race and ethnicity – fragmented and all-but-destroyed the original sociological foundations of the field in Britain, as it reacted against the 'old guard' of Rex and company (although Rex continued to be a key figure in countries with stronger sociological traditions such as Germany). The story of the rise and fall of the Centre for Research in Ethnic Relations (CRER) at Warwick – which split along exactly these lines – crystallised this intellectual genesis. The Centre was initially headed by Rex and nurtured many of the leading figures mentioned above. However, caught between its growing policy-oriented role and the increasing radicalisation of cultural studies approaches, the Centre fragmented in the mid-1990s. As in other places, it had to seek a new research identity through Europeanising itself on the new comparative (and EU funded) wave – as so many other research centres have done – but was a shadow of its former importance, as other centres rose in relation to new migration trends: Bristol (with Modood), University College London (John Salt), the University of Sussex (Russell King and Richard Black), and most dominantly, Oxford (with Vertovec's Transnational Communities Programme, and Castles' two centres COMPAS, later directed by Vertovec, and IMI, later directed by Robin Cohen). A bidding war in the late 2000s over the call for a massive cross-Europe research programme on migration under the auspices of New Opportunities for Research Funding Agency Cooperation in Europe (NORFACE) led to a framework dominated by economists and narrowly technical projects, many with little connection to previous work in the field, and managed out of University College London (Christian Dustmann). Cultural studies approaches, meanwhile, has been ascendent in place of sociology as a discipline, as it further diluted into media, communication, gender, identity, etc. studies. This process was exacerbated by the increasingly market-oriented dynamics of university teaching, which force syllabi to compete for students with fashionable subjects that focus on students' own identity concerns and lifestyle preferences. Self-styled marginal and radical approaches thus, ironically, became the mainstream. But with the growing demand for credible comparative work – in a more 'conventional' policy relevant social scientific style – work started to re-discover older, discarded ways of studying immigration that brought British research more in line with the rest of Europe. In this, cross-national research networks such as IMISCOE (directed out of Amsterdam by Rinus Penninx) have played a crucial role.

8. The return of T.H. Marshall, 1950, to everyone's theoretical agenda after the post-1989 collapse of the Marxist paradigm (which left the left looking around for a new one...), was emblematic of this 'progressive, but constructive' turn amongst scholars. No matter how false his theory can be shown to be, or how limited it is to British history (*see* Mann 1988), it nevertheless still offers a richly performative theoretical framework, which continues to inspire positive-minded academics trying to reconcile the normative and the historical/explanatory, and work with a rights and citizenship idiom (*see* Bulmer and Rees 1996; Soysal 2012).

Both radical and policy-oriented mainstream approaches are thus compromised in their relation to the object of study. We always need to emphasise the shifting role of the intellectual in relation to the social power of intellectual work in the nation-state context, and suggest how that has both disciplined and constrained their output, as a necessary condition, perhaps, for producing more engaged and socially meaningful work for others. As a system of thought, the progressive integration 'paradigm' (as I will call it) – of trying to imagine how Western nation-state-societies are going to deal with their ethnic dilemmas, resolving the achievement of social cohesion under conditions of cultural diversity and conflict – in fact forced a pragmatic discipline on thinking, which then had to also follow the logic of the mainstream integration discourse. This added up to a normatively-engaged mode of thinking about the problem of multicultural society which became the ubiquitous, apparently unavoidable, medium of progressive, constructive social thinking everywhere in the 1980s and 1990s: the idea of *citizenship* (Habermas 1992; Turner 1993; Kymlicka and Norman 1994; van Steenburgen 1994 and Beiner 1998). The key part of this line of thought – in practical terms that make it meaningful as a policy contribution – is to try to reconcile this rectifying impulse, with a recognition that there are always going to be *de facto* inequalities in society. The academic thus must engage in conceiving of a just 'equality of opportunity', which allows perhaps for special provisions and protection for the disadvantaged, but does not challenge the underlying need for common principles and rules that apply to all.[9] When linked to questions about integration or multiculturalism, the idea of citizenship gestures towards tolerance and recognition of difference, openness to diversity, perhaps even positive action or cultural rights for minorities. The apparent inevitability of the idiom of citizenship is perhaps not surprising once contemporary social thought went beyond Marxist critique, repositioning itself as offering practical interventions towards the construction of a multicultural society. But what is sometimes less honestly recognised in all this is that you cannot have citizenship without the historical social and state structures that make its various

---

9. This is the continuation of the basic liberal conundrum of the post-war period, whether we think of Marshall or Dahrendorf or Rawls: of how to reconcile *de facto* inequality and the persistence of dramatic social distinctions – and the threat of destructive social conflict over this – with the idea of a classless, just, welfare-state based society. The Rawlsian form of 'solution' became the triumphant default theoretical position of progressive liberalism: full citizenship with equal rights plus equality of opportunity, but individual freedom and any unequal distribution that remains compatible with these conditions (Rawls 1971). As a legitimising philosophy, thanks usually to a strong dose of nationalism and 'solidarity', and as long there was continued economic growth, it continued to hold firm in post-war Western societies. In the light of the growing critique of globalisation, and especially post-2008 crisis, critical currents focusing on the inequities of 'neo-liberalism' have, though, challenged the idea of acceptable inequality. 'Citizenship' has also occasionally been seized for more radical, *marxisant* projects, which however inevitably diffuse its specific legal and institutional definitions (Marx would have simply said that citizenship, like the idea of rights, is bourgeois 'nonsense on stilts'). In his later work (1993) Rawls went on to apply the same method to the reconciliation of cultural pluralism with liberal principles of freedom and equality. Lukes (1985) offers a sympathetic but acute analysis of the seismic paradigm shift – and new moral engagement – that intellectuals took in leaving behind Marx for contemporary liberal political theory.

component elements realistic and meaningful: the nation-state (Mann 1988; 1993). Many thinkers in the field may have started thinking of political and social entities 'beyond' the nation state, but invariably this involved projecting the features of the nation-state onto some supra-national construction. On this point, reflection about citizenship projected to a European level, or re-conceived as post-national citizenship, could often seem a misguided and mistaken reading of the European project (*see* debates in Meehan 1993; Wiener 1997; Weiler 1998; Maas 2007; Shaw 2007). Yet, at the same time, it is far from clear that the nation-state still exists in anything like the ideal type form that Ernest Renan or T.H. Marshall imagined in the past, except perhaps in the conceptions of those powerful social actors most embedded in the political forms which gave it its shape and power in the past. The reproduction of ideas of 'integration' and 'citizenship' in academic discourse – for all their progressive veneer – thus may be just reproducing a certain vision of a unitary modern nation-state/nation-society, that corresponds very closely to what those who speak from a powerful position within society most want to hear, but not how the society or societies out there really function (*see also* Bommes 1998).

Emergence of a cross-national comparative field

Talking about 'society' as a collectivity will naturally lead observers on to talking about the specific particularities of their own society: of projecting its distinctive nature, its mode of evolution, its future development. But, as any thinkers in the phenomenological tradition would readily point out, all talk about who 'we' are will depend in part on the simultaneous definition of the 'other', those whose differences enable us to see who we really are. We need to perceive and judge other societies in order to define our own. The urge to comparativism is, therefore, almost an epistemological necessity in all practical social thought; but it too is shot through with the distorting influence of partiality and unequal relations of power.

This, I would suggest, is a second important consideration in understanding the last thirty years or so of research on integration. For, in looking at how constructive thinking on integration and citizenship emerged in the 1980s and 1990s, the other key dimension was the return of a North American perspective on the European situation. This dimension has always been more or less present in European thinking about itself. In an era of post-war reconstruction and the cold war, Europeans bought seriously into Americanisation, eyeing up its version of market-based universalism, personal freedom and the paradigmatic immigrant nation/melting pot idea, as possible solutions to its own social future (De Grazia 2006). These ideas have also always been distorted by the asymmetrical power relations across the Atlantic, and Europeans' desire to define a different version of liberal democracy and the liberal market for itself: the EU emerged from this impulse as much as any other. European nations have always worked themselves up into paroxyms of love-hate in relation to the outside American cultural influence; none more so than the French. From the other side, Europe has always been seen as both the motherland origin of authentic cultures, and the hotbed of archaic nationalisms and histories; behind this, Americans have taken the same imperial developmentalist attitude to Europe which they took to every other part of the globe.

In thinking about race, ethnicity, multiculturalism or citizenship, the stock of American vocabulary has almost always been swallowed whole by Europeans trying to understand themselves in American (and then Canadian) terms. As I will argue throughout, this has not always been the most appropriate choice of social scientific language for study of European cases: Europeans, in fact, should be measuring their *distance* from settler countries built on immigration – and their very different social systems – not their similarities. The British, in particular, are particularly self-deluding in this sense: often seeing their society as closer to North America than 'Europe', that place just across the sea. This in turn is reinforced by the use of the completely meaningless adjective 'Anglo-Saxon' on the continent to lump English language societies together as one 'type' of society.

In other ways, the dominant intellectual influence of North America is abundantly clear. The very emergence of a policy-oriented sociological discipline, driven by the practical idea that the sociologists' primary role is to study, chart and offer remedies to social inequality, owes so much to the pioneering work of the Chicago school and its modelling of the social integration process in urban contexts (Bulmer 1984; Ballis-Lal 1990). American thus provided Europe with the whole model of immigrant integration, ethnic studies and race relations; as well as the nightmare vision of potential ethnic and social breakdown on a scale unimagined in European cities.[10] Again, these approximations have not always been so appropriate. The term 'integration' in the USA was, up to the 1960s, used not to talk about immigrants in American society, but the classic 'American dilemma' about the USA's native black minority population. Integration was promoted as the opposite of the official black and white segregation practised prior to the civil rights movement in many parts of the USA. It was used in sociological studies supporting the desegregation of restaurants, swimming pools, theatres and (especially) public schools. This usage went out of favour as anti-racist discourses in the USA changed. Integration, however, has now made a comeback in the context of the new immigration of the 1980s and 1990s, as new questions of cultural accommodation and assimilation (concerning Asian or Hispanic groups, for example) have emerged centre stage. The confusion in referencing these American-inspired terms and studies in Europe, lies in the fact that immigrants in Europe are usually *also* disadvantaged racial minorities: both American literatures, therefore, have inspired European work.[11] More generally, in

---

10. Classic texts by Burgess or Park are still the founding stones of urban ethnography and urban cultural studies. It was the Chicago school characterisation of migrant newcomers in Northern cities, assimilating via a step-by-step process of contact-conflict-accommodation-change, that provided scholars everywhere with the problematic of ethnic conflict leading to integration (or disintegration), and its ideal-type teleology. The connection with Parsonian forms of thinking about society and norms is made clear in Glazer (1976), to which Parsons contributes, alongside Gordon (1964). *See* my discussion in Chapter Four.

11. Glazer (1999) makes the case for regarding the USA as an exceptional case; Joppke (1999) meanwhile, does a good job of relating the USA to Europe, as part of a skilful asymmetrical comparison of the USA, Germany and Britain. The other key reference is Canadian: especially Kymlicka (1995, 1998), who I discuss in Chapter Two.

the Cold War period, Europe was taught to view itself on scales of comparative civic culture and democracy defined by the USA, that specified the ideal components of rights and democracy (Almond and Verba 1963). Yet, what was interesting in the 1980s and 1990s was that North Americans starting reversing this trend, and looked instead at Western Europe as a source of civic value and political and social virtues; often as a reaction to the perceived social breakdown of the USA, and the progress of a damaging social liberalism and individualism.[12] There was thus been a revival in looking at Europe comparatively, as if there was something to learn there.

What Europeanist Americans found, was the one thing the USA had been rolling back in recent years: resilient state-institutional structures, and 'thick' democratic cultures of civic participation and belonging. 'Rediscovering institutions' and 'Bringing the state back in', as the slogans go (Evans *et al.* 1985; Hollifield 2007). Behind this, among its leading proponents has been a constructive ambition: more than just understanding what it is that makes democracy work, but also what it is that makes multicultural citizenship work or not (Putnam 2007).[13] Again, the institutional focus signals that the crucial thing is the rooted, bounded and shared context of 'good' pluralist politics: the nation-state finding coherent democratic solutions to its integration dilemmas, with immigrants and minorities in Europe as the key focusing question. The evolving debate thus asked how nation-states have dealt with citizenship and integration questions for immigrants and ethnic minorities, seeking to distinguish between generically different national approaches and states of development across Europe, and then offering more prescriptive suggestions about the potential treatment of immigrants *vis-à-vis* what might be conceived as the full complement of citizenship rights in a revamped Marshallian scheme. Although there were European exceptions – which in the early 1980s took their cue from the growing realisation about how Western states had miscalculated that earlier immigrant workers would ultimately return home (Castles *et al.* 1984; Hammar 1985) – the true source of this comparative perspective was through the work of North American based scholars able to stand outside nationally-bounded European self-perceptions and interests. These innovations aside, the European scene at a national level often remained dominated by narrowly national perspectives, taking their cue from the predominant local political debates: these perspectives persist in spite of the growing outside and cross-national influences (*see also* my discussion in Chapter Ten).

---

12. I discuss the underlying origins of concerns expressed by, for example, Bellah *et al.* (1985), Schlesinger (1992), and Putnam (1993) in Favell (1998b), linking them to the re-emergent transatlantic citizenship research agenda. A slightly different aspect of the Europhilia among American Europeanists was the wave of interest in European Union studies after the Single European Act (1986). This was also an institutionalist movement in significant respects, and also drew strength from the obvious attraction of American academics for the EU as a kind of cosmopolitan, post-national project – a doubtful idealisation of the actual workings and dynamics of the EU.

13. Not all of the institutionalist turn in comparative studies was liberal in its conclusions. Putnam made great waves with his essentially conservative anti-immigration argument about how increased immigration across the Western world was leading to the destruction of social capital and trust, as measured in criminality rates, social problems and anti-immigrant politics. As a counter, *see* Banting and Kymlicka (2006).

The first and most obvious step was the formulation of cross-national European comparisons in terms of 'models': institutionalised state practices, rooted in nationally distinct historical 'cultures' or 'idioms' (Brubaker 1989, 1992; Hammar 1990; *see* my discussion and full references in Chapter Three). This in itself took its cue from the older civic culture type literature, which was concerned with identifying the national cultural bases of democratic political behaviour. The opening up of this perspective was crucial in forcing nationally located perspectives to encounter outside studies grounded in an autonomous academic discourse whose theorisation reflected wider disciplinary concerns from history, political science, geography and sociology. In other words, it gave the field both inter-disciplinary width and historical depth. For once, comparative method, coupled with some sensitivity towards the problems of interpretative comparatism, could be seen to ground cross-national understandings of national differences: quite a change from the perspectival influences of national policy contexts and self-comparisons. The result, arguably, was the creation of a genuine cross-national comparative 'research programme', with scientifically productive internal theoretical debates, and an evolving common framework of reference (Joppke 1998a).

Some of the initial value judgements of the 'models' approach were certainly superficial.[14] But the important thing was to inspire an evolving set of intellectual responses to an initially limited starting point. Thus the intellectual starting point of generic historical/cultural models has been challenged by more contemporary, institutionalist explanations of party politics and policy making;[15] local-level focused studies pointed out discrepancies between national rhetoric and local

---

14. For example, the now tediously well-trodden distinction between 'civic' France and 'ethnic' Germany (Weil 1996, critiquing Brubaker 1992). The citizenship models approach was however quickly adopted everywhere, above all in the edited collections that divide the subject by nation-by-nation case studies within a common comparative framework. For an archetypal collection, *see* Baldwin-Edwards and Schain (1994). Typical works that try to elaborate on the 'models' theme are Castles (1995), Bryant (1997), and the political cultural approach – needless to say – has always been very popular among French scholars, *see* e.g., Schnapper (1992), Todd (1994). Despite concerted criticism by myself and others (i.e. Scholten 2011) along the institutionalist lines outlined here and in Chapter Three, the stylised political cultural debates rolled on into the 2000s, i.e. Heckmann and Schnapper (2003); Alba (2005); Foner and Lucassen (2012). When the discussion gets comparative in this context, it often breaks down into fruitless ideological-philosophical stand-offs. In the context of trying to 'synthesise' an ideal model of European citizenship, large public funds have also been invested in comparative projects compiling information on national models of citizenship: for example, Preuß (1995). Carnegie's 'Comparative Citizenship Project' compiled a similar overview of citizenship practices in Western societies and elsewhere in its first stage. There was a lot of duplication of effort in many of these large-scale descriptive projects.

15. *See*, for example, Freeman, (1995), Favell (1997), Guiraudon (1997, 1998), Feldblum (1999), Fetzer (2000), Givens (2007). Joppke (1999) is another example. This last study, which sat at the end of a decade of such work, illustrated an emerging problem in this public policy-focused scholarship that has continued unabated among political scientists (i.e. Bleich 2008): that it can be done entirely through the discussion of secondary political debates and attendant scholarship, which talks about immigration, citizenship and integration issues with little or no genuinely sociological focus on the immigrant groups themselves, actual migration patterns, or theories of migration. By way of contrast, see the comparative policy framework set up from a bottom-up perspective (using migration patterns, post-industrial transformation and urban theory as the starting point) by migration scholars including Carmon (1996), Marcuse (1996) and Weiner (1996).

practice (Lapeyronnie 1992; Schain 1999); the institutionalist-slant led to more complex studies of mobilisation, participation and contestation of these state frameworks (Ireland 1994; Bousetta 1997, 2000; Kastoryano 1997; Vertovec 1999) and the idea of models was extended by classifying national differences in terms of typologies of incorporation regimes (Soysal 1994; Koopmans and Statham 1999). A cross-over was also made with other contemporaneous studies of welfare state regimes (Esping-Andersen 1990), with complex indices of rights and incorporation along a variety of scales (Janoski and Glennie 1995; Janoski 1998); and finally Europeans responded with the development of more thoroughly self-reflexive studies about how policy knowledge and constructions have been produced, tracing the accumulation of the institutional effects of these constructions which often overlap and flow into the construction of public perceptions of the subject.[16] In the 2000s, beginning with the Comparative Citizenship Project (CCP) (for which this chapter was a report), the focus then turned to the development of a concerted transatlantic agenda on immigrant incorporation, assimilation and/or integration.[17] Throughout, the interaction with the ever stronger political philosophical reflection on citizenship and multiculturalism also developed, often leading to a strong overt or covert normative flavour to otherwise comparative social scientific projects. Again, the North American – particularly Canadian – influence has been paramount (Taylor 1992; Kymlicka 1995). And, as might be expected, these transatlantic concerns very self-confidently translated themselves out of what has been a very successful emerging academic sub-field, into direct policy and public intellectual type work for many of the scholars involved.

---

16. *See* for example the work of Rath (1991), Alund and Schierup (1991), Martiniello (1992), Schierup (1993), Favell, (1998a), Blommaert and Verschueren (1998), Statham (1999), Castles (2000) on various countries, which was then continued into the prolific output connected with the International Migration, Integration and Social Cohesion (IMISCOE) project. On the pairing of the ostensibly similar, yet greatly variant Denmark and Sweden, *see* Hedetoft (2006). An historical example is Lucassen (2005), which makes the comparison both transatlantic and across centuries. Text book collections by Martiniello and Rath (2010, 2013, 2014) and overviews by Penninx *et al.* (i.e. 2006, 2008) offer the most comprehensive mapping of the field and its comparisons from a European point of view since the early 2000s. Another recent review is Koopmans (2013), who heads an important research team at Wissenschaftszentrum Berlin für Sozialforschung (WZB), Berlin. Koopmans' work again synthesises and develops a top down approach to comparatism in terms of policy and legal frameworks, which he then combines with a claims-making analysis of immigrant mobilisation in the media. Like Joppke and Putnam, he puts an emphasis on religion, and conflicts concerning Islam in Europe. The 'paradoxes of multiculturalism' most of these authors identify is linked to the fact that in each case the society incorrectly assumes it can seize itself from above as a collectivity and change itself through new hierarchical structures (policy, law, etc.) alone. This 'minorisation' where it occurs, as Rath calls it, also typically has significant perverse effects. For example, institutionalising policies also enables the policy sector to be seized by other policy actors for their own social power struggles: hence, the pervasive and distorting presence of go-between advocates and co-opted ethnic minority leaders in the 'representation' of minority or migrant interests (Favell 1998e, Kastoryano 1998a; Favell and Geddes 2000).

17. Before CCP there were already two large-scale efforts to formulate a global agenda: Massey and colleague's (1998) piecemeal attempt to overview world regions in terms of Massey's Mexico-US migration theory, and Hirschman *et al.*'s highly US-centric handbook (1999). The three publications for the CCP included two state-of-the-art collections and a final report with policy prescriptions (Aleinikoff and Klusmeyer 2000, 2001, 2002). Again, this was based on

Commissioned studies on integration policy

While it may ultimately be a matter for the history of ideas to chart the underlying intellectual reasons why a growing number of scholars began asking these constructive 'integration' and 'citizenship' questions in the 1980s and 1990s, the material and contextual reasons why such interests were generated in cross-national comparative research are fairly clear. Although clearly less central to party politics and government agendas than (for example) issues of macro-economic policy, the future of the welfare state, or regional development and devolution, ethnic minority and immigrant integration – and the multicultural questions surrounding it – have risen significantly on the political agenda everywhere during these past decades. In parallel to the evolving philosophical and sociological debates about citizenship, the question has come to be seen as an essential element of ongoing policy thinking about the future of liberal democracy and the distinctive possibilities of freedom and equality it may offer beyond mono-national conceptions of the nation. The treatment and accommodation of minorities and strangers is seen to be something that liberal democracy, of all systems of political organisation, does best; it is indeed widely assumed to be a defining trait of liberal democracy.[18]

---

a comparative 'best practices' model which I discuss in detail below in relation to the work of the Migration Policy Group in Europe. The American Social Science Research Council (SSRC) then, over the next few years, brought together many of the leading European scholars cited above, with leading American names such as Portes, Alba, Waters, Mollenkopf and others to develop the scientific transatlantic agenda. As a participant in some of these events, I can only comment that both the problems of transatlantic asymmetry discussed here, and the incommensurabilites in quantitatively identifying 'immigrant' populations in variable national contexts, were rarely brought into focus. American scholarship has instead imperialistically sought to impose its modes of analysis of immigration on fresh 'comparative' research material and unquestioned, yet problematic data sources (such as Labour Force surveys and European surveys). For many years, this had been impossible because of the lack of quality comparative data in Europe to match against US studies. A sample of these works would include: Portes and De Wind (2004, 2007); Alba (2005); Parsons and Smeeding (2006); Alba and Foner (2008; 2014); Hochschild and Mollenkopf (2009); Portes *et al.* (2010); Alba and Waters (2011); Crul and Mollenkopf (2012); Alba and Holdaway (2013); Hochschild *et al.* (2013). Many of these studies for operational reasons rely on the simple identification of 'immigrants' and 'second generations' solely by origin nationality: the classic notion of (disappearing) 'ethnicity' in the USA transposed to Europe, sidelining how problematic all of these concepts regarding minorities or migrants are in a European context, while entirely ignoring any examination of the invisible ethnicity of the assumed 'native' comparator population, and the unquestioned methodological nationalism of the assumed bounded national society. A sustained critique and alternative to these standard approaches is developed by Wimmer (2013). An example in French of a general programme strongly inspired by the American literature (in particularly Alba) is Safi (2011). *See also* Vermeulen (2010). Most influential on my own understanding has been the sustained critique of the competing dominant paradigms of Portes and Alba, developed over the years by Roger Waldinger. This has two key elements. One is that becoming an assimilated middle-class American is not just a process of losing origin ethnicity: it is a *re-nationalisation* into a new ethnicity, being American (Waldinger and FitzGerald 2004). The other is that immigrant trajectories cannot only be measured in relation to the receiving society; the sending society must always part of the picture. Alba and Nee's rational choice model (2003) suggests that immigrants who invest successfully in the norms of the receiving society, achieve returns which enable them to invest

National governments themselves thus began to generate a public research agenda around these questions: as well as direct policy and political debates, this led to media activity and the involvement of other actors in the policy process. And, of course, it sponsored the involvement and co-option of prominent academic scholars, willing to cross the line and take on the role of public intellectual in one of the various channels of policy thinking. In a parallel learning curve to that achieved by academics who broadened their intellectual resources by looking comparatively across nations, European states themselves developed an urge to cross-national self-comparison *within* Europe. In and of itself this did not necessarily produce fair-minded, non-perspectival thinking among public figures. At the early stages of developing public knowledge on the subject, this urge to comparison might often be seen as a kind of self-justificatory reflex, driven by an instinct for defending culturally distinct national ways of doing things, which seek to resist or adapt by pointing to negative contrasts in foreign countries as part of the study. Many examples of this kind of argumentation can be found in the leading countries with the most developed immigration and integration policy, often

---

more, and thereby become more 'invisibly' middle class and 'American'. Waldinger points out that many immigrants firstly are more concerned with measuring their success relative to their home society. Moreover, they often continue to invest their successful resources in investments back home – through remittances, or conspicuous consumption in their homeland, for example. These can certainly lead to the notorious downsides of bonding versus bridging capital (Portes and Landolt 1996). But it also pinpoints sources of social status and economic resources in the receiving society rooted in exterior transnational sources, as well as persistent, self-reproducing and influential 'foreign' ethnicity in American life – a good example being ethnic and homeland political lobbying in US politics (on these points, *see* Waldinger 2013; Waldinger and Soehl 2013; Waldinger 2015). Ignoring these concerns, the overall tendency of the transatlantic research field is to conclude that European nation-states – still troubled by what thereby seem purely atavistic issues of 'ethnic' nationhood or 'nationalist' sovereignty – are invariably to be seen as backward in relation to 'universalist' settler societies, including the multi-racial USA (whatever failings it has in other respects). Moreover, European societies always end up ranked in predictable ways, with great admiration for the Scandinavians and Dutch (at least before the recent turn in anti-immigrant politics), some puzzlement over the British or new Southern cases, criticism for chauvinist xenophobia masking as universalism in France, and, again, invariably Germany as the 'bad guy' in terms of racism and exclusion. The tendency at least certainly created many new opportunities for academic Atlantic crossings, something of which Deutsch (1957) would have certainly approved in terms of transactionalism and pan-regional integration.

18. It is by no means certain that this is true. The most genuinely 'multicultural' societies (in terms of cultural exchange and conflict not structured uniquely by a dominant nation-state) historically have been within non-democratic 'empires': *see* discussion in Brubaker (1995) and Grillo (1998). This, at least, becomes a possibility as a result of the power-based conceptualisation of multicultural relations of exchange that I work with, once it is detached from the nation-state-society integration framework. Another consequence is that this realisation also pushes most conventional liberal-democrats back to a straightforward defence of the (in fact) assimiliatory nation-state as the best grounds for delivering liberal philosophies of justice, equality or 'cultural pluralism': a sample of such 'honest' nationalist forms of liberalism (some of which are pro-multicultural, some anti-) are Kymlicka (1995); Goulbourne (1991); Miller (1995, 2000); Crowley (1998); Hansen (2009); Uberoi and Modood (2013).

with a goal to affirm the link between these policies and particularistic national ideas of citizenship or democracy along the way.[19]

However, the widening scope of policy thinking that encourages such cross-national initiatives, does also lead to new kinds of contact with foreign counterparts, that expands the national legal, political and bureaucratic policy community. As one can readily tell from the rapid international involvements of the Blair government (albeit confined to their early days in power), one of the big benefits of election to power is the opportunity to engage in all kinds of cross-national networking and synergy building, that would simply not be possible when in opposition. And, if it is possible to a little less cynical on this point for a moment, then it can be suggested that that the parties might overcome their national blinkers, and engage in some kind of cross-national *policy learning* while they are fraternising. The famous example in this field is, of course, the 'liberal hour' of 1960s race relations thinking in Britain and the Wilson administration courting of the American civil rights movement, in order to import ideas and moral justifications into Britain's proposed race relations legislation.[20] Of course, to engage in such an import of 'foreign' ideas can prove not only practical but a clear justificatory strategy, which diverts responsibility for the justification of ideas away from the smaller country's own national political traditions and discourses when internal justification is not possible. The weak position of exchange between European nations and the USA, has in fact enabled European governments to pursue potentially unpopular legislation under cover of the unequal superpower relations, in which they attempt a *self-assimilation* of national particularities to the outside, 'universal' moral and political model of North American *civilisation* (*see also* Favell 1998a: 121–4). The basically unequal transnational relations of power dictate that any 'common transatlantic' agenda, will ultimately remain a peculiar one, despite the growth in comparative knowledge of this kind. The asymmetric power relations distort any equal exchange of ideas, and Europeans are often likely to end up uncomfortably trying to implement American ideas and conceptualisations that do not necessarily fit the immigration and integration questions most salient in the European context (Favell 1999).[21]

An arguably more equitable venue for cross-national exchange of ideas across European policy thinking has emerged under the sponsorship of the EU.

---

19. Countless examples of negative comments about other countries' approaches and/or flattering self-comparisons could be found in official British, French, Dutch or Scandinavian policy statements and formulations. This is much less the case in countries which, for a variety of reasons, are more self-questioning or angst-ridden about their own national 'philosophies of integration': such as Germany, Belgium or Italy. Intellectuals in these countries are also often spectacularly critical and damning about their own country's policy shortcomings on immigration and integration. In Italy and Belgium, indeed, intellectual despair is almost the national sport.

20. *See* work by Hansen (2000), Bleich (1998, 2003). The theoretical paradigm for thinking about the role of ideas in policy making was developed by Peter Hall (1993) who has been involved as supervisor in a number of the more recent contributions to the comparative immigration politics field.

The bi-lateral relations between states within the EU is so heavily institutionalised as competition among equals, that it precludes states projecting themselves into the weaker 'learning' role, unless this giving up of 'sovereignty' (as the learning/policy justification process is constructed in public discussion) is seen to be part of wider pan-European co-operative effort. It is clear that the common history and similarity of European societies should dictate that they probably have a lot more to learn from each other than from a rather different society such as the USA. Where the central difficulty lies in relation to advancing cooperative research on immigrant integration, is that the EU officially has very little competence or jurisdiction over the kind of state policies that make up the domain of integration policy: not surprising given that nearly all are linked to nation-building operations in the traditional sense (Favell 2006). Despite starting to formulate European level ideas about integration from the Tampere agreement of 1999 onwards, in legislative and policy terms, it is still the case. Where opportunities for cross-national thinking did more easily arise then, it was in much less 'progressive' areas: in the strongly emerging security agenda on co-operative (restrictive) immigration policy in the EU, in terms of the security building 'compensatory measures' for dealing with the side-effects of building a free movement zone in

---

21. The Carnegie Endowment, the Ford Foundation, the Marshall Fund and others, all got involved in funding large cross-Atlantic research projects on immigration/citizenship/ethnic relations during these years, and there has never been such a high level of transatlantic policy consultation on the subject. The collection Cornelius *et al.* (1994) was a typical example of the products of these initiatives. A good example of the asymmetry involved is the Metropolis project (http://canada.metropolis.net), funded copiously by the Canadian government on one side, but with scant resources on the European side. What is troubling are the slightly warped reasons why academics get involved in these kinds of activities, which are financially rewarding, but do not entail real influence on the policy process, and can only be a diversion from pure academic research. On the other side, it is very unclear how and where their involvement can get translated, say, into Canadian city urban policy, even allowing for the fact that something might be learned from, say, looking comparatively at Dutch social policies or British race relations jurisprudence. As with the EU Commission, the Canadian civil servants tried over time to control the output of Metropolis more strictly: but when this happens it just decreases the side benefits for other research that academics themselves may get from involvement in such 'policy-relevant' projects. Another excellent example of a reverse, but equally distorted, transatlantic learning process is the fascination many left-wing American social scientists have for Swedish and Dutch social and welfare policies, such as legislated child care or the regulation of sex-work. This might be called the 'Amsterdam' phenomenon: being attracted by something very 'liberal' – that is unrepresentative and out of context in terms of the way these highly controlled, conservative societies actually function as social systems – and using it as a 'social policy other' in order to derive normative conclusions for one's own society. This phenomenon also often works in reverse: Europeans using America as a negative dystopian 'other'. A good example was the follow-up research to the Modood report (1997, discussed below), at the time the best recent research project on immigrant social mobility in Britain. Instead of pursuing the much needed but difficult path of cross-national European comparison, the authors instead opted to make a comparison of the findings with the USA (eventually published as Loury, Modood and Teles 2005). It is very hard to see how this could avoid the usual asymmetric distortions that render this kind of comparison hugely problematic. And, as might be expected, the first media reports of this ambitious new project (*The Guardian*, Aug 4th 1999) immediately saw the British claiming how successful some ethnic minorities in Britain are when compared to the black American population, despite the blatant inappropriateness of the analogy.

Europe (Guiraudon and Joppke 2001; Lavenex and Uçarer 2002; Boswell and Geddes 2011). There is, therefore, a great deal of co-operative policy thinking going on between home affairs officials and expert consultants on issues such as clandestine immigration, the trafficking of persons (the analogy being with drugs), the treatment of asylum seekers, and the uncovering of underground transnational criminal networks. Yet despite its official lack of competence on immigrant and minority integration questions, parts of the European institutions have seen the area as one where it can seek to expand its influence, thereby seeking further 'integration' of its own (in the EU-building sense of the word). It thus has followed the classic tactic of seeking to co-opt academics into its policy circles as a way Directorate General's (i.e. DGs or the main administrative units of the European Commission) may attempt to accrue new supra-national powers in areas where immigrant integration issues can be said to fall: the typical ones being social policy, regional policy, culture and communications and education and training. This in turn has generated very many lines of new research from which academics have been able to profit. The Targeted Social Economic Research (TSER) programme and the European Year Against Racism (1997) were two early examples of large policy programmes that had important benefits to academics working on issues in this area; the European Year of Workers' Mobility (2006) was a later example.[22] This new range of publicly funded integration research found itself able to seek EU funding that builds a rather different cross-national policy learning process and policy community in this area than national groupings. The ultimate aim of the EU in getting involved in this kind of promotional role is, of course, self-legitimisation: which is why so much of the thinking in this area has been linked with bolstering the idea of democracy and 'European citizenship'. The enormous growth in research networks and research institutes dependent on EU funding has been remarkable: a dependency that has only grown as national public funding for research has become more problematic.

The nature of this kind of work is clearly co-optive and self-reproducing. However self-critical one is of one's relationship with the EU, working

---

22. The TSER project ended up funding an impressive array of projects (either as full cross-national projects or funded international networks) that emerged from an intense bidding war among rival European academic networks. These included subjects such as police cooperation and immigration control (headed by Didier Bigo), immigrants and the informal economy (Robert Kloosterman/Jan Rath), migrants in cities (Malcolm Cross), models of European citizenship (Richard Bellamy), and comparative integration policies (Friedrich Heckmann). This latter, a large project located at the University of Bamberg (http://www.uni-bamberg.de/efms), published as Heckmann and Schnapper (2003), was particularly symptomatic of some of the limitations of this predominantly descriptive and documentary, network-based research. Its findings were archetypal of the mainstream 'comparative models' approach, something largely determined by the fact each network has to have a well-known national representative (in this case, Dominique Schnapper for France, Han Entzinger for The Netherlands, Roger Penn for the UK) who are each likely to have very conventional national viewpoints (because the best known figures are policy academics), and the fact selection of projects also is made by similarly established nation-by-nation figures. In the following EU Frameworks for research, there continued to be numerous calls for work on immigration, citizenship, integration and mobility, but terms of strict policy-relevance have been increasingly dictated by the Commission to researchers.

within their (EU) integration agenda will inevitably draw scholars into a pro-European integration stance that seeks to diminish exclusive national level control over these questions – although the logic of every network being made up of 'national' representatives mitigates this tendency somewhat. The benefits of this new kind of cross-national thinking in not automatically reproducing national policy perspectives should be clear. An additional dimension linked to this has been the involvement of professional non-governmental organisations (NGOs) in this kind of quasi-academic commissioned work.[23] Its necessarily schematic packaging and content means that this kind of work does not contribute much to critical knowledge about integration policies, but it can be an excellent source of descriptive facts and policy practice across national cases. What has been invariably argued in this kind of work is, again, that there are indeed clearly distinct national 'models' of justifying and implementing integration strategies, and that these frameworks may render the idea of policy transferability to other national cases problematic. One thing this kind of research has sometimes sustained, however, is the perception that European nation states are converging on similar kinds of policies and problems.[24]

---

23. The prolific output of the Migration Policy Group (http://www.migpolgroup.com), a tiny but very influential NGO in Brussels is a case in point. In the 1990s, two major examples of the projects they have mounted on citizenship and integration questions, were MPG (1996); and the Vermeulen report (1997), in collaboration with the Institute for Migration and Ethnic Studies, Amsterdam. The first was a massive synthesis of roundtable discussions conducted with policy makers in five Western European countries, and a further handful of East European countries; the second, a five nation survey of the different integration strategies and policies being used for integration policies, language, schooling and cultural organisation (in France, Britain, Belgium, Germany and The Netherlands). In the 2000s, the MPG became even more central, under the politically savvy leadership of Jan Niessen, leading to the enormous MIPEX (Migrant Integration Policy Index) database (http://www.mipex.eu), which tracks and compares relative migrant integration policies and laws across thirty one countries, including Eastern Europe, North America, Japan and South Korea. This is a starting point both for further campaigning and comparative research on the successes and failures of integration in different countries, as well as their progressive or conservative tendencies, ranking countries overall. It should be noted however that this index like so many others only reports top down legal and policy frameworks, and does not work with an independent sociological model of social processes. A recent systematic attempt to contrast the methodological merits of different indices of comparative immigration policies (mostly immigration law), covering thirteen different studies, is Bjerre *et al.* (2014).

24. The MPG reporting offers evidence of and normative arguments for convergence (as does the Heckmann project discussed above); what is less clear is whether this convergence comes about through policy learning, or isomorphism, or simple a 'garbage can' choice of policy (developed further by Guiraudon 2003). Randall Hansen and Patrick Weil (2000) put together a massive comparison of apparent convergence in naturalisation/citizenship practices across Western states, under the benevolent funding of the German Marshall Fund – but what explains this convergence? We should be suspicious of arguments which suggest it is pulled by some rational 'good'; as well of the functionalist consequences of allowing comparative research to be pulled by the teleological idea of harmonisation, the logic that has always been a driving rationale for the reproduction of European integration processes. *See also* Lapeyronnie's (1993) arguments about *de facto* policy convergence in Britain and France. A more recent comprehensive study on citizenship rights (Koopmans *et al.* 2012) finds little convergence, and evidence for the continued relevance of national policy models across national contexts; meanwhile inclusive citizenship rights have been in retreat since 2002 due to anti-immigrant politics.

This observation can then in turn be used to sustain claims for improving rights for minorities and non-nationals across Europe by campaigners at the European level.[25]

A slightly different inspiration and sponsor of cross-national research has been the Council of Europe in Strasbourg, which has wider interests in promoting pan-European relations and security.[26] Much of this work has over the years explicitly sought to link integration policy research on the position of migrants and minorities across West and East, with an interest in guaranteeing human rights and minority rights standards in the new democratising societies of the East under the auspices of Organisation for Security and Cooperation in Europe (OSCE) conventions. This kind of thinking represents a slightly different kind of internationalisation that posits conformity of nations to international law as the driving outside force of policy progression, rather than the discovery of common, convergent Western European standards (which is the case with EU funded research). There was, however, a growing interest in EU circles in the kinds of connections the Council of Europe draws between integration and minority rights, in connection with EU enlargement accession: East European candidates were being forced to accept minority rights and citizenship guarantees as part of the Agenda 2000 package on the Schengen *acquis* and so forth. The East became the new policy terrain for making multicultural citizenship work: the coercive way the European international community went about imposing its norms, offered a clear suggestion that more is at stake than the rights of minorities in the countries concerned. After all, Britain and France went out of their way to explicitly refuse any association of these East European minority issues with their own internal minority conflicts, despite their own little problems in Northern Ireland and Corsica (Burgess 1999; Chandler 1999).

One interesting consequence of the new European co-operative efforts has been the intellectual struggle over the progressive agenda at the European

---

25. Perhaps the best example of this was the Migration Policy Group's apparently success in using the example of existing British anti race discrimination legislation as a benchmark for new European standards which it campaigned for under the heading of The Starting Line group discussed below.

26. The best of its kind is the Bauböck report (1994a) for the Council of Europe, which is able to offer a much more panoramic and detached view than work sponsored by EU institutions. This is an entirely conceptual work, which succeeds in opening up migration and integration questions in Europe to the broadest possible schema. In fact, the Council of Europe sponsored a whole series of recent reports on dimensions of integration, within the framework of the European Committee on Migration: reports covered women and migration (1995), religion (1999), labour markets (1998) and social and political participation (1999). *See also* the meticulous documentary work of Banton for the Council and the UN on minority rights and discrimination issues – which is highly sceptical of the EU – and his briefings in *New Community/Journal of Ethnic and Minority Studies*. Another international organisation which sponsors research on immigrant integration is the International Labour Organisation in Geneva: *see* Doomernik (1998), a report which looks at economic data on labour market integration in France, The Netherlands and Germany.

level: whether it should follow more the British anti-discrimination focus or the French approach to citizenship and equality. The British initially were very suspicious of the EU's efforts to engage with anti-discrimination issues at the supra-national level, arguing that the EU was likely to dilute British standards, which were in any case the best in Europe (an argument reminiscent of Scandinavian arguments about welfare provisions).[27] For many years this lead to an almost contemptuous attitude on the parts of campaigners and race relations intellectuals in Britain towards the EU's own initiatives in this area, but this attitude began to shift during the 1996/7 IGC (Inter-Governmental Conference to revised European treaties), when certain strongly academic cross-national networks such as the Starting Line Group and the Dutch Experts Committee on Immigration began making lobbying headway on the anti-discrimination possibilities in the Amsterdam Treaty (1997) (the new Article 13, which introduced an anti-racist clause into anti-discrimination provisions) (Guiraudon 2009). It was noteworthy that it was their specifically legal knowledge that was the crucial factor they brought to bear in the policy discussions. With its sublime confidence in Britain's track record (as I discuss in Chapter Three), Blair's coming to power just before the signing of the Amsterdam Treaty then, in fact, gave the green light to more concerted efforts in this direction, made more likely by the fact that little progress was being made on the issue of citizenship rights for third country nationals (non-national, non-European residents in Europe). The Labour party giving the green light to the setting up of the Vienna-based Monitoring Centre on Racism and Xenophobia, was also the signal for encouraging British activists to seek leadership in this field, pushing Anglo-Dutch ideas on anti-discrimination against the French/continental conception. The Austrian connection has indeed become a key element in the development of large-scale surveys comparing the relative standards of integration policies and minority rights provisions. With the Austrian government itself keen to be seen getting involved in progressive efforts in this area (especially during its period of EU presidency), Vienna thus became one of the main centres for the production of research in this field: not least because the city has become the natural geographical base for NGOs and

---

27. The background to this was a series of large-scale reports on anti-discrimination provisions, and the attempt to rate existing provisions in different countries. The early comparative report by Forbes and Mead (1992), explicitly set up Britain as the model in Europe, against which other European countries measure on a declining scale. As the years went on, this message was conveyed more openly by the Commission for Racial Equality and the Runnymede Trust in Britain, who were conducting an audit of twenty five years of race relations in Britain, with one eye on 'selling' this experience in a positive way to the rest of Europe. A more nuanced report, drawing on ethnographic work on employment practices and discrimination in the workplace in sixteen countries is to be found in Wrench (1996). The external influence of ideas of anti-racism, however, had a positive effect on France, which, at the end of the 1990s, while the official government *Haut Conseil à l'Intégration* was headed by Patrick Weil, began to look seriously at the deficiencies of its own legal mechanisms on racism (Simon 2005).

international organisations (IOs) working with Central and Eastern European countries, just as businesses have chosen to move east to Berlin.[28]

The creation of the Monitoring Centre pointed towards the hooking up of knowledge production on discrimination, racism and minority rights with the existing machine for producing 'Euro-knowledge' such as the Eurobarometer surveys.[29] Reminiscent of the huge scale post-war American civic culture/democracy indices that were concerned with managing transitions to democracy, such work attempts to evaluate the relative level of development as regards integration policy and legislation according to a common European scale, that brusquely rides over the kind of arguments based on national distinctiveness/traditions so prevalent among national policy makers when they compare themselves to others in Europe. While clearly extending the range and repertoire of knowledge about what each country is doing and how each is officially dealing with the problems involved, the kinds of results produced by these surveys – that country x is less racist or more tolerant than country y because country x has better official legal provisions against discrimination and more rights than country y – can be highly dubious as indicators of integration as such. Predictably, highly state-centred countries, with a high level of co-opted academic policy production – such as The Netherlands or Sweden – often rate much higher than disorganised and intellectually divided countries such as Belgium or Italy. But these kinds of figures say nothing about the porousness of a particular national culture, or its propensity to change in relation to minority cultures. In fact, a culture such as Dutch – which is highly coherent, nationally oriented, and difficult to learn – may in fact be very resistant to integration, and is in some ways a much harder country for foreigners to live freely (or uncontrolled) in than, say, a less well-rated country such as Belgium.

The second problem with these kinds of studies and the knowledge they produce is equating integration and inter-ethnic relations with official state structures such as rights, policies, legislation and so on. Such indicators only really measure the extent to which the state succeeds in defining, controlling and managing the phenomenon: it says little about whether this control is benevolent, or in fact highly dominating in its effects. Intellectuals here, again, are involved in legitimising a view of society to

---

28. Among the output has been perhaps the most ambitious comparative integration policy project of all prior to MIPEX: the Çinar *et al.* (1995), project on 'legal obstacles to integration', which put together an index of legal and policy integration provisions and barriers in seven countries and the EU (*see* Waldrauch and Hofinger 1997; Waldrauch 2001). This concentration of legalistic knowledge offered a checklist of types of rights rated on a 0–1 scale, rating each country in term on separate issues of naturalisation laws, family reunification, civil, political and social rights etc,, giving each an overall final score between zero and one. In a similar line, with the strong involvement of Baubök and Jo Shaw, as part of the European Union Observatory on Democracy (EUDO) at the European University Institute (EUI), Florence, the Access to Citizenship and its Impact on Immigrant Integration (ACIT) developed similar indices of good and bad practice in law and policy (http://eudo-citizenship.eu/about/acit). The search for overarching schemes of comparing good practices on a common scale, often only confirms 'national' stereotypes, and ends up slanted towards more transparently 'organised', rights-based, state-dominated societies, because it mostly reflects what is 'on paper' rather than what is happening in the streets (Austria does very badly; Britain does less well than usual; the Dutch, French do better than the Germans and the Swiss; everyone loves the Scandinavians[...]). Methodologically, the weaknesses of this type of survey are linked to the weaknesses of Eurobarometer type surveys discussed below.

which they should in fact be offering a critique. Knowledge that is reproducing the kinds of categories and institutional schema that the state seeks to impose on ethnic relations in society, is itself part of the institutional process of enforcing hierarchical state power and jurisdiction on the subject. Intellectual work thus becomes part of the process whereby institutions enforce a coercive and constraining cognitive framing of societal phenomena, that might not necessarily be things that can or should come into the state's domain. It turns complex societal relations and interactions into a categorised object of 'policy', creating bureaucratic norms that can be imposed on social actors on the way to becoming law. The Dutch way of managing policy problems by funding nearly all academic production in this area – and hence turning academic research into a branch of state-sponsored knowledge creation on the subject – is one extreme on a scale which could also envisage totally disconnection between state policy thinking and the work of autonomous intellectuals. Dutch society puts such a central premium on the idea of rationally-produced, informed and structured *beleid* (policy), that nearly all leading social scientists have over the years been co-opted into the system of producing policy-relevant research for social engineering purposes, by a host of different ministries and independent research agencies

---

29. The existing Eurobarometer surveys contain questions on attitudes to immigration and race, and questions related to citizenship and identity. Indeed, one of the surveys (Eurobarometer 47.1, 1997) was devoted to these questions, sparking a whole new round of debate about the data and its dubious methods of collection (particularly in Belgium which apparently had very high levels of self-confessed 'racism'), but also launching a thousand research projects based on explaining it. For example, around a dozen quantitative PhD research projects were coordinated on this and related projects by social psychologist Peer Scheepers at Nijmegen. We have to be very aware of some of the limitations, indeed sometimes the absurd conclusions drawn by constructing this kind of comparative knowledge from this 'ready-made' kind of data. More often than not this data reflects what people think about themselves, not what they are. The parody of this, is the Dutch declaring themselves almost totally non-racist, while the Belgians declare themselves to be 40 per cent racist, and then setting out, as some researchers have done, to explain why Belgians are 'more' racist than the Dutch. Needless to say, we should be highly suspicious of these figures, which reflect the dramatically different self-perceptions of these two societies, and in particular the vitriolic rhetoric of the often 'racist' Flemish versus Walloon arguments. The Swedish government, it is said, once commissioned a survey of this kind about the Swedish, in order to prove that Swedish society was not racist (which was 'proven' when the survey population duly declared themselves to be overwhelmingly not racist). It is my feeling that the self-searching paroxyms of anguish and anger over these results in Belgium is far preferable to the kind of complacency it inspires in Sweden or The Netherlands. In France – where, because of the fundamental epistemological scepticism that underpins all French social science, there is often a greater sensitivity to deeper issues about the social construction of data – there has been better critical reflection on the Eurobarometer project: *see*, for example, Brèchon and Cautrès (1999). Given the over-reliance in mainstream research on Eurobarometer data from Inglehart (1990) onwards, there is clearly a need for someone to put a critical spanner in the works of this co-optive European machine of knowledge production, and the masses of social science work it structures. The Ethnobarometer project (1999), for example, offered the promise of a much larger scale comparison of ethnic conflicts and relations across Europe, based on a regional reports around a common framework that link up with NGO activities and interventions. The targeting of conflict was significant, given that it takes the issue away from comparing policies or governmental discourse. Ethnic and majority-minority conflict, of course, remains an enormous issue in many parts of Europe. One of the reasons why this work goes further is because it has been based on extensive epistemological reflection and consultation with NGOs and others in the field. See the extremely interesting reflections on this by Codagnone (1998).

(*see also* Scholten *et al.* 2014).[30] The result of this academic influence – the wonderfully well-organised schema of rights and provisions for minorities in the country – is both a measure of how seriously the state and government take policy on integration questions; but also, inversely, a measure of the scale of pathological effects that such top-down hierarchical structures can have on the social situation itself, if the significant presence of informal activities among immigrants in The Netherlands is any indication (Engbersen 1996; Burgers 1998; Kloosterman *et al.* 1998; Rath and Kloosterman 1998).

The deeper point here is that any discussion of integration which tries to measure it by evaluating the degree of state-institutionalised organisation in the country assumes a degree of coercive, state-powered pressure on immigrants to conform to this framework. Given the overwhelmingly one way direction of social integration pressures that living in Western social system imposes on anybody, positive, fully institutionalised indicators of integration in law or policy are thus also indicators of the state-organised assimilation pressures put on migrant and minority groups to conform to Western norms – the very opposite of where multiculturalism is supposed to lead.

Survey and census-based work on integration

Thus far, my overview of integration research has concentrated on works which approach the question from the point of view of top-down 'policy': that is, of already institutionalised legal and political structures in various national contexts in Europe. In a sense, to seek to compare integration strategies along this axis automatically reproduces as given many of the nation-state structuring influences that research should in fact be trying to control for, as possible structural factors among others. Moreover, the role of academics in structuring their knowledge-interventions in this way also, I argue, works to produce the tacit presence of the nation-state as the only meaningful context in which the integration of immigrants and minorities can be talked about in practical terms. Clearly, this kind of approach will be the one preferred by policy makers: practitioners who explicitly seek to reproduce and enhance the nation-state in their conceptual construction of the social problem. However, the close identification of scholars with the policy makers' role is not only a curious mis-identification of the role of the academic in producing independent knowledge on the subject; it also indicates the degree to which the material conditions of production of knowledge and the pressures of the immediate political context, are influencing and

---

30. On questions of immigration and integration, a handful of leading academics – with distinct power-bases in different universities – have over the years vied for central influence on policy making in The Netherlands as thinking has veered from pillorised multiculturalism to nationalist integration: among the leading figures are Han Entzinger (Utrecht), Rinus Penninx (Amsterdam), Justus Veenman (Rotterdam). These are academics able to step smoothly in and out of academic and public political roles (Entzinger indeed has held governmental roles), and are the first to whom the intelligent press turn when there is a new political development on which to comment. For an overview of developments in The Netherlands *see* Uitermark (2012), and for a deconstruction of Dutch integration research, Schinkel (2008).

distorting the basic research programme of this field. Yet the excessive institutional focus of policy and politics-based studies can, on the face of it, be quite easily side-stepped. What of the whole other range of integration research: independent survey based studies of integration perceived from the bottom up, as it were, charting the interaction of ethnic groups with the dominant population, their social mobility in their new host societies, and the changing perceptions of immigrants themselves in relation to majority population opinions on the subject?

Turning to the state-of-the-art in behavioural attitude surveys, social mobility and social psychological approaches to immigrant integration, we do indeed find that a range of far more ambitious integration surveys began to emerge out of the empirical expansion of this field in the 1990s, due in large part to the investment of public funding to address a subject seen to be of rising political and social concern, and thus due in effect to the recent technical possibility of doing this kind of work. The great advantage of survey-based work is the fact that it explicitly seeks to reduce questions about policy frameworks, laws and legislation, and so on, to background variables. Being highly 'positivist' in style, these studies also generally refrain in their methodologies from taking overtly ideological positions in advance about what states should be doing from a top-down perspective to achieve their policy goals, relying simply on the idea that facts, particular numbers and percentages, should speak for themselves. Drawing explicit conclusions is usually left to an explicitly secondary stage of interpretation, public framing and publicity, which may lead to normative conclusions or engage in post-publication interventions in the media and public debates. Because it aims for autonomy, it is correct therefore to take the self-styled 'scientific' credentials of survey-based work seriously: it is why such work may offer more insights about actual integration processes than explicitly policy and politics-focused work, which often in the final analysis has very little to say about immigrants themselves, if rather a lot about how elites view, debate and understand the question. However, as I will argue, this is not to say that the methodological choices and conceptual assumptions that survey-based studies make, reflect any less the material and contextual influences that shape other types of work on the subject.

One significant limitation with survey-based work was that before the attempts I describe in this report, there were virtually no existing examples of genuine cross-national comparative survey work in the field, and certainly no elaborated source of comparable data.[31] Most of the projects I describe below are indeed single national

---

31. One symptom of this was that it was still, in the late 1990s, a completely new frontier for the 'RC28 guys': the comparative social stratificationists and demographers who position themselves as the high church of empirical sociology. As was clear from their exploratory discussions at the Sept 1999 on the subject conference organised by Hartmut Esser (fn.1 Chapter Five), very few of the epistemological problems to doing work on migration and social mobility had yet been considered by researchers more familiar with doing cross-national studies on employment, educational mobility or inequality (i.e. Erikson and Goldthorpe 1992), even if their analyses were beginning to suggest that much of the mobility that could be found in Europe might be linked to immigration (Breen 2004). Just how little social scientists agree on in terms of basic social research categories across Europe has been revealed in recent years by the spectacular controversies and powerplays in which figures like Goldthorpe and others have engaged over which socio-professional categories the European research community would adopt as its basic standard (*see* Rowell and Pénissat 2012).

case studies studying diversity within one country (or in some cases, one city). Any comparative work would have to start here: with the diversity of national approaches and questions about their commensurability. In terms of international organisations providing standardised models, there is nothing on immigrant integration comparable to the database on migrant flows and stocks in various countries put together in the annual Continuous Reporting System on Migration (SOPEMI) reports produced by the Organisation for Economic Cooperation and Development (OECD), a report which gathers data individually from individual national experts in each of the OECD countries.[32] The OECD report does have a section on 'integration', but this is by far its weakest part, simply reproducing some of the usual debates about top-down national models or comparative rights-frameworks, on which there is now an overload of approaches, as we have seen.

A deeper and persistent problem is that all data on immigrant (or minority) numbers still follows the very different conventions in each country about collecting population data. On this basis, 'integration' – if it is so named – can only be quantified in the normatively specific and nationally-rooted terms that are set up by the individual national research technologies themselves. This is a basic constraint which limits the construction of survey-based knowledge in the field: as we will see, the difficulties of collecting meaningful cross-national data continues to be at the root of the many problems with which scholars have engaged.[33] As soon as anyone looks at the question from this level, it becomes apparent just how much even the basic elements of comparison – how we categorise the populations themselves – are incommensurable in terms of the ways different nation-states gather data on migrants and minorities.

Counting only non-nationals as the immigrant population is still the base-line norm across nearly all European countries except Britain, which has a famously idiosyncratic form of ethnic self-identification in its census, which I discuss below. Most basic comparative sources offer crude figures for non-nationals by nationality (the easiest part of the 'immigrant' population to count), which works up to a point in countries where original nationality remains a distinguishing factor: as, say, in Germany, Italy or Spain – although it runs into problems in Germany, for example, in counting the 3 million *aussiedler* (German-origin immigrants) from Eastern Europe. This method is clearly a criteria of declining usefulness, however, as increasing numbers of second and third generation immigrant children in fact accede to full national citizenship; it can indeed be simply a crude measure of administrative exclusion. Naturalisation rates over time are a second set of figures, which trace the absorption of immigrants over shorter, given periods of time. Other countries may also offer figures which count those people who identify older family members born outside of the country. From this, a great deal can be extrapolated

---

32. For access to the latest report published in 2013, *see*: http://www.oecd.org/migration/international-migration-outlook-1999124x.htm

33. On these issues, I owe great thanks to social psychologist Karen Phalet and quantitative political sociologist Marc Swyngedouw (Phalet and Swyngedouw 1999a, 2001, 2003), and to demographer Patrick Simon (1997, 2005, 2012). I further explore many of these issues about the construction of data and categories in France and Britain in Favell (1998a).

into the second and third generation, but a country such as France still maintains barriers sometimes for ideological reasons to researchers using this information, which means that some naturalised second or third generation citizens of migrant origin are lost to studies once they leave the immigrant household.

A strong moral prohibition, meanwhile, exists on the classification of people by race or religion across much of Europe. There is little more distasteful to continental Europeans than anything with a whiff of former Nazi racial classifications, or indeed the common practice in former multinational empires such as the Soviet Union or Yugoslavia to brand people permanently on their interior passports with an 'ethnic' nationality (*see* Brubaker 1995). However, a more racially heterogeneous population such as the Portuguese avoids these racial classifications for rather different reasons, to do with the cosmopolitan colonial conception of the nation. In Belgium, you are classified by language according to political records after you vote, religion after you choose university. Here, however, the census is banned by law to answer such questions up front. In The Netherlands, meanwhile, there is no national census at all, after a libertarian public revolt in the 1970s. Ethnic statistics here have to be reconstructed from local city and police records or special ministry surveys, something that has contributed significantly to the sense of unease about the numbers of 'undocumented' residents in the country. Other countries, however, such as Denmark and Britain – which in other respects have very different census methods – are prepared under certain circumstances to make available census data to track specified (anonymous) individuals over time between censuses, in order, for example, to analyses spatial mobility or rates of political participation. Such a babel of survey information is, to say the least, a difficult starting point.

The most popular dividing line – the narrow definition of immigrants as resident non-nationals – has the virtue of avoiding the integration issue entirely in some respects. It offers the normative panacea of equating citizenship with full integration, an idea which has long reassured republicans in France, for example, on the virtues of a cosmopolitan type of nationhood. A normative dogma such as this makes no sociological sense, of course, once anyone is willing to admit that host populations and migrants alike will continue to informally discriminate themselves and each other regardless of which passport they are holding. Once some outsiders become insiders, however, their formal categorisation (or 'recognition', in more affirmative terms) itself becomes a part of the integration process. Whether or not they are separated off for official monitoring purposes, and how and where they can be placed on some path towards full integration, become a crucial part of the integrative process itself, not least because the separation from one's original nationality may also be a coercive state-enforced act (*see* Simon 1997). There is a profound moral truth in the French refusal to actually recognise any French citizen of non-national 'ethnic' origin as such in official statistics, because the recognition itself can indeed be a form of inequality or discrimination. The power of naming does indeed count for something. The French refusal is also a dramatic statement of the nation-state's continued prerogative to nationalise a new citizen as indivisibly French. Yet, on the other hand, no policy can be devised for systematic integration of foreign-origin groups until the nation-state begins to collectively recognise and classify minorities of ethnic origin, with special claims – targeted policies, resources, legal allowances, etc. – that follow from this (the central problematic as we have seen in Chapter Two of Kymlicka 1995). I discuss some specific examples of the research dilemma in France in more detail below.

So some countries use censuses, some do not; some use Labour Force surveys and some construct their own data. Censuses and Labour Force surveys in turn use very different classification schemes, ranging from ethnic self-identification through parental country of origin and rates of naturalisation to only registering those classified as non-nationals in the country. Who, then, or what are we talking about? 'Races'; 'ethnic minorities'; 'immigrants'; 'aliens'; 'foreigners'; 'non-nationals'; 'third country nationals' or (as has become very common, albeit for the most crass political reasons), 'Muslims' (i.e. religious denomination; *see* Brubaker 2013)? Do these groups self-select their identity or are these identities objectively imposed by some family link, or by phenotypical category? What of mixed, ambiguous identities, or dual-nationalities and citizenships? Do we prioritise groups as ethnicity or races, or look for more sophisticated models of group identity (conscious or not) that recognise internal diversity and stratification? Even an independently constructed survey – if it has to work with official data of any kind – will find itself limited to a given external 'sampling frame', which is likely to be defined by the way the nation-state counts, classifies, delimits and controls 'its' population versus 'foreigners' on a given territory. Nothing whatsoever is agreed on by researchers or state agencies pursuing these questions in the vast numbers of studies on the question across Europe; and these basic difficulties only multiply as the questions move to asking the opinions, feelings or affiliations of particular populations, or how their behaviour, actions and choices relate to the so-called 'norms' of the majority population.

As this last point suggests, there is yet another side to the classificatory separation of populations. Integration cannot be conceived, identified, let alone measured as degrees of inequality and so on, until a *control group* representative of the national population has been specified. But this raises the question: we are talking about integration into *what*? Here, the logic of classification becomes even more slippery. Are they the indigenous population (*de souche* in French), but if so, what length of time constitutes 'roots'?; are they defined culturally, by their family origins, by their length of residence ('heritage' has become the politically correct term)?; are they, rather, simply to be identified as the majority 'white' or 'European' population?; or, are we in fact speaking of some representative sample or statistical mean of the citizenry as a whole, including all those new and culturally exotic recent additions? Moreover, as Banton points out (2001), it makes little sense to measure the integration of an immigrant or ethnic minority population, until we have some precise comparative measurement of how well the majority population are integrated as a nation. Leaving aside their immigrant populations, is Britain a more 'integrated' society than Germany? Does diversity of values and culture count most in this – or homogeneity? It is a rarely asked question. Whatever method is chosen – however the state chooses to classify, count and control its population or define those who are in and those who are out – it will again amount to a pre-determined national 'sampling frame', that is very closely linked to the ideological concept of nationhood which is present. Behind this, of course, lies the normative commitment to integration as societal end-goal, the underlying assumption that holds the nation-state-society unit together. Researchers who thus set out to objectively measure integration, without taking into account how much the nation-state unit has already determined the very quantitative tools they use, will fail to see how much the bounds of what they can discover have already been pre-set for them. If so, they are working no less to underwrite the predominance of the nation-state optic, than policy studies researchers who accept without challenge nation-state centred definitions of 'universal' citizenship or 'cosmopolitan' multiculturalism.

It should be stressed too that survey works of these various kinds, even with autonomous methodologies, are also invariably self-consciously aware interventions into an ongoing temporal domestic policy debate, which seek to affirm or transform certain assumptions about the correct currency and direction of the debate. Because they are high-brow, scientific works, they often carry enormous prestige and weight; in this sense, they can be much more significant than the academic fields of comparative politics and public policy which are often precariously journalistic or anecdotal in their approaches. Crucially, also, the work shadows the actual mechanical and material apparatus for conducting this kind of work, something which in some places has recently become possible through the adaptation of national census production, for example, to allow for sensitivity to ethnic minority monitoring and analysis.[34] Again, it cannot be stressed enough how important these material conditions of production are in determining the shape of the final work, which also critically reflect the current social coalition between different policy-interested actors who might be interested in the 'objective' and 'scientific' findings of a large-scale survey project. Although survey work is invariably inspired or forced as a 'progressive' reaction to some current perceived social crisis or danger, it is highly significant that they are almost always conducted under hot and pressing conditions: high profile studies on Islam and fundamentalism indicate what a dangerous fertile ground this is for sensationalist work.[35] Quality newspapers, in particular, love this kind of work when it produces shocking

---

34. I discuss more precisely details of French, British, Dutch and Belgian data collection below. As well as identifying and counting migrants or ethnic minorities, some census collections incorporate specific samples of sub-populations for other questions. The longitudinal sampling in Britain and Denmark is a good example, which enables the tracing of the small percentage of the population each time round in terms of, i.e. their social trajectories and physical movement (Fielding, 1995) or political participation (Togeby 1999). In both studies cited, this special data was used to analyse the behaviour of the specific migrant population.

35. Even prior to 9/11, there were obvious examples of this, such as Heitmeyer *et al.* (1997), which asked young Turkish adolescents provocative questions about their attitudes towards Islam, as 'proof' that their difficult social circumstances were leading them towards dangerously militant forms of fundamentalism.

or anxiety-inducing 'facts' from a research project of the kind which, by definition, everyday journalism is unable to mount.[36] Yet, as with policy and public funding elsewhere, scholars often enter into a Faustian pact when they sign up to do this kind of research work with heteronomous production and publication conditions attached.

The inevitable transatlantic influence felt on research on integration policy discussed in the previous section has similarly been felt on the shaping of survey-based research in Europe. There has indeed been an almost universal effort by academics in Europe to promote the idea that all European nation-states are now 'countries of immigration', often in polemical discussion with politicians who claim the opposite. The idea has always been that North American multiculturalism and its cosmopolitan idea of national identity is where European nations (or some pan-European EU construct) should be heading. However, this idea remains a rhetorical construction, one that can only be dubiously substantiated by the incoming numbers of migrants into Europe (especially in comparison to North America or Asia), or indeed the overall percentage population of non-European descendants in each country in Europe. This is not to say that Europe does not have an 'integration' problem: quite the contrary, in fact. This – and not immigration control or naturalisation – may indeed be the key immigration question that needs addressing, particularly in view of the weakness of research in this area. Going on from this, the American influence on 'integration' studies has broken down in one of two ways. One – the emphasis on managing race relations and treating integration through anti-discrimination measures – has been most reflected in Britain, and in The Netherlands to a lesser extent. The other – the idea of assimilation in countries built on immigration, of the melting pot or *creuset* – is one which has always retained its strongest reflection in France. Indeed, the historical reconstruction of the idea of France as a 'country of immigration' was the first big achievement of the new republicans of the 1980s.[37] It is no surprise, then, that the most advanced French thinking on integration have resembled most closely the kind of standard sociological works measuring different dimensions of assimilation in the USA, which date

---

36. Work such as this has indeed been frequently sponsored by newspapers such as *Volkskrant* in The Netherlands or *Le Monde* in France, while academics in small countries such as Denmark are on constant call from the newspapers for 'expert' data, argumentation and opinion.

37. The historical work of Noiriel (1988) – with its strong US links (Horowitz and Noiriel 1992) – was vitally important to this. His longstanding message – of France as a country of immigration that had forgotten this – was then repeated without question as the starting point for all the subsequent leading works, through Schnapper (1991), Weil (1991) – whose work has consistently explored French/US parallels – Todd (1994) and Tribalat (1995). It also became the motif of progressive political rhetoric on the subject at the time: for example Mitterrand's famous speech of May 1987 of the French being 'un peu romain, un peu germain, un peu juif, un peu italien, un peu espanol et (même peut-être maintenant) un peu arabe'.

back to the heyday of US sociology on the subject in the 1960s (Gordon 1964; Alba and Nee 2003).

The somewhat old-fashioned sound of the idea of assimilation is not at all reflected in the technology of research to be found in France. The massive state-apparatus that the French are able to muster in their official production of knowledge on the subject is quite breathtaking. Indeed, the reports of the government-appointed *Haut Conseil à l'Intégration* (HCI) have over the years not only sought to formulate the normative, historical and political grounding for the new republican philosophy it espoused, they also set in motion a machine of empirical evidence gathering, explicitly constructed to find the data that the public theory had set out to prove.[38] Since the early 1990s, all kinds of empirical work has been set up to look at the performance and social mobility of 'immigrants' in education or the labour market (Vallet 1996; Silberman *et al.* 2007; Safi 2009). Most quantitative or survey work, however, remains constrained by the basic sampling frame offered to it by the official national survey statistics produced by the French statistics office INSEE: surveys that continue to only generate data (albeit wonderfully elaborated data) on 'étrangers' (foreign non-nationals) in France in comparison with the French population. The basic ideological prohibition on gathering data on the 'ethnic' origin of naturalised French citizens of immigrant origin has reigned in official public circles, concerned that this will undermine the republican fiction that being French is an indivisible, universal political identity, that should not be linked to any ethnic or cultural classification: much 'integration' research is indeed thus limited to charting the social mobility of non-nationals only, or retracing second and third generations only through family-origin records. Family origin is a powerful corrective: going back three generations as much as 23 per cent of French people can be shown to have immigrant origins (Brouard and Tiberj 2005). Yet everyone – academics and political actors – continue to make claims about whether integration or assimilation is or is not working on the basic of reading relations between 'immigrants' and nationals. In a sense, then, the existing intellectual machinery for producing scientific knowledge to back up or disprove these claims, was in fact generating internal contradictions that necessitated the start of a dramatic shift in the methodology of French integration research: in the direction of recognising some kind of 'ethnic but French' classification of hitherto unrecognised populations in France in terms

---

38. The first report of the series, *Pour un modèle français de l'intégration*, written under the auspices of Jacqueline Costa-Lascoux (*see* Haut Conseil à l'Intégration, 1993), constructed a survey that was sent out to the town halls of some seventy-three communes across France, enquiring about general data on immigrants' integration into norms of national-belonging (*appartenance*), family behaviour, social advancement and social involvement (*sociabilité*) (Favell, 1998a: 72–4). This crude, politically oriented survey, provided the impetus for the much more scientific efforts of INED and Tribalat's research group which I discuss further below.

other than 'non-national' origin.[39] It should be stressed that this has not yet happened for the national census in France, nor are questions likely to start looking like the British 'ethnic question' or American 'race monitoring forms'.

This was the background to the controversies surrounding the report by Michèle Tribalat and associates, a major empirical survey of the assimilation of immigrants in France, which long represented the state-of-the-art in French integration research (Tribalat 1995; Tribalat *et al.* 1996). For the first time in an officially funded work, a rigorously constructed survey – derivative of official INSEE data – put together a sample and a series of questions which probed the 'ethnic' proximity of immigrants in France *and* naturalised French persons of immigrant origin to the norms of behaviour of *français de souche* (French of non-immigrant origin). Using geographical targeted, door to door sampling (widely used in studies on immigrant cities in the USA) and asking formerly taboo questions about persons' 'ethnic' national origin and their linguistic/cultural affiliation, the report came up with an unprecedented panorama of the diversity of France's immigrant population, linked to their different migration trajectories, cultural profiles, and political position. The report, which was put together under the auspices of INED (Institut national d'études démographiques), thus differed crucially from the regular population surveys done by INSEE, or with INSEE's data (i.e. Champsaur 1994). A murky internal bureaucratic struggle about the funding of the report almost in fact destroyed it at an early stage: quite a great ideological issue was at stake, and there were important figures who did not want to see it succeed. And, as was similarly the case with the enormously important historical public policy study by Weil (1991), it took a decisive behind-the-scenes political intervention by powerful civil servant and president of the HCI, Marceau Long, to ensure that

---

39. A strong critic of this problem in France has always been the Belgian francophone Martiniello (1995). The line of work focusing on potential 'ethno-racial' discrimination in France (notably against Africans and Turks) has been most strongly developed in quantitative terms by Simon, rebelling against the nationalist tone of Tribalat's work (on which he was part of the team), and Safi: *see* Simon (2005, 2012), Safi and Simon (2014), Safi (2013). Simon and Safi are two of the team members of the most recent major survey in France: *Trajectoires et Origines (TeO): Enquête sur la diversité des populations en France*. A joint effort of INED and INSEE, and conducted on a sample of 21,000 persons between 2008–9, it represented the most important step forward since the breakthrough Tribalat report discussed here. It was able to call selectively on assistance from the national survey to give an unprecedented portrait of the diversity of the French population traced through their parental origins, with migrant origin populations now contrasted with a majority population. With geographical data combined with these other data, French researchers could now talk with precision about the percentages of migrant origin populations in cities and neighbourhoods, which in parts of some cities now saw majority origin French in clear minorities. Notably, too, the survey asked questions about differential experiences of discrimination across migrant origin groups, and its protagonists were also willing to amalgamate migrant origin groupings into ethnic groupings (i.e. Arabic, Black-African, etc.) in some analyses such that both an anti-racist and ethnicity based research agenda became possible. The quality of this new data source has not been lost on US-based researchers who have been quick to start using the French data in new comparative and transatlantic projects (i.e. Soehl 2014). *See also* Beauchemin *et al.* (2010); Guiraudon (2014).

the project got the green light. Although, this was research still very different from the British way of doing it, a more 'ethnicity' based study of integration was evidently needed to continue to provide the evidence for the grand claims about assimilatory integration, being made everywhere by the ideologues of neo-republicanism among intellectuals, media and politicians alike.[40] The controversy is ironic, because in other ways, Tribalat's report was as traditional as a French study could be. It indeed offered a break with recent reconstructive formulations by going *back* to the word 'assimilation' rather than 'integration', to describe the end point of the social adaptation process in France, echoing the methodology of behavioural convergence to statistical norms established by Alba and Nee (2003) in the USA. The report thus presented integration/

---

40. The report was greeted with intense polemics in the press about its methodology. For example, rival INSEE professor Le Bras (1998) led a revolt against it. It is difficult to reconcile the modesty of the methodological step towards 'ethnicity' taken, with the spectacular intensity of its symbolic significance. Across a variety of questions which cover attitudes and behaviour on inter-ethnic marriage (a large part of the report), cultural orientation to the homeland, language and the maintenance of traditional cultural practices, housing concentration, intergenerational social mobility and labour market access, and political participation and associational activity, the report charts the socialisation of France's immigrants to national norms of the *population de souche* derived from a control group of non-immigrant origin French. Its explicit aim, and its empirical result, is to present positive findings about the ongoing success of these processes in the light of a thus confirmed public theory and framework of integration, understood as a *sui generis* French national achievement. Such a picture offers no way of gauging how migrant social trajectories might take creative or successful paths that are not convergent with French norms and its bounded social context. Perhaps most indicative of this is the key 'exception' to the findings of the report: that there is one clear ethnic outlier to the generally positive assimilatory progress of ethnic groups in France: the Turkish population in France, which can be consistently shown to perform 'worst' (i.e. the least 'French') in all of the main categories of enquiry. The reaction to Turkish resistance to French social norms and integration, is to classify them as a clear case of 'integration failure': that this group has failed to be socialised properly and constitutes an objective social problem group. However, it is not at all clear that this group has been performing badly according to other types of indicators of 'integration failure' that might be pointed to in Anglo-American studies: such as youth crime and disorder, social deprivation, poverty, etc. In fact, many of the high profile public order problems in France – as seen in films like *La Haine* (1995), and the streets of suburban cities almost weekly during the 2000s – actually have very little to do with cultural 'intégration' *per se* as the French conceived from the early 1990s onwards. It is fairly clear that these are socio-economic in origin: the cross-ethnic groups typically involved in these are united by poverty and housing concentration, the misery and exclusion of the *banlieues*. They are, in other words, occurring among groups who are to all extents and purposes well integrated by the Tribalat standards (the same can be said about militant Islamic movements in France). And this leaves the status of the Turkish increasingly anomalous within the French integration scheme. Taken as a group across Europe, it is not at all clear that they are can be said to be among the most deprived (as Crul shows in the TIES project, their status is very differentiated). The evidence of France thus seems fundamentally distorted by the fact that the behaviour and self-organisation of the Turkish cannot be described in terms of nation-state oriented integration (a similar thing might be said about the Chinese in France): the problem lies with the intellectual framework rather than with the group itself.

assimilation in France as 'business as usual', with diversity reported as minor exceptions and deviations.[41]

The Tribalat report and its methods had a significant influence on work in other countries: French-style work is in this sense a lot closer to the basic methods of survey work being done across Europe than British methods. A good example is the enormous scale survey project being conducted by Ron Lesthaege (1997) at the Vrije Universiteit Brussel (VUB), for which Tribalat was an external advisor, focusing on the socialisation to 'Western' norms of the Moroccan and Turkish population in Belgium (in particular women), again with the significant blessing, funding and technical support of the various Belgian states. What is noticeable here is not the weaker assumptions about integration or socialisation, but the much weaker nation-state policy context for interpreting the findings of this work, which focused on 'cultural' gender differences and the still significant integration gap between these ethnic populations and the 'Belgian' population (for other important work on Belgium, from a variety of positions, (*see* Blaise *et al.* 1997; Blommaert and Verschueren 1998; Jacobs 1998; Martiniello 1998). The situation offers potentially a very different type of policy context to France, given that no intellectual production in Belgium can comfortably fit within any one single policy framework or definition of integration, let alone a single unitary idea about the nation-state into which immigrants might be imagined to integrate. What is the 'Belgian' population after all but a political fiction? Integration rather has always been a field of conflictual positions in Belgium, which habitually imports its more grandiose conceptual vocabulary from the French, but which then faces significant differences in interpretations in the Walloon and Flemish communities (who themselves often look to the Dutch), and more local differentiations at regional, city, even commune level. The absence of a functioning nation-state context means that the norms of socialisation being identified as the gold standard of immigrant behaviour defaults in Lesthaege (2000) to simply generic 'Western' norms.

In the Belgian context, the really critical question is the language use of immigrants in relation to integration: crucially, of course, in the bi-lingual capital itself, Brussels, where it is thought that immigrants opting to learn French or Dutch

---

41. Despite its controversy, then, the report was received by many commentators as proof that good old-fashioned French republican assimilation was still working: arch-republican Emmanuel Todd, for example, made much of its findings about inter-marriage in France as opposed to other countries. The mystery remains as to why such ideological work is so powerful in France, given the fairly obvious *décalage* with what happens in reality at local levels. Commentators might cruelly observe how the most prominent Parisian researchers never need set foot in the *banlieues* – all that matters is what happens in the 5th, 6th and 7th *arrondissements* (this at least was the case until the state started dumping many of them into new offices in the 13th or, worse, la Courneuve!). However this perhaps misses the point: that the criteria for competition in this intellectual field is not empirical accuracy, but control of the ideological high ground – something that successful players such as Todd, Taguieff and Schnapper well-understand. I argue (1999) that this is rooted in the idealist philosophical tradition in French political thought which all these writers share: it is not what exists which matters, but what you name it. Even those who offer a different account of multiculturalism in France – such as Wieviorka (1996) – do so with the similarly idealist style of work.

might tip the political balance in the city one way of the other. Work on this question is highly controversial in Belgium, which, for reasons of political sensitivity, officially makes no census since the 1960s of language use in bi-lingual communes. Yet it is only via language that integration can be tracked. Deschouwer, Phalet and Swyngedouw's city level survey (1999) of over 1000 ethnic minority respondents in Brussels, immediately ran into public controversies over its findings about illiteracy among immigrants, and the apparent dominance of French. Researchers in Belgium have always been heavily dependent on their location in networks of political patronage and affiliation, which provide the major source of funding. Whatever work is published on a sensitive subject such as this, can spark both immediate and well-publicised debate, but also run foul of what the politicians expect to see for their money.[42] The determining factor here, then, is the reception of the report, rather than the careful methodology it pursued. Integration is ultimately all about the ongoing political struggle about populations in the city, and how the immigrant groups themselves may or may not be able to work the conflictual system to their own advantage (Favell and Martiniello 1999; Jacobs 2000). In the light of the best Belgian research – some of the most sophisticated of European survey output – there was the glimmerings of genuinely cross-national comparative work, showing how conceptually compatible integration studies might be produced.[43]

Meanwhile, systematic cross-ethnic comparative work has been more developed in Germany than in most countries. Research infra-structure is better in Germany, where there are very strong national data banks on populations by

---

42. Another study by the Swyngedouw group (by Bousetta and Swyngedouw 1999) found that the granting of votes to non-national immigrants and resident Europeans in Brussels (who are both assumed to be likely to vote Francophone rather than Flemish) would not in all probability affect political results in the city. One of the Flemish sponsors was not happy with these results and withdrew support, which then jeopardised the continued funding of various other projects the group had planned.

43. Jacobs' pioneering work in Belgium was later connected to great effect with cross-national work on political participation and incorporation, adapting the work of Robert Putnam on social capital by Fennema and Tillie (1999, *see also* Jacobs and Tillie 2004). This work has intriguingly shown how minorities mobilised around more radical, difference oriented politics (the Turks in The Netherlands, for instance) are better integrated in to the Dutch political system, than those incorporated more willingly into the existing party system; *see also* Odmalm (2005). Phalet and Swyngedouw, meanwhile (i.e. 2001), whose mechanistic, multi-levelled model in the Brussels research was a breakthrough for comparative cross-ethnic and multi-levelled research, similarly became key partners in the TIES project (as did Simon), a project I discuss further below. Their work on Brussels was original for modelling integration as a social psychological process that charted without integration end goal preconceptions, the varied strategies taken by different immigrant groups in relation to the spaces and opportunities they encounter in a variety of local, regional or transnational contexts. This open-ended approach might be contrasted with another ambitious contemporaneous study of integration (in Germany) from a social psychological perspective, by Nauck and associates (i.e. Nauck and Schönpflug 1997) which started off – like so many integration studies obsessed with state-centred typologies – by locating different trajectories within the reductive closed schema of types of integration (pluralist integration, assimilation, segregation, marginalisation) proposed most famously by the high priest of the social psychology of immigration, Berry (1997). Koopmans and Statham's (2000) framework for comparative immigration studies also takes this as its starting point.

national-origin available, such as the socio-economic panel commissioned yearly by the Deutschen Institut für Wirtschaft, which provides data on ethnicity, language, identity questions and participation (an example of such work being Diehl (2002)). Progressive researchers here have been even more sensitive to the de-categorisation of foreigners and consciously promoting the positive idea of Germany as 'a country of immigration'. There have been advantages to such research in the fact it has had to be diverted away from the ideologically dominated discussions on citizenship and naturalisation, where progress has been more difficult. German research is thus more likely to concentrate on conceptualising integration in technical socio-economic terms: in terms of participation in the welfare state, and in differences between federal or city level contexts. One consequence is the possibility of internal comparisons of integration geographically (by city or federal state) within the nation, something of which there is no trace in France and Britain. German research, however, has not escape the pervasively nation-centred frame which dominates its political debates. Negative evidence of non-integration – such as ethnic concentration or the failure of second and third generations to speak German – tend to get constructed as evidence of segregation or marginalisation, in contrast with more successful state-centred integration or assimilation.

Across the water in Britain, it would come as no surprise to find integration research has been significantly out of step with the rest of mainland Europe. Britain identified its 'race relations' problematic at an early stage with that of the native black population in the USA, and the evolution of what might be called 'multicultural race relations' has been shaped ever since by this peculiar self-assimilation to a part (but not all) of the US example. The message has always been that Britain does it differently, if not best. In the late 1990s, its own state-of-the-art survey on integration, offering a deep contemporaneous contrast in methodology and rhetoric to that of the Tribalat report, was the *Ethnic Minorities in Britain* survey, published in 1997. Reports such as this have been made by the influential Policy Studies Institute (PSI) on a decade by decade basis, and have offered a distinct, rather more autonomous picture from the kinds of official census and survey material produced by the state Quasi-Autonomous Non-Governmental Organisations (quangos) such as the CRE, which used to 'regulate' the implementation and progress of race relations laws, or clientalist pressure groups such as the Runnymede Trust. This slightly subversive role was underlined by the fact that the report was headed by Tariq Modood, who played quite a significant role in what can be looked at in hindsight as the break-up of ethnic and racial studies in Britain, partly under the challenge that new ethnic questions have brought to the dominant race relations establishment.[44] The PSI was also notable as one of a battery of new-left think tank groups that rose to prominence in the 1990s, and which had a strong presence in the policy circles of New Labour.

---

44. See his earlier attacks on the 'establishment' in Modood (1992) and (1994), based partly on experiences working within the 'race relations industry', in which he upset many established dogmas by putting Asians, and then Pakistani and Bangladeshi Muslims, on what had been up until then a black and white race relations map. In her socio-psychological work on Brussels and Rotterdam (i.e. Phalet and Swyngedouw (2001)), Phalet notes the possible comparative usefulness of Modood's other work on ethnic identities in Britain (Modood *et al.* 1994), if it can be adapted elsewhere.

The report therefore offered a distinct perspective on the key successes and deficiencies of British 'multicultural race relations' that stood at a certain distance from current orthodoxies. It was a very self-aware work: knowing its place in a long canon of similar national studies, and the often temperamental debates about multiculturalism and anti-racism in Britain. However, the report remained squarely 'British' in its overall perspective: with no hint of the research being at all related to, linked with, or aimed at, a wider European comparative agenda.[45]

---

45. The British construction of data on ethnic minorities here dictates a sampling frame – and hence a construction of the integration problematic – which follows the British convention of relativising more or less distinct 'ethnic groups' with one another, and, most importantly, an amorphous, under-specified, majority 'white' ethnic group. In the British census and other official data gathering devices (*see* Connolly and White 2006), each individual questioned self-identifies with a given ethnic category, from which wider patterns about groups are generated. In the Modood report, the identification of the sample and the 'ethnic' self-categorisation questions, followed generally the kinds of the categories created for the 1991 census, but also allowed cross-checking with declared family origin, and some recognition of the problem of mixed-origin, and distinctions within groups crudely clumped together in the official census. It limited itself, however, only to these, Britain's officially recognised 'ethnic minorities'. It was the 1991 census which introduced the generic post-colonial scheme of self-classification peculiar to Britain (on the details of the British ethnic census and its evolution, *see* Kesler and Schwartzman 2014). It identified White, Black-Caribbean, Black-African, Black-Other (please describe), Indian, Pakistani, Bangladeshi, Chinese, Any other group (please describe). This is quite different to the basic five way delineation of 'race' in American censuses, which are supposed to be such a source of British 'race relations': (essentially) White, Black, Native American, Asian, and Pacific Islander, with Hispanic or Latino an 'ethnic' category of 'any' race. In Britain, outside of family or parental origin, the migration history of individuals becomes irrelevant, and there is often no place for properly distinguishing many other substantial minority or non-national groups. The Modood survey differed primarily in separating out the Gujarati 'African Asians', who have had a quite different social trajectory than other Asian groups. The 2001 census offered even more boxes to tick and write in boxes for those feeling left out, and some pressure to open the Pandora's box of 'whiteness', for example, so that the Irish and Jewish in Britain could be recognised as groups suffering from 'racial' (sic) discrimination. The irony here is that in the USA, the typical immigration story is how a phenotypically disadvantaged group such as the Irish became 'white', whereas the story in Britain is how the Irish became (effectively) 'black' (i.e. able to bring race discrimination cases), as they become separated from 'White-British'. In Modood, 'disadvantage' is identified by cross-referencing findings with the kind of ABCDE occupational social class categories, famous from the British sociology of social mobility mentioned above (i.e. Goldthorpe, 1987). The Modood report explicitly rejected the use of the term 'integration', focusing on representing the diversity of experience, identity, and success of Britain's ethnic minorities, and the persistence of disadvantage for some (young Pakistanis and Bangladeshis alongside Afro-Caribbeans) amidst the above average success of certain other highly qualified Asian groups. Werbner (1999) problematised the still very individualistic notion of 'success' that this kind of study of social mobility is limited to identifying. This led to aggregating relative group success from individual paths of mobility, something which may indeed lead to big distinctions between, say, African Asians and Pakistanis. However, as she points out, if success is re-thought in anthropological terms as the creation of collective cultural value (and meaning) by groups, it can be argued that Pakistanis have often been very successful at creating rich community contexts in which the production of individualistic material wealth is negligible, and that those Asians who are materially successful often depend thus for their 'success' not on individual human capital but on the rich social capital that the ethnic group context produces for them. Moreover, the individualistic conception of success sells very short in social mobility terms, the kind of cultural difference and diversity elsewhere vaunted as the source of ethnic assertiveness. Werbner was also responding to some very stereotyping remarks by Ceri Peach and Roger Ballard (in Peach 1996) about diversity among Britain's ethnic minorities, in which the African Asians are said to be following a 'Jewish' path to integration, and the Pakistanis an 'Irish' path to social stigmatisation and segregation.

What this reflected was a reluctance to move outside of a framework in which Britain as a 'society' remains the one fixed and bounded background within which diversity and difference might be found.[46] As with Tribalat, then, what the Modood report represented was a bid for the national cultural high-ground: an argument to preserve the nation by imagining it to be as universal and inclusive as possible, in which the old nation is taught to face up to the consequences of 'immigration' – but not at all forced to acknowledge the consequences of 'globalisation' or the break-down of the nation-state as the dominant mode of social organisation. As such, it was a key move in the policy/knowledge struggle, in which British academics as elsewhere have had some considerable background influence. The 'multiculturalism in one nation' idea has certainly been a very powerful example for Europe. Yet, as we saw in Chapter Three, when British policy makers turn in that direction on these questions, it is not with a view to build co-operation, but rather to assert a kind of moral hegemony. This represents the re-assertion of nation-state primacy over integration policies, and of the superiority of the British way, over what it sees as an 'ethnicity-stricken' continent, unable to deal either with internal ethnic and national conflicts, or the multicultural difference brought by immigration.

What is perhaps remarkable is that during the early 2000s and after other smaller European states followed the neo-nationalist response of Britain and France, and took a similar turn in their thinking about cultural diversity and the changing nature of the nation. The 1990s decade of globalisation and the supposed decline of the nation-state in fact saw both the Scandinavian countries and The Netherlands return to a hard line nation-building idea of integration, after previous flirtations with strong state-sponsored versions of cultural pluralism and multiculturalism (Joppke and Morawska 2003).[47] In The Netherlands, immigrants found their access to welfare and rights made

---

46. A partial exception however may be the one scholar coming out of the RC28 social stratification camp who has most strongly engaged with the mainstream of ethnic and migration studies: Anthony Heath. In Heath and Cheung (2007), extending well beyond the national borders of the Modood study, and indeed well beyond Europe, they develop an alternate integration model which looks at diversity and discrimination in terms of 'ethnic penalties' on the labour market. The work is a prodigious compendium of secondary data available across Western Europe, North America, Australia and Israel. Its main weakness is that it relies on (and does not question effectively) nation-by-nation conventions about the different modes of counting ethnic or immigrant groups; nor does it factor in asymmetries between European and settler societies. Heath has also joined forces with Phalet (Phalet and Heath 2010). Building on this line of work using Labour Force survey data, Kesler (i.e. 2006, 2010) has produced a series of striking new comparative analyses, including cross-national (Britain, Germany and Sweden), cross-welfare states (effects on childcare and women's labour force participation), and cross-ethnic comparison (comparing old and new migration in Britain). With Safi, she is also broaching French-British comparisons (Kesler and Safi 2012). These studies rely on categorisation by non-national origin, so are less sensitive to typical British concerns about ethnic and racial relations, and to the challenge of super-diversity (Vertovec 2007), but they are the first to provide data on the comparative effects of inequality on recent East European migrants versus older, post-colonial minorities. For a comprehensive review of the variety of means for collecting ethnic minority statistics in Europe and the problems it is causing, *see* Simon (2012).

conditional on their attending structured tuition in the language and culture of their host country; and that left-wing thinking had shifted markedly to associate the goals of equality and anti-discrimination with a more successful and pro-active integration framework.[48] Unlike Britain and France, however, these small countries have the luxury of being small, cohesive states with very strong national identities and minimal regional tensions, that have long

---

47. One distinctive feature of Dutch research, which contributes to its diversity and highly contested nature, is the fact there is no official census since the early 1970s. Data and sampling frames (based on country of birth-origin of individual and parents, and attribution of religion) therefore have to be reconstructed either from official police and town hall population records of residence; or through the kinds of specific ministry sponsored official reports on policy, such as the annual *Sociale en Culture Rapport*. The Dutch system is noteworthy for its bifurcation of residents into *autochtone* and *allochtone* categories: 'originating from another country' or not. A person with one foreign origin parent is considered *allochtone*; a person born to non-foreign origin person living abroad is *autochtone*. Even more peculiarly given the absence of ethnicity statistics, schools and poor neighborhoods with predominant immigrant populations are referred to as 'black', and immigrant groups as 'ethnic minorities' (in the Anglo-American style). These peculiarities has quite an effect on the numbers game and stereotyping in Dutch discussions of immigration, and the unease in particular about unregistered and undocumented migrants in the country. For,a discussion on the limitations in The Netherlands of identifying ethnic minorities only by parental country of origin, *see* Guiraudon *et al.* (2005).

48. An early and influential example was the impressive integration survey work by Justus Veenman and team in Rotterdam (1997, 1998), which explicitly linked social capital and social mobility research to the persistence of racial discrimination for Dutch ethnic minorities in education and the labour market. It argued for the kind of pro-active national cultural education for immigrants and minorities that would enable them to overcome barriers and prejudice, and against the pre-existing multicultural approach in the country. Joining the growing critique of Dutch multiculturalism, Koopmans (2010) caused a stir by suggesting that multicultural rights and high welfare provision in The Netherlands (but also Sweden and Belgium) had caused higher rates of incarceration, worse spatial segregation and lower labour market participation than Austria, Switzerland, Britain, but especially (and most controversially) Germany. Critics disliked his mix of uneven secondary cross-national data sources. Also from the mid-2000s on, the challenge of a more consistent and systematic mechanistic comparative work was taken up by Maurice Crul, at the head of the Integration of the European Second Generation (TIES) and Pathways to Success (ELITE) projects (Crul and Vermeulen 2003; Crul and Schneider 2010; Crul *et al.* 2012; Crul 2013). Pulling together a strong European network of eight country partners, and inspired explicitly by the in-depth example of American work on assimilation and the second generation (Vermeulen 2010), TIES has developed a multi-level institutional analysis to explain the various school performances across countries of the migrant second generation of Turkish, Moroccan and ex-Yugoslavian children, showing quite convincingly how issues such as child-care provision, educational tracking, gender, and stereotyping have affected differentially the careers of young migrant offspring. The project was notable for its focus on in-depth biographical, family and professional information, yet still managing to cover 10,000 respondents in fifteen cities. The model is both dynamic in terms of agency and structure, and flexible in terms of institutional variety and mechanistic causality. Notably, Crul and associates challenge the overweening emphasis on ethnicity in American research to explain diverse or segmented outcomes, for example, showing how across the Turkish population in Europe (itself very diverse), there are quite dramatic differences between the major nation states in terms of educational and career performance. Although sensitive to intra-state (cross-city) diversity, the presentation does tend to still emphasise national variation as the bottom line, highlighting 'good' systems (such as Sweden and The Netherlands) relative to 'bad' ones France and, especially, Germany. In ELITE, Crul has focused more specifically on explaining the success of highly skilled and educated migrants within these groups, using a similar model. In this project, an even greater role is given to qualitative life story narratives and dynamics of self-selection, which offers interesting comparisons to my work in *Eurostars and Eurocities* and PIONEUR on young highly educated West European movers (Favell 2008a; Recchi and Favell 2009).

since mastered (through trade, exchange and open borders) a dual game of embracing international influences while preserving all kinds of particularist internal national traditions and ways of doing things.

The Dutch, however, do have something in common with the French and the British: their nationalism. They too are fiercely convinced of the superiority of their national political model and the kinds of characteristic policy methods that follow from this. This may be characteristic of the post-colonial condition, or indeed of countries that have not had to see themselves on the losing, 'bad guys' side of the century's wars in Europe. Yet it does seem that the shrinking of the generic 'British', 'French' or 'Dutch' civilisations into the original national territory in the post-war period, and the 'post-colonial' humiliation they were supposed to have suffered, has eventually only led on to the re-formulation of a universalist 'multiculturalism-in-one-nation' in these countries, built around re-worked ideas of integration and nation-building. Nationalising elites, competing for hegemony over the idea of the nation, have used these kind of 'universalist-nationalist' discourses to outflank old-fashioned culturally-exclusive competitors, refining an international role in the world for these perennial nation-states in decline. Yet at the same time, this openness to internalising and adopting to foreign imported culture, has come with the staunch refusal to see new immigrants as anything but re-located colonial subjects importing diverse but assimilable cultures into the nation-state. Yet could they not equally be the personification of other internationalising forces blowing holes in the idea of bounded nation-states – such as the global economy, or more transnational conceptions of civilisation grounded in universal human rights and personhood? I will explore this possibility briefly in a further section below.

Crucially, within this nation-state sponsored picture, the status and power of immigrants gets measured entirely in terms of a social mobility relative to norms of integration into the nation-society, or average national social mobility paths; yet, it is increasingly normal to think of elites in these countries as becoming more and more transnational and free-floating in their identifications and trajectories. Britain and France may be the countries in Europe with the longest immigration experience, and the most well-worked ideas of reconciling multicultural diversity with national unity; but this does not stop even the most progressive policy intellectuals from espousing nationalising ideologies which appear increasingly anachronistic in their conceptions of how to actualise multiculturalism in an internationalising world. It may be wrong, therefore, to continually take France and Britain as the ideal type 'integration nations', whose example will be followed by less 'advanced' nations, such as those in Southern Europe.[49]

---

49. This point was reflected in innovative PhD work by Barbulescu (2013), in which she showed how Italy and Spain had rejected the integration models of Britain and France, and were using variegated integration policies towards different groups and at different levels (local to Europe) to 'integrate' by differentiating and excluding immigrants.

The challenge of transnationalism

For all the return of 'integration' to the immigration policy agenda, the 1990s were also the highpoint of optimism about 'post-national' globalisation and cosmopolitanism. In migration research this was connected centrally to the notion of transnationalism and sending country influences, and its challenge to standard immigration models (beginning with, i.e. Basch *et al.* 1994; Portes 1996; Smith and Guarnizo 1998, Vertovec 1999, Smith 2001). It is worth asking, then, what the debates on transnationalism might have contributed to the question of integration? (*see also* Favell 2003a).

In fact, scholars of transnationalism sought – for exactly the kinds of reasons spelt out in this chapter – to purge 'integration' from their terms of research; for the most part the question was not addressed. By definition, they did not wish to be underwriting the nation-state in a new world which could be seen in terms of other networks, transactions, flows and imaginations on a transnational or global scale. Methodologically, too, their bottom-up, ethnographic preferences suited a style of work which drew large conclusions from the study of cases likely to be seen as exceptional, or indeed deviant from the conventional structural or survey-based integration-focused perspective. For sure, it was this too which may account for the often excessively celebratory tone of transnational studies. Seeking a new kind of cosmopolitan liberation, some studies fell into the longstanding problem that has distorted much radical ethnic and racial studies: the transfer of sympathy for the experiences, difficulties, and sometimes plight of migrants and ethnic minorities, into visions of these groups as some sort of heroic new 'proletariat'. Although the 'search for a new world' – and the slogan 'globalisation from below' – was indeed the rather romantic packaging chosen in the work of Portes (1998), or Castells (2000), for example, it should not deflect us from its key insights. Its major advance was the empirical uncovering of trans-state, trans-nation economic and cultural networks of transactions (and protean forms of social organisation) among new and developing migrant groups. These networks have thus been generating sources of collective social power outside of territorial state structures familiar from our conventional understanding of the world of nations. Whereas Portes principally recognises the source of transnational power as the global market, others pointed to diasporas, or informal ('illegal') sources of these same powers (*see* Cohen 1997; Phizacklea 1998).

The other crucial aspect of Portes' work, however, was its insistence on linking emergent transnational forms with classic integration questions. In connection with his notion of 'segmented assimilation' in the USA, it pointed towards an emergent structural relationship between the transnational 'survival' strategies resorted to by migrant groups when facing the unappealing 'downward assimilation' offered to them by the host societies state and societal structures (Portes 1995). European examples of this thus focused on the similar emergence of community resilience against negative socio-economic conditions, or excessive assimilatory pressures from the host society. The results can be seen in the innovations of the informal economy or inner-city Islam in many European cities. The integration path may indeed prove to be, in Kloosterman and Rath's terms, 'a long and winding road' (Kloosterman *et al.* 1998). As the Dutch state, for example, seemed to grow ever tighter in its heavily legislated attempt to discover, encompass, regularise and normalise the spontaneous economic activities of new migrants, so there seemed to be an ever-growing over-flow of undisciplined, self-organised informal activities in the country (Engbersen 1996). The best continental European work thus focused on precisely this issue of informality or non-institutionalised forms of social organisation; often focusing, unsurprisingly, on those groups identified in conventional integration research as the ethnic cases which fit worst into the kinds of automatically integrating schemes set up, for example, by French and British research (Kastoryano 1993; Césari 1994; Bousetta 1997; Fennema and Tillie 1999; Phalet *et al.* 2000). It is not surprising that this work invariably highlighted either Turkish or Moroccan groups in various countries: two newer, non-colonial migrant groups that have displayed some of the most pronounced sending country influences and transnational, non-integrating social trajectories in Europe.

Systematising these deviant tendencies among particular groups without simply reproducing the nation-state-society as the container unit has proven a lot more difficult. Some researchers offered a Polanyi-inspired way forward, for example, Faist (2000), Kesteloot (2000) or Werbner (1999), as a way of understanding the informal, infra-state social structures created by (especially economic) migrant transnationalism. Others have turned to the metaphor of transnational 'social spaces', likely to be found in non-spatial urban networks and global localities (Pries 2001; Levitt and Glick Schiller 2004; Glick Schiller and Çağlar 2009). These conceptual innovations enabled such scholars to analyse schemes of transnational or local integration in economic and community structures which cross-cut with national, citizenship-centred forms. Whether it is the bustling migrant markets of old Antwerp or East Amsterdam, or the mosque-centred inner city Islam of Turks and Moroccans in Brussels, or the textile trade of Pakistani Manchester, there is clearly a need to recognise these city-embedded activities as emergent forms of social organisation – and hence social power – largely unstructured or incorporated (in formal or informal terms) by the state. The somewhat anarchical multiculturalism of some European cities continues to suggest a new type of multi-ethnic culture in Europe, rather different to the multicultural citizenship shaped by integrating nation-states. It is not egalitarian, it is not anchored in rights, and it is certainly not conflict free; but it is, for better or for worse, much less disciplined by the nation-building pressures hidden in top-down policies of 'integration'.

Interestingly, however, even this kind of multicultural challenge to dominant European nation-state-centred cultures tends to still be anchored in deterritorialised 'nationality': the persistence of important political and social links with the 'homeland', as both a concrete and symbolic reference (Al-Ali *et al.* 2001; Al-Ali and Koser 2002). This fact – which is certainly the case with Turks and Moroccans in Europe – indicates a limit to these forms of transnationalism outside of their European context. Viewed from here they are not really transnational at all, but rather examples of deterritorialised nation-state building, familiar perhaps from the older diasporic histories of countries like Ireland, Italy or Greece.

As these overwhelmingly national sources for transnational ideas suggest, as well as the brute fact of international borders and international relations, we should be wary of seeing transnationalism as an end to the integration paradigm (Waldinger and FitzGerald 2004). Rather, transnationalism in Europe has to be seen as a growing empirical exception to the familiar nation-centred pattern of integration pattern across the continent. These remain the dominant focus for policy actors and migrant activists alike. Transnationalism perhaps points towards the new sources of social power accessed by migrant groups when they begin to organise themselves and their activities in ways not already organised for them by an integrating nation state. By setting these forms against the continuity of nation-state centred patterns of integration, we may be able to understand how and why new spaces in the empire of the state may develop. But the far stronger presence in institutional and structural terms of the nation-state centred integration paradigm, suggests that whatever emergent transnationalism we may find in Europe, it falls some way short of the global institutional structures of post-national personhood envisaged in the work of Bauböck (1994b), Jacobson (1996), Soysal (1997) or Sassen (2006).[50]

Directions for future research

The field of immigrant integration research has evolved dramatically since the early 2000s although, as I argue throughout, it has not always taken on board the kind of necessary critique of its basic assumptions and blindspots articulated here. In particular a new wave of comparative international studies in the slipstream of the work in the USA by Portes (1993, with Zhou; 2001, with Rumbaut) and Alba (2003, with Nee; 2005) has boldly proposed that European societies and their immigration processes can be easily assimilated to the basic US model: of immigrant ethnicities progressively disappearing in straight and/or segmented generational lines into a universal 'middle class' majority nationhood. While marshalling extraordinary new resources in terms of large-scale and increasingly compatible data sets across European countries and the Atlantic, much of this research may still lead to dead ends, if problems with comparative

---

50. The research project INTERACT ('Researching third country nationals integration as a three way process involving immigrants, countries of emigration and countries of immigration as actors of integration') headed by Philippe Fargues and Agnieszka Weiner at the EUI, Florence responds quite exactly to the call for a new kind of integration research able to identify and assess transnational factors identified in this section (which is adapted from Favell 2003a). Proposing to study from among a claimed 25 million third country nationals, the fifty-five sending country nationalities with more than 100,000 emigrés across the EU28, the project seeks to challenge the state-centred receiving country focus in typical integration/assimilation research, by charting how the institutions and communities of countries of origin differentially impact on integration. Nine dimensions of study are proposed: labour market, education, political participation, civic participation, social interactions, access to nationality, language use and acquisition, religion, and residential integration. Integration into 'what?', and whether the concept of 'integration' can be disembedded from its national-societal location – particular in terms of the macro-level aggregates of either populations (i.e. comparison with the integration norms of 'natives') or institutions necessary for any operationalisation (nearly all the dimensions mentioned above are bounded national domains) – was not yet fully addressed in the initial conceptualisation of the subject: *see* Unterreiner and Weiner (2014), Vincenza Desiderio and Weiner (2014), and the website: http://interact-project.eu.

conceptualisation and asymmetries are not seriously addressed. National majority populations – the 'society' into which immigrants are supposedly integrated – remains the great (white) black box in this research field. As I have discussed in detail in footnotes above and below, however, the elements of a more satisfactory approach can be amalgamated from the work of a number of scholars and projects. These would include work by Modood (*et al.* 1994); Bommes (1998; *see* Boswell and D'Amato 2012), Wimmer and Glick Schiller (2002), Phalet (with Swyngedouw 2001; with Heath 2010), Brubaker (2004), Waldinger (with FitzGerald 2004; 2013), Vertovec (2007), Glick Schiller and Çağlar (2009), Simon (with Beauchemin *et al.* 2010; 2012); Wimmer (2013), and Crul (with Schneider 2010; with Mollenkopf 2012; 2013; *et al.* 2013). The present essay also offers a foundational critique and introduction. Three key elements in this research agenda are apparent. The first is the shift away from nation-centred integration to the most likely alternative – the city context – as a site in which local, national, regional and global scales come together, amidst institutionally diverse sub-systems of a 'society' no longer exclusively bounded by the nation-state. The second is a strong scepticism towards essentialising 'groupism' about ethnicity in migration research, which opens the door to multi-variate 'super-diverse' categorisation, and variation within groups across local contexts, whether institutional or not. The third is a comprehensive commitment to find new and sometimes iconoclastic means of operationalising these qualitative concerns in systematic quantitative research.

As we have seen, though, such comparative research on integration processes and integration policy in Europe is a hugely difficult enterprise, as well as a hugely difficult field to span in any review. We are still some way from the stage when either official national data and conceptualisations or independent constructed academic approaches are sufficiently compatible for clear cut comparative studies to be made. The aim of this chapter has been to clarify why this is so, showing how the nuts and bolts of national and cross-national research must also be related systematically back to the political construction of the problem in each country, and the material conditions that academics working within these frameworks have had to face. Although seemingly negative in tone, my effort has in fact been to try to clear the way for the more genuine advance on cross-national comparative research that others are now developing. The question remains of how integration research might be conceived and executed in the future. By way of a brief and programmatic answer, I will conclude then by presenting how I think the subject should be approached as a problem of basic comparative research design. As this was originally conceived to respond to the goals and substance of the Carnegie project's central questions on citizenship, I will limit myself here to the comparative study of *political integration*: that is on research which might compare levels of participation and/or representation of migrants and minorities in their host societies, as measured through the rights they are offered or their 'social power' in the political system.

First of all, it needs be pointed out that a precondition for any new research is that some solutions to the dilemmas outlined at the preliminary stage – i.e. in this chapter – must now be found. These questions require detailed expert debate by all concerned. We need to determine a common set of categories for identifying migrants or minorities across Europe, and thus a suitably corrected set of official data for them. It is clear that these categories must be something other than the category of nationality, which renders many citizens of ethnic migrant origin invisible; but also that the self-attributing 'racial' categories of the British ethnic question are equally limited. Some kind of combination of subjective ethnic/racial and objective national migrant origin categories would seem a sensible compromise, but it must avoid pitfalls of ethnic groupism. We also need to specify in advance the relationship that academics doing this research envisage with actual politics and policy making. If the work is to be highly context specific – like so much that has been done before – it will inevitably end up more strategic and instrumental than scientific. In fact, the lesson from the Carnegie project was the importance of the relative autonomy it offered from other political and material demands, and the independent moral authority a non-specific transatlantic viewpoint – drawing on the best international specialists on the subject – can in fact claim. It is at this – admittedly quite Olympian level – that the research should be done.

Stage one of the research proper must be the gathering of existing research on the question. Obviously, this chapter is a step in this direction, albeit incomplete, which indicates the degree to which most existing studies have to be processed through an interpretative key of this kind, in order to understand how and why they have been written. This key is essential if we are to unlock and re-use the best existing national studies, which always need 'translating' out of context as it were, as well as pinpointing the weaknesses (usually flattening effects) of existing cross-national or transatlantic comparisons. However, in all the countries in question data exists on the numbers and concentration of migrants and minority groups, their social and political organisation, their political behaviour and access to existing political channels and so on.

Stage two must be the determining of what it is we want to compare and explain: our dependent variable. Much normatively directed work pitches this in a vague, indeterminate way: it seeks to compare levels of 'citizenship', 'democracy' or 'civil society', as if were in fact possible to measure these notions in an open-minded enough way, that did not already expect certain conditions to be fulfilled before the normative category can be said to be achieved. These concepts are also too often bound up with normative ideas about nation-building and the progress of national societies; they are too ideologically loaded. Narrower studies, however, such as those which seek to measure the degree of formal rights or the amount of formal legislation protecting migrants or minorities, are too literal, reproducing a certain kind of highly organised, top-down state perspective in their analysis. The key measure for political integration should be something in between, something linked to participation and the mobilisation of groups. The important thing will be to stress that it is not just the quantity of participation that needs measuring, but its quality: the degree to which migrant groups actually manage to influence political outcomes (whether it is influence on policy outcome, influence over agenda-setting or issue-definition, or indeed faces in parties or public positions). In other words, we must look for a measure of their relative social power in specific contexts.[51]

Stage three is the measuring of the dependent variable in different national situations, in order to set up a cross-national research question and identify the key possible independent variables (explanatory factors) that might be causing variance in outcomes in different contexts. Almost any stance on measurement here will contain a bias towards either disorganised libertarian states (measurements indicating degrees of freedom from state control for groups), or highly organised state-centred approaches towards integration (measurements indicating degrees of formal protection and policy for groups). It is here, then, that I suggest a rather idiosyncratic trick to make comparison in the European context possible. The bottom line of much cross-national research is to discover national variation: to compile 'league tables' of more less successful national approaches to or experiences with integration. But how useful is this really? In many instances, it just ends up confirming that there are indeed national differences in Europe, reaffirming national boundaries and distinctions, as much that asymmetric comparisons between (i.e.) small, homogenous, rich states and large, poorer, chaotic ones, or between North and South or East and West, actually only reveal incommensurability in comparing cross-nationally within Europe. A comparatist emphasis (in the literary or philological sense) on interpretative difference is often needed as much as the comparative social science search for explanatory commonalities (variables), in order to understand cross-national contrasts. Rather, my alternate strategy has always been to instead assume that all the states in Europe we are interested in are roughly equivalent in the degree of integration they enable, and that what is more important is to not to classify them as better or worse, but to compare the different ways in which they frame the question and seek to achieve it in practice. This move is in effect like creating a 'G7' of 'integration nations' who, as in the real G7, have different GDPs and degrees of economic performance, but who within this set of nations are nevertheless considered equals, with an equal status in the select group of developed, industrially advanced states. If, then, we take our 'integration nations' as essentially equal members of a select group – within which it is absurd to impose a hierarchy of advancedness – what we are left measuring is not absolute variance but rather qualitative variance across cases. Although this means we will not be able find out whether Sweden is 'better' than France or Britain 'better' than Germany in their treatment of immigrants,

---

51. Two models for this are the social capital based studies by Fennema and Tillie (1999), pursued in several European countries in the LOCALMULTIDEM project (Morales and Giugni 2011)); and the MERCI project, based on public sphere analysis of migrant and majority claims making, by Koopmans *et al.*(2005). Both developed innovative measurements of immigrant voice and social power across national and urban contexts using European and national funding. *See also* recent work by Maxwell (2012), Givens and Maxwell (2012).

the exercise may – via a series of paired bi-lateral comparisons – enable us to identify what is good and bad in a particular country's policies of integration relative to another.[52] If we then take on board the assumption that there is a kind of policy convergence going on across all these states, it may be possible to synthesise from across the various comparisons a set of 'best practices' that take the best of each.

Stages four would move on from this logical design to practical questions of what the unit of comparison will be across nations (i.e. at what level it should take place). Too many studies in the past have compared immigration politics or policies of integration using the general 'institutional' features of national political systems, read off from law and policy on the books. Although initially productive, this is now leading to repetitive and moribund research, that reproduces national stereotypes and assumptions about the nation-state. It is also inherently biased in favour of state-centred policy approaches. My suggestion, as mentioned above, would be that the city is far better unit of comparison, a level for studying political integration which enables both contextual specificity and structural comparisons that allow for the fact that immigrant integration might be influenced simultaneously by local, national and transnational factors. From this we can move to the selection itself of cities and immigrant groups for study. Here, a good deal of existing descriptive work exists that has already generated information and data about indicators of the independent variables that explain differences across cities and there would seem no reason why research cannot build on these studies, and develop a more extensive range of studies of migrant political integration in European cities.[53]

It is suggested, then, that a simple work through a step-by-step research design process such as this, may in fact help clarify how more effective cross-national

---

52. This was in fact the research strategy I used in my study of France and Britain, Favell (1998a). By refusing to answer the loaded and inherently flattening question of which country is 'better' at integration, I was able to contrast the two in such a way as to highlight their relative policy achievements and their distinctive pathological tendencies. The good and the bad are in effect two sides of the same coin.

53. An early example in the 1990s was the UNESCO-MOST project or the various reports produced by the Metropolis project on migrants in cities (*see* Hjarnø 1999). The former project produced a set of city reports on the participation and representation of migrants in cities that each followed a common template specifying indicators (for population numbers, types of political organisation, channels of representation, etc.). Some excellent academic studies which followed the kind of strategy suggested here were those by Ireland (1994) on migrants in four localities in France and Switzerland, by Bousetta (2000) on Moroccans in four cities in three national contexts (Lille, Liège, Antwerp and Utrecht), by Garbaye (2005) on two French cities and one in Britain, as well as the cross-national projects inspired by the work of Fennema and Tillie in The Netherlands (Jacobs and Tillie 2004). *See also* Body-Gendrot and Martiniello (2000). In the 2000s, perhaps the most promising work in this direction was the TIES project, headed by Crul, as it linked up with the interests of the urban studies scholar Mollenkopf in New York: *see* the agenda in Crul and Mollenkopf (2012). A further example of work from the fruitful CUNY-UvA partnership is Foner *et al.* (2014); *see also* Nicholls and Uitermark (2012) for another city-based comparison between Amsterdam and Los Angeles. A general rationale for shifting the study of migrant incorporation to the city scale is provided by Glick Schiller and Çağlar (2009).

comparative research on integration might be possible. It may indeed also be possible to envisage this kind research drawing conclusions about which are the more effective means of political integration of migrants and minorities found across Europe, as well as a sense of the specific problems that nation state policies have generated in their progressive attempts to build distinctive national 'philosophies of integration'. With this kind of procedure, it may *even* be possible to envisage the derivation of normative statements or guidelines of the kind that I have sought to isolate from the research process throughout this study. It is in this way, I argue, that social scientific research on integration may be able to redefine an autonomous role for itself in the policy making and politics of integration currently troubling so many European states.

Part Three

Highly Skilled Migration and Social Mobility

Chapter Six

The Human Face of Global Mobility:
A Research Agenda

with Miriam Feldblum and Michael Peter Smith

The nation state is *so* 20th century. A rising regionalism around the world is dissolving old national borders. The global city-region, cross-border region, and super-region is the new parlance of a borderless world of swashbuckling businessmen, high-speed commuters and jetsetting teenagers [...] If a borderless world is truly in the making, then the tool of choice for the 21st century cartographer won't be the pencil but the eraser. *Wallpaper* patiently awaits the new World Atlas *sans frontières*.

'The new world order', *Wallpaper* magazine, April 2000: 59–64.

What the world ranging activities of these major actors (large banks and corporations) do is to provide examples, incentives and technical means for common people to attempt a novel and previously unimagined alternative. By combining their new technological prowess with mobilization of their social capital, former immigrant workers are thus able to imitate the majors in taking advantage of economic opportunities distributed unequally in space [...] The long-term potential of the transnationalization of labour runs against growing international inequalities of wealth and power as well as intra-national ones in the countries of out-migration. What the process does above all is to weaken a fundamental premise of the hegemony of corporate economic elites and domestic ruling classes [...] that labour and subordinate classes remain 'local', while dominant elites are able to range 'global'.

'Globalization from below: The rise of transnational communities',
Alejandro Portes (1998): p. 18.

Talk of globalisation and regional integration in the 1990s and 2000s familiarised us with the idea that the continued liberalisation of world trade and the movement of goods, capital and services on which it is based, leads also to a spectacular liberalisation of the free movement of persons.[1] In terms of political economy and sociology, authors such as Sassen (1996, 2001) linked these developments with a consequent withdrawal in the controlling powers of nation-states over population movement, something seen as the fulfilment of a new 'age of migration' (Castles and Miller 2009). In more popular discussions – such as the queasy celebrations of *Financial Times* 'fast lane' columnist Tyler Brûlé above, or *New York Times* bestseller Thomas Friedman's 'flat world' (2005) – the free movement of stylised 'elites' and their business, political or cultural transactions took on almost utopian dimensions. Meanwhile, scholars of transnationalism, such as Alejandro Portes, foresaw also an extraordinary 'globalisation from below' (Smith and Guarnizo 1998), as lower status migrants would too seize on the potentials of multiple mobilities in a fast-evolving world (Papastergiadis 1999; Tarrius 2000).

The discussion was, of course, controversial, and remains so. After 9/11, but particularly after the global economic crisis of 2008, many of the higher hopes about globalisation have dissipated. Despite market forces, the control functions of states clearly continue to pose obvious obstacles to poorer international migrants. Labour, for other political and cultural reasons, is often not as mobile as other factors of production. Political scientists are also right to remind us that political and institutional factors – the drama of international relations, variation in national policy approaches, attempts to coordinate border control or the policing of movement and evolving modes of international governance – all pose significant constraints and boundaries on unfettered movement, at all levels of the economy (Freeman 1995; Zolberg 1999; Money 1999; Guiraudon and Joppke 2001; Waldinger and FitzGerald 2004).

Interestingly, though, these qualifications of globalisation do not normally extend to the upper realm of migration. We are in fact much more familiar with the processes, policies or politics shaping unskilled migration, than those behind highly skilled or professional migration. To be sure, when the focus turns to the movement of highly educated and talented migrants, many assume there are likely to be fewer barriers of all kinds to these forms of global 'free movement' and the phenomenon is, thus, still growing in magnitude and significance. To put it in the parlance of global city theorists (Castells 2000; Taylor 2004), the virtual 'space of flows' on which new global networks of capital and trade are based must also be peopled by mobile persons who, it is assumed, are embodied by the world's cadre of international highly skilled migrants (Beaverstock 2001). Some authors have even spoken of the emergence of new 'global elites' or a 'transnational capitalist class,' with unprecedented mobile and

1. Originally published in Michael Peter Smith and Adrian Favell (eds) (2006) *The Human Face of Global Mobility: International Highly Skilled Migration in Europe, North America and the Asia Pacific*. New Brunswick, NJ: Transaction. The collection was vol.8 of Michael Peter Smith's series on 'Comparative Urban and Community Research'. Republished with permission. An abridged version (2007) also appeared under the same title in the journal *Society*, 44(2): 15–25. The chapter reflects the intense three years of meetings (2002–5) at UCLA organised for the working group I founded on 'The Human Face of Global Mobility', funded by a cross-UC initiative launched by the Comparative Center for Global Research. Further details on the personnel, meetings and working papers of the group can be found here: http://www1.international.ucla.edu/ccgr/mobility. asp. With thanks to my co-convener, Miriam Feldblum, my co-editor, Michael Peter Smith, and all the participants in the group.

cosmopolitan lifestyles, presaging dramatic social change to the national order of things (e.g. Sklair 2001). These heroes of global free movement – top-ranked employees of multinational corporations, international finance, IT companies, scientific research agencies and so on – are, presumably, the human hands, brains and faces behind the impersonal dynamics of global markets and the transformation of the nation-state (Sassen 2006). Their continued mobility, meanwhile, is routinely cited as the most accurate index of global inequality when contrasted with the growing constraints face by immobilised lower classes (Bauman 1998; Wagner 1998; Kofman 2005; Berger and Weiss 2008; Castles 2012; Mau et al. 2012).

These popular images call for scholarly investigation. The lives and experiences of these frequent-flying, fast-lane, global elites are better known from the editorial and marketing content of glossy magazines or corporate brochures than they are from solid, social science research. And behind the image of global elites lie other socially differentiated realities. In fact, the skilled and educated among the globally mobile, also include: students, nurses, mid-level technical and clerical employees, ambitious or adventurous upwardly mobile middle-classes, migrants from a range of intermediate developing states, and many more it would be hard to describe as 'elites.' In addition, there are those international migrants, of course, who are counted as unskilled migrants in official statistics because of their menial employment destinations after migration but who may have attained high levels of skill and education in their home countries or who have had to move for political reasons. A whole range of types of international migrants, in fact, are not captured by the two stylised images counter-posed at either end of the social spectrum: high-flying corporate elites versus desperate, poverty-stricken labour migrants and asylum-seekers. Our chapter, which introduced a path-breaking volume on the subject (Smith and Favell 2006), thus, seeks to open up a whole new field of research that may begin to fully document the many worlds of international highly skilled, educated or professional migration, as well as integrate the various types of theory and methodology needed to account for these phenomena.

Lacunae in global and transnational studies

Academically speaking, there has been relatively little 'human level' research on the diverse, yet prototypical avatars of globalisation in the skilled, educated or professional categories. More broadly, there remains a call for more micro-level, phenomenological studies of the everyday reality of 'global mobility,' despite the avalanche of writings on globalisation in all its forms. Looking back, the first generation of global studies in the 1990s was nothing if not sweepingly macro in its scope and argumentation. Rarely did authors consider the 'human face' that might be found behind the aggregate data and structural logic that led to the recognition of global cities and global networks in the work of Sassen, Castells, Taylor, and others (see Loughborough University's *Globalization and World Cities* project, for a panorama of this work).[2] The grounded ethnographic work by authors such

---

2.   Their excellent website can be found at: http://www.lboro.ac.uk/gawc.

as Beaverstock (2002, 2005), or Yeoh and Willis (2005) on corporate employees and business networks was, in fact, exceptional in relation to the general body of work in urban and regional studies on global cities.

A second-generation of global studies heeded, to some extent, the limitations of the macro-bias with more 'agent-centred' studies in anthropology, human geography and sociology on transnational networks, transmigrants and the new 'spaces' of the transnational global economy and politics (e.g. Pries 2001; Conradson and Latham 2005). The move to 'locate' transnationalism was a positive one, not least in showing how global processes always have locally inflected and mediated expressions (*see*, i.e. Eade 1997; Gupta and Ferguson 1997; Scott 1997; Smith and Guarnizo 1998; Smith 2001; Burawoy *et al.* 2000; Glick Schiller 2005). On the other hand, transnationalism in these debates, was, more often than not, presented normatively as a blow against the capitalist, nation-state centred order of things, emphasising transnational actors' resistance and freedom in its conceptualisation of 'agency.' Building on this, a new wave of social theory focusing on 'mobility' then sought to dissolve the category of 'society' itself (Urry 2000), celebrating a variety of new forms of social, gendered or transnational 'citizenship' beyond the nation-state supposedly enjoyed by mobile and networked populations (Benhabib 2002). Writing in this vein often tended to be thin on empirical research and reify the lives and cultures of such groups in order to make theoretical (and political) points rather than empirical ones. Even more problematically, the cultural and critical theory leanings of much of this work led to a complete disconnect from quantitative studies of migration by demographers and economists as well as institutional studies of the politics of immigration by political scientists and sociologists.

This may be less of a problem within the more specific field of migration research where truly interdisciplinary work using multiple methods has been more common. Here it is the contrast between the volume of interest in research topics that is most striking. On highly skilled migration, there were one or two early attempts to define a broad research agenda (Cornelius *et al.* 2001; Iredale 2001) alongside the more policy-targeted work of demographers and economists (Borjas 1989; Salt 1992; Findlay 1995; Lowell 1996; Peri 2005; Martin 2012). The quite considerable body of empirical work during these years on transnational communities, meanwhile, focused on documenting the transnational strategies and resources of more typically lower-end labour- and asylum-seeking migrants – and, hence, those more likely to be subject to control and restriction. Many convincing transnational studies of this kind can certainly be cited: of Mexicans (Smith 2005; Smith and Bakker 2007), Ecuadorans (Kyle 2000), Moroccans (Bousetta 2000; Salih 2003), Turks (Faist 2000), and Senegalese (Riccio 2001). Such work has been usually driven by an ethnographic interest in ethnicity and inequality and linked to the ways ethnic networks and cultures facilitate the economic and political actions of relatively powerless or underprivileged actors, as well as providing the means for evading the control efforts of states (Portes 1996; Levitt 2001).

As we saw, the transnational theorists pointed to these findings as 'globalisation from below' (Portes 1998). But the migrants they portray are also those *more* likely to be subject to control and restriction. A better test case of the supposed liberalisation of human mobility in the world economy then, would be international professional, highly skilled or technical migrants whose mobility is linked more to choice, professional career and educational opportunities. That is, of those who face the *least* barriers linked to exclusion, domination or economic exploitation. Their experience may reveal not just how far liberalisation can go under ideal conditions but also reveal, in sharp relief, what persisting limitations there might still be to a completely unfettered global economy of mobility. As everyone is aware, such migrants are clearly the most likely candidates to fill the role of genuine 'transmigrants' (Glick Schiller *et al.* 1995), privileged as they are by the global economy, recruited by nation-states still keen to slam the doors on many other forms of global migration and endowed with the kinds of levels of human and social capital most likely to facilitate the real construction of global lives in new national destinations.

The lack of research on these migrants, as well as the empirical weaknesses of many other debates on transnationalism and global mobility, has left a clear opportunity for a new kind of integrated research agenda on global mobility and the international migration of the highly skilled. The political economy of globalisation can too easily become an overly structural and faceless account of the capitalist logics of global investment and labour demand. Yet, without a structural dimension – without an emphasis on the constraining nature of global economic and demographic trends or of efforts to control and/or liberalise migration flows by governments – the imagined 'agency' of migrants and movers also becomes an insubstantial, de-contextual, reified thing. Both lead to an idealisation of social processes we need to understand from *both* a structural and agent-centred viewpoint. To a large degree, their agency depends on just how distinct this form of highly skilled migration is from other more constrained kinds – in both top-down demographic and policy terms and bottom-up ethnographic ones. There is little or nothing to connect these two sides – partly because they are likely so separated by the distinct theories and methodologies that the different generations of global and migration scholars have used.

Our goal, then, must be to transcend the methodological barriers that leave demographers, economists, political scientists and ethnographers of international migration unable to fully integrate their diverse macro, meso and micro interests – indeed, unable to even *talk* to one another. Methodological divides have ensured there is rarely an attempt to cross-reference their distinctive contributions: the highly structural quantitative analyses of demographers and political economists; the explanatory process-based approach of comparative policy and institutional analysts; and the qualitative approaches based on ethnography, interviews or life-stories. Qualitative work is rarely in an authoritative position by itself to generalise its case study or small sample findings; a quantitative backdrop is always necessary. Explanatory efforts to isolate causal factors determining political processes still, always, benefit from interpretative work about the meanings and contexts of specific actors. Yet macro-level analyses equally, should always be carried through meso-level institutional mediation to micro-level insights into an appreciation of the very real consequences of these structures on the lives of actual individuals and groups. Context, too, is vitally important, particularly in the context of regional integration: the discussion below spans work on Europe, on North America, and on the evolving trans-regional context of the Asia-Pacific.

The organisation of the following discussion reflects these concerns. Along the way several key themes are highlighted. These take the form, in turn, of first challenging assumptions often made in global and migration studies about highly skilled migrants and migration; and then, second, of rethinking three of the major regional contexts in which such migration is taking place. Together, the discussion identifies the components of an ambitious research agenda, reflected in some of the works cited as well as more recent contributions to the research field.

Challenging assumptions

Despite its visibility as a conceptual reference point in migration studies there has, as we have argued, been a lack of research on international skilled and professional migration; both from the experiential point of view of migrants and in terms of a more structural analysis of demographics and politics. What we find instead in much of the global and transnational literatures is an explicit, or implicit, discussion about highly skilled migration, often lodged in studies of other kinds of migration or global phenomena, in which a series of 'assumptions' about this kind of migration can be found. These assumptions may be true or false but all need to be interrogated in the light of concrete empirical studies. Working through *five* such assumptions then, in fact, leads to the emergence of a new, more-specified and more-differentiated research agenda on 'elite,' 'professional,' 'highly skilled or 'highly educated' international migration – in all its forms.

A polarised world of 'elites' and 'proles'?

The first assumption concerns the question of who and what constitutes highly skilled migration. Authors routinely refer to higher-end migrants as 'elites,' usually as a stylised contrast to the disadvantaged, lower-class, typically ethnically distinct, putatively 'proletariat' migration that is the concern – for other political reasons – of most researchers in the field. The dichotomy of highly skilled versus unskilled migration glosses over the stratifications within and across categories as well as significant mediating factors such as the gendered nature of some highly skilled movements like nursing (Hardill and MacDonald 2000; Kofman 2000). Further, the dichotomy obscures the hard realities of the many highly skilled, educated migrants who cross borders as unskilled migrants leaving their unconvertible human capital, as it were, behind at the border. Finally, the terminology – if dependent on education, profession and migrant status – can leave out key populations; particularly international students who, perhaps more than nearly all other groups, are the quintessential avatars of globalisation. This will determine data sources as much as the theoretical arguments that might be made from them (Batalova and Lowell 2006).

The explosion of literature on migration is linked – quite rightly – to concerns with global inequalities, development and the exclusionary workings of ethnicity and race. But with these kind of concerns uppermost for most researchers, it has not been well equipped to study or understand other forms of apparently 'less disadvantaged' migration except through a dismissive ('they are all just elites') lens. The globalisation literature cemented this two-sided view of international migration with the social polarisation theme promoted by the leading scholars of the global city (Friedmann and Goetz-Wolff 1982; Friedmann 1986; Sassen 2001). The image of high-rise corporate downtowns populated by a sharp-suited global elite service industry workforce, but serviced by an army of lower-class immigrant cleaners, shop owners, domestic home help and sex workers, is a powerful one that rings true in many contexts. A graphic example is Kloosterman, van der Leun and Rath's study (1998) of the two sides of the tracks that bifurcate the *Bijlmer* suburb of Amsterdam. But it belies many other forms of migration and work in a mobile global mobile context that would be better seen as 'middling' in class terms (*see* Conradson and Latham 2005). All forms of migration require thorough empirical investigation, and one of the effects of globalisation has, in fact, been a downward 'massification,' through the middle-classes, of international migration opportunities linked to careers and education such that it is by no means only those who might be thought of as 'elites' who are able to move. Moving beyond the image of free-moving elites brings to the fore differential questions of mobility and incorporation for these other highly skilled migrants (Blitz 2014). As Batalova shows (2005), evidence suggests that highly skilled foreign-origin workers in the USA are systematically underpaid – i.e. discriminated against – in relation to the qualification levels of domestic workers.

The real action in international migration is, in fact, to be found in the broad middle of society. Highly developed societies typically have fat, bell-shaped, class structures that mean the massification of hitherto 'elite,' professional, career opportunities internationally – particularly within an integrating Europe – become the acid test of whether transnational mobility beyond the nation-state is, in fact, a sociologically significant reality. It may turn out so-called 'elites,' who have opted to move internationally under present conditions of globalisation, are often not at all from elite backgrounds but often provincial, career-frustrated 'spiralists' (Watson 1964) who have gambled with dramatic spatial mobility in their educations and careers abroad to improve social mobility opportunities that are otherwise blocked at home. Now, as in the past, 'real' elites tend to have routine access to international travel and experience through family connections and schooling – as well as a far better chance of success in their chosen career at home – without needing to propel themselves individually on an international stage. They are not necessarily the ones using new educational opportunities such as the EU's *Erasmus* and *Socrates* schemes (King and Ruiz-Gélices 2003). In research on different graduate student nationalities in the USA, Szelenyi (2006) shows the less-developed the country internationally, the more the elites of this country tend to choose to move internationally in their educations and careers. Favell (2008a) argues it is no surprise that the North Africans and Latin Americans one meets in finance or the media in London are from relatively elite backgrounds – one *has* to be an elite in these countries to have the chance to move. This is not the case with the nationals from the more highly developed countries where mobility opportunities are more broadly shared and where people who move internationally have made much more marginal, risky, career decisions compared to those in nationalised careers from welfare-states with stable pay-offs at home. They may have been free to move out in order to move up but this, as always, has costs; it is not for the risk-averse or psychologically conservative and will not be chosen if they already have easier, elite-based access to success in their own societies. As more countries move into the ranks of the highly developed then, we are likely to observe more migrants of a modest, middle-class backgrounds amongst the highly skilled as the economies of their home countries afford more broadly distributed opportunities for migration.

A demand-driven migration?

Demographers and economists have often battled to assert the demand-driven nature of much migration to suggest it is much less of a threat than politicians suggest (Piore 1979; Fischer and Straubhaar 1996). Yet, clearly, it is much harder to defuse the relevance of such sending conditions regarding lower-end, poverty- and conflict-related migration. As a corollary, one might assume higher-end migration much more perfectly fulfils market demand. Consequences follow from this assumption: that skilled migration is always 'selected' by the receiving country; that it is governed by efficient not sub-optimal politics; and that such skilled workers are not replacing or suppressing the job opportunities of natives. If this view were true it would reflect migration at its Pareto-efficient best, operating in a George Borjas-type neo-classical world (Borjas 1989).

This neo-classical worldview can be challenged in several respects. First and foremost, it can be shown in the case of skilled, no less than unskilled, global migration the macro-economic logic of market forces is mediated by institutional barriers and channelling mechanisms (Freeman and Hill 2006; Money and Zartner Falstrom 2006). State policies regarding entry and exit, the granting or withholding of visas and work permits and the establishment of numerical quotas on certain categories of migrants, set the permissions and constraints under which various regimes of immigration are established by receiving nation-states. A good example is the complicated politics behind the number of skilled workers allowed H-1B visas, the principle legal channel of temporary labour migration in the USA. While the politics of low-skilled migration may be more visible and contentious, both highly skilled and unskilled migration are shaped by distinctive policy processes and political structures (Cornelius et al. 2001).

It is within the context of such mediating state policies and political processes that other institutional-level factors challenge simplistic notions of global demand-driven migration. For example, Lavenex's (2006) work on the competition state and global governance structures, shows how the World Trade Organisation's (WTO) negotiations on General Agreement on Trade in Services (GATS) have reshaped international migration of this kind. Corporate and professional steering mechanisms also structure the opportunities and constraints experienced by skilled professionals who wish to advance their life chances by transnational migration.

These include, but are not limited to, intra-corporate transfer policies, the existing division of labour within transnational corporations, professional information networks and social connections and corporate and professional training regimes. All of these institutional-level policies and practices shape the contours of skilled global migration, often in ways quite different from Pareto-optimal assumptions about market efficiency. Finally, neo-classical assumptions about the efficient operation of markets ignore the normative and ideological constraints that may affect the dynamics of the global mobility of skilled migrants. For example, the norms of multinational corporate cultures, as well as the prevailing national cultures of sending and receiving societies, may affect processes of global mobility in different ways. Such conceptions can help create subtle forms of social exclusion or set internalised limits on the vision and imagination of potentially mobile subjects.

So is there an efficient global competition for skills in which countries with 'points based' quotas come out on top (Freeman 1999; McLaughlan and Salt 2002)? This is a familiar refrain from 'immigration reformers' seeking to make the case for more high-end immigration, usually at the expense of the putatively less desirable. The argument is made US immigration policy must place greater emphasis on attracting skilled migrants if a nation in a global era is to efficiently compete for the skilled with such countries as Canada and Australia whose skill-based approaches are the models. No one would claim the Byzantine US system was a model. It has created a plenitude of peculiar migration channels sustained by vested client interests and a veritable alphabet soup of visa categories. But it might be argued US immigration policy reflects more of an efficient *political* process than an efficient economic competition for skills (Money and Zartner Falstrom 2006). Politics, here, clearly matters.

Brains keep on draining?

In decades past, highly skilled migration raised the spectre of 'brain drain' from developing countries with resulting enormous attendant literature and policy debate. Since then highly skilled and educated mobility has become far more complex and diversified with the 'brain drain' assumption challenged on numerous fronts (Straubhaar 2000; Stark 2004). From 'brain drain' to 'brain gain' and 'brain circulation,' in a competitive global economy, the migration literature and popular press now underscore the new patterns in which engineers and services can be more easily found, and more cheaply located, in regions previously identified as 'brain drain' origin regions, especially in China and India. This, in fact, is the very root of the 'outsourcing' phenomenon now so prevalent in the global economy.

Again, a simple equation lies behind the supposed distinctiveness of higher-end migration: that the highest skilled are freer to move; that they are more than able to carry away with them the benefits of their own human capital; and, hence, that they automatically represent a 'brain loss' for their countries of origin. The 'brain drain/gain/circulation' question has, in fact, become the biggest single area of research on skilled migrants (for reviews, *see* Batalova and Lowell 2006; Szelenyi 2006). This is because of its sharp policy implications in developing countries in terms of economic development and political stability. Such fears of the developmental costs of 'brain drain' assume a zero-sum game in which sending countries lose as the developed world creams off the brightest and best. But is it always the brightest and best who move?

As global movement becomes easier, in fact, this need not be the case. In a more global world the brightest and best might, in fact, be potentially hyper-mobile entrepreneurs who are now able to stay at home with the new emergence of technical industries in developing countries or, when they do move, use transnational networks and contribute to the economic development of their countries and regions of origin. In fact, these new patterns are already evident. Whereas in the past thirty years large numbers of Asian students came to the USA for graduate study, today many more, including top students, are staying in Asia for their higher education. More Asian scientists, schooled in the USA, are returning home. In particular, the Chinese and Indian governments are investing heavily in university systems and hi-tech and science infrastructure in their respective countries; as are American companies by opening up engineering facilities and laboratories in these countries (Saxenian 2006). Chakravartty (2001) contrasts the everyday experiences of Indian entrepreneurs from Bangalore, who are very successfully developing that region as a high-tech global metropolis, with the often unhappy, mid-level educated Indian migrants to the USA who now come to the USA on H-1B visas because they were not 'good enough' to break into the elite schools and best high-tech operations in India.

A second problem with the zero-sum assumption underlying the 'brain gain/drain' debate is this formulation ignores, or, at best, understates, the frequent back and forth movement of migrants, ideas, knowledge, information and skill sets, that are now a routine part of contemporary transnationalism. These back and forth movements are part of a pattern of trans-local interconnectivity that many skilled migrants, like their unskilled counterparts, maintain to their regions and localities of origin (Cheng and Yang 1998). In fact, their relative affluence and privileged status may, in fact, encourage them to be more transnational in outlook and allegiance, contrary to individualist expectations. Although very different in other respects, the evolving ties of, for example, international students in the USA, high-tech workers from India in Silicon Valley and workers in a multinational corporations in Finland and Sweden, lead to continuing kinds of global circulation and incorporation. The implications of this complex interconnectivity clearly weaken the 'brain drain' hypothesis. Zhou and Tseng (2001) show in the case of Chinese high-tech and accounting business in Los Angeles, that these types of network-based translocal connections implicate the economic growth of LA with the activities of overseas investment networks from Taiwan and Hong Kong, thereby contributing to the economic benefit of both sending and receiving locations rather than just draining the sending locales. This kind of scenario may be coming the norm rather than the exception.

'Controlled' immigration versus 'frictionless' mobility?

International migration studies have benefited considerably from geographers and critical theorists reminding them that geographical mobility in all its forms is something they should consider part of the subject, even when it is not officially classified as typical state-to-state 'immigration' (Hardwick 2007; McNevin 2014). One of the benefits of this has been the recognition that those forms of spatial mobility – moving from place *a* to place *b* – that get classified as *im*-migration are so classified for *political* reasons. They signal the historical state monopoly on freedom of movement that was one of the key emergent 'pastoral' features of the modern territorially-defined nation-state and its growing bureaucratic powers to 'penetrate' society and, thus, shape society in its own image (Torpey 2000). Without sovereign political regulation of movement – in the shape of citizenship and naturalisation laws, welfare rights for members only, and the control and classification of border crossing and re-settlement – migration would just be people moving around (Joppke 1998b; Zolberg 1999). Typically, among those moving across the borders of territorial 'container' states, there are the immigrants (e.g. refugees and the economically desperate), who are moved by forces beyond their control; and then there the others, most generally thought of as 'international travellers' (e.g. tourists, businessmen, expats, exchange students, retirees) who move by choice alone. The first form – the story goes – elicit categorisation and strict state control of numbers; the second melt through borders, untouched by the state, their uncapped numbers reflecting only market demand, commercial interests and the dictates of economic and human capital accumulation. In a globalising world, these are the masters of collapsing time/space coordinates, to echo the much-discussed thesis of Bauman (1998) on mobility as the new index of global stratification. The clarity of the stark official lines between the two are such that even many questioning scholars do not put into doubt the construction of such routine bureaucratic legal classifications.

Trends in global mobility support these distinctions in some senses but go quite against it in others. On the affirmative side, as Lavenex (2006) points out, even after two successive decades of control rhetoric and all kinds of efforts at international police cooperation, there is evidence of new forms of mobility slipping through the immigration category. There is, she argues, a reinforced disassociation of regulated or unwanted migration, as officially viewed, from other forms of international mobility that can be allowed, even encouraged and institutionalised, under various international business and trade agreements such as the GATS. In some ways, these latter forms of migration are becoming more like trade in goods and capital, transformed into a temporary mobility that is less visible on the state's radar. Tourist migration and the business migration of temporary 'non-immigrant' workers or 'posted' service personnel are cases in point, illustrating the multiple new ways temporary mobility is possible. In cases that are more politically visible, such as the outsourcing of skilled services, national attempts to enact 'clawback' measures at the national level have been blocked by WTO regulations. These are part and parcel of the process of supra-national private governance that authors such as Sassen (1996) and Strange (1996) have discussed in terms of states 'losing control.' These new developments do not mean the national governments have ceased to be a player in the politics of skilled labour migration but rather that they are no longer a clearly controlling player.

Look closer however, at the apparently clear disassociation and the two kinds of mobility are approaching each other. Migration is clearly not what it used to be given the ever-increasing diversity of channels and opportunities. Many of those moving into and through these mobility channels are not rich white folk from Europe and America but Indian software engineers, Central and South Americans able to get six-month tourist visas to the West, or Koreans and Chinese using US immigration loopholes to get their children educated in the USA and on a fast track to US citizenship. These movements are using visa categories available to anyone who can get enough money together and who happens to come from a US- or Europe-approved country; all can only be thought of very ambiguously as 'immigration', although 'temporary' in these cases can mean anywhere between three months and five years. However, this time dimension can often lead to a kind of immigrant experience. The experience of an international traveller is often assumed to be that of a 'sojourner' and no more; a 'frictionless' mobility characterised by an absence of any kind of meaningful encounter or incorporation in the host society. But, in fact, highly skilled migration brings with it both different mechanisms for entry and distinctive challenges and opportunities for incorporation. It is not a frictionless mobility but rather a differently tracked mobility with its own costs and constraints.

While the unchallenged transnational sojournment of the highly skilled and educated might once have been seen as evidence of the state losing control, this is no longer so as migration bleeds into mobility. There is a *re*-regulation of these new forms, such that immigration is arguably becoming a *less* important focus of control than the new global mobility. In the aftermath of 9/11, it was increasingly these *other* forms of movement/mobility that became the big state security concerns. There was a growing perception the 'alien threat' might come more from the ranks of students, tourists and business travellers – hitherto a massive blind spot in border scrutiny – rather than official immigrant categories. After all, 'true' immigrants are subject to much more stringent screening than others coming through on a waiver basis or study visa and they have also, of course, expressed a desire to become (for example) American rather than simply exploiting mobility opportunities as free floating global movers. The new control technologies of the American state have since 9/11 been targeted at these now suspect movers, turning to bio-metric monitoring and multiple new layers of bureaucratic paperwork, as the fulfilling of an almost Foucauldian effort in bio-power to cleanse a globalising world from 'terrorists' (De Genova 2010).

The cooperative attitudes of other major world players indicate states might seek to outdo each other technologically in their enthusiasm for these new forms of bureaucratic 'governmentality', The compliant stance of the EU – the USA's supposed nemesis in international relations – is hard to square with the continent's extraordinary transnational commitment to freedom of movement as a legal right for European citizens. In fact, the USA is exploiting some of the EU's experience of new modes of control as this has shifted inwards to the welfare state and policing of access to the interior society rather than the border (Brochmann 1999; Guiraudon and Lahav 2000). Although formal 'immigration control' still ends the moment the agent stamps your passport and lets you by, current developments suggest states are becoming more concerned with heretofore unregulated elites and the affluent in other ways. The US state is clamping down on tax loopholes for the hyper-mobile and looking to enforce more citizenship responsibilities. A side effect of the new security environment appears to be an increase in governments' technological capacity and motivation to monitor all transnational activities, whether it be the financial transactions of religious charities with alleged 'terrorist' connections, or squeezing expats and permanent residents on long-term, hidden tax obligations to the US state. At the other end of the scale, 9/11 licensed new powers for states seeking to escape the binding constraints of international law; arrogating human rights in cases when 'terrorists' can be tried outside of the law for reasons of 'national security.' The spectre of 'stateless persons' being held indefinitely in legal quarantine outside of international law is an Arendtian reminder of how vulnerable all so-called 'post-national' populations still are to the claims of the sovereign state.

Human capital: All you need to succeed?

The all-purpose lubricant of the (allegedly) frictionless world of elite global mobility is human capital in which the 'human' part is measured in terms of internationally recognised qualifications and quantifiable talent and is every bit as universal and inalienable as human rights. Economic capital might indeed matter less in a truly neo-classical market for migration in which talent and enterprise would drive the migration calculus and where internationally recognised education or experience (rather than the right family background) would be the one way ticket to global elite status (Borjas 1994). Again, an economist's theory here does not match empirical realities. It turns out that faster social and spatial mobility, based on the 'universal' metric of skill and talent, does not, in fact, remove the challenge of incorporation. Culture and particularistic know-how still impose all the difficulties of integration on these kinds of migrants. Moreover, even if mobility itself has become a form of privileged capital, not all other forms of capital are as mobile as elite status is supposed to guarantee.

Social networks (i.e. who you know and how this can help you) might be the secret of success globally as much as nationally or in your home town but the real power of the global mobility myth stems from its individualist faith; the idea the human capital of education can take you where you want to go regardless of social structure or social reproduction. The globally talented are supposed to be able to make it work anywhere, even without local connections or embedded networks. One assumption of this kind would be that the human capital-rich face fewer problems of discrimination, exploitation and/or exclusion from receiving societies than do other foreigners.

On many straightforward issues regarding attitudes to migrants, this is still likely to be true. However, the very idea of a world uncritically open to the globally mobile is premised on the idea, promoted by some theorists of mobility (i.e. Urry 2000), that societies (for the highly mobile at least) no longer exist – and therefore that non-spatially located forms of capital have essentially interchangeable values in different locations. Were this the case, the obstacles encountered and submitted to by other migrants less rich in capital (the less talented) – forces of integration, such as national norms, sanctions for difference or hierarchies of insider/outsider status manifested as privilege and exclusion – should simply not apply here. Those with human capital mobility are thought to be able to exist 'outside' of society and yet be effortlessly able to integrate when they choose to in their host destination. Integration, for them, would somehow escape the coercion of a sociological process and become more of an *à la carte* set of individualistic choices in which one can always out-trump the imposition of any particular norm or constraint by an appeal to post-national rights or one's mobility right of exit/entry.

Evidence on this question needs to be qualitative. We must look at the experiences of some of the most mobile, talented, human capital-rich migrants on the planet and see just how they get along in their chosen host societies. High earnings, comfortable unquestioned status and accelerated professional success through mobility are not uncommon. These migrants are indeed choosing their own paths and garnering rewards from corporate or educational systems that reward universal rather than local standards. However, the picture muddies a great deal over time. It is rare to find selective integration really works. We find instead their power to choose only means they are choosing to stay *out* of local societies (Bozkurt 2006). They may be very functional parts of the cities in which they live in terms of economic consumption but they have no voice politically or socially. Their ability to change or impact the places to which they have migrated is limited. This might seem a negligible drawback for the globally mobile until we remember over time 'everyday' issues of housing, taxation, health, child-care, schooling and retirement, all require some engagement and negotiation with local social structures that inevitably favour insiders. Failure to master the local rules of the game, in fact, may lead to a subtle exclusion from the benefits of long-term residence. Freed of the less pressurised, coercive adaptation imposed on less capital-rich immigrants, they may remain constrained to live the expensive life of the permanent expat exploited by the city around them and forced, instead, into a less than easily sustainable transnational lifestyle that debars them from any meaningful 'settlement'.

For the highly mobile, the work environment is at least meant to function as well as a place where human capital is recognised and convertible. Here too, however, mobility has costs as well as benefits. Skilled migrants, because of foreign status, can face 'glass ceilings' in professional advancement not commensurate with education, experience or professional attainment (Csedö 2008). Because of the precariousness of the H-1B type immigration status, it can be argued skilled migrants to the USA have frequently been exploited by employers having become the equivalent of 'high-tech *braceros"* (Smith 1999). Batalova and Lowell (2006) find there has been a persistent downward transnational mobility of skilled workers in the USA and elsewhere – data that would be even more dramatic if it included the highly educated migrants forced to leave their human capital behind at the border when they cross borders as unskilled labour with no recognition of their experience or education. Flexibility and mobility can also equal vulnerability when there is a turn down or as age creeps up and family responsibilities begin to weigh. This can become a form of transnational 'fragility' of lifestyle, if the host state decides to start pressurising the non-integrated to clarify their residency status or commit themselves to cultural and linguistic rites of passage – as has been the case for expats in The Netherlands, for example, in recent years. Whatever else they are experiencing, their privileged formal position also does not prevent exploitation of precariousness in other ways. Skilled migrants from developing countries can still be easily racialised or ethnicised negatively. Expats can also still be stigmatised culturally for non-conformity to local ways. The 'post-national' mover in the USA, for example, can also be viewed as 'un-American' if they too openly affirm a lack of interest in long-term immigration and citizenship in the country.

In his incendiary manifesto on offshore living for the globally mobile, libertarian Ian Angell recommends living like a 'new barbarian' as a way to escape the burdens and responsibilities of nation-state membership in a fast globalising world (Angell 2000). Like master thief Robert de Niro in the classic Michael Mann movie, tax-and citizenship-evading barbarians have got to be able to take everything they own or care about and run the moment they feel the *Heat* around the corner. But states are always catching up and globalising their reach too. US citizens abroad, for example, always have to file a tax return or they may lose their citizenship. This can turn into a nasty catch-22 for dual citizens or permanent residents when they then find they cannot voluntarily 'lose' their citizenship or residence status unless they can demonstrate they are not giving it up for financial reasons. In short, the offshore world in which it is easy to be a transnational barbarian may not really exist. Life outside of such everyday structures, as we have, is a life impossible to imagine (*see also* Andreotti *et al.* 2015). The permanently mobile and moving need to remember: live like a barbarian and you might just die like one.

Rethinking regional contexts

The second part of a research agenda in this field should be to look again at the major world regional contexts in which highly skilled migration is happening. This involves thinking through and differentiating the specific contextual research questions that might be asked in different global locations and in relation to different forms of mobility such as international students, workers in multi-national corporations and high-tech professionals. Across the board, one issue that immediately arises is the dearth of instruments to calculate and break down the magnitude of highly skilled migration *wherever* it is occurring. One immediate research agenda, therefore, concerns the question of what are the best analytical frameworks for ascertaining both the scale and specificity of such mobility. Research in future is likely to have to think creatively about combining official national and international sources with other kinds of investigative procedures.

Europe

In terms of free movement of persons, the EU is the global leader, as it were, of regional mobility possibilities, far outstripping those to be found within the regional groupings of the North American Free Trade Association (NAFTA) or the Association of South East Asian Nation (ASEAN, which sometimes meets as ASEAN 'plus four', i.e. the big four of Japan, South Korea, China and Taiwan). Only in Europe has a genuine freedom of movement of persons been legally institutionalised alongside the freedom of movement of capital, goods and (more problematically) services, although free movement arrangements exist within MERCOSUR (Common Market of the South). EU laws – which date back to the 1950s and Italy's insistence on framework for the migration of its workers to the North of Europe – have, over time, strongly undermined the state monopoly on free movement in Europe in the post-war period. The anti-discriminatory provisions about the employment of foreign Europeans have proven quite dramatic in European jurisprudence as they have been extended over time to non-economically active persons such as spouses, students and retirees. With the accession of thirteen new members from mostly Central and East Europe in 2004 and after, the issue took on a huge geo-political significance, as I explore further in Chapter Eight. Although new members states have usually faced a transition period before attaining full freedom of movement, the *de facto* free movement of East European workers, tourists and visitors in the West is in any event long established through existing bi-lateral agreements and the open call for labour in the construction, homemaking and agricultural industries in many countries. The logic is economic, the willingness to see the freedom of movement of labour alongside trade and services as an efficient factor of production that does not admit other political or cultural forms of restriction for national reasons. To block this in an integrated regional economy is now seen straightforwardly as an example of discrimination, hence unfair competition, in this frame.

Ironically, the dramatic institutional encouragement of free movement in Europe has not been accompanied by a dramatic rise in the small number of European nationals actually moving and resettling within Europe. Recchi (2006; 2013) sees evidence of a growth in mobility and it is certainly true that new forms of cross-border movement, linked to tourism, retirement, shopping and so on, have become more significant (Tarrius 1992; Benson and O'Reilly 2012). But in another sense there has been a decline in intra-EU mobility since the early 1970s as working class South-to-North migration has dried up. Other issues in relation to highly skilled migration might be suggested in terms of the encounter of non-Europeans with receiving host countries struggling with the long-term consequences of immigration. Much work has been done on the immigrant experience in post-war Europe but much less has been done on the putatively more privileged, skilled, educated or 'elite' migrants that have been a growing part of these flows. For example, where do the new migrants fit alongside older post-colonial immigrants in France or Britain? How are highly skilled Asians or Africans getting along in unlikely new multinational destinations such as Sweden or Finland? What are the reasons for the apparent failure of the so-called German 'green card' scheme to recruit highly skilled technical workers from India and elsewhere in recent years? In recent years, there has been a proliferation of new research projects, particularly PhDs, addressing these and other issues.[3]

North America

In a North American context, it is Canada that is often seen as the model for highly skilled migration policies rather than its dominant Southern neighbour. On this question, at least, Canada is typically seen as a globally open immigrant nation efficiently offering all potential newcomers access to the country through a rational talent and human capital-based evaluation of immigrant applications. In the USA, family- and ethnicity-based immigration has long trumped skills-based criteria, something often blamed for the declining quality of 'selection' in the USA. Reitz (1998) challenges the economic rationality of the Canadian model, but the model itself still seems to appeal strongly to reformers pushing for new high end immigration channels in countries such as the USA, Britain and Germany.

As shown by Freeman and Hill (2006), and Money and Zartner Falstrom (2006), the US system of multiple visa categories and the often distorting business interests behind these point to a far from rational economic construction of policy. They indicate the difficulties of reform, even in the absence of strongly organised public opposition, and the degree to which path-dependence seems to determine overall outcomes in the policy process. Curiously, these discussions suggest that highly skilled migration policy in the USA is a wholly self-contained national affair. National politics, rather than global economic pressures, drive the twists and turns of US immigration policies with key roles being played by high-tech employers, professional associations, pro- and anti-immigrant organisations and even associations of immigration lawyers. There appears to be little space in the US context for the kind of global legal/institutional influences signalled by WTO reforms, or by the importance of global multinationals as employers, as studied elsewhere (Bozkurt 2006). Further work on highly skilled migration in the USA might look to see how far US policy is also subject to the same kind of global economic pressures forcing other nations to give way on control over some forms of economic mobility.

The questionable self-containment of the USA is likely to be challenged in other ways as the consequences of new empirical trends begin to be felt. How, for example, will the more mobile 'brain circulation' and new global competition – evidenced by students staying in or returning to their countries of origin, especially

---

3.   I have been pleased to be involved as a mentor or examiner for several PhDs that have begun to fill in this agenda: Csedő (2009) on Hungarian and Romanian professionals in London; Kiriakos (2010) and Koikkalainen (2013) on Finnish migrations; Amadou Dia (2011) on highly skilled Africans and Asians; Morosanu (2011) on Romanians; Losada (2011) on students; van Bochove (2012) on highly skilled migrants in Rotterdam; Malyutina (2012) on Russians in London; and Yanasmayan (2013) on Turkish professionals.

India and China – reshape the landscape of highly skilled migration in the USA? Will the benefits of open-door policies on students and highly skilled migrants continue to accrue to the USA or are these influential factors in national GDP also mobile across borders? What new types of translocal geographical, business and social connections are likely to be forged between sending and receiving regions of skilled and business migration along the lines of those now established between Taipei and Los Angeles? Are these likely to be significant enough to constitute future new global city regions? Alternatively, might hostility towards highly skilled migrants grow as they increasingly become identified as 'un-American' in their footloose attitude to residence in America? What, in fact, are going to be the medium- and long-term effects of the US's new bureaucratic controls on international students which led to such a dramatic drop-off in new arrivals in the years immediately after 9/11? On the other hand, political science models, such as Freeman's well known adoption of Wilson's model of diffuse versus concentrated interests in policy explanations (Freeman 1995) need testing in other contexts and times. The politics of visa categories in the USA are a remarkable site of competition between business and societal interests as well as the different scales of local and national interest. Further qualitative studies of migrants in and between particular regions and industries – as suggested by Chakravartty's research project on Boston, New Jersey and the Silicon Valley (2006) – could be usefully developed.

Asia-Pacific

No work has done more to cement the image of Asian migrants across the Asia-Pacific as the paradigmatic transnational global movers than Ong's widely read work on *Flexible Citizenship* (1999), about Chinese transmigrants in the region. Further ethnographic work of this kind is still called for on the forms of migrant 'agency' displayed by Chinese, Korean, Japanese migrants and others using loopholes in national immigration regimes in the USA and Canada to create new kinds of networks and practices across the region. The social organisation of 'astronaut' and 'wild geese' families jetting between Asia, Australia and North America, is often extraordinary (Fan 2008; Ley 2010): for example, the strategic planning of pregnancies and schooling these families use to gain US citizenship for their children as well as access to the US educational system. The relatively invisible migration of long-term, overstaying visitors from Japan and Korea, and the dramatic role they play in their remarkable 'offshore' cultures in cities such as Los Angeles, is also a highly suggestive transnational topic.

Increasingly, Mexicans and Central Americans deserve to be seen in a similar light, as participants in a Pacific-Rim regional space, centred on porous economic opportunities for some categories moving in and out of the USA. This has developed into research on the increasing social differentiation within Mexican migration, for example, that looks at the movement of highly skilled Mexicans within migration systems between particular US and Mexican cities in a post-industrial context (Hernández-León 2004, 2008). Mexicans themselves count among some of the new 'high tech *braceros*' using various visa channels to work in the US economy (Alarcón 1999).

Research on migration in the Asia-Pacific or Pacific Rim needs, above all, to differentiate between sending countries in terms of their political relationship with the USA: the dominant defining factor in migrant flows between countries (Waldinger and FitzGerald 2004). The post-war emergence of South Korea, for example, owes everything to the privileged economic position given to the fast developing nation because of its geo-political significance in Cold War politics and the very easy forms of mobility established as a side effect of ever-increasing business flows between these unequal partners. Similar things can be said about US-Japanese, US-Filipino or US-Indian relations, and China has emerged as the biggest transnational question of all in the last decade. Sending countries have, however, found there are ways to subvert the dominated position they find themselves in by opening their arms to former expats and their children and seeking to pull back reserves of economic and human capital through the open business and education channels with the USA (Chavravartty 2001). Given the economic success enjoyed by India in pro-actively managing its migration relations with the USA, it is unlikely other notable sending countries will remain passive in their attitudes to the crucial national resource represented by their most mobile native populations. As a result of these various migration patterns, the changing character of inter-ethnic relations within transnational cities like Los Angeles and New York and the effects of these relations on future trends in global mobility along the Pacific Rim in particular, remain important research questions (Bozorgmehr and Waldinger 1996).

Conclusion

The empirical study of highly skilled, professional or educated migrants needs to be brought back on to research agendas in migration or global studies more attuned to thinking about immigration at the lower end of the labour market, and then usually in terms of minority race, ethnicities or cultures. Instead, there are manifold opportunities for new research topics seeking to resist the clichéd opposition of 'elite' and 'ethnic' migrants in a polarised global economy.

There are, for sure, different views on whether highly skilled migration is fundamentally different from unskilled migration as well as how the idea of 'global mobility' differs from more conventional notions of 'international migration.' Highly skilled movements are certainly looked upon more favourably in the context of liberalising international trade regimes: this fact only argues for their growing importance in national and international policy. The distinctive dimensions of national policies on highly skilled migration show, however, that it is just as important to differentiate among different instances and types of highly skilled migration, as it is to recognise differences between highly skilled and unskilled migration. Recent discussions mentioned here have suggested that the economic impact of highly skilled migration has moved beyond mere 'brain drain' in many contexts and is now encouraging 'brain circulation' to include new forms of global competition. There is also good qualitative evidence for thinking that, although mobility *across* and integration *into* receiving societies may differ quite considerably in its patterns to the experiences of less skilled migrants, these privileges far from remove the challenges and difficulties involved in global mobility and international relocation. As always, a research agenda such as this is an invitation to further research. Mobility is clearly a feature of the globalising contemporary world and mobility breaks open and extends many of our conventional ideas about international migration. What is needed now is a whole new range of empirical studies that can begin to fill out the research agenda sketched here.[4]

---

4. A large conference at the University of Middlesex in May 2012 for graduate students and young researchers on 'Highly Skilled Migration in the 21st Century' organised by Jon Mulholland and Louise Ryan – the culmination of their project (2010–12) 'French capital: a study of French highly skilled migrants in London's financial and business sectors' – was testimony to how much this research agenda has developed during the last ten years or so. *See* the website: http://frenchlondon.co.uk/dissemination/events/conference-on-highly-skilled-migration-in-the-21st-century. Another example, at which I was also a keynote speaker alongside Eleonore Kofman and Louise Ackers, was 'Women in Movement' organised by Ana Maria Gonzáles Ramos in Barcelona in February 2013. The agenda also converged broadly with a European Science Foundation conference (August 2010, in Linköping, Sweden) 'Home, Migration and the City: New Narratives, New Methodologies', headed by Ayonna Datta and Kathy Burrell, at which I was an invited speaker. *See also* Nohl, Schittenhelm *et al* (2014).

Chapter Seven

Social Mobility and Spatial Mobility

with Ettore Recchi

There is no subject more central to sociology than social mobility.[1] The degree to which modern industrialised societies enable talented, ambitious or lucky individuals to move up in status, or conversely the extent to which they reproduce inherited inequalities or social hierarchies from one generation to the next, are questions that still dominate much of the empirical mainstream of the discipline under the general rubric of stratification. Some of the most longstanding and detailed debates in the mainstream have centred on attempts to measure and distinguish the patterns of social mobility of European societies in comparison with others (Ganzeboom *et al.* 1989; Erikson and Goldthorpe 1992; Treiman and Ganzeboom 2000; Breen 2004). In particular, Europe is generally taken to be less fluid than America: the stereotype of the 'old world' of ingrained privilege, tradition, and slow moving social change, set against the 'new world' of opportunity, achievement and flux. Yet the emergence of a European society built largely on legal and institutional structures that facilitate free movement – that is, the spatial mobility of capital, goods, services and persons – poses an interesting question for a sociology of the EU. Has the spatial mobility enabled by the breaking down of barriers to movement and the notion of European citizenship – i.e. the establishment of a borderless labour market, sustained by the norm of non-discrimination to foreign nationals – also done something to the likelihood of social mobility within the European population? To put this in other terms: can people now move *out* of their own country in order to move *up* socially in relation to where they come from, and if so, who is moving and where are they moving to? It is not hard to see that operationalising this question might be one of the most direct and fruitful ways of conceiving of an empirical sociology of the European Union. Such a sociology might bring new facts and phenomena to EU studies, but also engage in debate with the mainstream of the sociology discipline, which has hitherto largely ignored the EU as a subject of interest.

In this chapter, we offer a guide to how the question of social and spatial mobility can be posed as part of a new sociology of the European Union. Doing empirical sociology is all about issues of operationalisation. One of the interesting aspects of studying social and spatial mobility in the EU lies in the

---

1. Originally published in Adrian Favell and Virginie Guiraudon (eds) *Sociology of the European Union*. London: Palgrave (2011): 50–75. Republished with permission. The chapter was conceived jointly by the two authors. Ettore Recchi was the principal author of 'Operationalisation 1' section and Adrian Favell the principal author of 'Operationalisation 2'. All other sections were written equally together.

necessary complementarity of quantitative and qualitative strategies of research. Designing a study that can genuinely work across national borders in Europe also highlights some of the great methodological problems in avoiding the pervasive methodological nationalism of cross-national comparative work. In our chapter, after a brief review of the relevant literature and theoretical concerns, we thus present first a quantitative, then a qualitative take on the subject, both based on original empirical research. A constructed survey on social and spatial mobility in the EU reveals both that Europeans do not move much spatially, and that there is not much social mobility associated with the building of a borderless Europe. Quantitative evidence in fact underlines the structural marginality of mobility in Europe today despite its visibility and apparent ubiquity. On the other hand, qualitative strategies, that home in on ideal type cases of mobility in Europe, reveal a different picture of Europe: of European Union as a process, in which hidden populations and crucial pathways to social mobility can be revealed, and in which marginal or improbable behaviour (in statistical terms) can have a much larger symbolic impact on the continent as a whole than its structural size would suggest. Both structure and process, and structure and symbolism, are a necessary part of the empirical sociology we propose.

Social and spatial mobility in Europe

Mobility and immobility in Western societies

Europe is not famous for its social mobility. Unlike the USA, which is widely seen as a society that enables anyone to become an American, make money, and claw their way up the social ladder, European societies have traditionally been preoccupied by subtle and not so subtle struggles over the reproduction of class privileges and distinctions: how one generation manages to transmit to its children (or grandchildren) status and class assets, and the social identities that go with these. On the structural side, ample evidence shows that Europeans, predominantly, are more fixed than Americans into their parents' status ranks and class positions, with Sweden being the only significant exception. Such a finding is corroborated by research carried out with different theoretical and methodological approaches (*see* Treiman and Ganzeboom 2000; or Breen and Luijkx 2004a: 49–50, for a guide to this). The story of upper-class children attaining upper-class lives and working-class children getting working-class jobs is still very common. Maybe even more relevant is the transatlantic difference in cultural terms – that is, in the solidity and capacity of class cultures to reproduce themselves across generations. Comparative cultural sociology has shown how class (in the USA and France) is cemented by distinct sets of values, morality, and sense of community among different classes and social groups in each country (Lamont 1992, 2000; on Britain, *see also* Willis 1981).

Likewise, spatial mobility. The USA is seen as a country where working, middle and upper classes routinely move around the country from job to job, often changing states and major cities of residence several times over a lifetime. Rates of cross-state mobility are historically set at around 3 per cent of all Americans per year (Theodos 2006); moreover, the dynamism of mobile talent, especially among the more educated, is seen as a crucial historical engine of the American economy. In Europe, if we may take it for a moment as a 'United States of Europe', rates of such mobility (across states, in this case nation-states) are dramatically lower – at 0.3 per cent of the population per year (Herm 2008), and Europeans move less *even* from region to region inside nation-states (at 1 per cent per year) than Americans across states (Ester and Krieger 2008: 2).

These at least are the conclusions one would draw from standardised definitions of class, occupational and residential mobility in the two continents. Social mobility in Europe has occurred but at rates typically lower than in the USA or other settler countries. Some of the most recent studies on this have added that in so far as mobility is growing in Europe, it is likely to be due to its immigrant populations (Breen and Luijkx 2004b: 401–402). This is an as yet untested, but intriguing, thought for linking social and spatial mobility in Europe. Human geographers meanwhile have, since the more marked social flux of the 1950s and 1960s, observed very interesting couplings between internal migration and social occupational mobility (Fielding 2012). Typically, the move of younger citizens from the rural or provincial location they grew up in to the metropolitan city is accompanied by an escalator effect: it is a spatial move linked to a social mobility outcome, like stepping on a moving escalator that sweeps you along and upwards faster than your peers. Talented and ambitious individuals have historically always moved out of the local worlds they live in, in order to move up: this was a key dynamic of industrialisation and the formation of the nation-state in the modern world (Weber 1976; Moch 2003), and it continues today – although arguably less now than in the more meritocratic and egalitarian era of *les trente glorieuses*, that is, the post-war boom years of continental European economies.

Reflection on this subject links back to classic distinctions in the structural functionalist literature (Merton 1957: 387–420; Gouldner 1957, 1958) between 'locals' and 'cosmopolitans'. According to this model, one of the key dynamics of modernising societies, as mentioned in the previous chapter, is 'social spiralism' (Watson 1964) as a way of moving up in society. Talented or educated persons from provincial places and social locations might feel blocked in their career aspirations if they stay local to where they come from: the social mobility ladder may be fixed, or only reproduce existing status hierarchies. To get on, then, they may choose to move out, spiralling up through society by taking a detour away from their place of origin. Residents in cities used as destinations for spiralist ambitions thus often display a tension between the ambitions of 'insider' locals – to move up through existing work structures that reward incumbency and patience – and those of 'outsider' cosmopolitans ready always to exit and move elsewhere if their efforts are not rewarded. This tension is a familiar feature of all kinds of locations under conditions of globalisation or regionalisation where (local) natives compete with (cosmopolitan) newcomers. In an apparently ever more mobile world, ingrained structures are often being swept away by the forces of change represented by those who moved. On the other hand, there is also a tension between the obviously visible examples furnished by qualitative studies – that focus on movers, migrants, transnationals, cosmopolitans, and so on, and the change they bring – and aggregate structural studies that often arrive at sceptical conclusions on the overall impact of the mobile minority on the broader established social order. Sadly, preferences in the debate and the conclusions that are drawn are often tied dogmatically to the methodological option that is chosen to study it, but it may be possible that both observations are truthful – in the manner of Schroedinger's famous cat in Quantum physics – if one approach is viewed as a snapshot of an emergent process, and the other a depiction of temporal background stability.

Analysing social mobility data

The mainstream sociology of social mobility tends to be carried out on a grand cross-national comparative scale. Variations in rates of mobility are thus studied across different national societal units, each assumed to be a more or less bounded, single systems coterminous with individual nations. This approach is driven by the available statistics and modes of generating data internationally which are typically linked to national state techniques of counting, measuring and classifying resident populations (in terms of income, occupation, education level, etc.). As a simple example, Table 7.1 presents the basic information on intergenerational class mobility in the five largest national societies of the EU15 (EU member states up to 2004). These tables are based on the European Social Survey, one of the largest scale independent representative surveys of the European population.

When examining a social mobility table, diagonal cells are the first to be inspected as they include those individuals who stay put in their parents' class. Overall, this corresponds to about one third of respondents in every country. The totals on the rows and the columns represent the overall class structure of each society, before and after generational change respectively. We can thus quickly note how, across the board, in each country there are now higher percentages in upper- and middle-class categories, and a lower percentage in the working-class

Table 7.1: Intergenerational social mobility in the five largest countries of EU15 (inflows, column %)

Germany	Class of destination					
	I–II	III	IV	V–VI	VII	Total
Class of origin						
Bourgeoisie (I–II)	29.3	13.6	20.2	9.3	11.4	17.3
Routine non-manual (III)	28.2	31.0	22.7	25.1	19.4	26.3
Petty bourgeoisie (IV)	11.6	12.5	28.6	8.3	11.8	12.8
High-skilled manual (V–VI)	16.5	21.8	15.3	28.8	25.5	21.7
Low/non-skilled manual (VII)	14.4	21.2	13.3	28.6	31.9	22.0
Total	27.6	27.3	8.6	17.0	19.5	

N=2350

Table 7.1 (continued)

France	Class of destination					
	I–II	III	IV	V–VI	VII	*Total*
Class of origin						
Bourgeoisie (I–II)	31.8	9.9	12.9	11.0	7.0	*16.2*
Routine non-manual (III)	18.0	17.4	11.2	13.6	9.8	*14.9*
Petty bourgeoisie (IV)	20.2	19.5	41.4	10.7	20.5	*20.0*
High-skilled manual (V–VI)	10.8	20.1	6.0	19.5	11.6	*14.5*
Low/non-skilled manual (VII)	19.3	33.1	28.4	45.2	51.2	*34.4*
Total	*28.8*	*23.3*	*9.2*	*21.6*	*17.1*	

N=1258

Britain	Class of destination					
	I–II	III	IV	V–VI	VII	*Total*
Class of origin						
Bourgeoisie (I–II)	30.7	20.6	21.9	10.6	11.9	*20.7*
Routine non-manual (III)	18.7	20.0	15.6	15.9	10.3	*16.5*
Petty bourgeoisie (IV)	15.5	11.6	24.4	11.2	12.8	*14,2*
High-skilled manual (V–VI)	16.8	20.6	18.1	27.1	22.1	*20.2*
Low/non-skilled manual (VII)	18.3	27.1	20.1	35.3	42.9	*28.3*
Total	*30.1*	*27.7*	*8.9*	*9.4*	*23.8*	

N=1799

Italy	Class of destination					
	I–II	III	IV	V–VI	VII	*Total*
Class of origin						
Bourgeoisie (I–II)	20.5	9.3	7.2	7.0	0.9	*8.5*
Routine non-manual (III)	26.3	20.9	11.1	14.1	10.2	*16.1*
Petty bourgeoisie (IV)	27.6	34.6	47.3	33.8	32.6	*35.9*
High-skilled manual (V–VI)	10.3	10.4	6.3	9.9	10.7	*9.4*
Low/non-skilled manual (VII)	15.4	24.7	28.0	35.2	45.6	*30.1*
Total	*18.8*	*21.9*	*24.9*	*8.5*	*25.9*	

N=831

Table 7.1 (continued)

Spain	Class of destination					
	I–II	III	IV	V–VI	VII	*Total*
Class of origin						
Bourgeoisie (I–II)	22.8	7.9	4.9	2.5	2.8	*7.8*
Routine non-manual (III)	17.3	14.3	4.4	3.1	4.7	*8.2*
Petty bourgeoisie (IV)	23.2	24.3	51.7	33.1	22.7	*29.2*
High-skilled manual (V–VI)	11.0	12.9	6.3	14.4	9.9	*10.4*
Low/non-skilled manual (VII)	25.6	40.7	32.7	46.9	60.0	*44.4*
Total	*20.7*	*11.4*	*16.7*	*13.1*	*38.1*	

N=1226

Source: European Social Survey, 2004

category. This change has been found to be principally driven by the structural transformation of the occupational structure of Western societies over the past decades, which has enlarged the size of middle and upper classes and reduced that of the bottom of the pyramid. Because of these structural changes, upwardly mobile people are in larger numbers than people moving the other way around. As a matter of fact, in all countries there are higher proportions of working-class children who make it to the bourgeoisie than offspring of the upper class in working-class occupations. This is especially the case in Southern Europe, where the transformation of the occupational structure has been more marked in the late twentieth century. In Spain, for instance, 25.6 per cent of the bourgeoisie is made up of working-class offspring, while only 2.8 per cent of the non-qualified working class stems from upper-class families. In other terms, sons and daughters of the working class are 'more than sufficient', so to speak, to fill in the ranks of manual occupations in post-industrial societies. This leaves out the question of immigrants, who are, symptomatically, not included in these tables – an issue to which we will turn momentarily.

The highest rate of social immobility is found among low/non-skilled workers: in France and Spain, where more than half of them (51.2 per cent and 60 per cent, respectively) perpetuate the social class position of their family of origin. That about one third of Europeans are intergenerationally immobile is also shown in a larger scale comparative study on social mobility in Europe (Breen and Luijkx 2004a). This study also reveals that the percentage of upwardly and downwardly mobile individuals has remained substantially the same in the last three decades of the twentieth century, with the exceptions of Ireland and Poland, where it increased substantially, and Hungary, where in fact it declined. Overall, however, there are two widespread long-term tendencies in the social mobility regimes of European national societies, that counter to some degree the perception that there is limited social mobility in Europe: first, towards higher levels of social fluidity – that is, a reduced association between parents' and children's social class (Breen and

Lujikx 2004a: 73); second, to a 'high degree of similarity among countries [..] in all the measures of mobility' (ibid.: 49). Such a convergence in patterns of social mobility is rather unique to Europe, making national boundaries less significant both substantially and analytically. Nevertheless, on all these measures, it can be shown that there is substantially more mobility overall in the USA than Europe.

One of the problems with such analyses is, fairly obviously, that they assume closed social systems of mobility and class structure, congruent with the idea of a bounded nation-state-society. Immigrants' mobility can only be measured *within* the system – i.e. by comparing, say, the first with second and third generation. This says nothing about how the family is doing relative to the country where they came from – which might be a far more salient issue for them, particularly subjectively. It is now routine in other research areas to question the bounded form of the nation-state-society as a given closed social order. Globalisation has been all the rage in social theory, and transnationalism 'beyond the nation-state' a dominant focus of attention, in most European sociology at least. Furthermore, we would never dream of arguing that economies and the multiple transactions that sustain them end at national borders – even if it is true that nearly all international measurements of aggregate societal outputs – of the kind for example produced by organisations such as the OECD – are still measured in stylised, bounded, nation-by-nation GDP terms. But what of cross-border mobility, hence mobility compared *across* societies and *across* categories of individuals moving in and out of stable national boxes? Nation-by-nation data itself reproduces the fiction of there being bounded national societal systems; only what lies within the national box makes sense, the rest is noise; people who move across borders by definition mess these units up (Joppke 1998b).

The problem of methodological nationalism

This problem lies under the general heading of the pervasive methodological nationalism found in the social sciences, in particular in empirical studies that rely on state-derived technologies of counting populations necessarily bounded by conventional politically defined territories. Some scholars have recognised this problem and proposed programmatic solutions (Beck 2000; Wimmer and Glick Schiller 2002). However, the question of social mobility is not one they pose. Meanwhile, the discussion on this point in sociology has been mostly theoretical, reducing it to a conceptual issue and neglecting concerns on how to deal with it empirically (exceptions are: Breen and Rottman 1998; Berger and Weiss 2008). The anthropologists' case studies and the social theorists' metaphors and problematisations are not enough. What is really needed are some empirical analyses that work through ideas of how to operationalise a genuinely transnational approach to social and spatial mobility.

Spatially mobile Europeans form a clear test to the usual cross-national comparative findings on social mobility in Europe. There are two reasons. One is the structural possibility that spatial mobility will alter the relatively stable patterns of social mobility and social reproduction in the Europe of national societies. The second has to do with the transformation of the categories with which units of society (i.e. classes) are recognised and rendered comparable. Formal comparative work often misses this aspect of temporal and categorical change, a point that has been emphatically developed by Abbott (2001). In moving across societies, spatially mobile Europeans might also be messing the clear units of migrants, natives, residents, workers and classes by which other comparative assessments are made: mobility may lead to categories changing, emerging or disappearing. So, if we could somehow compare a subset of European 'movers' (EU citizens who have chosen to live and work abroad in another EU member state) with the majority of 'stayers' (the average national population sampled by conventional social surveys), we might be able to ask new questions about flux and mobility in Europe, both structurally *and* conceptually. There is good reason to think that mobile Europeans are having a substantial impact on the continent, even when statistics suggest they may number as little as one-in-fifty of the population. In fact, official figures on intra-European migration suggest that only 2 per cent of European nationals live in another EU member state, and only about 4 per cent have an experience of living abroad (Vandenbrande *et al.* 2006: 14). As seen in Table 7.2, numbers of EU citizens in different countries range from highs of almost 10 per cent in Ireland, 6.4 per cent in Belgium or 4 per cent in Austria or Sweden, to barely more than 1 per cent in Italy, The Netherlands or Denmark, and less than 1 per cent in Greece, Hungary and Poland (for an elaboration, *see* Zaiceva and Zimmermann 2008). Moreover, EU-born foreign residents (i.e. intra-EU migrants) invariably number between about a third and a quarter of the totals of non-EU born residents (i.e. traditionally perceived 'immigrants').

Yet the small minority of international mobile Europeans lies at the heart of conceptualisations and idealisations of European citizenship. They are highly symbolic of some of the ideas of a unified Europe conceived by the founding fathers of European integration. More concretely, economic theories of European integration – particularly policy-driven analyses of how a more fluid and dynamic European economy can be built in the wake of the EU's 2000 Lisbon Agenda (i.e. Sapir *et al.* 2004) – suggest that more mobility is likely to be a good thing for Europe as a whole, both in (re)deploying workforces where and when they are needed within a single market, as well as politically helping people identify more with the idea of Europe. Thought of as rational actors, people who chose to make the big move abroad might well be expected to be selected for their frustration at home, hence be talented individuals looking for more opportunities, and more willing to take risks. This positive selection is often postulated under pure economic conditions of the kind that the removal of barriers to free movement in Europe has supposed to ensure: the basic economic models for this selection process under 'free' labour market conditions (Borjas 1989). If they are the folkloric 'brightest and best', they are more likely to be a population that would kick start again social mobility effects in Europe or at least be a potential vector for economic growth (*see* Borjas 1999 for an application of his theory to an integrating Europe).

Table 7.2: Proportion of foreign-born residents in EU member states (% of total population, end of 2006)

	Born in the EU	Born outside the EU	Total
EU15			
Austria	3.8	7.5	11.3
Belgium	6.4	6.3	12.7
Denmark	1.5	3.7	5.2
Finland	1.1	1.7	2.8
France	2.7	6.8	10.3
Germany*	2.1	4.5	6.6
Greece	0.7	4.4	5.1
Ireland	9.6	0.7	10.3
Italy*	1.1	3.1	4.2
Luxembourg	23.8	4.3	28.1
The Netherlands	1.7	6.3	8.0
Portugal	1.0	3.5	4.5
Spain	1.0	4.5	5.5
Sweden	4.3	7.9	12.2
UK	2.7	6.3	9.0
EU12			
Bulgaria	0.1	0.2	0.3
Cyprus	4.9	8.6	13.5
Czech Republic	1.4	0.6	2.0
Estonia	0.6	11.0	11.6
Hungary	0.3	1.1	1.4
Latvia	1.1	11.0	12.1
Lithuania	0.3	3.8	4.1
Malta	-	-	-
Poland	0.4	0.8	1.2
Romania	0.0	0.0	0.1
Slovakia	0.7	0.1	0.8
Slovenia	0.6	6.0	6.6

Source: Labour Force Survey data (2006)
*Proportion of foreign citizens

Hypotheses about social and spatial mobility in Europe

From these kinds of considerations, we can now move to formulating empirical hypotheses that might assess the impact of EU free movement opportunities on spatial and social mobility within Europe. In particular, we elaborate on the class position and the patterns of social mobility of movers in a context of free movement opportunities.

Firstly, we might expect spatial mobility to be class insensitive (Hypothesis 1). That is, the likelihood of moving from one country to another within Europe should not be influenced by individuals' social class. This is because open and universal EU freedom of movement laws (for EU citizens) should have levelled the playing field, evening out the kind of bias of mobility towards elites supposed to be a feature of more general global mobility – in effect democratising intra-EU migrant opportunities. It would therefore be creating the kind of ideal conditions under which the social spiralists – talented and dynamic movers who self-select as the 'brightest and best' – might be able to use spatial mobility as a social mobility strategy regardless of class background.

Secondly, EU movers are expected to experience no discrimination in their occupational opportunities (Hypothesis 2). They are not like traditional immigrants who face discrimination or glass ceilings according to their 'ethnic' non-European origins. Rather they enjoy European citizen status, on a legal par with natives in the labour market; moreover, they are ethnically and culturally proximate, and often relatively invisible as migrants. Downward career mobility – which is in fact frequent among immigrants from less developed countries – should be quite exceptional among EU movers taking jobs abroad in the Union. Given the converging levels of salaries in Western Europe, moreover, possible downward class movements at migration are not justified – on average – by significantly higher monetary returns in the host country. At the very least, EU movers should at least be able to preserve their pre-existing class positions, if not do better – otherwise there would be no economic or symbolic rationale to their mobility.

The analyses that follow will control to what extent these *ex ante* suppositions, predicated on a rational choice view of spatial movements driven by the maximisation of socioeconomic benefits in open, pan-European free labour market, describe the real trajectories of class mobility of intra-EU migrants.[2] However, as the focus of this chapter is on social mobility achieved through occupation in a foreign country, EU movers without any job experience in the host country – such as students, non-working spouses, pensioners – are left out of the analysis.

Operationalisation 1: A quantitative approach

How might we control these hypotheses? An obvious move would be to construct data that can be directly related to the kinds of data sets being crunched on social mobility in cross-national comparative terms. The required data have to describe the class and/ or occupational status of movers before and after their international move(s).

---

2. The dataset used in this chapter merges two similar sources: EIMSS (for movers) and ESS (for stayers) for Germany, France, United Kingdom, Italy and Spain. *See* Recchi and Favell (2009), in particular appendix A, on this methodological strategy and the data sources used.

To answer these questions, an original survey was needed. Survey data always has to be found or generated. In this case, nation by nation statistics and studies were not much use. Studies on foreign and migrant populations are often not comparable across nations, due to the very different way of classifying, counting and observing foreigners, immigrants and minorities in different countries. A classic example is the difference between the data produced on these populations in Britain and France, discussed extensively in Chapter Five. Even restricting the issue to foreign residents clearly distinguishable by nationality of origin, a second problem arises with foreign European nationals, in that as populations they are generally far too small to generate adequate sample sizes from the largest scale national surveys that are made. Even national Labour Force surveys – the widest existing surveys in the continent – have sample sizes that are too small to fill the cells with enough foreign European residents from even the largest neighbouring countries. Generally a minimal number of cases – a good rule of thumb would be 1000 – would be needed for reliable samples. If EU movers are 2 per cent of the population we would need a random sample of 500,000 residents to find 1000 of them. These kinds of sample sizes are far beyond the capacity of even the biggest national survey operations. Some surveys at this point give up on the criterion of representativity and start generating cases by non-random means – i.e. snowballing or hunting down foreigners through networks or localities with known concentrations. Others content themselves to generalise about immigrant groups from very small numbers.

The PIONEUR project (Recchi and Favell 2009) adopted a different and original strategy, generating the European Internal Movers Social Survey (EIMSS). EIMSS turned out to be one of the largest ever original comparative surveys made on immigrants. How was this data collection achieved? The PIONEUR project in fact developed an innovative procedure based on the probability of finding foreign national residents in the host country through their first and family names. It thus collected information on the rankings of the most popular first and family names from each country – for example, in Spain: Pedro, Carlos, Ramon; Lopez, Hernandez, Garcia, and so on – discarding names also likely to be found amongst nationals of the other nations in the study. It then sampled these 'most likely' names in publicly available telephone directories, to find the requisite number of Spanish in Britain, Germans in France, and so on, generating lists of telephone numbers for the survey operators. Despite some obvious problems, such as the heterogeneity of immigrant origins in countries such as France (where there are many 'Italian' names among French citizens), or problematic frequencies in border regions (where cross-national mixed backgrounds are common), the method in fact worked in terms of the high proportion of telephone answers made by people who were indeed foreigners of the nationality targeted. A total of 5,000 30-minute telephone interviews across the five countries were thus completed using a battery of questions about class background, migration motivations, cultural adaptation, identification with Europe, political behaviour, media consumption, and so on. At the core of the interviews lay the spatial/social mobility question as perhaps the key sociological issue tied to the process of European integration. Data from EIMSS provides some structural answers to the hypotheses posed above.

The short answer to the two hypotheses posed is that neither of them – sound as they may seem in rational choice or economic theory terms – are borne out by the systematic evidence, with only the second being partially fulfilled. In relation to Hypothesis 1, in terms of class positions before leaving their country of origin, upper-class individuals are over-represented and members of the working class are under-represented among EU movers (Table 7.3). Across the board, the figures for residents in class category I-II (bourgeoisie) is higher for resident migrants than natives of the country (the left hand figure in italics). Upper- and upper-middle-class movers reach their highest number in Italy: around 45 per cent of British, French and Germans in Italy are drawn from class I-II. Only Italians and Spanish in Germany (about 45 per cent and 60 per cent respectively) are exceptions to this rule, fitting in larger number with the traditional immigrant profile as low-skilled or manual workers. High-skilled workers leaving their home country are particularly unusual, although there are cases: Italians (in France, Germany and Spain), Spanish (in Germany), and British (in Germany, where some go as posted workers, and Spain, where they move as retirees). Overall, though, the free movement regime appears to widen the opportunities of social reproduction of the higher social strata rather than creating a comparable avenue of social mobility for all. Intra-EU migration is thus not notably democratised by the removal of borders or the economic convergence of Western Europe.

Regarding Hypothesis 2, looking at patterns of career mobility when changing country of settlement – here considering only respondents who had a job before and after moving – a similarly cautious set of conclusions emerges. Overall, with little variation by nationality and country of residence, more than two thirds of EU movers (71.3 per cent) did not change social class when taking up their first job after migration (Table 7.4). Moreover, four out of five (80.7 per cent) held the same class position in the transition between first and current job in the host country. Contrary to our hypothesis, though, the work-with-migration transition – i.e. transition no. 1 in Table 7.4 – is in fact associated with some risk of downward mobility. This is the case for 14.3 per cent of respondents, while 8.5 per cent are upwardly mobile. However, in line with the hypothesis, the subsequent career in the host country is much more likely to be on the upside (12.8 per cent) than on the downside (3 per cent). Apart from this, the overwhelming majority of occupational shifts for intra-EU migrants occur within the classes to which they belong, qualifying these shifts as either progress within an already class-tracked career or fine-grained changes that hardly alter the overall class structure in which they occur.

Interestingly, though, elsewhere in our analysis an escalator effect does emerge for one national destination for younger migrants – Britain – which, given the disproportionate importance of the capital in terms of migrant destination in this country, corroborates what is frequently claimed about London as a 'Eurocity' enabling a new kind of mobility for ambitious, young European movers (Favell 2004). This is an aggregate finding that would be worth further exploring with qualitative case study data – a classic methodological rationale for the quantitative-then-qualitative strategy being presented here.

Table 7.3: Class position of EU stayers and movers (before their movement) by country of residence and nationality (column %)

	Nationality									
	Germans					British				
COR	*DE*	GB	FR	IT	ES	*GB*	DE	FR	IT	ES
Bourgeoisie (I-II)	*27.6*	57.7	41.9	44.4	30.9	*30.1*	38.3	53.1	46.1	33.5
Routine non-manual (III)	*27.3*	28.8	32.4	35.9	38.8	*27.7*	30.2	24.5	36.8	27.1
Petty bourgeoisie (IV)	*8.6*	2.5	5.4	8.6	9.7	*8.9*	3.2	7.5	4.8	6.8
High-skilled manual (V-VI)	*17.0*	8.0	14.9	6.1	14.5	*9.4*	19.8	9.5	6.1	16.3
Low/non-skilled manual (VII)	*19.5*	3.1	5.4	5.1	6.1	*23.8*	8.6	5.4	6.1	16.3

	French					Italians				
COR	*FR*	GB	DE	IT	ES	*IT*	GB	FR	DE	ES
Bourgeoisie (I-II)	*28.8*	37.2	34.3	45.4	41.1	*18.8*	29.7	35.9	2.9	25.0
Routine non-manual (III)	*23.3*	42.4	39.5	35.1	29.2	*21.9*	31.2	18.2	14.5	25.0
Petty bourgeoisie (IV)	*9.2*	2.3	4.7	3.9	9.4	*24.9*	6.9	6.1	5.8	15.8
High-skilled manual (V-VI)	*21.6*	7.6	13.4	5.9	13.5	*8.5*	7.9	16.7	21.0	16.8
Low/non-skilled manual (VII)	*17.1*	10.5	8.1	9.8	6.8	*25.9*	24.3	23.2	23.2	17.3

	Spanish				
COR	*ES*	GB	FR	IT	DE
Bourgeoisie (I-II)	*20.7*	28.6	39.9	31.1	19.5
Routine non-manual (III)	*11.4*	31.3	20.8	34.4	18.3
Petty bourgeoisie (IV)	*16.7*	1.8	6.6	4.6	3.0
High-skilled manual (V-VI)	*13.1*	9.8	12.6	10.6	16.5
Low/non-skilled manual (VII)	*38.1*	28.6	20.2	19.2	42.7

Note: 'Stayers' data in italics
Source: ESS 2004=7464 and EIMSS=3671
(COR = Country of Residence)

Table 7.4: Patterns of intragenerational class mobility of EU movers (%)

		Transition 2 (from first to current job in host country)				
		Immobile	Non-vertically mobile	Upwardly mobile	Downwardly mobile	Total
Transition 1 (from last job in home country to first job in host country)	Immobile	62.1	1.8	5.8	1.7	*71.3*
	NV mobile	4.2	0.9	0.6	0.1	*5.8*
	UP mobile	6.7	0.5	0.2	1.1	*8.5*
	DOWN mobile	7.7	0.4	6.1	0.1	*14.3*
	Total	*80.7*	*3.6*	*12.8*	*3.0*	*100.0*

Note: Reference is made to social classes and forms of class mobility as defined in Erikson and Goldthorpe (1992)
Source: European Internal Movers Social Survey, N=2180

Overall, then, the picture we get from the quantitative survey is one of little change. The European Union appears not to be having significant mobility effects, with one or two unsurprising exceptions. Indeed, it appears to be having a reverse effect to one that might be hoped for by the builders of the EU: enabling *more* not less elite social reproduction in the continent. Advocates of migration and mobility here might find the results rather gloomy. We cannot presuppose the dynamising of the European economy, or the beneficial selection effects of migration if in fact the integration of the continent is only benefitting the most privileged (on this, *see* Fligstein 2008; Haller 2008). If we stop here with the study, we might well conclude that the well-known social theoretical claims about globalisation and mobility – that the ability to be globally mobile increasingly indexes social inequality (Bauman 1998) – is in fact unproblematically true. This would be an empirically substantiated finding that would go well beyond the speculative rhetoric that has mostly sustained this particular critique of the globalising and regionalising world.

Operationalisation 2: A qualitative approach

A quantitative approach can tell us a lot about the structural background and aggregate effects of Europe in change. It allows us to question appearances and determine what is and what is not statistically meaningful in a range of behaviour or values that may or may not be changing with European integration. As we can see with the example above, it invariably takes a sceptical line towards hypotheses that might otherwise be hastily reached as conclusions through untested theorising. This, at least, gives us a reason as to why an empirical sociology of European Union is likely to look quite different to the outpouring of social theory of Europe and European integration that has become quite visible in EU studies in recent years. Empirical methods and operationalisation here can make all the difference.

Aggregate structural analysis also typically reveals norms: that is, statistical averages which indicate the most probable and hence most stable forms of social behaviour or values in a given society. Variation from norms is measured from the statistical mid-point, and the odds of a deviation lessen dramatically the further one moves from the norm in any standardised distribution. Societies or social aggregates pictured this way have fat 'bell curve' shaped structures that point to how society reproduces itself through most recognising behaviours or values that conform to the 'fat' average part of the distribution (i.e. what the mainstream does or thinks), rather than the much more scarcely populated extremes. Visualising society, as conventional statistics does, in terms of a 'bell curve' distribution – something which technically speaking is inevitable when variation is enumerated, as it is conventionally done, in terms of non-scalar degrees of variation from the statistical norm – thus inevitably links recognisable norms (statistically significant results) to an explanation of how societies work. A certain bell-shaped distribution of values, behaviour, or social positions, locking in upper limits (i.e. variation) on mobility can, as the next step, then be assumed as the cause of the stable functioning of the society in question. One might describe such a society as well 'integrated': this kind of pattern becomes a definition of societal 'integration'. Wild or disruptive deviations from these norms might threaten disintegration or revolution. But statistically represented, they are inherently, numerically insignificant observations. Mostly, then, theories about societies in this account function well, when everything is 'in its right place'. Building a theory atop the most stable norms and probabilities as the core *modus operandi* of empirical sociology is thus bound up, in classic sociological theory, with the doctrine of 'structural functionalism': associated above all with Talcott Parsons, but present already in the sociology of Emile Durkheim. As well as being an inherently conservative vision of society, there is also clearly a blindspot in this form of theory about radical possibility of change to the system – i.e. the possible impact of populations that are located at the margins or tail end of the bell-curve distributions.

Structural functionalism, which had a massive impact on the social sciences during their most confident modernist, developmentalist phase in the 1950s and 1960s, is thought to be a largely redundant theoretical doctrine nowadays. Its logic though is inescapable in any structural analysis that posits some kind of stable reproduction of social structure – through aggregates such as 'culture', 'institutions', 'norms' or 'ideology' – and it has thus crept back into much recent social and political science under the heading of 'new institutionalism', particularly the fashion for explanations using the term 'path dependency'. Path dependent analyses that stay close to the concept's origins in institutional economics (i.e. North 1990; Pierson 2004) are not necessarily functionalist in their logic. The lock-in effect of social reproduction in the accounts of these pioneering authors is specified, in actor-centred terms, in the discrepancy between long- and short-term pay offs to actors thinking about changing course. Yet as the term has been used more and more metaphorically by others, referring to self-reproducing forces such as norms, ideologies or discourses that cannot think and act, it often takes on a functionalist character (*see* Barry 1971, or Coleman 1990: Ch.1). In EU studies today, popular institutionalist and constructivist arguments claiming to be 'sociological' thus often use implicitly functionalist logics.

There are obvious problems here. An analysis based on norms and statistical significance is clearly important in an account of stable structures and reproduction, but it is not well equipped to detect change, process or flux. In looking only at the aggregate distributions of mobility or occupations in intra-EU movement, we may, in short, be missing a lot of the most interesting stories. Critiques of mainstream bell-curve statistics often point to the disproportionate impact in reality of marginal actors or events – the 'black swans' that cannot be predicted by aggregate statistical methods (Taleb 2008). This can be related to the analysis of marginal international movement in Europe vis-à-vis the dominant patterns of staying put in national locations of origin. Actors stepping away from dominant norms – particularly those associated with stable nationalised patterns of, say, educational and career attainment, or family life – may embody the process of a different Europe in the making, and be pointing towards a ferment of change not detectable in the aggregate analysis. Plus, as in many studies dependent on problematic statistical information, there is a great 'hidden population' problem associated with spatial and social mobility across borders. In part this is a category problem (Abbott 2001) of the target population moving in and out of the groupings – the usual, stable, nation-by-nation categories – with which statistical comparisons might be made. Yet, look on the streets of major European cities, and we seem to be able to see in abundant numbers the people we think embody the new European social and spatial mobility. Official numbers and surveys of foreign populations – particularly relatively invisible ones such as mobile Europeans, who are ethnically and culturally proximate, and able to come and go as they please – might thus be missing in some if not most of the data. Another possibility is that it is precisely the marginality of the movers in the 'long tail' (Anderson 2008) of the European population distribution that has given them unique social powers to succeed in a Europe in flux. As pioneers they may find rich and unique pay offs precisely in being and doing differently to the mainstream norms, although as their numbers rise, there will be a threshold effect and hence diminishing returns relative to the mainstream.

As suggested by our Hypothesis 2 above, EU free movers are interesting as a case of international migration which *prima facie* has nearly all the inbuilt disadvantages of typical migration processes taken out. With political and legal barriers down, and cultural or ethnic disadvantage and exclusion at a minimum, they should in theory be avatars of a Europeanised economic selection process that is undistorted by these other (typical) factors in the workings of international labour market – a perfect market, so to speak. That we don't necessarily find this in the quantitative analysis might be a question of their marginal numbers, rather than a problem with the theory as such. Their quantitative marginality suggests rather a qualitative 'ideal type' based approach. What if we were to empirically go out and look one by one for prototypes of the ideal European mobility proposed in theory, and then assess these different exceptional cases in relation to the mainstream European norms (of dominant national values, immobility, stable class positions, etc.)?

The ideal type approach to empirical work has its own venerable tradition in Weberian sociology. The theoretical construction of such cases also can be used profitably with the logic of counterfactual analysis – that is, searching precisely for what might be the outcomes under theoretical conditions explicitly different to the actual dominant situation as established by empirical statistical analysis (Hawthorn 1991).

This was precisely the methodological logic in *Eurostars and Eurocities* (Favell 2008a). We know that free movers in Europe are numerically scarce, yet their theoretical and symbolic valence in thinking about the sociological impact of European Union is undeniable. Moreover, go to any of the major cosmopolitan centres of Europe, and we find them in quite large concentrations – a whole new generation of mostly young, mobile, ambitious or adventurous Europeans using their free movement rights to live and work abroad, regardless of whether they are showing up in official statistics or surveys. Eschewing a conventional quantitative approach, I sought rather to 'construct' my empirical sample by actively seeking out the most likely individuals who might embody the propositions about spatial and social mobility in Europe, its social spiralism and transformative effects on a possible new European society. I went looking, in other words, for the most likely 'highly Europeanised' Europeans in the most likely 'highly Europeanised' places, eventually settling on the foreign EU populations in three of the major hubs of internal European migration in Western Europe: Amsterdam, London, and Brussels. Each of these cities can lay claim to being a 'capital' of Europe: in cultural, economic, and political terms, respectively. I sought to put flesh and blood on the theoretical construct of an ideal type European 'free mover', among a population that ranged from the young, freely mobile, individual movers in their 20s, through to older people in their 30s and 40s who might now be settling into cosmopolitan single or family lives in the three cities.

The study used a variety of snowball and networks-based sampling techniques to find this population, varying interviews by age, gender, nationality, marital and professional status. Given the fact that so many of these foreign residents are missed in the official possible 'sampling frames' – such as national survey statistics or foreign consulate registries – it also sought to juxtapose the found cases with studies of populations made by commercial organisations interested in selling products or services to this target population of foreigners: for example, 'expat' magazines or websites. Through this variety of statistical sources on the population, a broader picture of the overall moving Europeans emerged, from which particular under-represented categories of individuals in each city was then sought in a second wave of interviews. This method, for example, allows the correction of stereotypes of the European foreign population in any given city: a case in point being the conception that all the foreign European residents in Brussels are EU employed 'eurocrats' or corporate 'expats'. The technique follows a distinctly francophone current in social research that emphasises 'constructing the object of research' as a key empirical step, and never taking the empirical object as 'given' or immediately 'readable' from given preconceptions (Bourdieu *et al.* 1968; Champagne *et al.* 1996). It is nevertheless an eminently empirical, rather than social theoretical strategy – an issue that it is mistaken in much of self-styled 'social constructivism' in the Anglo-American literature, which is often predominantly only conceptual in its approach.

By thus constructing the object of research, a total of sixty primary interviews was completed in the three cities, alongside over five years of intermittent participant observation, numerous secondary interviews, and extensive documentary research about the foreign EU population in the three cities. The small *n* of interview cases could, by the constructivist methodology by which the sample was made, claim a certain kind of representativity of this elusive population. Moreover, the long interviews were conducted using a narrative 'life history' approach – asking questions in the manned of an oral history – which has been promoted by maverick social stratification scholars such as Bertaux (i.e. Bertaux and Thompson 1997), precisely as a way of capturing process and flux in social mobility structures that are missed by the dominant quantitative approaches. *Eurostars and Eurocities* also foregrounds a 'phenomenological' or 'grounded' technique of research, that is, allowing actors to speak for themselves in order to inductively reveal their everyday *habitus*: the kinds of everyday social practices and habits they embody as Europeans today (Glaser and Strauss 1967). Indeed the book simply reproduces many of the *in situ* interviews, to offer a direct window into the lives and experiences of these prototypical free movers.

The study thus discovers phenomena that remain largely undetected in the quantitative survey. It also puts flesh and blood on those exceptional currents in spatial/social mobility that were found in the broader aggregate data. The most prototypically rational, individualistic, social spiralist EU movers emerge qualitatively as those young, ambitious, career-minded, highly educated career women from the South of Europe, who have deliberately moved to the North West of the continent as part of a planned international career. They sought to differentiate themselves from their peer group back home, opting out of more reliable, mainstream, but heavily gendered national career and marriage paths, that would lead to professional and family stability much more quickly had they stayed. In describing her reasons for moving, Nicole, a mid-twenties IT programmer, who moved to London from the North of France, speaks for many of these women:

> 'There was a big sense of frustration about the personal development thing. The Latin countries are absolutely not flexible on the work market. I can do anything I want there but it's not going to change my situation. You are just young, so your opinion doesn't count. They say you don't have any experience – even though you have! – and I was working crazy hours, and being paid peanuts, no rewards. And still you live in Paris and it is very expensive. At the end of the day I didn't study five or six years for that [...]'

Following the perfect logic of an economist's theory of European integration – where the 'brightest and best' of young EU citizens would just 'get on their bike' to go look for work and a better life across national borders – Nicole also speaks for the droves of young French people, in particular, who abandoned an economically depressed

France during the mid to late 1990s to go to the global Eurocity of choice, London, in search of their fame and fortune (Favell 2004; Ryan and Mulholland 2014). London's role as an escalator region is thus also corroborated in the qualitative findings, which are able to personify structural trends that showed up in the quantitative analysis (*see also* Ryan and Mulholland 2013).

Beyond this data, though, we begin to find things not in the quantitative survey. Social spiralism *is* found to be a feature of many of these younger movers to the three cities. Many have come from relatively obscure provincial regional origins, choosing a path out of their own country as an alternative to the well-trodden elite national path through their own national capitals. Frustration at home can be the motivation for a chancy move abroad, that gives new impetus and, eventually, mobility through the liberational effect of what can thus be called a de-nationalising experience. European free movement has effectively created a new kind of regional 'freedom' in the world, uniquely available in terms of European citizenship status rather than elite privilege. European movers discover themselves as individuals, learn to free themselves from norms they learned as nationals, to play around and instrumentalise their identities, to try out new social pathways. This perhaps accounts for why among the most unique movers there is an important selection effect that accentuates talented people able to think differently or take risks, as the economic theory of European integration predicts. Franz, now a highly successful banker in London from Germany, with experience also working in France and Spain, pinpoints how this works:

> 'Why are people moving? My first move was from Frankfurt to Paris. I was looking for a job in Paris, because it would mean I am not number 15,907 of Germans in Frankfurt looking for a job as a banker [...] I think I was quite unique there, to say, listen, I quit my job now, I take my little car, I go away and see what I can do.'

Their difference is valued in the new location, as long as they are relatively scarce. Moreover, with all these moves it is an important element that they are movers between relatively close and easily accessible locations. Many of the Eurostars also emphasise that a key to their European move is the ability to go 'home' at weekends – perhaps to catch up with a doctor or dentist's appointment, if not sometimes to take some washing back to mum. Cross-national commuting and split households also become a possibility. This points to a new, Europeanised mode of social and family organisation, enabled by ease of mobility on a regional scale, particularly through new high-speed train links and abundant low cost intra-European airlines.

A further self-selection operates with people using mobility to opt out of the standardised mainstream values that impose themselves on lives lived only on local scale. Family life is changed irrevocably by mobility and distance. For some, the choice of a 'third' international city becomes the way that couple of different nationalities reconcile their difficult to balance private and professional lives across borders. Their children will necessarily grow up as cosmopolitans outside of familiar national structures, with new forms of social capital, but also perhaps disadvantaged relative to traditional nationalised elites. For others, mobility is associated with an individual move out of conventional family norms. Hence the high prevalence in my sample of childless couples, gay people and single people, particularly women. Amsterdam, London and Brussels all have lively gay sub-cultures, that provide a home for mobile individualists adrift from family and social norms – and pressures – that would have been felt that much stronger if they were still living in their home countries. Amsterdam, not an easy place for foreigners to settle in many ways, has functioned as a comfortable capital in this sense, precisely because it is easier to identify with the city and Dutch culture as a progressive identity if you are gay. The internationally mobile, career-minded attitude becomes a justification for the choices single women have made to live their lives away from typical family norms. Helen, a very successful logistics manager, who has constructed a happy life in Brussels and then Amsterdam away from her native Northern Ireland, puts it this way:

'I'm a very lucky person in life, I've just been a cat landing on its feet [...] I don't need anybody around me that much. On the one hand you do want to move on, it's what you like doing. On the other hand, it's a big emotional upheaval. You are not married, so you are in it by yourself [...] But I wouldn't have it any other way. This is what I want.'

These Eurostars are, in short, pioneers. Not statistically significant enough maybe to alter aggregate social mobility charts, but symbolically the very emblem of the new, de-nationalised Europe that European Union has enabled. They embody the process, flux and change that European Union has released, albeit around the edges of European society. On both counts, they are statistical 'black swans' whose impact extends well beyond their structural location in the margins. Moreover, their unusual lives and experience cast sharp light on the background norms and patterns that continue to hold much of Europe in place. Indeed, many of them could never have succeeded in their lives if those norms were not there, and they were not rather unique statistical exceptions. Their category crossing experiences – which is neither conventional migration, nor conventional social mobility – also points to elements of flux and change in Europe linked to urban-periphery distinctions, growing individualism, and new forms of spatial-temporal organisation across borders. All of this would have been undetectable 'noise' in the conventional quantitative approach. Social theorists have been quick to point to the transformative effects of highly 'mobile' (Urry), 'liquid' (Bauman) or 'reflexive' societies (Giddens, Beck). The new Europe might be what they have in mind. But they have not investigated these claims empirically. When all we have otherwise to assert these transformative social currents is speculative social theory, the ethnographic/documentary approach detailed here is revealed as an essential empirical complement to the quantitative mainstream approach, a vital part of the apparatus needed for a true sociology of the European Union.

Conclusion: A European field of mobility

When Caterina moved to Brussels from Northern Italy to work as a medical administrator she was already in her 30s. A wholly individual choice, it was a rather speculative move, given she had no specific interest in or connection to Brussels, and had never previously visited. She just thought it was a good 'somewhere' to find work, and give the international life a try, to 'see how it was' and 'look for something else'. 'I wanted to challenge myself in a different environment, discover things and enrich my life', she says – a prototypical Eurostar reasoning. Although a relatively adventurous move compared to her peers back home, the fact the scale was European made all the difference. European citizenship meant formal barriers were down, and it was still close enough to home in Italy. She would not have moved otherwise. Now nearly 40, she left behind a cosy and stable life in her native Italy, to which she still dreams of returning – maybe to 'go in a hole', she laughs – someday when she gets old.

This is the pioneer attitude, typical of so many EU movers: the EU as a new European field of mobility on a regional scale, picking up on the conceptualisation of structure and action proposed in the sociology of Pierre Bourdieu (*see also* Favell 2003a; O'Reilly 2012). This is not a defined metric of rational choices with a clear, easy to assess pay off, but an open, undefined, protean horizon beyond the nation, a place for self-discovery and adventure as much as possible opportunity and advancement, that works because of its relatively bounded scope. As the PIONEUR project (Recchi and Favell 2009) also finds quantitatively, it is often not rational economic motives that caused people to move, so much as ideas about adventure, quality of life, or – a big factor for post-Erasmus students – romance with a European of another nationality. These factors perhaps account for why the strictly rationalist models on which economic theories and structural hypotheses about mobility and European integration are built do not work so well in practice. They do not measure the qualitative dimension of mobility and change, let alone the symbolic and cultural energies unleashed. The de-nationalised European freedoms enabled by the freedom of movement is, in many ways, not yet a recognised currency. This may be the EU's most precious invention: a new sense of regionalised freedom – since it is wrapped up in very European virtues of security, welfare, quality of life, and lived out on a European scale – but freedom nonetheless. And indeed 'the freedom to travel, work and study anywhere in the EU' is what the majority of Europeans constantly cite as the most important benefit of EU membership according to Eurobarometer data. Free movement is the EU in Europeans' minds. Much of this freedom is experienced by those that try it as a shot in the dark: there is no clear feedback to others who might want to try, the rational calculation is unclear if not obscure, and there are clearly diminishing returns if too many free-thinking, de-nationalising individuals start moving. A shift in too many people upsetting national norms and patterns might undermine much on what European social structure – ultimately its distinctive balance of economy and society – is built. The one-in-fifty who move are likely to remain a marginal niche, statistical exceptions, albeit individuals who point to how Europe has and can change the most.

Some of the effects of this movement may be inherently temporary. The mid- to long-term evaluation of the European move of the Eurostars is often not so encouraging. Long-term settlement, in even the most cosmopolitan of cities such as London and Amsterdam, often proves elusive. Home countries of origin and foreign countries of residence alike have their way of re-asserting their norms, value systems and social hierarchies over the lives of these pioneers. They see their experiences and opportunities being *re*-nationalised by the weight of mainstream lives lived in national structures; they are often caught out on a limb in their life choice, out of time and place in terms of both the peers they left back home, and the natives living and working around them. Structures outside the standard nationalised society for things like child care, education, welfare, and pensions – issues that increasingly form the terrain of struggle for middle classes seeking better quality of life in urban settings (Butler and Robson 2003) – are often very vulnerable. But the few that do dare to move are perhaps a symbol of a better, brighter Europe as is has been hoped for by the founders of European Union.

The marginal mobility of the Eurostars points to how social mobility opportunities have been extended to a far wider range of European citizens than clichéd images of European elites allow. When enumerated one-by-one, mobile Europeans are often provincial, upwardly mobile, middle- and lower-middle-class individuals with high education. The aggregate structural evidence about European mobility, though, continues to suggest that spatial mobility opportunities are still dominantly monopolised by upper- and upper-middle classes in Europe. The symbolic and structural potential of the EU thus co-exist: the European Union enhances both social fluidity and social reproduction.

However, the relation may shift once the question is extended to the economic integration and social changes associated with the new East-West movers, now able to enjoy free movement rights in the EU after the accessions of new East European members to the EU in 2004, 2007 and after. While these forms of migration cannot be directly assimilated to the free movement of West Europeans prior to 2004 – despite theoretical arguments about the integration of the European labour market which suggest this may one day be the case – there is strong evidence for the Poles, Lithuanians, Romanians and others moving westwards of distinct social mobility, income improvement, and return development effects relative to their countries of origin, even when in status terms the move West is a move down the occupational hierarchy. In a few short years, a marked effect of EU enlargement and integration on new member states has been visible via the new intra-EU mobility it has enabled. Studies of Western Europe may not conclusively provide a sociological base for claims about European integration and spatial or social mobility. But to put a face on the very visible and striking social structural impact of European Union on the continent, we may need only to think of these new highly mobile East-West workers – a very real spatial and social mobility that may prove the most significant demographic change in the continent since the end of the Second World War. I turn to these new migration and mobilities in Europe in the next chapter.

Part Four

New Migration and Mobilities in Europe

Chapter Eight

The New Face of East-West Migration in Europe

The enlargements of the EU eastwards in May 2004 and January 2007 signalled a geo-political shift in post-1989 Europe, that – in terms of the migration and mobility of populations – poses the biggest demographic change in Europe since the devastation and flux at the end of the Second World War.[1] The Cold War was finally over, and Europe united again – with new Central and East European citizens able to access now, or in the near future, the same free movement rights that have been enjoyed for years by West European citizens of the EU. Freedom of movement of persons from the new Member States remains a contentious issue, and some borders remain in place: not all temporary accession limitations to free movement are yet down. West European states have shown themselves politically to be far less keen on the movement of people westwards than they are on the gold rush of Western capital to the East. Yet one by one, formal restrictions on the free movement of East Europeans have been given up, in many cases enabling legal regularisation of migration and mobility that has long been occuring in practice. Borders have come down, and a new East-West migration system has been established in the continent.

These dramatic changes represent a new frontier in European migration research. Most of the studies completed before the enlargements focused on large-scale demographic trends or their political framing (for overviews, *see* Wallace and Stola 2001; Favell and Hansen 2002; Kaczmarczyk and Okólski 2005). Less has been done on the ethnographic micro-level: on the lives, experiences, networks and social forms that this new migration in Europe has taken. As was stressed earlier in this volume, fresh research is called for on the 'human face' of this migration as others, and this is being answered in large part by a new generation of Central and East European researchers, themselves often academic migrants pursuing education and careers in the West. In this introduction to the subject, I offer a framework and

1. Originally published in Adrian Favell and Tim Elrick (eds) (2008) *The New Face of East-West Migration in Europe*, special edition of *Journal of Ethnic and Migration Studies*, 34(5): 699–841. Republished with permission. The volume showcased new work by a range of younger scholars first presented at the Hamburg Institute for International Economics in November 2005, in a conference organised by the KNOWMIG project ('Expanding the knowledge base of European labour migration policies'), led by Christina Boswell, which subsequently moved to the University of Edinburgh. *See* its website: http://www.migration-networks.org. I also organised a special event on the subject at the Danish Institute for International Studies, Copenhagen in October 2006. With thanks to Christina Boswell for the original invitation, to demographer Philip Muus for his contribution to the discussion in Copenhagen, and to Simon Turner (DIIS) and my co-editor Tim Elrick for their comments.

overview for understanding the importance of this new research, emphasising two key points. The first is that our tried and tested narrative and models of post-war immigration in Europe – the standard discussions of immigration, integration and citizenship, based on post-colonial, guest worker and asylum models, and historical distinctions between pre- and post-1973 trends – is finished. The second is that the new East-West migration finally provides scholars with a European context comparable to the Mexican-US scenario that has inspired the largest and most sophisticated body of migration theory and research available in the social sciences. East-West migration can be read through these theories, providing a rich empirical material that will enable the development of better, more comparative views on the driving forces of international migration, as well as the role of free movement and migration in regional integration processes taking place around the globe today.

Systematising what we can learn from this body of theory and research, I evaluate four different hypotheses that might best account for the new East-West migration system in Europe. The dominant trend in Europe appears to be towards the emergence of a more regionalised system, in which West European societies come to rely on East European movers to fill secondary labour market needs in the service economy – in an exploitative fashion – as well as encouraging a more effective racial or ethnically-based exclusion of migrants from the South or further afield.

Political and policy context

Policy advocacy on East-West migration, as well as most of the credible demographic and economic scholarship, has consistently suggested that the West has little to fear from post-enlargement migration. Early scholarship in the days after the Berlin Wall came down – usually by German or Austrian scholars – did suggest that there was a huge pent-up demand for East-West migration that might provoke a flood to the West (Hönekopp 1991; Fassmann and Hintermann 1997; Bauer and Zimmerman 1999). Much of this research was based on surveys of migration intentions among a population recently freed to dream about being part of the West. Later scholars rightly pointed out the unreliability of this work. A much better guide to future enlargements were the past enlargements of Southern and Mediterranean states (Kupiszewski 2002; Wallace 2002). The accession of Spain, Portugal and Greece did not lead to floods of new migrants, but manageable flows, positive trends in terms of trade and development in the new Southern Member States, and high levels of return migration. The integration of these nations into the European fold in fact stands as an unqualified success in the history of the EU – as well as clear inspiration to later enlargements.

The consensus among policy makers aware of the underlying demographics – particularly reflected in the most influential policy advocacy in Brussels (ECAS 2005, 2006; ACA 2006) – is that Europe as a whole has benefited from a greater degree of manageable East-West movement. Not only has Western Europe received a new influx of highly educated, talented or (in any case) ambitious East Europeans, driven by the very positive selection mechanisms working in the European context (Borjas 1999). These migration trends are also quite different from the post-colonial, guest worker and asylum immigration that has proven such a long-term political issue of contention in Europe. East European migrants once accession is complete are in fact regional 'free movers' *not* immigrants; and with the borders open, they have been much more likely to engage in temporary circular and transnational mobility, governed by the ebb and flow of economic demand, than by long-term permanent immigration and asylum seeking.[2] Many East Europeans in any case were able to move and work in the West before 2004; the enlargement regularised a situation well established in *de facto* practice on the ground.

For all the good arguments to encourage open borders and free movement, the political calculation on these issues has pointed to a different rationality. Particularly in the ongoing aftermath of the 2008 economic crisis, there has been great electoral reward to be had by populist politicians using the 'threat' of open doors eastwards as a tool for berating the impact of the EU, in particular the liberalisation of West European labour markets or employment legislation. The ugly French debate about the 'Polish plumber' during the EU constitutional vote of spring 2005 was but the start of this phenomenon. Little matter that the handful of Polish plumbers in France have been outnumbered vastly by their Polish counterparts who chose Britain instead, and who went on to dominate this sector in London or Manchester – or apparently that the British economy during this period did much better than the French on the back of this informal workforce. It was the failed Bolkestein directive on freedom of movement of services (2006) that opened the spectre of European nation states no longer being able to control employment legislation on their own territory. France baulked at the possibility of the rights of workers or the rules of the working week, in certain sectors now coming under the jurisdiction of say, Polish or British law, both of which are more lax. Critics call this competitive imbalance in the system 'social dumping', and 'a race to the bottom'. In reality, though, what is not harmonised (and thereby regulated) by the EU with planned legislation, may instead simply get accomplished by market-driven forces, when they are able freely post workers *within* Europe wherever and whenever in the absence of meaningful border controls.

As regards the members that joined in 2004, West European nations one by one accepted the inevitable and brought down transitional barriers to freedom of movement for new Member States after much lobbying from the European Commission. Initially only three countries opened their borders: Ireland, Sweden, and Britain. All reaped economic benefits from the inflows that followed, that

---

2. This point is controversial, not least for policy makers. A report for the Rowntree Foundation (Spencer *et al.* 2007), based on interviews with East Europeans resident in the UK before and after enlargement, was presented by the British press as evidence that more of them were now intending to settle in Britain than expected. In fact, only around a quarter stated this intention, the others still engaging in dominantly circular and temporary mobility patterns. The economic crisis and increasing harassment with cross-border travel may well have persuaded more East Europeans to attempt longer term settlement – in case the doors close again. Intentions in migration are notoriously unreliable, and the presentation says nothing about the everyday transnational practices that have been made easier by the regularisation processes, as documented in the work cited by Garapich (2008) and Anghel (2013). The Rowntree report's interpretation was also influenced by the heavily normative integrationist perspective of the COMPAS (Oxford) researchers involved.

have proven higher than expected in the Irish and British case. By February 2007, The Netherlands had become the ninth country to drop restrictions to the EU10 Member States, joining Finland, Greece, Italy, Portugal, and Spain. Belgium, France, Luxembourg and Denmark in the meantime reduced their barriers. Only Austria and Germany – where hostility post 1989 has always been greatest – maintained restrictions for the maximum period possible of seven years. Numbers of such workers have always been high, however, in both these countries, whether legal or not. Restrictions across the board were harder on the new members of 2007, Bulgaria and Romania, only expiring in 2014. Britain, for example, backed off from its openness towards the new members of 2004, announcing from the start that doors were to remain officially shut to Bulgarians and Romanians when these two countries joined in January 2007 – although again, this did not stop significant migrations by other means. Spain and then others quickly followed suit, even though in both cases it simply meant that large numbers of workers already there in the two countries will not be able to regularise their status – or begin to pay taxes. The latest member to join, Croatia in 2013, also faced accession restrictions in an environment now much more politically hostile to open doors.

The slow political acceptance of open East-West borders confirms the underlying fact that Europe in future has an almost desperate structural need, in both demographic and labour force terms, for increased intra-European population movements. For the next twenty to thirty years, regardless of what happens to birth rates, this demand will persist; and if more countries come to resemble the Italian or Spanish rates of birth, the situation will get worse. These demands notably have not been satisfied by the intra-EU movement of West Europeans, with regional disparities between the North and South evening out through development, structural funds and welfare provision. Intra-EU migration among West European countries has only risen slightly over a thirty period since the migration stop of the 1970s, despite the extension of freedom of movement rights through successive EU treaties (Recchi 2005). Labour markets instead have looked East. As I argued in Chapter One, European economies – with some variation according to how much they continue to preserve nationally specific welfare state provisions and employment legislation – have increasingly come to resemble the USA: in which these free-moving migrants fill a vast range of low-end service sector, manufacturing and agricultural work that nationals no longer accept. Who better to fill these 3D ('dirty, dangerous and dull') jobs, than fresh faced European neighbours from the East, who are likely to be temporary rather than permanent, and are ethnically 'similar' and/or culturally 'proximate'? There is a strong suspicion here that West European economies, whatever the politics, have been quite happy to reduce their reliance on non-white, non-European immigrants by the development of a more internal and regional European labour market. This new migration system can even be seen to extend beyond the nominal frontiers of the official Member States, to include candidate countries and other near neighbors, albeit tacitly. The European Neighbourhood Policy, although noted normally only for its security aspects, is also creating regulated cross-border markets along these lines, in some cases to enable new Member States (such as Poland) who are losing their own workforce, to replace them with migrant workers from their immediate East (such as Ukrainians). The EU thus must be seen as a concentric, territorial project in regional integration that has used its external partner agreements to set up new mechanisms of managing regional migration flows, while closing doors to others (Rogers 2000; Carling 2002; Mau *et al.* 2012; Triandafyllidou 2013).

Idealist pro-EU federalists see the economic migration of East European as a win-win-win scenario. West European economies benefit from dynamic labour market effects, East European movers cash in on the premium of working in the higher paid West, and East European economies develop through the two way circulation of talent and capital. The EU, they think, can successfully govern and manage this scenario if political action is pooled at the supra-national level. These rosy scenarios have been celebrated especially in the European Year of Workers' Mobility (2006), organised by the Directorate General for Employment, Social Affairs and Equal Opportunities in Brussels, which has lobbied hard for the breaking down of transitional barriers. Neo-liberal economists share their optimism, but are much happier to let the whole scenario play out in terms of the inter-national 'competition for the brightest and best', where the more powerful Western economies may indeed benefit disproportionately from the 'brain drain' of the most employable talent and skills from the East (Borjas 1999). The political rationality in the meantime hangs in the balance: national politicians are tempted by populist rhetoric towards hostility, that has started to reap spectacular rewards for new right and nationalist parties, while all the economic, demographic, and geo-political arguments point in the opposite direction. Below I elaborate on these positions in terms of four different hypothetical scenarios.

European research and North American theory

The new wave of research on East-West migration and mobilities has documented, as it was happening, the emergence of a new European migration system (*see* Favell and Elrick 2008). Looking back, it is perhaps ironic that Massey and colleagues completed their round-up of the post-war European system in a global context at the moment when everything was changing again (Massey *et al.* 1998). The standard text-book story of post-war colonial and guest-worker immigration driven by industrial growth, followed by post-industrial closure and the contested emergence of multi-ethnic nation-states, multiculturalism and new conceptions of citizenship (i.e. Castles and Miller 2009; Hollifield 1992) now has to be rewritten (on this, *see* especially King 2002). The paradigm of immigration and integration, in particular, looks redundant in the face of the emergent, regional scale, European territorial space. Within this, European citizens – old and new – can move freely against a wider, transnational horizon that encourages temporary and circular migration trends, and demands no long-term settlement or naturalisation in the country of work. Post-colonial theories of race, ethnicity and multiculturalism – that still clutter the shelves of bookstores and the pages of syllabi in the Anglo-American dominated field of 'ethnic and racial studies' – are also ineffective and largely irrelevant in relation to these new movements in Europe.

To theorise and interpret the new East-West migration in comparative context, researchers have instead turned to the most substantial existing body of theory and research in international migration studies, work largely developed in relation to studies of Latin American, especially Mexican migration to the USA. This is no coincidence: the question of East-West integration, and the movement and mobility it encourages, is directly parallel to the regional integration processes in North America, that have led Mexican migration to the USA to be the single largest international migration flow in the Western world, and the biggest migration-related component of the US economy, itself the world's biggest. Like Europe, the USA wrestles continually with the political pressure for more effective closure of its Southern borders, while – again, like Europe – being dependent on the undepletable reservoir of cheaper skilled and unskilled labour it provides. It is a relation above all characterised by the profound cross-border, territorial, regional embeddedness of the US South-West with Mexico, at every level of the economy and demography.

The Mexican Migration Project (MMP), for example, headed by Durand and Massey, is the single most ambitious empirical project ever developed on a major international migration system.[3] With roots in an ethno-survey methodology, reflected in the early anthropological style work on sending communities (Massey *et al.* 1987), since 1982 MMP has developed and elaborated a huge, publicly accessible quantitative database, centred on surveys of potential migrant populations in key Mexican cities and their patterns of movement to the USA. As well as providing the biggest source of data about Mexican migration to the USA, it has also been the basis for Massey's concerted attempt to summarise, frame and extend migration theory into a more comprehensive networks-based migration system approach that illustrates the exponential dynamics and social structures beyond simple push-pull explanations (Massey *et al.* 1993). On the back of this research, these core migration theories were pushed to encompass the whole globe (Massey *et al.* 1998).

A second body of work, hailing from economic sociology, has focused rather on the direct impact of these migration flows on the US economy and its internal labour market dynamics (Portes 1995; Cross and Waldinger 1999; Waldinger 2001). The free-flowing, massively informal labour market of California for domestic work, agriculture, household and construction work – the dynamo that powers this, the largest corner of the US economy – are proving a model for the rest of the post-industrial world, as it shifts increasingly into a highly informalised and structurally unequal dual labour market model (*see* Piore 1979). While this is a boon for capitalist exploitation of cheap mobile labour, it can also be read as leading to a potential 'globalisation from below', as pointed out in literature on ethnic economies (Portes 1998). Domestic work, and the feminisation of migration it underlines, is a key sector in which these processes play out (Hodagneu-Sotelo 2001). These theories also link in with attempts to show how the emergence of networks and territorial-based ethnic economic niches are often the primary channel of incorporation of migrant labour into the post-industrial economy

---

3.   *See* its website: http://mmp.opr.princeton.edu.

(Aldrich and Waldinger 1990; Light and Gold 2000), pointing the way forward to future limitations of US urban change in even the most global of cities (Light 2006), and to emerging new labour market conflicts with the Latino workforce (Milkman 2006).

Rather different in style, but no less influential, has been the body of work grouped together under the rubric of 'transnationalism'. Again, the extraordinary cross-border flows, social forms, economic and political structures that have developed among Mexicans in the USA, particularly in California, have provided the material for a thorough rethinking of the nation-state centred immigration/assimilation paradigm, that sees the phenomenon only through the receiving country's eyes (Glick Schiller *et al.* 1995; Smith and Guarnizo 1998; Levitt 2001). This work has gone on to detail the interpenetration of Mexican and US political, economic and cultural dynamics (Smith 2005; Smith and Bakker 2007), and changing patterns of Mexican migrant settlement in the USA as they penetrate ever further the receiving society (Zuniga and Hernández-Léon 2005).

A fourth relevant literature is the work of labour market economics inspired by the Mexico-USA scenario. These focus on two main questions: either the potentially positive 'win-win-win' relation of migration, trade and development to receiving and sending societies and migrants alike (Martin 2006); or the question of selection mechanisms, and the conditions under which receiving societies best capitalise on the potential human capital of immigrants, and even are able to select for the 'unobserved skill' that is carried by the most motivated and dynamic of immigrant (Borjas 1989; Chiswick 2007). Borjas notably argues that the USA's ability to select for the 'brightest and the best' is declining, as policies have increasingly favoured family reunification and migrant networks over demand-driven criteria; he does however see great potential for positivity in the European scenario (Borjas 1999). The European context in fact has seen the emergence of a much 'purer' open borders system, in which the conditions of an ideal cross-border labour market are better achieved. Here, the dilemma is likely to be the threat of 'brain drain', and its negative effects on sending countries. On the other hand, developments with the American system as regards other migrants who have a preferential access to the American economy and American jobs, shows that highly skilled global mobility is just as likely under global conditions to lead to positive development dynamics and 'brain gain' (Stark 2004). Free moving entrepreneurs can use their sojourn working in the US to develop ideas, networks and sources of capital that will allow successful entrepreneurship to be established back in their home country – as has been graphically the case with recent Chinese and Indian migrants (Saxenian 2006). Martin's analysis, meanwhile, extends the question to the European neighborhood, in his comparison of Mexicans and Turks. He sees qualified positive aspects of the migration, trade and development relationship in terms of Turkey and Europe when compared to the more unstable Mexican-USA relation (Martin 2011).

Hypotheses

We can systematise the existing literature on East-West migration, as well as what can be derived from the North American migration and immigration literature, by distinguishing a number of distinct hypotheses. Migrants to Western Europe from East and Central Europe can come from countries that are either, post-accession, full members of the EU (subject to transitional barriers on free movement in some countries); or from actual and potential candidate countries (who have different external association agreements with the EU). They might either be easily and well received, with positive personal experiences and observations of life and work in Western Europe, or not. And their movement to the West might follow economists' and geographers' predictions – leading to the emergence of an efficient Europe-wide labour market, and a new intra-EU mobility regime – or it might have political and economic consequences that reflect or lead to a rather different exclusionary or exploitative political economy of migration in Europe.

Hypothesis One – Neo-liberal Europe

Borjas (1989) identifies mechanisms why post-communist immigration to the USA was far more beneficial economically, both to the USA and the immigrants themselves, than more recent low income immigration from Central America. Both the analogy with communism and with Mexico can be drawn for East and Central European migrants, but in Borjas' terms, it is the former situation that ought to prevail. These migrants are relatively well educated and/or skilled, but they are moving from countries that have not valued or prized this human capital to the degree it will be in the West. Mobility can thus lead to dramatic economic payoffs for themselves and their hosts, and they pose few cultural problems of adjustment, having accepted the host country's (capitalist) ideology. In this hypothesis, then, Central and East European migrants should be well received, happy and successful, and achieve successful mobility. From the receiving side, they are migrants preferable to non-Europeans because of their 'cultural' closeness, their education levels (the costs of which were borne in the sending countries), and other political/ideological links – they should not, therefore experience negative discrimination or hostility. Being spatially close to home, they are unlikely to want to stay or pose long-term burdens on the welfare state; they are a largely costless migration, with significant benefits for both migrants and receiving states. We should expect no big difference between their experiences and internal West European movers, or between migrants from different status sending countries (this being a 'market' governed process); and most migrants should offer a strongly positively evaluation of the experience. Receiving societies will also be positive as long as the wider economic climate is good. However, the model is a view of benefit from the receiving side, and a zero sum game: on the sending side, the migrants' human capital can only be seen as a loss, with likely significant effects of brain drain.

Hypothesis two – Exclusionary Europe

A rather different reading of this situation suggests an analogy closer to migration to the USA from Mexico or Central America. It also suggests that the regional, cross-border closeness of these migrants from the East could in fact pose a serious problem for West European states, whose dealings with immigration in the post-war period have generally been based on postcolonial models of integrating more distant migrants, who have some close cultural and political socialisation to the receiving country from global historical and cultural links. In this hypothesis, the experiences of the East and Central Europeans will be stratified according to perceptions of how willing they are to adapt culturally and ethnically to the receiving countries. They will be negative in so far as these migrants are seen as a 'parasitical' movers – taking the benefits of economic opportunities in the West, but not interested in participating or integrating in the host country, let alone any kind of cultural assimilation. The situation might vary according to what extent the receiving country's immigration paradigm is based on a post-colonial model. Eastern European movers may even be seen as an economic threat to indigenous working classes and existing ethnic minorities in working class positions (an extension of Castles and Kosack 1973). The 'new migration' they represent (Koser and Lutz 1998), is seen as a chaotic threat to the migration system that has developed with European enlargement, which prior to 1989 was relatively settled and politically manageable, as I argued earlier in this volume. The migrants' experiences will be largely negative, and highly conscious of these reactions among natives. It reflects a systemic response mostly governed by national political conceptions of citizenship.

Hypothesis three – EU Europe

A third hypothesis elicits evidence on the degree to which the new East-West patterns are in fact fulfilling the theories and observations of economists and demographers. As well as generating the kind of payoffs for migrants and receiving states envisaged in hypothesis one, the new freedom of movement from East to West presages a new European migration system in which East Europeans fill European labour market needs, while engaging in mostly temporary and circular forms of mobility (Wallace 2002; Williams and Balasz 2002) that have positive effects *also* back home: a win/win/win scenario. There are thus significant development and trade payoffs to the East, and the well governed new system rapidly settles down – as EU policy makers expect – into an enlightened and integrated European free movement regime (a 'political economy') in which all sides are happy. As the model – which is very popular amongst EU free movement advocates (*see* ECAS 2005) – is premised on effective political regulation of the market, we would expect to see big differences in the ease of mobility between citizens of countries that have acceded and those that have not, as well as between migrants going to countries without transitional barriers and those where they were maintained or made difficult. Migrants' happiness with the movements, as well as their support for the EU, may well reflect these legal and political constraints.

Hypothesis four – Exploitative Europe

The final hypothesis puts a critical spin on the idealised economic scenario, by positing that, yes, market integration is occuring, but that it is occuring anyways regardless of the EU efforts of governing East-West labour migration through coordinated free movement policies. This scenario is suggested as the actual one closest to the reality in Mexican-US migration (in the work of Massey *et al.* 2002), and has been picked up in work by Favell and Hansen (2002), and Samers (2004). This questions the existence of a well-controlled 'fortress Europe', either before or after enlargement, and points towards the exploitative dimensions of the rampant market-led system governing migration in Europe. In this hypothesis, political talk of controlling free movement is largely a game of electoral 'smoke and mirrors', to disguise the degree to which economic interests in Europe are now actively exploiting easy East-West migration possibilities, in advance of accession and transition barriers coming down. There are few *de facto* political or legal barriers in fact to moving. Migrants from the East find easy ways of entering the West, taking up '3D' jobs, in low end service, agriculture and sweat shop manufacturing, replacing racially less desirable non-European migrants, but being exploited in advance of their rising to meet labour standards and wages of the East (*see* classic studies of how it works in the USA, such as Piore 1979; Waldinger 1996). In this scenario, we would expect ease of mobility, but seriously negative experiences across the board, a strong sense of exploitation and vulnerability, and a sense that 'official' EU enlargement is not likely to make the situation much better (*see also* Meardi 2012). This downward migration would apply to all East and Central European migrants, regardless of educational status or which country they come from.

Findings from research on new East-West migration

East-West migration is a fruitful context for testing the hypotheses that may thus be derived from elaboration and modification of the bodies of theory and research discussed above which compare and contrast Europe and North America. The enlarged Europe in fact offers a rival model of regional integration to the North American one. As an institutional construct, the EU can boast of a much more developed corpus of policy and legislation seeking to politically govern the underlying economic processes that are rapidly constructing an interpenetrated, regional and international labour market – along with its social and cultural consequences – in both parts of the world. EU migration trends, because of this, might be expected to attain a more manageable and a rationally organised form than the largely informal and desperately unequal relations that characterise the Mexico-USA border.

Until recently, though, very little research had been done with this broad comparative view of the European migration system in mind. In terms of the early assessments Favell and Hansen (2002) made this point, arguing for the primacy of market-led forces over political efforts at control, and Samers (2003, 2004) developed a broad political economy analysis of Europe's tacit US-style reliance on undocumented and irregular migration. Düvell and Jordan, meanwhile, both explored the necessary emergence of migration networks to facilitate and structure an East-West migration taking place largely 'beyond control' (Jordan and Düvell 2002; Düvell 2005). From another angle, and a much broader quantitative analysis across forty-six countries, Ruhs (2013) acutely charts the uncomfortable trade-off of protecting migrant rights (both human and labour market protections) versus liberalisation of labour markets. This is a trade-off substantially disrupted by the EU freedom of movement rights that grant equal rights to foreign workers within the EU. He points to how companies have increasingly sought to evade these workers' rights and associated costs, by using 'posted' workers under freedom of movement of services provisions which allow workers to be paid according to (lower) sending country standards.

These perspectives offered starting points for the work brought together in collections such as Favell and Elrick (2008), some of which I summarise below (*see also* Burrell 2009; Black *et al.* 2010, Krings *et al.* 2013). The question of networks facilitating irregular migration is picked up here by Elrick and Lawandowska (2008) which details the migrant networks and agents that facilitate Polish domestic worker migration in Italy and Germany. A telling criticism of Massey's networks-based theory that they and other make (Krissman 2005; Collyer 2005; Garni 2010), has been its emphasis on networks being conceived predominantly in terms of family and friends. This leads to an over-emphasis on symmetrical community-based dynamics of reciprocity, and an over-weighting on supply side factors at the expense of the structural and contextual impact of economic and political factors. This critique points to the fact that networks almost always facilitate business demand as a factor, often explicitly via the role played by Mexican bosses in the USA looking for migrants to fill certain needs (the 'patrón' in Krissman's critique), as well as the role of migration agents in making border crossing, and matching migrants to jobs (in Krissman, the 'coyote'). A migration industry emerges, in particular centered on the necessary financial flows and transactions needed to make this labour market work. Migrant agents, sponsors and go-betweens have a bad reputation: they are often associated with trafficking and illicit international activities, and have become the target of many moralistic crusades in recent years. However, they may well be a necessary part of any and every informal migration channel found facilitating movement across formally closed borders (Hernández-León 2005, 2012). In work on the Polish community and new commercial activities linked to migration, in London, Garapich (2008) illustrates the potential beneficial effects of an emergent migrant industry. As he argues, the market-led dynamics behind these emergent social and organisational forms, in fact provide a channel for political activism and incorporation, an outcome that has both changed the face of migration in Britain in recent years, and questions the classic opposition of economic and political rationality encapsulated in standard accounts, such as Hollfield's well know 'liberal paradox' (*see* Hollifield 1992).

Turning to the Polish population in Germany, Miera (2008) documents their effect on the economic life of small- and medium-sized businesses in the city. Germany long played a deceitful political game, denying formal access to Poles, while relying on a *de facto* and largely accepted temporary Polish presence in the country, a population who have been finding ways to move economically across its borders since the early 1990s. Miera develops both the US inspired work on ethnic economies and its European derivations that focus on the notion of 'mixed embeddedness' where urban contexts and policy interventions are factored in (Kloosterman *et al.* 1999), as well as an emphasis on the spatially driven transnational and circular flows that have been studied by scholars of East European, particularly Polish migration (Okólski 2001; Williams and Baláž 2002; Morawska 2002). Using these references, she draws a very fruitful comparison with the more visible, but less extensive Turkish entrepreneurial activity in the city. The research substantiates very concretely the kind of broader theoretical arguments that have been put forward on globalisation and networks effects (i.e. Portes 1998; Faist 2000). Here is a very real instance of an emergent, spatially organised, transnational ethnic economy that has had a clear influence from below on regional integration – and in direct opposition to the stated national German policy.

Another legacy of the early ethno-survey based work of MMP on Mexican sending communities, was the focus on the 'cultural of migration': getting inside the minds of migrants, understanding their local options vis-à-vis migration choices and the local economy, the pressure of peers and family, and the allure of Western wealth. A good case in point is Horváth's study (2008) on the culture of migration in the sending context of East European migration, in this case from the Transylvanian context, itself cut across by inter-ethnic conflicts and an ambiguous territorial relationship with the Hungarian and Romanian nations (Brubaker *et al.* 2006). The emphasis Horváth makes here, however, is on the structural context of de-industrialisation and rural depopulation, cross-referenced to the social psychology of youth processing signals from their peers and the West during their difficult transition to adulthood. This echoes the work of another associate of MMP, Hernández-León (2004), on the de-industrialising context of Monterrey, Mexico and the dynamics of migrant networks with Texas and Georgia. Anghel (2008, 2013) meanwhile provides the other receiving side of the Romanian story in a rich ethnographic portrait of Romanians in Italy. Documenting both the practical social forms that they have established and developed in rich Northern Italy, the receiving context dynamics in the city of Milan, and the social role of migrants when they return to the home villages, Anghel's study is extraordinarily reminiscent of US transnational studies – particularly the 'second generation' of these studies which have moved to localise the transationalism observed (Smith 2001). Similar work putting an accent on migrant voices and experiences can be pointed to among human geographers regarding Poles and other European migrations in Britain (Burrell 2006; Datta 2009).

Thus far, in terms of labour market destinations, most of these migrants – who are far from un-educated or unskilled – appear destined to languish in undervalued roles in temporary and low-paid labouring, domestic, agricultural or construction work; although some may also be making use of EU's parallel freedom of establishment laws to set up their own ethnic businesses. These sorting mechanisms offer very positive returns for West European economies, exploiting a relatively skilled, hard-working, ethnically unproblematic and highly available labour source for low wages and no job security. The British and Irish economies have been the most spectacular beneficiaries of these selection processes, and the apparent willingness of East European migrant workers to accept work there under these conditions. But the East-West story is also one of highly skilled migration. Whether these selection processes are fair and effective, and whether the outcome is one of brain drain, or some other more virtuous dynamic, is the question here. Csedö's extensive London-based research (2008) homes in on the recognition and rewarding of 'skill' among Hungarian and Romanians in the global city of choice. The economic literature has often worked with fixed notions of 'objective' human capital, but she argues that social context and power relations construct what is perceived as 'skill', evaluating what is worthy and what is not. London may be one of the most open labour market destinations in Europe, but even here the 'brightest and best' are potentially undervalued and relatively 'wasted' in their labour market participation – largely because of residual language and cultural barriers. In the worst case scenarios it can lead to a downward assimilation into lower end labour market positions typically marked out for ethnic minorities – as often found in US assimilation research (Portes and Zhou 1993) – and at best an outcome that is some way short of the win-win-win scenarios on which global and regional theories are based. In a large scale project, MOBEX2 ('Promoting Balanced Growth in an Enlarging Europe') the vexing issue of the apparent dramatic brain drain of scientific personnel from Bulgaria and Poland, was attacked, laying out the costs and benefits of opportunities that have emerged for mobile scientists in Britain and Germany (Guth and Gill 2008; Ackers and Gill 2008). They temper the more cataclysmic accounts of the westward flux, noting the return and circular benefits that continue to accrue to the sending countries, while also contributing a nuanced account of the 'economic' motivation of such migrants in the context of broader issues of training, experience and career building.

The new European migration system

With such a wealth of new research on the table, it is to be hoped that international migration researchers will begin to look to East-West migration in Europe as a potential source for controlling and modifying theories that have been built exclusively on US-centred scenarios. Because of EU enlargement, the European migration system is probably the most dramatically evolving and changing context of migration in the developed world. It offers reason to question the automatic assumption that the USA is the automatic paradigm of immigration for the rest of the world, while also posing the issue of whether Europe is in fact sliding ever closer to the USA-Mexico migration model.

In sum, what do these studies add up to? What is the big picture here? Taken together along with other more systematic surveys underway, a much less happy scenario than those promoted by advocates of EU integration is suggested.[4] Here I will close by synthesising the view of the European migration system that might emerge from a broader reading of these various studies. Which of the four hypotheses is most substantiated?

As strongly suggested by many of the studies cited above, *Exploitative Europe* is the dominant scenario. Both higher and lower end migrants from the East are attracted by the West, and certainly see their movements as temporary, opportunistic and circular. In fact there is little evidence that formal borders or barriers have made a lot of difference between, say, Poles and Romanians, although the latter are more likely to find themselves in precarious situations for want of official papers. But where their experiences are strikingly similar is in their strong sense of exclusion and exploitation. Many of these migrants accept sharp downward mobility in terms of status and qualifications in order to fill some low-end niche in the labour market, that is grimly justified in terms of its payoff for family back home. The jobs they take are the ones that Western citizens no longer want – those 3D jobs that have become a familiar range of employment 'opportunities' in the post-industrial service economy. Where there is conflict with the 'natives' over jobs and resources, the reaction gets expressed in populist and xenophobic terms. Where there is not, they slip into the background as an invisible but functional 'secondary' part of the economy. As I argue in the next chapter, the one destination where might be found some more positive effects, in economic and demographic terms, is Britain. In Britain today, for example, it is almost impossible to be served dinner or drinks in a rural pub or get your bathroom fixed in a big city, without encountering an East European worker. The effects here have been so much more developed and extensive than in other parts of Europe, where selections dynamics were less positive. Still, downward assimilation in the short run is often a reality, as Csedö (2008) suggests. Many accept jobs they would have not dreamt of while studying at school back home. Much depends on whether they have established an upward foothold in the British labour market before the effects of the downturn have taken hold (Kesler and Safi 2012). Moreover, the politicisation of the issue by the United Kingdom Independence Party (UKIP) – however symbolic and devoid of economic substantiation their case is – has seriously pushed the British case back towards the second, *Exclusionary Europe* scenario. A nationalist Britain with formal barriers to the free movement of EU migrant will lose all the selection benefits of an open labour market, as well as breeding a senseless and economically damaging xenophobia. Elsewhere in Europe an even more negative scenario prevails, as I argue in Chapter Nine.

---

4. Results here are also systematised from two large-scale projects in which I was a research partner: PIONEUR (2003–6) 'Pioneers of European Integration 'From Below': Mobility and the Emergence of European Identity Among National and Foreign Citizens in the EU', EU Framework V project, directed by Ettore Recchi, which is described elsewhere in this volume (*see* the website: http://www.obets.ua.es/pioneur); and MIGSYS (2006–7) 'Immigrants, policies and migration systems: an ethnographic comparative approach', International Metropolis funded project directed by Anna Triandafyllidou, which compared external borders and migration in both the North American and European regional contexts (*see* the website: http://www.eliamep.gr/en/migration/migsys-immigrants-policies-and-migration-systems/migsys).

Professional and college-level East Europeans, meanwhile, attracted West for educational opportunities also find themselves blocked in their careers in most locations. For them, too, the emergent structure is of a discriminatory labour market, that keeps them provisional and precarious, in order the better to extract cheaper labour. The payoffs if any are in terms of their status in relation to their peer group back home. That might be enough to dampen the feeling that they are treated as if they do not belong in the West, or that their hopeful European mobility might lead to serious long-term consequences in terms of social isolation. The sentiment many still express is that West European societies may put on an increasingly open economic face, but the reality is that they still believe the USA one day will offer far more recognition and reward for their talents and entrepreneurship – if they can get there.

The American dream, thus, does indeed still lie behind so many of the ideas driving the opening of the European economy, for all the emphasis placed in Europe on governance and the rational political management of the economy. Europeans may well ask whether this is the kind of society they want to see built in the name of economic growth and competivity – the mantra of the Lisbon Agenda (2000), that puts mobility and the liberalisation of labour markets at the heart of its strategy. As I also argued in Chapter One, in most major cities in the USA today, the faces likely to be flipping burgers, cleaning cars, tending gardens, or working as *au pairs* for young children are Latino; in Europe today, these same figures speak with Balkan or Slavic accents. There is perhaps one more irony built into to this apparently inevitable asymmetry between East and West, and the structural inequalities it reinforces. These new migrants may sometimes face hostility, but from the point of view of populist politicians, they are usually still much more desirable than other, more visible, actual and potential immigrant populations. It might be speculated that, in the long run, West European publics are likely to be more comfortable with the scenario of getting used to Balkan migrants, rather than seeing black and brown faces in the same jobs, or (especially) hearing them speak the language of Allah. There is indeed a racial and ethnic logic inherent in the EU enlargement process: borders to the East have opened as they have been increasingly rammed shut to those from the South. The positive thought was the East might provide the population resources to tide Europe over in a time of big demographic change. Demography, though, has a sting in the tail. East Europeans may well be willing to move on a regional scale well beyond the reluctant numbers of West Europeans so tempted. But their birth rates, both under communism and after, are a not little different to some of the lowest ones in the West. East-West migration is thus unlikely to be a long-term solution to the West's coming demographic crisis.

In an environment in which there are electoral gains to be had from talking tough on immigration, it is no surprise that most research on migration focuses on policies of immigration control or security. But, just as in the USA, much of this discussion is in fact a game of political 'smoke and mirrors' (Massey *et al.* 2002), to mask just how little control governments or the EU have over migration and mobility trends, let alone the globalising international labour market essential to national economies. The underlying political economy of Europe, rather, is one that is not closing but opening borders to the East. The compelling but distorting focus on the open party politics of immigration in Europe masks underlying economic and demographic realities. Debates on immigration policy would therefore benefit from paying more attention to the population trends and labour market dynamics that underwrite the policies that elected politicians defend or extremist politicians challenge. As a first stop, they would do well to consider the ethnographic evidence amassed by those researchers closest to the ground where it is happening.

Chapter Nine

The Fourth Freedom: Theories of Migration and Mobilities in 'Neo-liberal' Europe

Marxist and Social Democratic commentary on the EU has converged in the years since the 2005 constitutional vote and the 2008 global financial crisis on a 'neo-liberal' interpretation, that castigates 'free market' driven European integration as the 'wrong Europe', undermining principles of democracy, justice and/or community that may – perhaps – still be better protected at the national level (Anderson 2009; Schulz-Forberg and Stråth 2010; Crouch 2011; Streeck 2013; Schmidt and Thatcher 2013).[1] Defending arguments about the desirability of well-regulated, labour protecting institutions at the national level against so-called 'Anglo-Saxon' or 'Anglo-American' liberalism, their implicit normative models discount or overlook migration and mobilities as a now core structural feature of all European societies; and something much better handled in more open labour markets such as Britain, than in more closed ones such as France, Germany, The Netherlands, or Denmark.

Scholars of international migration and mobilities, meanwhile, cannot share the hostility to one of the main consequences of liberalising (i.e. reducing state control of) labour markets internationally. They would generally see the consequences of 'free market' migration in terms of the diversification of society and cultural change. Nor can they agree that the presence of informality rooted in cross-border economic activities or the avoidance of state oversight is inherently bad: transnational and unregulated 'ethnic economies' are celebrated as a crucial means by which migrants establish a financial foothold in contemporary societies. Are progressive-minded migration scholars thereby part of the neo-liberal conspiracy promoting the domination of 'market fundamentalism' (Peck 2010)?

I address this theoretical question by focusing on the one innovative dimension of market freedom created by the EU in contrast to other regional market integration projects such as NAFTA: the 'fourth freedom', of free movement of persons. After first contrasting basic Marxist and liberal positions on international migration in analytical terms, I go on to argue how since 2004, under certain conditions, market-driven migration and mobilities in Europe have fulfilled the promise of an

1.   Originally published in *European Journal of Social Theory* (2014). Republished with permission. With many thanks to Gerard Delanty for the invitation to write on this subject for the special edition on the post-2008 European crisis. I have also been strongly influenced by discussions with Sciences Po colleagues Michael Storper, Patrick Le Galès and Tommaso Vitale on this subject, as well as continued inspiration from a longstanding dialogue with Yasemin Soysal. The paper was first presented publicly as a lecture at the Blinken European Institute, Columbia University, in March 2014.

ideal liberal economic theory of migration: where migrants, receiving states and sending states, accepting migration according to the canonical EU legal/economic principles, have all been 'winners'. Moreover, I challenge head-on the limitations of the 'neo-liberal' interpretation of the present European crisis by heading straight to the alleged greatest culprit: Britain, the heartland of the supposedly 'neo-liberal' 'Anglo-Saxon' free market model undermining the potentials of a democratic, progressive EU. On the contrary, I argue that Britain in the 1990s and 2000s was the best illustration of EU ideals as well as the potential all-round benefits of the fourth market freedom. On *this* dimension – the egalitarian openness and dynamism of its labour market – Britain has long been the most highly Europeanised, or EU integrated, member state. Amidst the current crisis, Britain's potential vote on EU membership, and its sharply growing political hostility to the very migration and mobilities that drove its recent boom years, would therefore also be a vote about the future of freedom of movement of persons in Europe: the one progressive dimension of European economic integration that has done the most to break down nationalist barriers, mentalities and seclusions.

Negatives and positives of economic migration

Left-wing critics of 'neo-liberal' Europe mischaracterise or ignore the progressive dimensions of its market-driven regional integration because of an unadmitted Marxist, or at least strongly *marxisant*, tendency in recent debate. Straight Marxists should have no problem knowing where they stand on international labour markets; that is, open migration across national borders driven by economic dynamics. Markets are for Marxists essentially the root of evil; the fact that the labour being alienated is an African escaping from poverty does not change the fact that in selling themselves to international labour market demand they are selling themselves into wage slavery. Contemporary globalisation, particularly in the light of the current crisis, has thus to be seen as deeply negative in its consequences (De Genova and Peutz 2010; Castles 2011). Critical opinion routinely cites the 'polarisation' effects of globalisation: with elite capitalists enjoying the benefits of a free-flowing world, while exploiting low-end, mainly service sector, migrants. International justice in a Marxist world might at some utopian point in the future necessitate abandoning oppressive nation-state borders, but this is not aided by the border busting movement of individuals driven by unhampered (what will be called 'neo-liberal') forces of capital. An older Marxist literature bluntly also considered in negative terms the conflict these migrants would bring to existing labour-capital settlements (Castles and Kosack 1973). Similarly, Marxists should not support informal economic activities which seek to avoid the taxation and regulation that pay for communitarian re-distribution and labour protection. The 'anti-liberal' upshot has to be that states (i.e. national governments) should control and regulate borders: that is, restrict or prevent these (poorer) foreigners with intentions of working and settling from crossing them, thereby protecting migrants from exploitation and developing states from loss of human capital, and protecting insider workers from labour market and wage competition or a dilution of their citizenship privileges. Marxists, strongly communitarian social democrats as well as nationalist conservatives, may indeed converge on the justice of state restriction of open migration on these grounds (Miller 2000). Outside of this, progressive views which wish to sympathise with the attempts of the poorer workers of the world to move – and hence the benefits and desirability of international migration within a more globalising world – will have to settle for some or other view of international labour markets that is basically 'liberal' in some way (compare with Cohen 2006; Hampshire 2012).

In contrast, the liberal position is that states do not have an unquestioned sovereignty on whether they may restrict labour migration (Hollifield 1992). A case can be made for limiting state governance, either when open migration is of overall benefit for all in utility (i.e. economic) terms; or because of the stronger claims of a human right to move over citizens' rights to restrict access to their community; or – in the special case of an integrated regional labour market – because there is an equity-based principle of non-discrimination making it illegal to disfavour foreigners in employment contracts. Some go so far as to argue for completely open borders on humanitarian and global justice terms, or to compensate for the arbitrary accident of birth (being born Congolese rather than British) (Carens 1987); and further support can be taken from arguments about the beneficial effects of international diversity in promoting more tolerance or cosmopolitanism (Papastergiadis 1999). Opposing the idea that national citizenship gives special privileges to insiders in a territory to restrict the access of others, liberal support for open borders breaks open the 'state monopoly on the freedom of movement' that was one of the great social disciplining achievements of nation-state building and consolidation of the late nineteenth century and early twentieth century (Torpey 2000).

For sure, for liberals, international labour markets can be, often are, indeed perhaps *mostly* are negative, empirically speaking: that is, liberals may recognise the kind of points Marxists would make, that labour markets can be exclusionary or exploitative. In exclusionary labour markets, discrimination (i.e. racially or ethnically based) leads the market to systematically categorise, restrict and shuffle migrants into badly paid, low status jobs (the secondary labour market), failing to recognise skills and qualifications, or imposing glass ceilings and barriers to getting jobs in the primary labour market (i.e. full time, secure, unionised and regulated work status) (Piore 1979). In exploitative markets, these exclusions lead to the migrant worker failing to earn the salary they are due, systematically being underpaid. This can be accompanied by an inefficient mismatch of actual skills and qualification to demands in the host labour market (Waldinger 1996).

But whereas for a Marxist the very notion of alienated wage labour is anathema, for a liberal, the critique of an inefficient or unjust labour market presupposes its opposite: that a non-exclusionary, non-exploitative – and therefore non-coercive – market is possible. State intervention is justifiable, but only in order to correct situations where there is clear market failure. This leaves the way open to the liberal belief that it is state borders – including the kind of internal borders favouring insiders on the labour market – that may be the problem here. A more rather than less open international labour market may, under certain conditions, bring more benefits to all – the migrant, the receiving state and even the sending state: in terms of social mobility and the circulation of human capital, skills and education; the complementary filling of sectoral demand (in the case of jobs not taken by native workers) and/or the entrepreneurial creation of new employment niches by business-minded migrant workers; and (in some cases) the circulation of capital back to the sending state (through remittances, return investment) (*see* Light and Gold 2000).

Much of the debate in migration theory therefore is not about the general desirability of migration – most migration scholars tend to be liberal on whether states should restrict free movement – but to what extent better state regulated (i.e. managed) migration might temper the possible negative consequences of completely unregulated (informal) migration (Koser 2007). On this, the most familiar scenario internationally is far from optimal: the clearly hypocritical 'smoke and mirrors' type political economy, which mixes political bluster about controlling or stopping migration – mostly symbolic actions designed at policing the borders (military operations, fence construction and deportation) – with tacit acceptance that domestic labour markets desperately need a constant supply of cheap, easy to hire and fire (informal) markets to do all the dirty, dangerous and dull work required (Massey *et al.* 2002). This has long been the scenario in the USA as regards Mexican and Central American migration; for all the anti-immigration rhetoric there is massive labour market demand in the USA for fruit pickers, domestic workers, cleaners, and fast food attendants, and the state tacitly allows US economic interests, favouring migration, to call the shots; there is much to suggest that Europe's Southern borders work similarly (Samers 2004). The recent tendency in the last decade to stage more overt enforcement at these two sets of borders only underlines the hypocrisy more.

Again, though, there are potentially better managed alternatives, in which the state can be engaged in facilitating various kinds of wanted migration and free movement – even cultivating *laissez-faire* attitudes to certain forms of migrant mobility and entrepreneurship – while trying to limit the extent to which the migration is governed by untamed market forces alone. This is signalled by the notion of 'managed migration', at the centre of most applied policy debates about migration internationally. The problem with 'smoke and mirrors' policies is that coupling *laissez-faire* with heavily securitised borders tends to lead to the rise of mafia-like migration businesses, in which bosses (*patrón*) collude with traffickers (*coyote*, or migrant agents) to secure the exploitable labour they crave (Krissman 2005). What is often forgotten – again with all the emotiveness of migration control and policing issues – is that at any given border, even some of the most restrictive such as the USA-Mexico border, the amount of cross-border 'migration' daily (formal or informal) is dwarfed by the vast number of other border crossings linked to trade, the movement of goods, commuting, tourism, shopping, temporary stays, and so on (Pastor 2001). In the name of better trade relations, liberal states may enable and often cut loose all of these 'mobilities' (Urry 2007) under the rubric of free movement, thus operating a lighter hand in controlling migration.

Somewhere, there may be an optimal balance to be found: in which a flow of positive labour migration, driven by economic supply and demand, is openly allowed and recognised by the state, while negative migration (those proven to be harmful to migrants and/or unwanted by the host society) is minimalised.

Migration in the European Union

What do critics of 'neo-liberalism' have to say about these issues? Debates on the political economy of 'neo-liberalism' mainly focus not on the migration of labour or freedom of movement of persons, but on the injustices that have followed the removal of state control or governance over the three other 'core' freedoms of movement – of capital, goods and services – as part of the rampant global era of the 1980s, 1990s and 2000s. These variously include the triumph of financialisation, the rise of unaccountable transnational corporations, the cutting of welfare states and protective legislation, and the growing inequalities between super-elites and the rest of the population. Much of the ire expressed by critics centres on how the liberal 'freeing' up of market forces, justified by aggregate measures of growth and production, has seen the benefits accrued and monopolised by a narrow band of large-scale, internationally evasive, corporate interests. It is also a top-down story: governments and bureaucracies are seen to be part of these same elites, and in cahoots with the corporations. The 'roll back' is then not an abdication of power; it is also the aggressive use of state power in the name of an 'anti-state' philosophy and economic theory – the 'roll out' of neo-liberal policies (Peck 2010). Extending this to the EU, in recent work on the allegedly neo-liberal underpinnings of the European integration project by Anderson (2009), reprised by Schulz-Forberg and Stråth (2010), and Streeck (2013), it has been argued that the idea of the European institutions' elite autonomy from democratic governance at the national level can in fact be traced to the high priest of neo-liberalism, Hayek (*see also* Höpner and Schäfer 2012).[2]

Where these critics of neo-liberalism address the question of labour, it is always to see it as another abstract factor of production in the throes of the same neo-liberal logic. The varieties of capitalism literature thus sets up a negative, reified 'Anglo-American' model, supposedly ascendant against a 'continental' one (Hall and Soskice 2001), anchored in a Keynesian social democratic past, whose welfarist provision and legislation protecting workers was embedded in older national social compromises that emerged from conflicts between capital and labour. Neo-liberalism is apparently sweeping these away – with the EU

---

2. A more nuanced account of the global historical effects of neo-liberalism can be found in Hall and Lamont (2013). While this collection certainly flirts in parts with the Marxisant and Foucauldian style critiques, its introduction draws important distinctions between the values of liberalism and their corruption by neo-liberalism, and the main overview chapter (Evans and Sewell 2013) offers a comprehensive yet subtle account able to distinguish the variable and often paradoxical effects of both liberalism and neo-liberalism in different global and regional contexts. The focus on bottom-up 'social resilience' in the face of political economy trends is also a welcome analytical resource in relation to the underestimated effects of migrant agency and mobility argued for here.

as the primary source of these reforms at the national level. When alternatives are imagined – for example, in Esping-Andersen's defence of a Nordic system (1999) – they are idealised versions of nationalised political economies, in which (democratic, communitarian) politics curb markets through the decommodification of service provision, particularly child care and household work, which is sustained as a highly paid, regulated and taxed sector (Esping-Andersen then complains that his dry cleaning or a haircut costs him two or three times more in Copenhagen than New York!) As this suggests, the missing part of Esping-Andersen's brilliant, albeit imaginary Danish model, is the structural role of migration and migrants in all post-industrial economies today. The comparative varieties of capitalism literature continues to theorise (continental) European economies – i.e. labour markets – as if they can be nationally self-contained. Any migration is minimal or discounted as a factor. The stylisation is that we find migrants driving down service sector protection (and prices) in the USA, but not in Europe today – except, perhaps, in the Americanised 'Anglo-Saxon' Trojan horse economies (Britain and Ireland).

Yet migration across *all* of Europe is far from being a peripheral or exogenous factor: it is in fact the structural component of all European economies which – in Europe as America – allows the middle classes the life (and the service sector provision) they enjoy, as much as the central flow of new human capital keeping these economies fluid and dynamic. Migrants take the jobs that nationals do not want; they work in sectors where social protection or labour benefits are scarce. Migration everywhere has thus moved to become a central structural feature of late capitalist societies juggling the legacies of social democracy with global capitalism (*see also* Menz 2008). Even in Denmark, there is a sizeable black market in some sectors of the economy; where there is not, migrants are peripheralised and caricatured in populist terms and openly discriminated against in terms of non-recognition of skills and qualification. In a similar case, The Netherlands, a further symptom sees migrants forcibly 'integrated' into national cultural and linguistic norms as a condition of labour market incorporation. At the same time, informal migrant organisation and entrepreneurship – much of it transnational in basis – cut across these forced nationalisations. For much of the rest of the continent, then, the late 1990s and 2000s saw a remarkable liberalisation of the international labour market in many sectors, particular in services, that has seen the emergence of significant transnational economic spaces across Europe. Certainly, the informal scope and entrepreneurial nature of Southern Europe enabled migrant workers to find a place in the economy to an extraordinary degree; even corporatist France and Germany shifted in these informalising directions, while retaining sclerotic labour markets in some sectors – particularly in the heavily pensioned public sector, closed off to youth as much as foreigners. Anything that might be said about Britain or Ireland, therefore, as a migration destination in these respects is far from exceptional; rather they are setting a structural norm that most of Europe is following.

Critics, of course, may just see all this as evidence of 'neo-liberalism' triumphant. But labour here is not just a blind factor of production enabling capital to profit and escape state control; at least not in anything other than a hard-line structuralist Marxist view. Migrant labour also has agency, and experiences the benefits of social mobility relative to countries of origin; it brings change to the system from below (Smith 2001). Particularly, the inevitable transnationalism of migrants in informal economic spaces undermines and subverts the pretentions of states to re-impose national welfarist governance (Faist 2000). *Marxisant* scholars have often dealt with this challenge by a shift to Foucauldian territory: the apparent agency and individualism of the migrant and mobile work force is just a mark of how well the global capitalist system now produces easily exploitable 'flexible', hyper-mobile, adaptable 'subjectivities' attuned to a neo-liberal world (Sennett 1998; Mitchell 2003). Market freedoms are but a mark of a higher level form of state-disciplinary 'governmentality', albeit now located at a 'post-national' European level (Jensen and Richardson 2003).

Outside the dismal ontology and epistemology of Foucauldian Marxism – which renders any modern form of individual freedom impossible, as well as being wholly unfalsifiable in its logic – there remains a need to assess the negative or positive impact of free movement of persons within the changing European migration system. The critique of 'neo-liberalism' appears insensitive to the patent ways in which freedom of movement of persons might not lead to the same consequences as the free movement of capital, goods or services – for the migrants, as much as the receiving and sending economies.

Responding to the inequities of the emerging European migrant system, the EU – far from only unleashing free market forces, or moving towards a purely American model – has in fact sought to create conditions in which an optimal liberal outcome is possible. An alternate view of migration in Europe can thus be made by looking at different dimensions of the EU's attempt to develop policies that respond to the post-national scale of international labour markets no longer contained in their logic or substance by national borders.

Regarding migration from outside the EU, in search of a more optimal and just policy beyond 'smoke and mirrors' logic, the EU has officially made a great investment in the idea of 'managed migration'. Again, while much of the focus in academic debate has been on the failures and harshness of the restrictive regime to the South, European migration policies have also quietly smuggled in much more enlightened notions into the external partnership policies to the East and selective Southern states. In these agreements, improved trade relations and agreements on possible future membership negotiations have been accompanied by free movement accords or visa-free travel for different categories of person (for example, tourists, students and business movers). The goal is to liberalise top-down control and enable more open, back and forth-type borders rather hostile closed ones, which tend to have the negative informal effects detailed above. The nature of Europe's relations with, say, Morocco, Turkey or Ukraine has thus changed over the years in a liberal direction, albeit tentatively. Although these countries participate heavily in the conditional security and control operations, the migration regime has overall been liberalised. Similar effects for Romania and Bulgaria preceded their accession (Jileva 2002). The external policies amount to a concentric expansion of the realm of European integration beyond its internal borders, creating incipient new market-based rights to residents derived from the four freedom market principles of the EU. Under the right conditions, there will also be development benefits to the sending state; migration becomes governed more by demand and the choice of migrants to move or engage in economic activity.

These points are certainly empirically controversial. Turks in Europe, for example, feel indignant about persistent restrictions; but this is because they already sense they have justifiable rights and claims in the European territory derived from the market integration logic – they are already able to travel, study and work in Europe in unprecedented numbers. *Prima facie* it certainly cannot be denied that the EU scenario vis-à-vis the migration chances of its near neighbours certainly looks better than the 'smoke and mirrors' scenario in the USA-Mexico case. Damning criticism of the 'neo-liberalism' of NAFTA does not simply translate into the European scenario without ignoring one side of the story about European borders (as does Rumford 2006).

The impact of the idea of freedom of movement of persons outside the strict territory of the EU is one of the most surprising dimensions of the European integration project, albeit equivocal. Internally meanwhile, it is the very hallmark of why the EU is not like NAFTA or other purely top-down 'neo-liberal' regional integration projects (*see also* Bruszt and McDermott 2014). The fourth freedom makes all the difference: the fact that *all* citizens of the EU are in principle free to move live, study, work, retire in other member states – subject only to economic demand in another member state. They enjoy equality of employment, and rights of non-discrimination; they can study at the same cost, or (as workers) claim the same benefits as residents; they even have incipient political rights. The progressive reading likes to accent the more political and societal ambitions of these rights (Maas 2007), or attribute them to human rights (Soysal 2012); the fact is they are firstly grounded in market building principles (the EU's distinctive political economy), even if they allude in some ways (certainly not truly Marshallian) to a kind of European citizenship. The vast majority of Europeans using these rights are economic migrants: i.e. workers from both higher and lower sectors of the economy, to which can be added the individualistic choices of students and retirement migrants. Free movement of persons, which dates back to the insistent position of the Italians in negotiations about the European community in the 1950s, would be a radical concept in a Europe restricted to core economically rich states; yet, every successive accession has seen these rights extended eventually to new and often much poorer member states. By early 2014, nearly all transition barriers were down to the East and Central European member states; even Romania and Bulgaria. In theory, but also substantially in practice, this is a liberal migration dream scenario. There are no visas; there are no quotas or bizarre entry categories to fulfill; and even in non-Schengen countries, there are only the most perfunctory controls on cross-border movement. There is no visa scrutiny or application procedure preceding the move: you can just get on a plane or a train. The daily scene at London Stansted Airport says it all: dozens of flights pouring in from Poland or Southern Europe, just as the outbound flights take British residents off to their second home or back to see their families for the weekend.

Some may want to call this kind of thing 'neo-liberal', and to see the free choices of European citizens as nothing more than the expression of disciplined 'subjectivities' coerced by illusory notions of individual flexibility and mobility; but it has to be admitted that the effects of this part of regional integration – or European globalisation, if that's what it is – have been quite different to the effects of other freedoms of movement. Firstly, there is a light albeit marked evidence to show that unlike in open globalisation – which is dominated by arguments on how mobility has become an index of growing inequality – in European free movement the opportunities and effects are massifying (expanding) downwards, albeit partially, from top to bottom. European migrations are a mass middle-class phenomenon: characterised typically by educated, upwardly mobile or 'spiralist' movers (those socially ascending from provinces to cities) (Recchi and Favell 2009). European free movement have provided many more mobility opportunities for middle classes; not just elites. This includes far more than those who move physically. Even for the much bigger majority of European middle classes that don't, European mobilities are having a considerable impact on their daily lives in terms of the experience and organisation of their everyday lives: expanding social networks, wider travel experiences, the mobility of their children as students, financial mobilities, knowledge of other countries; it is, also, interestingly associated with growing cosmopolitanism (Mau 2010). One can agree with Fligstein (2008) in aggregate terms that it is upper and middle classes who have more benefitted more from European integration – hence his 'Euroclash' over the EU's legitimacy – but the people for whom their lives have been changed most radically by Europeanisation (and the regional elements of globalisation) are relatively speaking lower down the class scale – via new but increasingly banal consumer possibilities, travel, holidays, routine knowledge of foreign places, and so on (Mau and Verwiebe 2010). In terms of sending countries, self-selection has tended to put talented, adventurous, pioneering types on the road; there is certainly a danger of brain drain in many cases. On the receiving end, however, the benefits of such migration cannot be doubted: it is the most realistic vision of how the 2000 Lisbon Agenda could be fulfilled in terms of creating a Europe of maximised skill and knowledge in a dynamic, specialised economy.

This progressive case for the effects of West European migrations can be contested empirically, as I discussed in Chapter Seven. But the impact of Europe's extension to the East in these socially transformative terms is stronger, as was also emphasised in Chapter Eight. Here, the impact is bigger because it is also geo-political; soldering a new Europe across the massive divisions of the past. Europe has also seen a much larger scale migration of these citizens, driven by individual choice (to move), and market demand (selection of destination); highly educated or skilled migrants, facing low returns to these skills in their home countries, the migration also had positive self-selection effects. This holds positively in comparison to the much less open or liberal North American regime, with its perverse restrictions on skill and talent, its alphabet soup of visa categories, and its tendency to favour lower quality family reunification over selective self-motivated migration (Borjas 1999). For sure, East and Central European member states face a sharp danger of brain drain; however, in an open borders scenario, the migration is more likely to lead to circulatory and pendular migration, with high levels of remittances and return investment, particularly since so much of the migration activity is entrepreneurial in character (Morawska 2002). With longer-term settlement less likely as long as borders are easy and open (and cheap airlines plentiful), there are also fewer long-term family-related costs for receiving countries.

Faced with these theoretical and at least partially substantiated empirical views of the positive effects of the liberal idea of free movement on European migration and mobilities, social democrats should feel discomfort. Marxists cannot but see these trends as negative: this is where the reliance on the slogans condemning 'neo-liberalism' has made it easy. But can what they say about the free flow of capital, goods or services be applied to these apparent heroes and heroines of Europeanisation from below? If the issue is national welfare states, then yes: open European migration can damage welfare states when they take jobs from natives, drive down wages, or undermine ties of community. These are Polanyi's 'shiftless migrants' transforming the continent, as capital undoes the old coherence of political and social cohesion (Streeck 2013). But how to assess the conflicting evidence about complementarity in labour markets, positive effects of entrepreneurship, positive trends in human capital, significant cultural effects of diversity, or boosts towards post-national cosmopolitanism? Polanyi is often cited in a Marxisant way, but his view also allows for a liberal view, a positive potential balance between the competing poles of state, market and community (on this, *see* Caporaso and Tarrow 2009). Could it be with internal European migration, the EU actually achieved or at least offered a glimpse of a new, plausible and defensible balance between growth, flexible labour markets, political control, and social cohesion, re-located at a new post-national territorial level, that renders nationalist welfare-state positions outdated?

Britain as the future of Europe

While the boom years held, this optimistic reading could certainly find some empirical justification. The question is now, how has the crisis changed all this? Without a doubt, liberal Europe – the Europe of free movement that was ushered in by Delors in the 1980s, from the Single European Act, through Maastricht, to the single currency, the Lisbon agenda and treaty – is in deep crisis. This much in the accounts of Streeck, Anderson and others is true. The issue of democratic deficit – and the 'Euroclash' – sits at the heart of this. There has clearly emerged a popular resistance to the forces of post-national globalisation, expressed very clearly in the *non* and *nee* of France and The Netherlands in the constitutional referendum of 2005. These votes turned on middle-class anxieties about the liberalisation of the economy and the loss of national social and labour market protections. Critics of neo-liberalism call on democracy to be a bulwark to the consequences of an unfettered free market (Crouch 2011; Streeck 2011). What this will mean in practice, as we are beginning to see, is a democratic reaction against freedom of movement of workers, which will close borders in

Europe. Romanticism about 'another Europe' is thus shot through with the same contradictions as the left wing 'neo-liberal' interpretation: that it is possible to imagine a Europe somehow more attune to the demands of global justice, yet which has closed itself to the mobile factors of production and consumption that are most transforming the world elsewhere. This is particularly an unresolved contradiction in far left parties, who are emotionally cosmopolitan but viscerally nationalist in their conception of how markets are to be controlled or governed. The utopian solution of a European superstate which might engage in top-down management of the economy or large-scale redistribution in an up-scaled welfare state above all is a misconception of the progressive novelty of the EU, which lies rather in its promise of an unbounded cosmopolitan and post-national politics and society (Delanty and Rumford 2005). Less not more state has been the EU's greatest achievement: bringing liberalism and individualism as an antidote to the deeply ingrained fascist impulses of European governments and (especially) bureaucracies (Mazower 1998).

With democratic anti-EU unrest in many member states and struggling ratings in Eurobarometer, it is surely right that a certain limit has been reached to European integration. Beyond this, the danger is a nationalist 'roll back' of certain market freedoms. In February 2014, in a populist referendum, Switzerland, who were part of the open borders Schengen area, voted to curb freedom of movement and impose quotas on EU citizens working in the country. The next immediate threat in this sense is Britain, whose membership is very likely to come up for a vote in 2016 or 2017, especially after UKIP's triumph in the May 2014 European elections. A rising, democratic, anti-free movement tide drives the anti-EU case. The present government is threatening to opt out of free movement accords entirely, raising the spectre of imposing quotas and visas, removing all non-discrimination clauses, and restricting benefits for EU citizens: there is surely nothing 'neo-liberal', let alone liberal, about this blunt reassertion of state sovereign power over borders, driven by populist appeal.

Cameron's political gamble specifically brings into play the possibility of a decisive negative vote driven by the irrational misperception of the country's relationship with the EU, particularly a populist schizophrenia about the very freedoms of movement that the British economy perhaps best incarnates. Prior to the crisis, this could not be doubted. Britain's supposed distance to Europe – even its peculiar self-construction that sees Europe as its other, that 'place across the sea' – is perverse given the obvious fact that Britain is more closely involved and connected with the rest of the continent that at any point in its modern history, and that it has benefitted hugely throughout the 1990s and 2000s as an off-shore member of the club; having all the benefits of membership with fewer of the collective costs. This applies as much to trade (both exports and imports) and foreign direct investment, as to the banal everyday way the British have integrated European experiences, knowledge and (especially) forms of consumption into their lives. And, more than anything, it ignores the absolutely extraordinary way in which Britain has absorbed massive and disproportionate amounts of internal European migration, creaming off labour market selection benefits at all levels of the economy. This everyday willingness to receive European citizens as workers on legal terms is one important measure of European integration: on this dimension Britain can count as the *most deeply integrated* member state – only paralleled by the willingness of its own citizens to take up free movement benefits of retirement migration and buying property abroad. In many ways, the growing political hostility in elections or opinion polls thus sits in sharp contradiction to most British people's open-minded behaviour in practice. Meanwhile, what may be seen as 'neo-liberalism' by some, is also a mark of the market driven fluidity of a society that has been much less likely to use legal or illegal means to close the market, discriminate outsiders (via non-recognition of qualifications, parochialism, or cultural and linguistic barriers), or artificially protect the insider privileges of national citizens.

In terms of migration, a strong case can thus be made that what happened in Britain corresponded rather closely to the ideal liberal migration theory under optimal regional integration conditions. It *was* the brightest and best, those with talents and skills that might work in the entrepreneurial environment, who were drawn to Britain. With continental labour markets stagnant – especially in countries like France or Southern Europe – London became *the* Euro-destination of choice (Gordon *et al.* 2007). The youth of Western Europe could get work in London, and outperform natives. Their profile – a high proportion in their twenties, almost all under forty five, mostly highly educated, highly motivated – made them perfect workers. The best years of their working lives were given to the hugely competitive London labour market. Longer term, there were few costs to the receiving society: a large proportion would not stay once they had families, relying on going back to the more protected welfare states and education systems of continental Europe (i.e. social dumping).

A parallel dynamic applied to the much larger East European migration that followed the 2004 accessions. Given the numbers (well over 500,000 Poles in the first couple of years after accession, and large numbers from many other states), it is remarkable how long it took for any kind of significant political reaction. The migrants were given unquestioned labour market access, opportunities for niche sector entrepreneurship and received with equity by a market able to recognise the skills and talent on offer. And the migrants duly responded to this demand, by penetrating deeply many sectors of the economy (domestic work, household work, construction, hospitality and entertainment services, food service, transportation, agriculture), much of it entrepreneurialism which created new jobs (Garapich 2008). Unlikely any previous migration in modern Britain, they also penetrated widely out into provincial, small-town Britain.

It can argued that Britain's boom years were substantially fuelled by these European dynamics (Favell 2008a). But has this situation now changed? The sense of crisis has given the anti-immigration case a certain valency. But the point here is that from the anti-EU point of view, the question is not really empirical but symbolic and emotional. This has become increasingly clear in the government's inability to marshal any evidence that might be able to support its own official position that the decision should come down to the balance of national interest;

i.e. that this question somehow *does* hang in the balance (Portes 2013; Rigby and Parker 2014). On the face of it, compared to most of Europe, Britain has suffered the depression less deeply and recovered more quickly – for sure, monopolised by the London and the South East region which is most embedded in Europe. There has been some evidence of growing ethnic tensions over the presence of foreign Europeans, and certainly a growing awareness that some of the migration would have typical settlement consequences, particularly as it became progressively more difficult to come and go freely internationally. This lay the ground for UKIP's eventual ability to put a specific face on its Europhobia; but even in the years since the economic crisis – in which there has been tougher labour market competition, shrinkage of business and increased likelihood of settlement – there remain an certain abstractness to the hostility. Britain, as a whole, and the South East of England most strikingly, is a markedly more cosmopolitan place. The transformation – mostly a Europeanisation from below – since the grim years of the 1980s is extraordinary. 'Super-diversity' indeed sits well on its proudly established multi-racial history (Vertovec 2007).

The arguments above summarise an existing balance of evidence. On all these questions, there is now a furious debate, and there are certainly academic voices marshalling strong views on the anti-immigration side, right and left (Coleman 2011; Goodhart 2013). Meanwhile, the stakes involve a lot more than just the British population. Not only is the British European story one dramatically underplayed in the country itself; it is little recognised or understood on the continent, where clichés about its stripped-down, Americanised 'Anglo-Saxon' economy abound. British openness to foreign Europeans in its labour market and a certain degree of flexibility, flux and dynamism in an economy still structured significantly by social democratic legacies, might be argued as a model sorely needed elsewhere in Europe. Those countries which most closely align to the liberal market model within a social democratic framework, The Netherlands and Denmark, are – unfortunately and not coincidentally – also the ones with some of the worst track records on crude anti-immigration politics. This hinges on them being small countries with very exclusive cultural conceptions of national integration compared to Britain's more expansive post-colonial cosmopolitan nationalism. Britain meanwhile is much better governed and has a much more effective welfare state – also open on more equal terms to its migrant workers – than the more 'wild west' informal migration trends of Italy and boomtime Spain, all of which has turned very bad in the post-crisis period. Germany's structural dependency on manufacturing means its economy has a different kind of resilience, but it can eye with envy the much better governed results of open migration when compared to the problems of irregularity caused by its longstanding refusal to bring down transition barriers to Poles: it got the same migrant workers in large numbers, but with much worse selection dynamics. France, meanwhile, has been nothing but a tale of stumbling sclerosis for years. It saw a generation of its brightest and best graduates flee to London as Paris was eclipsed by its binary rival; unable to reform and open up its primary labour markets, immigrants and young French people alike were cast into immobile secondary labour market roles, while East European migrants were stigmatised, despite being numerically fewer than in neighbouring countries. From the point of view of the European Commission, on migration, Britain in Europe can only be seen as its star pupil.

Conclusion

The EU faces a decision of enormous moment with the British deliberation on Europe. As I have argued, it threatens to negate the example of a member state which has best embodied the radically transformative potential of the fourth freedom, itself the most distinctive element of the European regional integration project as a variant on globalisation. Open EU migration in Britain not only offered a solution to the conundrum of an optimal liberal migration scenario, but also a glimpse of its cosmopolitan potentials.

Yet this fact is far from visible. Both in Britain and in continental Europe, there is an assumption that Britain is both economically and politically an outlier; even that it is not really part of Europe. In Britain meanwhile, there is precious little recognition of how much it owes its recent success and power internationally to its geographical position; how its relationship with Europe was the secret of its re-ascendence and the boom times of 'cool Britannia'. The crisis since 2008 shows how much this success was effectively monopolised by London and the South East, where during and after the Olympics, it has continued to be business as usual, even as anti-Europeanism swells across the country.

Critics of liberal market economies can, from a left-leaning perspective, rightfully point to inequities, imbalances and harshness in the British economy. But there is little doubt that in terms of economic productivity as well as openness to the benefits of freer migration, most of continental Europe would benefit from *more* not less liberalisation on this question. Proponents of alternative political economies for Europe – re-imposing strong, top-down, state-governed controls on the factors of production and consumption, and labour market restrictions and protections – should own up clearly to the anti-European nationalist implications of their positions, if not their latent Marxism. In other words, sloganeering about the evils of 'neo-liberalism' masks and obscures an honest recognition that European economies in opening themselves to regional integration, must necessarily find a new balance between the prerogatives of the managed economy, flexible or open labour markets, and the privileges of insider communities and citizens.

Chapter Ten

Conclusion – Rebooting Migration Theory: Interdisciplinarity, Globality and Post-Disciplinarity in Migration Studies

Such has been the explosion of interest in international migration in the past two decades, that no scholar nowadays can feel adequate when confronting the avalanche of literature that has followed.[1] Any complete survey of migration theory or of empirical agendas for research would have to cover a full range of disciplines from the arts and literature through to psychology and economics, as well as spanning cases that might come from any part of the globe. The best approach perhaps has been in volumes such as Brettell and Hollifield's series of handbooks (2000, 2007, 2014) in which disciplinary perspectives were allowed to speak for themselves in a congenial dialogue, rather than attempting a unified theory – the most prominent of which have typically emerged from a base in economic theory (Hammar *et al.* 1997; Massey *et al.* 1998). The present collection, however, has a much narrower goal: to offer a set of strategic interventions into the field of research – mostly but not exclusively related to Europe – which identify a number of emerging agendas that may lead to new research in the future.

Although migration studies is an inherently global topic, questions of immigration, integration and mobility do not necessarily look the same in every part of the globe. Immigration is such a central part of the self-narrative of the USA, for example, no-one would today question the relevance of studying it in the mainstream social sciences and humanities. This may also be the case in settler societies such as Canada or Australia. Elsewhere in the world, migration is no less a significant subject, but it has taken time for it to be established as a serious academic topic. A major problem in anglophone countries has been that it is often lumped together – on syllabi and in bookstores – with 'ethnic and racial studies'. It took the great effort of some scholars to delineate a research program on migration that is quite distinct from the intersecting field of race and ethnicity (King 2002; Castles and Miller 2009), although this clearly now is well established. I hope this volume, too, will be useful ammunition to that end – to the consolidation of migration studies as a fully-fledged interdisciplinary field. In this brief bookend to the collection, my goal then is to not only explore some other dimensions raised by the question of interdisciplinarity in migration studies, but also offer

1. Originally published in Caroline Brettell and James Hollifield (eds) *Migration Theory: Talking Across Disciplines*. New York: Routledge (2007, 2nd edn). With thanks to the editors, Irene Bloemraad, Roger Waldinger and Russell King for their comments on the earlier version.

some thoughts as to what the core theoretical building blocks of this field might be (*see also* Smith and King 2012). In attempting to synthesise these ideas, as I have throughout, I aim to diagnose the weak spots and miscommunications in the research field, pointing the way forwards to the next decades of (hopefully) increasingly multi-disciplinary, multi-methods research.

Interdisciplinarity in migration studies

On the face of it, there could hardly be a topic in the contemporary social sciences more naturally ripe for interdisciplinary thinking than migration studies. This should be obvious to anyone sitting down to design a comprehensive course in international migration. In such a course, there is always a need to somehow marry quantitative data sources and basic economic or demographic analysis of migration, with an ethnographic or oral historical sense of the lives and experiences of migrants themselves. Sociology and political science readings are needed to broach the structural background of immigration and incorporation processes; and there is so much interesting work coming out of anthropology and geography – particular looking at transnational processes – that these approaches clearly must not be overlooked. Migration studies needs a simultaneously top-down as well as bottom-up approach, and it needs history to temper the overwhelming topicality of the present. A course such as this ought also to be comparative and global – although that part is the hardest to achieve.[2]

Yet interdisciplinarity – in the social sciences at least – is a struggling ideal. To talk across disciplines in the USA is also to speak against one's the disciplinary career interests, which often wholly reflect the business of reproducing the disciplinary canons and professional hierarchies that takes up so much of the everyday academic enterprise. Reading authors from different disciplines it is clear how much all of them have been socialised in the *habitus* of their own disciplines, however open minded their explicit intentions (Bourdieu 1984). In the disciplinary mindset, the canon in each is presented like an accumulation of sanctified knowledge stored in a tall farmyard silo. This is a very American problem, although research assessment exercises are making it a problem everywhere. As part of their training, students are taught to prepare for disciplinary 'field exams', which teach them to read and reread only familiar literature. Alternative methodologies are sidelined, they are often forced to study the USA (out of practical accessibility), and to pose the questions in a classical mode. The only

---

2. My experience teaching at UCLA, where I co-taught an ambitious programme with Roger Waldinger, Ivan Light, Ruben Hernández-León and others, as well as co-organising a large interdisciplinary summer school for the SSRC, is that – contrary to the constant advice in the USA about the need for specialist technical training – students are well able to appreciate and assimilate readings from across disciplines and methodologies when migration is the singular focus. A course such as this can play a vital role in prising open the disciplinary closing of the American mind that is often hammered home in departments riven by fruitless quantitative/ qualitative divides, and in universities where disciplines rarely talk to each other. In studying migration, multi-disciplinarity with a multi-methods approach should be a basic premise *even* if the case study focus of the course is exclusively immigration in the USA.

space for interdisciplinary social studies in the USA has been in international studies units, which often do not have their own faculty, and which are always less prestigious positions than mainstream disciplinary professorships. Woe betide the young graduate student who wanders too far from the disciplinary path. It can be professional suicide in terms of scoring those job-talk essential first publications in the 'top' recognised journals of the given discipline. Young academics in the USA are basically taught that their dream someday should (only) be to become chair of their respective disciplinary association. It is ironic and unfortunate that the wilfully diverse, and distinction-obsessed social sciences are behind the times in this sense. Interdisciplinarity is becoming a rule of thumb for natural scientists in science fields unifying across old boundaries: for example, in the intersection of biological and physical sciences; or in the pathbreaking work in complexity science, in which natural sciences are marching boldly into social scientific territories.

In Europe, interdisciplinarity is threatened by the grim progress of bureaucratic research assessment exercises, spearheaded by the British model, and self-inflicted by a generation of compliant Stakhanovite academics re-cast by policy makers as standardised organisation men (and women). Intellectual production has suffered hugely as a result. In these assessments, all academic output is reduced to scoring major journal articles, the ranking of which is inevitably defined by disciplinary canons. Citations accumulate most effectively in closed networks of friends and acquaintances citing each other's work. Inevitably, then, interdisciplinary or eclectic journals such as those in migration studies carry much less weight, and it has become much harder to make a career as a multi-disciplinary migration studies scholar. Interdisciplinarity across Europe is now associated with the failure of 1970s and 1980s experiments in university structures.[3]

Different disciplines can, however, provide a base for a multi-disciplinary approach. Sociology – at least when it breaks clear of classical questions – has the virtue of being a space in which interdisciplinarity is fairly automatic. The most important areas of sociology are in effect interdisciplinary dialogues – political sociology, economic sociology, comparative historical sociology, ethnography (with anthropology), demography (with economics and statistics), conversation analysis (with linguistics), communication and media studies, and so on. This leaves the difficulty of defining who or what a sociologist is – as opposed, say, to economists, political scientists or anthropologists, who have a clearer conception of who they are. But this can be a virtue as well as an identity problem.

Geography – which, although rather marginal in the USA, is arguably the most exciting discipline in the social sciences in Europe – has, at its best, a similar quality (King 2012). With its central concern about flows, networks, space, place and transactions across the planet, geography's advantage is that it is much less automatically wedded to methodological nationalism than sociology, whose master concept of 'society' is almost impossible to extricate from the historical context

---

3.   As a member of faculty at the Universities of Sussex and Utrecht I experienced the dismantling of two innovative interdisciplinary structures because of outside funding pressures structured by research assessment imperatives, in both cases against the will of those who worked there.

of the nation state (Wimmer and Glick Schiller 2002). Historians, meanwhile, often stress sensitivity to context and the unique complexity of specific migration experiences, but in comparative historical mode they inevitably reach out to political science theories of the state, and sociological theories about immigrant integration processes: one thinks of the essential work of Moch (2003), Morawska (2011) or Gabaccia (2000) and their struggle to open the US-centric bias of so much historical production on immigration. There are parallels to this in the intersection of demography, economics and sociology. Where would migration theory be today without the work of Massey (*et al.* 1998), Portes (with Rumbaut 2001), or Sassen (2001) – or the very fruitful ethnography and theory dialogue going on in contemporary cultural approaches in anthropology or geography, exemplified by Ong (1999)? There will be no problem with interdisciplinarity in migration studies if these are the inspirations in future.

Globality in migration studies

That said, certain dimensions of interdisciplinarity are curtailed by the all-enveloping national focus of study in the USA. Navel gazing is, for sure, a pastime of academics in every major and minor national tradition. It is often at its worse in small, self-regarding nations – as the often very local intellectual debates of many West European countries suggest – but Americans in particular have a propensity for a lack of awareness of how so much of what they take to be 'canonical' or 'universal' to their respective disciplines is *nothing but* the view from within this particular nation-state, however large and powerful it is in the intellectual landscape. 'We are the world', Americans like to think. No, you are not. Parts of my essays here, particularly Chapters Four and Five, seek to diagnose this (*see also* Schmitter-Heisler 2004). The biggest problem is that academic studies reflecting above all the political concerns of local national debates, always turn discussion of international migration and global mobility into debates about the ethics of immigration – which inevitably prioritises the view from the receiving society, and the variable transformation of foreigners into (American) citizens.

It is particularly frustrating that leaders in the field in the USA make frequent calls for more cross-national comparativism in migration studies to help advance the American debates – one thinks of Portes's very sharp manifesto (1997) – but that the agenda has continually proven difficult to deliver. As Portes and DeWind (2004) put in a summary of one such meeting, many transatlantic dialogues rarely get much further than discovering, 'the wide differences in perspective arising from diverse national contexts and intellectual traditions' (p.843). Some of the very best European scholars are too busy in their local struggles and commitments to join these efforts as much needed experts, and often do not publish much in English. Americans weaned on the US canon, meanwhile, often rely on short summer visits to develop their local knowledge. As I argue in Chapter Five, a thorough transatlantic agenda, fully alert to problems of asymmetry and conceptual translation difficulties, is likely to necessitate rethinking many of the theoretical assumptions and data reflexes on which the American canon is based. There has been much recent work published by US scholars, with often heroic international comparative ambitions and in collaboration with some of the best European researchers.[4] But there is still a suspicion that European material is being flatly used as an extension of American concerns and American theory, in an arguably imperialist manner. But why should America and its experience with immigration be the automatic benchmark for anywhere? When leading American observers, re-applying American theory to fresh comparative cases, find that the USA has a more 'universal' track record when compared to Germany as a more 'ethnic' nation, or that French republicanism masks cultural particularism (i.e. Alba 2005), it can be questioned if these judgements have much meaning. What is missing is a realisation that US tools and theories have to be completely rethought in the European context. The scale of these societies, the historical nature of nation-building and migration, the institutional structures, and the transnational context of the EU, are all factors that ensure European national cases are not directly comparable or amenable to the habits of analysis that work so well in the USA. Comparativism is a wonderful thing, but it also has to be tempered by an awareness of the complete asymmetry in the US-Europe relationship, and the power relations that distort it (Favell 1999). The new crop of US-European immigrant integration studies, discussed in Chapter Five, need careful interrogation along these lines. However, as I also argued earlier, the explosion of comparative political sociology style work on citizenship and immigration *was* one genuine example of a fruitful internationalisation of a research field – a case where a far more sophisticated comparative social science was able to cut through the parochial concerns that dominated the debates of national scholars in countries such as France and Britain, and introduce a new scientific quality to the work being done.

Because of such widespread parochialism, even in such a closely interrelated continent such as Europe, the most basic cross-national awareness is often lacking. European scholars often hold highly stereotypical albeit operational views of near neighbours – the French see British ethnic and race relations as 'racist', the British see French republicanism as 'homogenising', and so on – that are linked to the usefulness of stereotypes in political debates within the country. This points to a distinctively politicised aspect of migration studies in Europe that in fact has its weaknesses and strengths. With the exception of some of the scholars circling around the Washington-based think tanks, American academic production about immigration, as on any other subject, takes place with splendid, Olympian distance from the dirt of everyday politics. Given just how dirty American politics is, this is perhaps a good thing for the academics concerned. It certainly helps academic production establish a credible power of autonomy, by not playing the journalistic game (Bourdieu 1996). At their best, American institutions *are* formidable institutions of independent science, that Europeans could only dream about matching. Social science in the USA is clearly much cleaner and therefore more scientific – in the positivist sense – than in Europe.

---

4.   For example, Parsons and Smeeding (2006); Crul and Mollenkopf (2012); Alba and Holdaway (2013). I discuss these and several others in Chapter Five, fn.17.

European research could hardly be described as politically clean, in continental Europe especially, and even more so in the smaller countries or ones – such as Spain, France or Denmark, for example – where academics, opinion makers and policy makers are concentrated on top of each other in the metropolitan centre and capital city. In these contexts, leading academics are almost always also highly politically engaged, and their careers and appointments are themselves are often political. When you are constantly running after ministry money or trying to catch the eye of newspaper editor, the danger again is navel gazing. Work gets framed exclusively in terms of the national political debates of the day, and you certainly do not have time to waste flying to international conferences in the USA. Being an international studies expert in certain countries does not principally mean doing international work or being part of an international network; it means being an international expert who observes the world outside and translates it to users involved in furiously inward-looking debates about national politics and national identity. Yet the academic production on a topic such as immigration or international migration can have a political relevance and impact in shaping debates in small European countries of which Americans could only dream. Leading academics are routinely invited to appear on TV as experts or write op eds in the leading newspapers. They have a status and visibility in the local society that is only ever matched in the USA by academics who have renounced the scientific academic game and become despised 'public intellectuals'.

One upshot of this is that there might be different criteria for evaluating the value of scientific production in different contexts. Pure research is different to policy situated research: those locally minded European scholars are not necessarily mistaken in their assessment of what counts most in their research. It might also lead to different theories. The situation means that European research is less naively positivistic. Europeans generally have no problem seeing that the difference between facts and values is very blurred or that political interests lie behind the production of most scientific knowledge. There can be found then a more sophisticated *reflexive* consciousness about the way in which power and knowledge-interests shape academic production. Roughly speaking – I will go on to elaborate the latter two – the Habermasian, Foucauldian and Bourdieusian approaches in social science are the three main paradigms for understanding this process (*see* Zimmermann and Favell 2011). The upshot of this is not so much that everyone becomes postmodern. This is actually a bigger problem in the USA, where there the rejection of positivism has often led to a dogmatic (qualitative) postmodernism, which mirrors the dogmatic (quantitative) positivism advanced by others. Rather, arguably, there is a more sophisticated awareness, especially in continental Europe, that you don't just throw out good empiricist instincts with the positivist bathwater. In other words, that an empirical post-post-positivism is possible (on this, *see* especially Bourdieu and Wacquant 1992). Even more obviously, the fact/value distinction is routinely crossed in the very large body of normative theorising in the social science of migration and immigration in Europe, which I discussed in detail in Chapters Two and Five.

Beyond Europe, of course, there is an even bigger question here about the ethnocentrism of much migration theory in *both* Europe and North America.

Decentring America in migration studies in the name of globality, would also be a process that ought to decentre Europe too. This continues to be a problem in many of the leading text books.[5] There is still remarkably little reflection in migration studies from the bottom of the heap up, as it were – from the sending side, the 'rest' of the world – at least in terms of dominant theory development. This point ought to be leading us to conceive of migration as a global topic embedded in post-colonial and development studies. We ought to be encouraging the production of far more work about migrations in all the regions of the world not just those in the West, looking far more at how sending country contexts influence and shape migration trends.[6] It is perhaps surprising that the study of international migration today has lost so much of the world systems or global development perspective that was much more present in the earlier work of Piore (1979), Castles (and Kosack 1973) or Portes (and Walton 1981), for example, work that stressed relations of power and of economic dependency between the West and the rest of the world.

Part of the problem, again, though is epistemological. We are right to want to foreground the role of power in knowledge construction. But the road to decentring the social sciences can also be a road out of social science entirely. The call to transcend ethnocentrism has often gone hand in hand with a broader philosophical agenda, coming out of cultural anthropology and radical geography, critiquing the whole modernist, developmental paradigm that privileges the view from the West: that is, those old school views that evaluate development in terms of its benefits for the (Western) global economy, and/or the performance of developing economies and political cultures in Western terms. The disciplinary mentality of the sciences can certainly be diagnosed as part of this problem: that the notion of knowledge and the techniques for establishing it, always rely on and mask the influence of power and dominant ideology. This broadly Foucauldian view of science and modernity, of the disciplining power of bureaucratic systematisation and technical specialisation – richly illustrated by the technical training components of post-graduate professionalisation in the USA – can be a very effective macro-history of the scientific West and its evaluative relations to 'backward' others. Given the relatively uncontroversial acceptance that the developmentalist paradigm and science it was built on was indeed in large part a self-deluding cover for Western self-justification, ethnocentrism and exploitation, the post-colonial inversion of the Western perspective seems good sense. We all want and need a truly 'global' social science – that speaks with and for the multitude, not only the global elites – and not one embedded in discredited Western political means of planetary control and dominance. Geography and anthropology indeed went through revolutionary change in this sense, when previous paradigms used for mastering and dominating

---

5. Brettell and Hollifield's otherwise admirable handbooks were a case in point (2004, 2007, 2014).

6. We should however applaud the Castles and Miller volumes – the leading textbook of the field, now in its fourth edition (2009) – for at least re-thinking international migration in an overtly global sense. The work of Massey *et al.* (1998), although very much driven by the Mexico-USA scenario, which is so close to home, can similarly be endorsed. Another recent, excellent overview volume is Gold and Nawyn (2013). *See also* King *et al.* (2010).

the colonies became discredited. Departments were closed and heads rolled. We might await a similar realisation that, say, the highly Americanised and US-centric disciplines of economics and political science – with their often brittle scientific self-presentation – might go through a similar self-critique as their embedded relation to American political and economic hegemony is revealed. But this call has to be made in the name of better science and truth itself.

Unfortunately, however, the pessimistic currents of postmodernism and cultural relativism which raised these doubts, and that began to creep across all the social sciences and humanities from the 1980s onwards, also led practitioners of such 'critique' to develop a thoroughgoing scepticism and deconstructive attitude to *all* the procedures and goals of the now despised 'enlightenment project', not only those that were perverted in the name of Western hegemony. The victim of this revolution, then, has more often not been power, but truth itself (Hollis 1994). Relativism all the way down is not an option for social science – a real cost of the over-enthusiastic postmodern anglophone interpretations of Foucault, Latour, Lyotard, Bourdieu and company.[7]

Positive and postmodern social sciences thus co-exist in mostly mutual distrust and ignorance. Sociology and political science, for example, are greatly lacking because of their disconnect with the highly creative growth of post-colonial cultural studies in the humanities. In disciplines that begin with novels, theatre or television as windows to the social world, but very soon move to claiming the whole world is a text to be deconstructed, there is in fact an alternate social analysis of the world being made, that often extends far beyond the realm of literary studies *per se*. The influence of textual and critical discourse analysis techniques can certainly be seen to work to good effect on the representations of migrants in newspapers, public debates and governmental policy documents and so on. The post-structuralist and post-colonial methodology that cutting-edge literary studies now embraces as a kind of orthodoxy, has indeed gone hand in hand with a huge outpouring of work on transnationalism, hybridity, cultural resistance, and the empowerment of subordinate and minority voices through representing the experiential dimension of migrant life. To not reflect more on this kind of post-disciplinary work is an oversight for sure (good examples are Papastergiadis 1999; Lionnet and Shih 2005).

Post-disciplinarity in migration studies

The post-disciplinary path being blazed by contemporary humanities and literary studies is, however, not the one I want to follow here. A different notion of post-disciplinarity can, I think, be retrieved for research approaches to migration other than the textual or wholly idealist in epistemological terms (*see* Sayer 1999; 2000). On some level, I would argue, the social scientific enterprise – perhaps

---

7.   This dominant anglophone reading of 'French theory' has typically been caused by the over-enthusiastic *mis*-reading of poor English language translations. The same scholars are read and understood very differently in France (*see* Cusset 2005).

in distinction to cultural and literary studies – relies in the end on an underlying possibility of realism in observational methods and representations of the world. Realism is often opposed in epistemological terms to constructivism, but this is in fact an unsophisticated philosophical schism. On some very basic level, *all* social sciences since at least Durkheim have or at least should be constructivist in their self-understanding (*see also* Hacking 2000). That is, accept the idea that the social world is a humanly constructed (i.e. not naturally or essentially given) reality, that our very methods of data gathering, categorisation, and representation themselves construct in a certain way. It accepts that the social scientist is a part of the social world about which they are constructing knowledge – and techniques of knowledge gathering. But it is no less *real* for that – and no less *true* when successful – especially if these techniques are embedded in a socially shared *habitus* of scientific practice (as opposed to literary, journalistic, political practice, etc.), that sustain the autonomous social power of recognised academic work (*see* Bourdieu *et al.* 1968).[8]

What a constructivist empiricism might enable is a re-thinking of migration theory that helps us re-build a more politically autonomous and scientific form of studying the subject, while not letting go of the incontrovertible need for a less disciplinary and more global approach. The point here is that we do not want to endorse procedures or methods that remove for us the very material 'fact' that migration is something that happens when a real (physical) person moves in real (physical) space. The suggestion that can be read in much radical geography that space itself is a wholly subjective or mentally constructed fiction seems to go too far. People move, and the material physical distance of those moves matter, as do the physical borders that separate different social units in space and define what counts as spatial movement. The postmodern cultural turn in population geography, in rejecting the 'objectivist' or 'positivist' old geography, unfortunately has tended to want to collapse all material space into socially constructed space, thus in a sense negating geography's most interesting and valuable contribution to the social sciences.

The approach to migration studies suggested by the post-disciplinary approach here, is however one that begins to question and dismantle some of the fixed points and conceptualisations provided by our standard definitions of international migration in the international state system. These, clearly, are political constructions of the modern world, exhaustively carved up as it is into distinct nation-state units. This world should, in our migration theory, be subject to political and historical deconstruction. Yet nearly all conventional approaches in migration studies assume that we know what migration is, and that we can accept the units – from which people move to which they move – given by the political world we live in. But these are only conventions that happen to be the case here and now. The basic definition they assume is the standard one. Citizens or (at least) residents of one nation-state are migrants or have migrated, firstly when they leave that nation-state and cross an international border to set foot in another; and secondly, when their move has a

---

8. Bourdieu and Wacquant (1992) speak of this as transcending the false opposition of 'social physics' and 'social phenomenology'. They offer perhaps the most successful and sophisticated paradigm for empirical social science research based on a kind of constructivist realism.

time dimension – decided by convention (one year in the statistics) – after which they can be considered to have moved residency. It is only a short step to fall into the full 'immigration' optic by accepting the third assumption that the move creates a particular relationship with the receiving society, defined by the new residence: that the migrant is an outside, foreign body that has to be absorbed in some way into the receiving, given 'society'. Other movers, who are not staying and whose presence is relatively indifferent to the receiving society, cross borders – such as tourists, business people, students, posted workers or international lorry drivers – but they remain largely invisible forms of movement from the migration/immigration perspective. The literature on transnationalism, it is true, questioned the one way assumptions of these migration definitions, stressing the interplay or interrelations of the two places, and the migrant networks between, but it did not much enlarge or question the notion of migration itself as a form of mobility. The second generation of this literature, responding to the accusation it was ignoring the state by stressing only flows and networks has, with the notion of 'simultaneity', in fact fallen back into describing the binary interaction of migrants in sending and receiving contexts, and hence retained a focus on essentially the same kind of movers as immigration scholars (Levitt and Glick Schiller 2004). In all these approaches, no-one examines whether migration is in fact something only defined and derived from the state's need to classify and carve up spatial mobility in a certain way – and that it could be defined in another way.

What might happen if we shut down the disciplinary canons for a moment, and reboot our computer? The filing system in the computer has collapsed and we are forced to re-describe our object of study out there in the real world. Nothing appears natural any more: certainly not our definition of what constitutes a migrant or an event/action of migration in the world. We would have to draw new lines and new conventions.

Would sending and receiving 'societies' today still automatically appear as units coterminous with the borders of actually existing, politically defined, nation-states? Or would this historical convention now appear a redundant, or certainly a questionable starting point for building a science of spatial movement? We take it for granted but it wholly defines our idea of who is a citizen and a resident, and who therefore is a foreigner and a migrant, in relation to specific territories and space. But the world is not only one of nation-state units. Some aspects of society are aggregated in very different units, in which social relations, networks, transactions and events, spanning both physical and virtual spaces, have local, regional, or global patterns that do not correspond in any way to the container that the nation-state view might wish to impose on them. Biologists studying pollination or meteorologists studying the patterns of hurricane formation would never think that the phenomena they describe were in any way defined by the given nation-state borders and definitions of the everyday political world. Should we continue to describe and file human spatial mobility in the same way?

The issue, in a sense, is a reverse of what is argued typically by political scientists and historians, who are mostly concerned with bringing the state back in to a scientific field in which the political view was missing. I would argue this is not the most urgent problematic for a re-booted migration theory. In fact, the political (i.e. the conventional) mode of carving up the world into nation-states is pervasive and ever present in *all* the existing disciplines and their debates. A similar thing might be said about history. To be able to theorise freely, we may need to *remove* our understanding of migration away from the urge to account for everything in terms of time and place specific narratives; that is, the way the world looks to us conventionally because of our history, and our inherited political modes of understanding. History and political science almost always end up reproducing the conventional nation-state point of view of spatial mobility, because it is (still) the dominant conventional view of the world. Sociology, as I have stressed throughout this volume, is also deeply embedded in the nation-state view of the world – not least because nearly all the statistics that it and demography uses are generated by nation-states classifying territorially fixed populations, in relation to collectivities imagined as national 'societies'. We might hope or expect economics – which claims to be methodologically individualistic in its approach – to challenge the convention that the world is divided up only into macro units called nation-states, but in fact nearly all economic theories of migration take the conventional definition of international migration from nation A to nation B as their starting point for discussing economic differentials between spatial units, or the costs and benefits of migration to pre-given national societies. Geography and anthropology, it is true, have a less automatic reliance on methodological nationalism in their modes of analyses. But they are prey to a different problem: of reifying a culturalist view of the world – which then often falls in line with the idea of a world divided up into national 'ethnic' cultures, languages, institutions, etc.

The point here is that in foregrounding the pervasiveness of the nation-state in our conventional understanding of migration, we might in fact reverse the relationship and show how the nation-state gets constructed and reproduced in and through these conventional understandings. Instead of telling a story about how foreign objects (migrants) fit into or challenge the given (nation-state) narrative and institutional structures by which we recognise the world, we might instead look at how the very process by which collectivities manage movers by naming and counting them – and thereby distinguishing them from non-movers or residents – is the fundamental way by which the territorial nation-state-society constitutes itself in the first place. Physical movement across space is the natural, normal given of human social life; what is abnormal, changeable and historically constructed, is the idea that human societies need to construct political borders and institutions that constrain and define spatial mobility in particular, regularised ways, such that immobility becomes the norm.

The step I am advocating here is essentially to expand and redefine migration studies as a subset of (spatial) mobility studies. This is a project that has been advocated by several social theorists in recent times (Castells 2000; Urry 2000). Unlike them, however, my concern is also with preserving the focus, uppermost to migration studies, on real people moving in real space – not virtual and non-human forms of mobility and flows. The issue, in fact, is quite simple. What is it that makes the 'illegal' migrant crossing a given border different to the 'legal' immigrant, the foreigner on a holiday visa, the lorry driver, or the shopper over for the day? The mobility of goods and services, and even sometimes capital, also involves the physical movement of persons across borders. Minus the nation-state, we might very easily see the fruit pickers on the other side of the sea, who pick the bananas we enjoy at breakfast, as part of *our* society; they are certainly an essential part of *our* economy, that is, our market for fruit. Similarly, there is a deep truth to the Mexicans in California who complain, when accused of illegality, that they did not cross any borders – *the borders crossed them*. What makes the 'illegal migrant' different is that a nation-state has decided to name the movement *that* way – as a way of asserting its own sovereign existence.

Just taking the border at Tijuana would make this point very clear. A very small proportion of the cross-border mobility found at this junction of the political world – that is the most stark political dividing line between the West and the rest – is actually 'migration' – illegal or otherwise. As well as the fun-loving tourists, the commuters, and the shoppers looking for cheap deals, there are a vast number of goods-related crossings that never count, and would never be recognised as migration. These open, mostly economic transactions, in fact dwarf movements counted as migrations. Yet some people have rights to physically move over the border while others do not; an even smaller number have a (nationally sanctioned) *right* to migrate. Some movements are counted as immigration, others illegal migration, still others asylum seeking, and so on. All these distinctions are more or less arbitrary and defined wholly by conventions imposed by the nation-states in question. As citizens we have to recognise the legality of nation-states and what it sanctions; but there is no reason why we have to take this power for granted as autonomous scholars, who should be free from such political blinkers. These conventions, we can see, can change or vary over time and space. The border itself only exists because it is the place where all these classifications are made; it is being made and remade every time the state (or one of its representatives) puts into action criteria in its name that classifies a movement as migration or not. In other words, minus the border, there would be no state, or state governance, here. The (American) nation-state in fact constitutes itself in the very act of recognising, classifying and then sanctioning or not (i.e. governing) the physical movements that are going across its self-declared borders.

Conventional views of governance, sovereignty and control entirely reproduce the taken-for-granted convention of state power. To think of this power as continually constructed and enacted also brings into sharp focus the absurdity of many of the discussions on incorporation or integration, especially since academic discussions in these sub-fields so tamely follow political ones. Spatial movements can be highly integrated in social networks and relations – whether familial, communal, political or economic – regardless of whether they are organised or even fall within the receiving society's political perception of incorporation and integration. But again, by recognising, classifying, and then reshaping the social interactions that follow from movement as 'incorporation' or 'integration', the receiving society itself is constituted. America is, we know, the sum of all immigrants; that is, immigration *is* the very story of the nation. But look again. It might be possible to see there really is no society here other than the controlled, hierarchical system that calls itself a nation because enough 'Americans' – who were once foreigners and immigrants – at the same time believe it is the primary social and political entity of which they are part. The historical emergence of the nation-state is one by which collectivities have found ways to cage and penetrate social and economic interactions that would otherwise be unbounded. One of the key historical ways that the state has constituted its powers over society has been to classify movement as migration, and thereby invented a fixed immobile territorial population that can call itself a nation.[9] That, in a globally porous world, this process still works so effectively for nations like America – which feels very little ontological insecurity at a political level – is a remarkable fact.

The effect of understanding how the state works to create itself and society in its own image need not be one that belittles its basic power. We simply see this power for what it is. In a basic social theoretical sense, some such collective entity as a state may well be necessary to the functioning of society. This is the old Hobbesian argument about a Leviathan as basic to the non-destructive functioning of social order. But historically, and even in the modern age, there are a range of possible social orders other than the modern nation-state-society (*see* Sassen 2006). Putting it this way in fact underlines just how remarkably dominant and powerful is our taken-for-granted carving up the world into nation-states. The modern nation-state's sharp ability to designate and recognise which spatial movers are foreigners is a remarkable political achievement – so effective that scholars of migration rarely question who are migrants or not by this definition.

What is of interest in the current global age, is the extent to which this conventional patterning and defining of populations, distinguishing citizens, residents, migrants and movers, is or has been changing because of the changing relationship of the global and regional economy to nation-state sovereignty. The subject matter of international political economy, in fact, is principally concerned with the politics of this shifting relationship, and the governance of mobility on which it turns: of *all* forms of movement–capital, goods, services and persons. Amongst these, the global economy is, of course, challenging the preeminent power of nation-states themselves to define who is and who is not a citizen or a migrant; who is an immobile resident and who is a mover who has crossed some border. The re-booted approach to migration theory I present here, may help us recognise the empirical significance of work focusing on these changes, which might otherwise look like fringe questions in migration studies.[10]

---

9. Here the story becomes something more familiar to comparative historical sociologists: the rise of classes and nation-states, the invention of the passport, and the containing of otherwise mobile or ambiguously defined populations in the late nineteenth century – a core moment in the forming of the modern nation-state system (Mann 1993; Torpey 2000). *See also* Scott (1998).

10. Two examples I have pursued elsewhere are the anomalous migrations of GATS Mode 4 service workers (posted workers), mentioned in Chapter Six and discussed in depth by Lavenex (2006); and the free movement of European citizens discussed in Chapters One, Seven, Eight and Nine, and conceptually explored in Favell (2008a), Recchi (2008; 2015), Favell, Recchi et al. (2011).

These thoughts suggest that while the nation-state remains the modern world's great disciplining device, we ought to be able to devise through migration studies a way of seeing how and why this disciplining happens. Perhaps this can be cited as the broadest agenda for migration studies offered by this volume. The nation-state has created the world in its own image, and science for centuries has also been harnessed to these goals. Migration is one of the key anomalies of a world divided up into more or less fixed population containers – which is why the state politically takes its challenge so seriously, and why migration is, by most observers, so conventionally understood. Power is at work here; it is pervasive in our social science of migration. It is perhaps disappointing that social science disciplines today still seem so wedded to these given conventions for understanding migration. Breaking with the disciplinary nature of the social sciences, and developing a post-disciplinary view may well help scholars think, for once, outside of the box.

The theory this re-booting generates need not be anything other than a straightforwardly empirical, historical and comparative enterprise, but it will have to recast the subject of migration in a thoroughly decentred, global perspective. We need to renew the conceptual tools with which we think of and recognise migration. The ones we have inherited from scientific disciplines are not ideally sensitive to this need. Disciplines themselves think and see like a (nation) state, to borrow James C. Scott's famous phrase (1998). To really talk across disciplines would also mean finding a way to escape the nation-state dominated conceptions that conventionally make sense of the world and the migration that takes place within it.

Works by the Author

Favell, A. (1995) *Philosophies of Integration: The Theory and Practice of Ethnic Minority Policies in France and Britain*, European University Institute (EUI), Florence, PhD.

Baumgartl, B. and Favell, A. (eds) (1995) *New Xenophobia in Europe*, The Hague: Kluwer Law International.

Favell, A. (1997) 'Citizenship and immigration: pathologies of a progressive philosophy', *New Community*, 23(2): 173–195.

Favell, A. (1998a) (2001, 2nd edn) *Philosophies of Integration: Immigration and the Idea of Citizenship in France and Britain*, London: Macmillan-Palgrave; New York: St Martin's Press.

Favell, A. (1998b) 'Multicultural race relations in Britain: problems of interpretation and explanation', in Joppke, C. (ed.), *Challenge to the Nation State: Immigration in Western Europe and the United States*. Oxford: OUP, pp. 310–349.

Favell, A. (1998c) 'A politics that is shared, bounded and rooted? Rediscovering civic political culture in Western Europe', *Theory and Society*, 27(2): 209–236.

Favell, A. (1998d) 'Political philosophy at the Rubicon: Will Kymlicka's *Multicultural Citizenship*', in *Ethical Theory and Moral Practice* 1(2): 255–278, http://www.uclouvain.be/cps/ucl/doc/etes/documents/DOCH_022_(Favell).pdf [Online expanded version]

Favell, A. (1998e) 'The Europeanisation of immigration politics', *European Integration online Papers* (EIoP), 2(10): 1–16.

Favell, A. (1999) 'Comments on Glazer, Schain and Fassin: how can we be European?' in Joppke, C. and Lukes, S. (eds), *Multicultural Questions*, Oxford: Oxford University Press, pp. 242–257.

Favell, A. and Martiniello, M. (1999) '*Multi-national, multi-cultural and multi-levelled Brussels: national and ethnic politics in the "Capital of Europe"*', ESRC Transnational Communities Working Paper Series, WPTC-99-04. Oxford: Oxford University Press, http://www.transcomm.ox.ac.uk/working papers/favell.pdf

Favell, A. and Geddes, A. (2000) 'Immigration and European integration: new opportunities for transnational political mobilisation?', in Koopmans, R. and Statham, P. (eds), *Challenging Immigration and Ethnic Relations Politics: Comparative European Perspectives*, Oxford: Oxford University Press, pp. 407–428.

Favell, A. (2001a) 'Integration policy and integration research in Western Europe: a review and critique,' in Aleinikoff, A. T. and Klusmeyer, D. (eds), *Citizenship Today: Global Perspectives and Practices*, Washington DC: Brookings Institute/Carnegie Endowment for International Peace, pp. 349–399.

Favell, A. (2001b) 'Multi-ethnic Britain: an exception in Europe?', *Patterns of Prejudice*, 35(1): 35–57.

Favell, A. (2001c) 'Multicultural nation-building: 'integration' as public philosophy and research paradigm in Western Europe', *Swiss Journal of Political Science*, 7(2): 116–124.

Favell, A. and Hansen, R. (2002) 'Markets against politics: migration, EU enlargement and the idea of Europe', *Journal of Ethnic and Migration Studies*, 28(4): 581–601.

Favell, A. (2003a) 'Games without frontiers? Questioning the transnational social power of migrants in Europe', *Archives Européennes de Sociologie* XLIV, 3: 106–136.

Favell, A. (2003b) 'Integration nations: the nation-state and research on immigrants in Western Europe', *Comparative Social Research*, 22: 13–42. [Republished as: Favell, A. (2005) 'Integration nations: the nation-state and research on immigrants in Western Europe', in Bommes, M. and Morawska, E. (eds), *International Migration Research: Constructions, Omissions and the Promise of Interdisciplinarity*, London: Ashgate, pp. 41–67.]

Favell, A. and Modood, T. (2003) 'The philosophy of multiculturalism: the theory and practice of applied political theories', in Finlayson, A. (ed.), *Contemporary Political Philosophy: A Reader and A Guide*, Edinburgh: Edinburgh University Press, pp. 484–495.

Favell, A. (2004) 'London as Eurocity: French free movers in the economic capital of London', *Global and World Cities Research Bulletin*, 150: 1–16, http://www.lboro.ac.uk/gawc/rb/rb150.html

Favell, A. (2006) 'The nation-centered perspective', in Giugni, M. and Passy, F. (eds) *Dialogues on Migration Policy*, Lanham, MD: Lexington, pp. 45–56.

Smith, M. P. and Favell, A. (eds) (2006) *The Human Face of Global Mobility: International High Skilled Migrants in Europe, North America and the Asia Pacific*, New Brunswick, NJ: Transaction Press.

Favell, A. (2007) 'Rebooting migration theory: interdisciplinarity, globality and postdisciplinarity in migration studies', in Brettell, C. and Hollifield, J. (eds) (2nd edn) *Migration Theory: Talking Across Disciplines*. New York: Routledge, pp. 259–278.

Favell, A. (2008a) *Eurostars and Eurocities: Free Movement and Mobility in an Integrating Europe*, Oxford: Blackwell.

Favell, A. (2008b) 'The new face of East-West migration in Europe', *Journal of Ethnic and Migration Studies*, 34(5): 701–716.

Favell, A. and Elrick, T. (eds) (2008) *The New Face of East-West Migration in Europe*, Sp. ed. of *Journal of Ethnic and Migration Studies*, 34(5).

Favell, A. (2009) 'Immigration, migration and free movement in the making of Europe', in Checkel, J. and Katzenstein, P. (eds), *European Identity*, Cambridge: Cambridge University Press, pp. 167–189.

Favell, A. and Guiraudon, V. (2009) 'The sociology of the European Union: an agenda', *European Union Politics*, 10(4): 550–576.

Recchi, E. and Favell, A. (eds) (2009) *Pioneers of European Integration: Citizenship and Mobility in the European Union*, Cheltenham: Edward Elgar.

Favell, A. and Guiraudon, V. (eds) (2011) *Sociology of the European Union*, London: Palgrave.

Favell, A. and Recchi, E. (2011) 'Social mobility and spatial mobility', in Favell, A. and Guiraudon, V. (eds), *Sociology of the European Union*, London: Palgrave, pp. 50–75.

Favell, A., Recchi, E., Kuhn, T., Solgaard Jensen, J. and Klein, J. (2011) *The Europeanisation of Everyday Life: Cross-Border Practices and Transnational Identifications among EU and Third-Country Citizens*, EUCROSS Working Paper #1: 1–54, http://www.eucross.eu/cms

Zimmermann, A. and Favell, A. (2011) 'Governmentality, political field or public sphere? Theoretical alternatives in the political sociology of the EU', *European Journal of Social Theory*, 14(4): 489–516.

Favell, A. (2014a) 'The fourth freedom: theories of migration and mobilities in "neo-liberal" Europe', *European Journal of Social Theory*, 17(3): 275–289.

Favell, A. (2014b) 'Migration theory rebooted: asymmetric challenges in a global agenda', in Brettell, C. and Hollifield, J (eds) (3rd edn) *Migration Theory: Talking Across Disciplines*, New York: Routledge, pp.318–328.

Bibliography

Abbott, A. (2001) *Time Matters: On Theory and Method*, Chicago: University of Chicago Press.

Academic Cooperation Association (ACA) (authors: Kelo, M. and Wächter, W.) (2006) *Brain Drain and Brain Gain: Migration in the European Union after Enlargement*, Brussels: Academic Cooperation Association.

Ackers, L. and Gill, B. (2008) *Moving People and Knowledge: Scientific Mobility in an Enlarging European Union*, Cheltenham: Edward Elgar.

Ahsan, M. M. and Kidwai, A. R. (eds) (1991) *Sacrilege versus Civility: Muslim Perspectives on 'The Satanic Verses Affair'*, Leicester: Islamic Foundation.

Akhtar, S. (1989) *Be Careful with Muhammad!*, London: Bellew.

Al-Ali, N., Black, R. and Koser, K. (2001) 'The limits to transnationalism: Bosnian and Eritrean refugees in Europe as emerging transnational communities', *Journal of Ethnic and Migration Studies*, 24(4): 578–600.

Al–Ali, N. and Koser, K. (eds) (2002) *New Approaches to Migration: Transnationalism and Transformations of Home*, London: Routledge.

Alarcón, R. (1999) 'Recruitment processes among foreign–born engineers and scientists in Silicon valley', *American Behavioral Scientist*, 42(9): 1381–1397.

Alba, R. (2005) 'Bright versus blurred boundaries: second generation assimilation and exclusion in France, Germany and the United States', *Ethnic and Racial Studies*, 28(1): 20–49.

Alba, R. and Foner, N. (2008) 'Immigrant religion in the U.S. and Western Europe: bridge or barrier to inclusion?', *International Migration Review*, 42(2): 360–392.

—— (2014) 'Comparing immigrant integration in North America and Western Europe: how much do the grand narratives tell us?', *International Migration Review*, 48(S1): 263–291.

Alba, R. and Holdaway, J. (eds) (2013) *The Children of Immigrants at School: A Comparative Look at Integration in the United States and Western Europe*, New York: NYU Press.

Alba, R. and Nee, V. (1997) 'Rethinking assimilation theory for a new era of immigration', *International Migration Review*, 31(4): 826–874.

—— (2003) *Remaking the American Mainstream: Assimilation and Contemporary Immigration*, Cambridge, MA: Harvard University Press.

Alba, R. and Waters, M. (eds) (2011) *The Next Generation: Immigrant Youth in a Comparative Perspective*, New York: NYU Press.

Aldrich, H. and Waldinger, R. (1990) 'Ethnicity and entrepreneurship', *Annual Review of Sociology*, 16: 111–135.

Aleinikoff, A. T. and Klusmeyer, D. (eds) (2000) *From Migrants to Citizens: Membership in a Changing World*, Washington DC: Brookings Institute/ Carnegie Endowment for International Peace.

— (2001) *Citizenship Today: Global Perspectives and Practices*, Washington DC: Brookings Institute/Carnegie Endowment for International Peace.

— (2002) *Citizenship Policies for an Age of Migration*, Washington DC: Brookings Institute/Carnegie Endowment for International Peace.

Alexander, J. (1987) *Twenty Lectures: Sociological Theory since World War II*, New York: Columbia University Press.

Almond, G. A. and Verba, S. (1963) *The Civic Culture: Political Attitudes and Democracy in Five Nations*, Boston: Little, Brown and Company.

Alund, A. and Schierup, C. -U. (1991) *Paradoxes of Multiculturalism*, Aldershot: Avebury.

Amadou Dia, I. (2011) *High Skilled International Migration and Transnationalism*, Université de Genève, PhD.

Andall, J. (1998) 'Catholic and state constructions of domestic workers: the case of Cape Verdean women in Rome in the 1970s', in Koser, K. and Lutz, H. (eds), *The New Migration in Europe*, London: Macmillan, pp. 124–142.

Anderson, B. (1991) *Imagined Communities*, London: Verso.

Anderson, C. (2008) *The Long Tail: Why the Future of Business is Selling Less of More*, New York: Hyperion.

Anderson, P. (2009) *The New Old World*, London: Verso.

Andreotti, A., Le Galès, P. and Moreno-Fuentes, F.J. (2015) Globalised Minds, Roots in the City: Urban Upper-Middle Classes in Europe, London: Wiley-Blackwell.

Angell, I. (2000) *The New Barbarian Manifesto: How to Survive the Information Age*, London: Kogan Page.

Anghel, R. (2008) 'Changing statuses: freedom of movement, locality and transnationality of irregular Romanian migrants in Milan', *Journal of Ethnic and Migration Studies*, 34(5): 787–802.

— (2013) *Romanians in Europe: Migration, Status Dilemmas and Transnational Connections*, Lanham, MD: Lexington.

Appignanesi, L. and Maitland, S. (eds) (1989) *The Rushdie File*, London: Fourth Estate.

Asad, T. (1990) 'Multiculturalism and British identity in the wake of the Rushdie affair', *Politics and Society*, 18(4): 455–480.

Bade, K. (2000) *Europa in Bewegung: Migration vom späten 18, Jahrhundert bis zur Gegenwart*, München: C. H. Beck Verlag.

Baldwin-Edwards, M. and Schain, M. (eds) (1994) *The Politics of Immigration in Western Europe*, London: Sage.

Ballis-Lal, B. (1990) *The Romance of Culture in an Urban Civilisation: Robert E. Park on Race and Ethnic Relations in Cities*, London: Routledge.

Banting, K. and Kymlicka, W. (2006) *Multiculturalism and the Welfare State: Recognition and Redistribution in Contemporary Democracies*, New York: Oxford University Press.

Banton, M. (1955) *The Coloured Quarter*, London: Cape.

— (1967) *Race Relations*, London: Tavistock.

—   (1985) *Promoting Racial Harmony*, Cambridge: Cambridge University Press.

—   (2001) 'National integration in France and Britain', *Journal of Ethnic and Migration Studies*, 27(1): 151–168.

Barbulescu R. (2013) *The Politics of Immigrant Integration in Post-Enlargement Europe: Migrants, Co-Ethnics and European Citizens in Italy and Spain*, European University Institute, Florence. PhD.

Barry, B. (1965) *Political Argument*, London: Routledge & Kegan Paul.

—   (1971) *Sociologists, Economists and Democracy*, Chicago: Chicago University Press.

—   (2000) *Culture and Equality*, Cambridge: Polity Press.

Basch, L., Glick Schiller, N. and Szanton-Blanc, C. (1994) *Nations Unbound: Transnational Projects, Post-Colonial Predicaments and Deterritorialized Nation-States*, Amsterdam: Gordon and Breach.

Batalova, J. (2005) *Crossing Borders in the Information Age: The Impact of Highly Skilled Migrants on the Labor Market Outcomes of the U.S. Highly Skilled Workers*, Dept of Sociology: University of California, Irvine. PhD.

Batalova, J. and Lowell, L. B. (2006) '"The best and the brightest": immigrant professionals in the US', in Smith, M. P. and Favell, A. (eds), *The Human Face of Global Mobility: International High Skilled Migrants in Europe, North America and the Asia Pacific*, New Brunswick, NJ: Transaction Press, pp. 81–102.

Bauböck, R. (1994a) *The Integration of Immigrants*, CMDG–Report. Strasbourg: The Council of Europe.

—   (1994b) *Transnational Citizenship: Membership and Rights in International Migration*, Aldershot: Edward Elgar.

Bauer, T. and Zimmerman, K. (1999) *Assessment of Possible Migration Pressure and its Labour Market Impact Following EU Enlargement to Central and Eastern Europe*, Bonn: IZA and London: CEPR.

Bauman, Z. (1998) *Globalization: The Human Consequences*, Cambridge: Polity Press.

Baumgartner, F. (1989) *Conflict and Rhetoric in French Policy Making*, Pittsburgh: University of Pittsburgh Press.

Beauchemin, C., Hamel, C. and Simon, P. (2010) *Trajectoires et origines: enquête sur la diversité des populations en France, Premiers résultats*, Oct. Paris, INED: Document de Travail 168.

Beaverstock, J. (2001) 'Transnational elite communities in global cities: connectivities, flows and networks', *Globalisation and World Cities Research Bulletin* 63, http://www.lboro.ac.uk/gawc/rb/rb63.html.

—   (2002) 'Transnational elites in global cities: British expatriates in Singapore's financial district', *Geoforum*, 33(4): 525–538.

—   (2005) 'Transnational elites in the city: British highly-skilled inter-company transferees in New York City's financial district', *Journal of Ethnic and Migration Studies*, 31(2): 245–268.

Beck, U. (2000) *What is Globalisation?*, Oxford: Blackwell.

Beiner, R. (ed.) (1998) *Theorizing Citizenship*, Albany, NY: SUNY Press.

Bellah, R. with Madsen, R., Sullivan, W., Swidler, A. and Tipton, S. (1985) *Habits of the Heart: Individualism and Commitment in American Life*, Berkeley and Los Angeles: University of California Press.

Bellah, R., Madsen, R., Tipton, S., Sullivan, W., and Swidler, A. (1991) *The Good Society*, New York: Knopf.

Benhabib, S. (2001) *Transformations of Citizenship: Dilemmas of the Nation State in the Era of Globalization*, Amsterdam: Koninklijke van Gorkum.

— (2002) *Claims of Culture: Equality and Diversity in the Global Era*, Princeton, NJ: Princeton University Press.

Benson, M. and O'Reilly, K. (eds) (2012) *Lifestyle Migration: Expectations, Aspirations and Experiences*, Farnham: Ashgate.

Benton, G. and Frank, P. (eds) (1998) *The Chinese in Europe*, London: Macmillan.

Berger, P. A. and Weiß, A. (eds) (2008) *Transnationalisierung Sozialer Ungleichheit*, Wiesbaden: VS.

Berry, J. (1997) 'Immigration, acculturation and adaptation', *Applied Psychology*, 46(1): 5–34.

Bertaux, D. and Thompson, P. (eds) (1997) *Pathways to Social Class*, Oxford: Clarendon.

Bjerre, L., Helbling, M., Römer, F. and Zobel, M. (2014) 'Conceptualizing and measuring immigration policies: a comparative perspective', *International Migration Review*, Available online, 22 May: 1–46.

Black, R., Engbersen, G., Okolski M., Pantiru, C. (eds) (2010) *A Continent Moving West? EU Enlargement and Labour Migration from Central and Eastern Europe*, Amsterdam: University of Amsterdam Press.

Blaise, P., Coenen, M. –T. and Lewin, R. (1997) *La Belgique et ses immigrés*, Bruxelles: De Boeck University.

Bleich, E. (1998) 'From international ideas to domestic politics: educational multiculturalism in England and France', *Comparative Politics*, 31(1): 81–100.

— (2003) *Race Politics in France and Britain: Ideas and Policymaking since the 1960s*, Cambridge: Cambridge University Press.

— (2005) 'The legacies of history? Colonialization and immigrant integration in Britain and France', *Theory and Society*, 34(2): 171–195.

— (2008) 'Immigration and integration in Western Europe and the United States', *World Politics*, 60(3): 509–538.

Blitz, B. (2014) *Migration and Freedom: Mobility, Citizenship, Exclusion*, Cheltenham: Edward Elgar.

Blommaert, J. and Verschueren, J. (1998) *Debating Diversity*, London: Routledge.

Body-Gendrot, S. and Martiniello, M. (eds) (2000) *Minorities in European Cities: The Dynamics of Social Integration and Social Exclusion at the Neighbourhood Level*, London: Macmillan.

Bommes, M. (1998) 'Migration, nation state and welfare state: a theoretical challenge for sociological migration research', paper presented to the European Forum on Migration, EUI, Florence, 16 Feb.

Bommes, M. *see also* Boswell and D'Amato (eds).

Bommes, M. and Morawska, E. (eds) (2005) *International Migration Research: Constructions, Omissions and the Promise of Interdisciplinarity*, London: Ashgate.

Borjas, G. (1989) 'Economic theory and international migration', *International Migration Review*, 23(3): 457–485.

— (1994) 'The economics of immigration', *Journal of Economic Literature*, Vol.XXXII: 1667–1717.

— (1999) *Economic Research on the Determinants of Immigration: Lessons for the European Union*, Washington DC: World Bank Technical Paper 438.

Böröcz, J. (2010) *The European Union and Global Social Change: A Critical Geopolitical-Economic Analysis*, New York: Routledge.

Boswell, C. (2009) *The Political Uses of Expert Knowledge: Immigration Policy and Social Research*, Cambridge: Cambridge University Press.

Boswell, C. and D'Amato, G. (eds) (2012) *Immigration and Social Systems: Collected Essays of Michael Bommes*, Amsterdam: University of Amsterdam Press.

Boswell, C. and Geddes, A. (2011) *Migration and Mobility in the European Union*, London: Palgrave.

Bourdieu, P. (1984) *Homo academicus*, Paris: Les éditions du minuit.

— (1996) *Sur la television*, Paris: Liber.

Bourdieu, P., Chamboredon, J. -C. and Passeron, J. -C. (1968) *Le métier du sociologue*, Paris: Mouton.

Bourdieu, P. and Wacquant, L. (1992) *An Invitation to Reflexive Sociology*, Cambridge: Polity.

— (1999) 'On the currency of imperialist reason', *Theory, Culture and Society*, 16(1): 44–58.

Bourne, C. and Whitmore, J. (1993) (2nd edn) *Race and Sex Discrimination*, London: Sweet & Maxwell.

Bousetta, H. (1997) 'Citizenship and political participation in France and the Netherlands: reflections on two local cases', *New Community*, 23(2): 215–232.

Bousetta, H. (2000) 'Political dynamics in the city. Citizenship, ethnic mobilisation and socio–political participation: four case studies', in Body–Gendrot, S. and Martiniello, M. (eds) *Minorities in European Cities: The Dynamics of Social Integration and Social Exclusion at the Neighbourhood Level*, London: Macmillan.

Bousetta, H. and Swyngedouw, M. (1999) 'La citoyenneté de l'union européen et l'enjeu de Bruxelles: le droit supranational européen confronté aux réalités d'une société multiéthnique et multinationale divisée', Courrier Hebdomadaire no.1636. Bruxelles: Centre de recherche et d'information socio-politiques (CRISP).

Bowen, J. (2007) *Why the French Don't Like Headscarfs: Islam, the State and Public Space*, Princeton, NJ: Princeton University Press.

— (2009) *Can Islam be French? Pluralism and Pragmatism in a Secularist State*, Princeton, NJ: Princeton University Press.

Bozkurt, Ö. (2006) 'Wired for work: highly skilled employment and global mobility in mobile telecommunications multinationals', in Smith, M. P. and Favell, A. (eds) *The Human Face of Global Mobility: International High Skilled Migrants in Europe, North America and the Asia Pacific*, New Brunswick, NJ: Transaction Press, pp. 213–248.

Bozorgmehr, M. and Waldinger, R. (eds) (1996) *Ethnic Los Angeles*, New York: Russell Sage Foundation.

Brèchon, P. and Cautrès, B. (eds) (1999) *Les enquêtes eurobaromètres*, Paris: L'Harmattan.

Breen, R. (ed.) (2004) *Social Mobility in Europe*, Oxford: Oxford University Press.

Breen, R. and Luijkx, R. (2004a) 'Social Mobility in Europe between 1970 and 2000', in Breen, R. (ed.) (2004) *Social Mobility in Europe*, Oxford: Oxford University Press, pp. 33–75.

— (2004b) 'Conclusions' in Richard Breen (ed.) *Social Mobility in Europe*, Oxford: Oxford University Press, pp. 383–410.

Breen, R. and Rottman, D. (1998) 'Is the national state the appropriate geographical unit for class analysis?', *Sociology*, 32(1): 1–21.

Brettell, C. and Hollifield, J. (eds) (2004) *Migration Theory: Talking Across Disciplines*, New York: Routledge.

— (2007) (2nd edn) *Migration Theory: Talking Across Disciplines*, New York: Routledge.

— (2014) (3rd edn) *Migration Theory: Talking Across Disciplines*, New York: Routledge.

Brochmann, G. (1999) 'The mechanisms of control', in Brochmann, G. and Hammar, T. (eds) *Mechanism of Immigration Control: A Comparative Analysis of European Regulation Policies*, Oxford: Berg, pp. 1–27.

Brouard, S. and Tiberj, V. (2005) *Français comme les autres? Enquête sur les citoyens d'origine maghrébine, africaine et turque*, Paris, Presses de Sciences Po.

Brubaker, R. (ed.) (1989) *Immigration and the Politics of Citizenship in Western Europe*, New York: University Press of America.

— (1992) *Citizenship and Nationhood in France and Germany*, Cambridge, MA: Harvard University Press.

— (1995) *Nationalism Reframed: Nationhood and the National Question in the New Europe*, Cambridge: Cambridge University Press.

— (2001) 'The return of assimilation? Changing perspectives on immigration and its sequels in France, Germany, and the United States', *Ethnic and Racial Studies*, 24(4): 531–548.

— (2004) *Ethnicity and Groups*, Cambridge, MA: Harvard University Press.

— (2013) 'Categories of analysis and categories of practice: a note on the study of Muslims in European countries of immigration', *Ethnic and Racial Studies*, 36(1): 1–8.

Brubaker, R., Fox, J., Grancea, L. and Feischmidt, M. (2006) *Nationalist Politics and Everyday Ethnicity in a Transylvanian Town*, Princeton, NJ: Princeton University Press.

Bruszt, L. and McDermott, G. (eds) (2014) *Levelling the Playing Field: Transnational Regulatory Integration and Development*, Oxford: Oxford University Press.

Bryant, C. (1997) 'Citizenship, national identity and the accommodation of difference: reflections on the German, French, Dutch and British cases', *New Community*, 23(2): 157–72.

Bulmer, M. (1984) *The Chicago School of Sociology: Institutionalization, Diversity and the Use of Sociological Research*, Chicago, IL: University of Chicago Press.

Bulmer, M. and Rees, A. (eds) (1996) *Citizenship Today: The Contemporary Relevance of T. H. Marshall*, London: UCL Press.

Burawoy, M. with Blum, J., George, S., Thayer, M., Gille, Z., Gowan, T., Haney, L., Klawiter, M., Lopez, S. and O'Riain, S. (2000) *Global Ethnography: Forces, Connections, and Imaginations in a Postmodern World*, Berkeley. University of California Press.

Burgers, J. (1998) 'Formal determinants of informal arrangements: housing and undocumented immigrants in Rotterdam', *Journal of Ethnic and Migration Studies*, 24(2): 295–312.

Burgess, A. (1999) 'Critical reflections on the return of minority rights regulation to East/West European affairs', in Cordell, K. (ed.) *Ethnicity and Democratisation in the New Europe*, London: Routledge, pp. 49–60.

Burrell, K. (2006) *Moving Lives: Narratives of Nation and Migration among Europeans in Post-War Britain*, Aldershot: Ashgate.

— (ed.) (2009) *Polish Migration to the UK in the 'New' European Union: After 2004*, Farnham: Ashgate.

Butler, T. and Robson, G. (2003) *London Calling: The Middle Classes and the Remaking of Inner London*, Oxford: Berg.

Byrnes, T. and Katzenstein, P. (eds) (2006) *Religion in an Expanding Europe*, Cambridge: Cambridge University Press.

Caporaso, J. and Tarrow, S. (2009) 'Polanyi in Brussels: Supranational institutions and the transnational embedding of markets', *International Organization*, 63(4): 593–620.

Carens, J. (1987) 'Aliens and citizens: the case for open borders', *Review of Politics*, 49(2): 251–273.

Carling, J. (2002) 'Migration in the age of involuntary immobility: theoretical reflections and Cape Verdean experiences', *Journal of Ethnic and Migration Studies*, 28(1): 5–42.

Carmon, N. (ed.) (1996) *Immigration and Integration in Post-Industrial Societies*, London: Macmillan.

Case, H. (2009) 'Being European: East and West,' in Checkel, J. and Katzenstein, P. (eds), *European Identity*, Cambridge: Cambridge University Press, pp. 111–131.

Castells, M. (2000) (2nd edn) *The Rise of the Network Society*, Oxford: Blackwell.

Castles, S. and Kosack, G. (1973) *Immigrant Workers and Class Structure in Western Europe*, Oxford: Oxford University Press.

Castles, S. (1995) 'How nation-states respond to immigration and ethnic diversity', *New Community*, 21(3): 293–308.

— (2000) 'Thirty years of research on migration and multicultural societies', in Castles, S. (ed.) *Ethnicity and Globalization: From Migrant Workers to Transnational Citizens*, London: Sage.

— (2011) 'Migration, crisis and the global labour market', *Globalizations*, 8(3): 311–324.

— (2012) 'Cosmopolitanism and freedom: lessons of the global economic crisis', *Ethnic and Racial Studies*, 35(11): 1843–1852.

Castles, S. and Davidson, A. (1999) *The Citizen Who Does Not Belong: Citizenship in a Global Age*, London: Macmillan.

Castles, S. and Kosack, G. (1973) *Immigrant Workers and Class Structure in Western Europe*, Oxford: Oxford University Press.

Castles, S. and Miller, M. (2009) (4th edn) *The Age of Migration: International Population Movements in the Modern World*, Basingstoke: Palgrave Macmillan.

Castles, S., Booth, H. and Wallace, T. (1984) *Here For Good: Western Europe's New Ethnic Minorities*, London: Pluto.

Castles, S., Korac, M., Vasta, E. and Vertovec, S. (2002) *Integration: Mapping the Field*. London: Home Office, Centre for Contemporary Cultural Studies

— (1982) *The Empire Strikes Back*, London: Hutchinson.

Césari, J. (1994) *Être musulman en France: associations, militants et mosques*, Aix-en-Provence: IREMAM.

Chakravartty, P. (2001) 'The emigration of high-skilled Indian workers to the United States: Flexible citizenship and India's information economy', in Cornelius, W., Espenshade, T. and Salehyan, I. (eds) *The International Migration of the Highly Skilled: Demand, Supply, and Development Consequences in Sending and Receiving Countries*, Boulder, CO: Lynne Reiner, pp. 325–350.

Chakravartty, P. (2006) 'Symbolic analysts or indentured servants? Indian high tech migrants in America's information economy', in Smith, M. P. and Favell, A. (eds) *The Human Face of Global Mobility: International High Skilled Migrants in Europe, North America and the Asia Pacific*, New Brunswick, NJ: Transaction Press, pp. 159–180.

Champagne, P., Pinto, L., Lenoir, R. and Merllié, D. (1996) *Initiation à la pratique sociologique*, Paris: Dunod.

Champsaur, P. (ed.) (1994) *Les étrangers en France: contours et caractères*, Paris: INSEE.

Chandler, D. (1999) 'The OSCE and the internationalisation of national minority rights', in Cordell, K. (ed.) *Ethnicity and Democratisation in the New Europe*, London: Routledge, pp. 61–76.

Checkel, J. and Katzenstein, P. (eds) (2009) *European Identity*, Cambridge: Cambridge University Press.

Cheng, L. and Yang, P. (1998) 'Global interaction, global inequality, and migration of the highly trained to the United States', *International Migration Review*, 32(3): 626–653.

Chiswick, B. R. (2007) 'Are immigrants favourably self-selected? An economic analysis' in Brettell, C. and Hollifield, J. (eds) (2nd edn) *Migration Theory: Talking Across Disciplines*, New York: Routledge, pp. 63–82.

Çinar, D., Hofinger, C. and Waldrauch, H. (1995) *Integrationsindex: Zur rechtlichen Integration von Ausländerinnenin ausgewählten europäischen Ländern*, Political Science Series No.25, Vienna: Institute for Advanced Study.

Codagnone, C. (1998) 'Monitoring ethnic relations in Western and Eastern Europe: concepts, indicators, sources and comparative issues', Ethnobarometer Project Working Paper. http:\\www.ethnobarometer.org

Cohen, R. (1997) *Global Diasporas: An Introduction*, London: UCL Press.

—— (2006) *Migration and its Enemies: Global Capital, Migrant Labour and the Nation-State*, Aldershot: Ashgate.

Coleman, D. (2011) 'The changing face of Europe' in Goldstone, J., Kaufmann, E. and Toft, M. (eds), *Political Demography*, Boulder, CO: Paradigm, pp. 201–18.

Coleman, J. (1990) *Foundations of Social Theory*, Cambridge, MA: Harvard University Press.

Collyer, M. (2005) 'When do social networks fail to explain migration? Accounting for the movement of Algerian asylum-seekers to the UK', *Journal of Ethnic and Migration Studies*, 31(4): 699–718.

Commission de la Nationalité (1988) *être français aujourd'hui et demain*, Paris: La documentation française.

Commission on Citizenship (1990) *Encouraging Citizenship*, London: HMSO.

Commission on the Future of Multi–Ethnic Britain (2000) *The Future of Multi–Ethnic Britain* (The Parekh Report), London: Runnymede.

Commission for Racial Equality (CRE) (1985) *Immigration Control Procedures*, London: CRE.

Commission for Racial Equality (CRE) (1990) *Schools of Faith: Religious Schools in a Multicultural Society*, London: CRE.

—— (1994) *Second Review of the Race Relations Act 1976*, London: CRE.

Commission on Urban Priority Areas (1985) *Faith in the City: A Call for Action by Church and Nation*, London: Church House.

—— (1990) *Living Faith in the City: A Progress Report*, London: Church House.

Connolly, H. and White, A. (2006) *The Different Experiences of the United Kingdom's Ethnic and Religious Populations*, Population report, London: HMSO.

Conradson, D. and Latham, A. (2005) 'Transnational urbanism: attending to everyday practices and mobilities', *Journal of Ethnic and Migration Studies*, 31(2): 227–234.

Cordell, K. (ed.) (1999) *Ethnicity and Democratisation in the New Europe*, London: Routledge.

Cornelius, W., Espenshade, T. and Salehyan, I. (eds) (2001) *The International Migration of the Highly Skilled: Demand, Supply, and Development Consequences in Sending and Receiving Countries*, Boulder, CO: Lynne Reinner.

Cornelius, W., Martin, P. and Hollifield, J. (eds) (1994) *Controlling immigration*, Stanford, CA: Stanford University Press.

Crouch, C. (1992) 'Citizenship and community in British political debate', in Crouch, C. and Heath, A. (eds) *Social Research and Social Reform*, Oxford: Clarendon Press.

— (2011) *The Strange Non-Death of Neo-Liberalism*, Oxford: Polity.

Cross, M. and Waldinger, R. (1999) 'Economic integration and labour market change: a review and a reappraisal', in Hjarnø, J. (ed.) *From Metropolis to Cosmopolis*, Esbjerg: South Jutland University Press, pp. 29–93.

Crowley, J. (1993) 'Paradoxes in the politicisation of race: a comparison of the UK and France', *New Community*, 19(4): 627–643.

— (1995) *Immigration, 'relations raciales' et mobilisations minoritaires au Royaume-Uni: la démocratie face à la complexité sociale*, Paris: Fondation Nationale des Sciences Politiques, PhD.

— (1998) 'The national dimension in T. H. Marshall', *Citizenship Studies*, 2(2): 165–178.

Crul, M. (2013) 'Snakes and Ladders in educational systems: access to higher education for second-generation Turks in Europe', *Journal of Ethnic and Migration Studies*, 39(9): 1383–1401.

Crul, M. and Mollenkopf, J. (eds) (2012) *The Changing Face of World Cities: The Second Generation in Europe and the United States*, New York: Russell Sage Foundation.

Crul, M. and Schneider, J. (2010) 'Comparative integration context theory: participation and belonging in new diverse European cities', *Ethnic and Racial Studies*, 33(7): 1249–1268.

Crul, M. and Vermeulen, H. (2003) 'The second generation in Europe', *International Migration Review*, 37(4): 965–986.

Crul, M., Schneider, J. and Lelie, F. (eds) (2012) *The European Second Generation Compared: Does the Integration Context Matter?*, Amsterdam: Amsterdam University Press.

— (2013) *Super-diversity: A New Perspective on Integration*, Amsterdam: VU Press.

Csedö, K. (2008) 'Negotiating skills in the global city: Hungarian and Romanian professionals and graduates in London', *Journal of Ethnic and Migration Studies*, 34(5): 803–23.

— (2009) *New Eurostars? The Labour Market Incorporation of East European Professionals in London*, Dept. of Sociology, LSE. PhD.

Cusset, F. (2005) *French Theory: Foucault, Derrida, Deleuze & Cie et les mutations de la vie intellectuelle aux États-Unis*, Paris: La Découverte.

Dahrendorf, R. (1988) *The Modern Social Conflict: An Essay on the Politics of Liberty*, London: Weidenfeld & Nicolson.

Datta, A. (2009) 'Places of everyday cosmopolitanisms: East European construction workers in London', *Environment and Planning A*, 41(2): 353–370.

De Genova, N. (2010) 'The deportation regime: sovereignty, space and the freedom of movement' in De Genova, N. and Peutz, N. (eds) *The Deportation Regime: Sovereignty, Space and the Freedom of Movement*, Durham, NC: Duke University Press, pp. 33–65.

De Genova, N. and Peutz, N. (eds) (2010) *The Deportation Regime: Sovereignty, Space and the Freedom of Movement*, Durham, NC: Duke University Press.

De Grazia, V. (2006) *Irresistible Empire: America's Advance Through the Twentieth Century*, Cambridge, MA: Belknap Press.

Delanty, G. and Rumford, C. (2005) *Rethinking Europe: Social Theory and the Implications of Europeanization*, London: Routledge.

Deschouwer, K., Phalet, K. and Swyngedouw, M. (eds) (1999) *Minderheden in Brussel*, Brussel: VUB Press.

Deutsch, K. (1957) *Nationalism and Social Communication*, Cambridge, MA: MIT Press.

Diamond, J. (1997) *Guns and Germs and Steel: The Fates of Human Societies*, New York: W.W. Norton & Co.

Diehl, C. (2002) *Die Partizipation von Migranten in Deutschland: Rückzug oder Mobilisierung?*, Opladen: Leske und Budrich.

Diken, B. (1998) *Strangers, Ambivalence and Social Theory*, Aldershot: Ashgate.

Doomernik, J. (1998) 'The effectiveness of integration policies towards immigrants and their descendants in France, Germany and the Netherlands', *International Migration Papers*, no.27, Geneva: International Labour Organisation.

Dummett, A., and Nicol, A. (1990) *Subjects, Citizens, Aliens and Others: Nationality and Immigration Law*, London: Wiedenfeld & Nicolson.

Dunn, J. (1979) *Western Political Theory in the Face of the Future*, Cambridge: Cambridge University Press.

—— (1990) *Interpreting Political Responsibility*, Oxford: Polity Press.

Düvell, F. (ed.) (2005) *Illegal Immigration in Europe: Beyond Control*, London: Palgrave Macmillan.

Eade, J. (ed.) (1997) *Living the Global City: Globalization as a Local Process*, London and New York: Routledge.

Economist, The (1995) 'Why Bradford burned', 17 June.

Elrick, T. and Lewandowska, E. (2008) 'Matching and making labour demand and supply: agents in Polish migrant networks of domestic elderly care in Germany and Italy', *Journal of Ethnic and Migration Studies*, 34(5): 717–734.

Elster, J. (1992) *Local Justice: How Institutions Allocate Scarce Goods and Necessary Burdens*, Cambridge: Cambridge University Press.

Elster, J., Offe, C. and Preuß, U. (1998) *Institutional Design in Post-Communist Societies*, Cambridge: Cambridge University Press.

Engbersen, G. (1996) 'The unknown city', *Berkeley Journal of Sociology*, 40: 87–111.

Erikson, R. and Goldthorpe, J. (1992) *The Constant Flux: A Study of Class Mobility in Industrial Societies*, Oxford: Clarendon Press.

Esping-Andersen, G. (1990) *Three Worlds of Welfare Capitalism*, Oxford: Polity.

— (1999) *The Social Foundations of Post-Industrial Society*, Oxford: Oxford University Press.

Esser, H. (1999) 'Inklusion, integration und ethnische Schichtung', *Journal für Konflikt und Gewaltforshung*, 1(1): 5–34.

Ester, P. and Krieger, H. (2008) *Labour Mobility in a Transatlantic Perspective: Conference Report*, Dublin: European Foundation for the Improvement of Living and Working Conditions.

Ethnobarometer Project (1999) *Ethnic Conflict and Migration in Europe*, First report. Rome: CSS/CEMES, http:\\\www.ethnobarometer.org

European Citizenship Action Service (ECAS) (2005) *Who's Afraid of EU Enlargement?*, Brussels: ECAS.

— (2006) *Who's Still Afraid of EU Enlargement?*, Brussels: ECAS.

European Foundation for the Improvement of Living and Working Conditions (EFILWC) (2006) *Mobility in Europe: Analysis of the 2005 Eurobarometer Survey on Geographical and Labour Market Mobility*, Dublin: EFILWC.

European Year of Workers' Mobility (2006) *Europeans and Mobility: First Results of an EU-wide Survey*, Brussels: European Commission.

Evans, P. and Sewell, T. (2013) 'Neoliberalism: policy regimes, international regimes and social effects', in Hall, P. and Lamont, M. (eds) *Social Resilience in the Neoliberal Era*, Cambridge: Cambridge University Press, pp. 35–68.

Evans, P., Rueschemeyer, D. and Skocpol, T. (eds) (1985) *Bringing the State Back In*, Cambridge: Cambridge University Press.

Faist, T. (2000) *The Volume and Dynamics of International Migration and Transnational Social Spaces*, Oxford: Oxford University Press.

Fan, C. (2008) *China on the Move: Migration, the State and the Household*, London: Routledge.

Fassmann, H. and Hintermann, C. (1997) *Migrationspotential Osteuropa: Struktur und Motivation potentieller Migranten aus Polen, der Slowakei, Tschechien, und Ungarn*, Vienna: Austrian Academy of Sciences.

Feldblum, M. (1998) 'Reconfiguring citizenship in Western Europe', in Joppke, C. (ed.) *Challenge to the Nation State: Immigration in Western Europe and the United States*, Oxford: Oxford University Press, pp. 231–271.

— (1999) *Reconstructing Citizenship: The Politics of Nationality Reform and Immigration in Contemporary France*, New York: SUNY Press.

Fennema, M. and Tillie, J. (1999) 'Political participation and political trust in Amsterdam: civic communities and ethnic networks, *Journal of Ethnic and Migration Studies*, 25(4): 703–726.

Fermin, A. (1999) 'Inburgeringsbeleid en burgerschap', *Migrantenstudien*, 15(2): 99–112.

Fetzer, J. (2000) *Public Attitudes toward Immigration in the United States, France, and Germany*, Cambridge: Cambridge University Press.

Fielding, T. (1995) 'Migration and social change: a longitudinal study of the social mobility of "immigrants" in England and Wales', *European Journal of Population*, 11(2): 107–121.

—— (2012) *Migration in Britain: Paradoxes of the Present, Prospects for the Future*, Cheltenham: Edward Elgar.

Findlay, A. (1995) 'The future of skill exchanges within the European Union', in Hall, R. and White, P. (eds) *Europe's Population: Towards the Next Century*, London: UCL, pp. 130–141.

Fischer, P. A. and Straubhaar, T. (1996) 'Is migration into EU-countries demand based?' in Corry, D. (ed.) *Economics and European Union Migration Policy*, London: Institute for Public Policy Research, pp. 11–49.

Fligstein, N. (2008) *Euroclash: The EU, European Identity, and the Future of Europe*, Oxford: Oxford University Press.

Foner, N. and Lucassen, L. (2012) 'Legacies of the past', in Crul, M. and Mollenkopf, J. (eds), *The Changing Face of World Cities: The Second Generation in Europe and the United States*, New York: Russell Sage Foundation, pp. 26–43.

Foner, N., Rath, J., Duyvendak, J. W. and van Reekum, R. (2014) *New York and Amsterdam: Immigration and the New Urban Landscape*, New York: NYU Press.

Forbes, I. and Mead, G. (1992) *Measure for Measure: A Comparative Analysis of Measure to Combat Racial Discrimination in the Member Countries of the European Community*, Sheffield: UK Department of Employment.

Freeman, G. (1979) *Immigrant Labour and Racial Conflict in Industrial Societies: The French and British Experience 1945–1975*, Princeton, NJ: Princeton University Press.

—— (1992) 'Migration policy and politics in the receiving states', *International Migration Review*, 26(4): 1144–1167.

—— (1995) 'Modes of Immigration politics in liberal democratic societies', *International Migration Review*, 29(4): 881–902.

—— (1999) 'The quest for skill: a comparative analysis', in Bernsteinn, A. and Weiner, M. (eds), *Migration and Refugee Policies: An Overview*, London: Pinter, pp. 84–118.

Freeman, G. and Hill, D. (2006) 'Disaggregating immigration policy: the politics of skilled labor recruitment in the U.S.', in Smith, M. P. and Favell, A. (eds) *The Human Face of Global Mobility: International High Skilled Migrants in Europe, North America and the Asia Pacific*, New Brunswick, NJ: Transaction Press, pp. 103–30.

Friedman, T. (2005) *The World is Flat*, New York: Farrar, Strauss and Giroux.

Friedmann, J. (1986) 'The world city hypothesis', *Development and Change*, 17(1): 69–84.

Friedmann, J. and Wolff, G. (1982) 'World city formation: an agenda for research and action', *International Journal of Urban and Regional Research*, 6(2): 309–339.

Gabaccia, D. (2000) *Italy's Many Diasporas*, London: UCL Press.

Gans, H. (1992) 'Acculturation, assimilation and mobility', *Ethnic and Racial Studies*, 30(1): 152–164.

Ganzeboom, H., Luijkx, R. and Treiman, D. (1989) 'Intergenerational class mobility in comparative perspective', *Research in Social Stratification and Mobility*, 8: 3–84.

Garapich, M. (2008) 'The migration industry and civil society: Polish immigrants in the United Kingdom before and after EU enlargement', *Journal of Ethnic and Migration Studies*, 34(5): 735–752.

Garbaye, R. (2005) *Getting into Local Power: The Politics of Ethnic Minorities in British and French Cities*, Oxford: Blackwell.

Garni, A. (2010) 'Mechanisms of migration: poverty and social instability in the post-war expansion of Central American migration to the United States', *Journal of Immigrant and Refugee Studies*, 8(3): 316–338.

Geddes, A. (1995) 'Immigrant and ethnic minorities and the EU's democratic deficit', *Journal of Common Market Studies*, 33(2): 197–212.

— (2000) *Immigration and European Integration: Towards Fortress Europe?*, Manchester: Manchester University Press.

— (2005) 'Migration research and European integration: the construction and institutionalization of problems of Europe', in Bommes, M. and Morawska, E. (eds) *International Migration Research: Constructions, Omissions and the Promise of Interdisciplinarity*, London: Ashgate, pp. 265–280.

Gellner, E. (1992) *Postmodernism, Reason and Religion*, London: Routledge.

Gerholm, T. and Lithman, Y. G. (eds) (1988) *The New Islamic Presence in Western Europe*, London: Mansell.

Gilroy, P. (1987) *There Ain't no Black in the Union Jack*, London: Hutchinson.

— (1990) 'The end of anti-racism', *New Community*, 17(1): 71–83.

Givens, T. (2007) 'Immigrant integration in Europe: empirical research', *Annual Review of Political Science*, 10: 67–83.

Givens, T. and Maxwell, R. (2012) *Immigration Politics: Race and Representation in Western Europe*, Boulder, CO: Lynne Reinner Publishers.

Glaser, B. and Strauss, A. (1967) *The Discovery of Grounded Theory*, New York: Aldine de Gruyter.

Glazer, N. (ed.) (1976) *Ethnicity: Theory and Experience*, Cambridge, MA: Bellinger.

— (1983) *Ethnic Dilemmas 1964–82*, Cambridge, MA: Harvard University Press

— (1999) 'Multiculturalism and American exceptionalism', in Joppke, C. and Lukes, S. (eds) *Multicultural Questions*, Oxford: Oxford University Press, pp. 183–198.

Glick Schiller, N. (2005) 'Transborder citizenship: an outcome of legal pluralism within transnational social fields', in Bender Backman, F. and Bender Beckman, K. (eds) *Mobile People, Mobile Law: Expanding Legal Relations in a Contracting World*, London: Ashgate.

Glick Schiller, N., Basch, L. and Blanc, C. (1995) 'From immigrant to transmigrant: theorizing transnational migration', *Anthropological Quarterly*, 68(1): 48–63.

Glick Schiller, N. and Cağlar, A. (2009) 'Towards a comparative theory of locality in migration studies: migrant incorporation and city scale', *Journal of Ethnic and Migration Studies*, 35(2): 177–202.

Gold, S. J. and Nawyn, S. (eds) (2013) *The Routledge International Handbook of Migration Studies*, New York: Routledge.

Goldstein, J. and Keohane, B. (eds) (1993) *Ideas and Foreign Policy*, New York: Cornell University Press.

Goldthorpe, J. (1987) *Social Mobility and Class Structure in Modern Britain*, Oxford: Clarendon.

Goodhart, D. (2013) *The British Dream*, London: Atlantic.

Gordon, I., Travers, T. and Whitehead, C. (2007) *The Impact of Recent Immigration on the London Economy*, Corporation of London, London.

Gordon, M. (1964) *Assimilation in American Life: The Role of Race, Religion and National Origins*, New York: Oxford University Press.

Goulbourne, H. (1991). *Ethnicity and Nationalism in Post-Imperial Britain*, Cambridge: Cambridge University Press.

Gouldner, A. (1957.)'Cosmopolitans and locals: toward an analysis of latent social roles - I', *Administrative Science Quarterly*, 2: 281–306.

— (1958) 'Cosmopolitans and locals: toward an analysis of latent social roles - II', *Administrative Science Quarterly*, 2: 444–480.

Gray, J. (1993) *Beyond the New Right: Markets, Government and the Common Environment*, London: Routledge.

Grillo, R. (1998) *Pluralism and the Politics of Difference*, Oxford: Oxford University Press.

Guiraudon, V. (1997) *Policy Change behind Gilded Doors: Explaining the Evolution of Aliens' Rights in Contemporary Western Europe*, Harvard University, Dept of Govt. PhD.

— (1998) 'Citizenship rights for non–citizens: France, Germany and the Netherlands,' in Joppke, C. (ed.) (1998) *Challenge to the Nation State: Immigration in Western Europe and the United States*, Oxford: Oxford University Press, pp. 272–319.

— (2000) *Les politiques d'immigration en Europe: Allemagne, France, Pays–Bas*. Paris: Harmattan.

— (2003) 'The constitution of a European immigration policy domain: a political sociology approach', *Journal of European Public Policy*, 10(2): 262–282.

— (2009) 'Equality in the making: implementing European non–discrimination law', *Citizenship Studies*, 13(5): 527–549.

—   (2014) 'Economic crisis and institutional resilience: the political economy of migrant incorporation', *West European Politics*, 37(6): 1297–1313.

Guiraudon, V. and Joppke, C. (eds) (2001) *Controlling a New Migration World*, London: Routledge.

Guiraudon, V. and Lahav, G. (2000) 'A reappraisal of the state–sovereignty debate: the case of migration control', *Comparative Political Studies*, 33(2): 163–195.

Guiraudon, V., Phalet, K. and Ter Wal, J. (2005) 'Monitoring ethnic minorities in the Netherlands', *International Social Science Journal*, 57(183): 75–87.

Gupta, A. and Ferguson, J. (eds) (1997) *Culture, Power, Place: Exploration In Critical Anthropology*, Durham and London: Duke University Press.

Gusfield, J. (1981) *The Culture of Public Problems*, Chicago, IL: University of Chicago Press.

Guth, J. and Gill, B. (2008) 'Motivations in East-West doctoral mobility: revisiting the question of brain drain', *Journal of Ethnic and Migration Studies*, 34(5): 825–841.

Gutmann, A. (ed.) (1994) *Multiculturalism: Examining the Politics of Recognition*, Princeton, NJ: Princeton University Press.

Habermas, J. (1992) 'Citizenship and national identity: some reflections on the future of Europe', *Praxis International*, 12(1): 1–19.

—   (1995) 'Reconciliation through the public use of reason: remarks on John Rawls's Political Liberalism', *Journal of Philosophy*, 92(3): 109–31.

Hacking, I. (2000) *The Social Construction of What?*, Cambridge, MA: Harvard University Press.

Haferkamp, H. and Smelser, N. (eds) (1992) *Social Change and Modernity*, Berkeley, CA: University of California Press.

Hall, P. (ed.) (1989) *The Political Power of Economic Ideas: Keynesianism across Nations*, Princeton, NJ: Princeton University Press.

—   (1993) 'Policy paradigms, social learning and the state: the case of economic policy making in Britain', *Comparative Politics*, 25(3): 275–96.

Hall, P. and Lamont, M. (eds) (2013) *Social Resilience in the Neoliberal Era*, Cambridge: Cambridge University Press.

Hall, P. and Soskice, D. (eds) (2001) *The Varieties of Capitalism: The Institutional Foundations of Comparative Advantage*, Oxford: Oxford University Press.

Hall, P. and Taylor, R. (1996) 'Political science and the three new institutionalisms', *Political Studies*, 44(5): 936–957.

Hall, S. (1995) *New Ethnicities*, London: UCL Press.

Haller, M. (2008) *European Integration as an Elite Process: The Failure of a Dream?*, New York: Routledge.

Hammar, T. (ed.) (1985) *European Immigration Policy: A Comparative Study*, Cambridge: Cambridge University Press.

—   (1990) *Democracy and the Nation State: Aliens, Denizens and Citizens in a World of International Migration*, Aldershot: Avebury.

Hammar, T., Brochmann, G., Tamas, K. and Faist, T. (eds) (1997) *International Migration, Immobility and Development*, Oxford: Berg.

Hampshire, J. (2012) *The Politics of Immigration: Contradictions of the Liberal State*, Cambridge: Polity.

Hansen, R. (1998) 'A European citizenship or a Europe of citizens? Third country nationals in the EU', *Journal of Ethnic and Migration Studies*, 24(4): 751–768.

—— (2000) *Citizenship and Immigration in Post-War Britain*, Oxford: Oxford University Press.

—— (2009) 'The poverty of postnationalism: citizenship, immigration and the new Europe', *Theory and Society*, 38(1): 1–24.

—— (2011) 'The two faces of liberalism: Islam in contemporary Europe', *Journal of Ethnic and Migration Studies*, 37(6): 881–897.

Hansen, R. and Weil, P. (eds) (2000) *Towards a European Nationality: Citizenship, Immigration and Nationality Law in the EU*, London: Macmillan.

Hardill, I. and MacDonald, S. (2000) 'Skilled international migration: the experience of nurses in the UK', *Regional Studies*, 34(7): 681–92.

Hardwick, S. (2007) 'Place, space and pattern: geographical theories in international migration', in Brettell, C. and Hollifield, J. (eds) (2nd edn) *Migration Theory: Talking Across Disciplines*, New York: Routledge, pp. 161–82.

Hatton, T. and Williamson, J. (1998) *The Age of Mass Migration*, Oxford: Oxford University Press.

Haut Conseil à l'Intégration (1993) *L'intégration à la française*, Paris: La documentation française.

Hawthorn, G. (1991) *Plausible Worlds: Possibility and Understanding in History and the Social Sciences*, Cambridge: Cambridge University Press.

Heath, A. and Cheung, S. Y. (eds) (2007) *Unequal Chances: Ethnic Minorities in Western Labour Markets*, Oxford: Oxford University Press.

Heckmann, F. and Schnapper, D. (eds) (2003) *The Integration of Immigrants in European Societies*, Stuttgart: Lucius and Lucius.

Hedetoft, U. (2006) 'Multiculturalism in Denmark and Sweden', Copenhagen: DIIS Brief, Dec, http://subweb.diis.dk/graphics/Publications/Briefs2006/hedetoft_multiculturalism_dk_sweden.pdf.

Heitmeyer, W., Müller, J. and Schröder, H. (1997) *Verlockender Fundamentalismus*, Frankfurt: Suhrkamp.

Helbling, M. (ed.) (2012) *Islamophobia in the West: Measuring and Explaining Individual Attitudes*, London: Routledge.

Held, D., McGrew, A., Goldblatt, D. and Perraton, J. (1999) *Global Transformations: Politics, Economics and Culture*, Oxford: Polity.

Herm, A. (2008) 'Recent migration trends: citizens of EU–27 member states become ever more mobile while EU remains attractive to non–EU citizens', *Statistics in Focus* 98, Eurostat, http://epp.eurostat.ec.europa.eu/cache/ITY_OFFPUB/KS–SF–08–098/EN/KS–SF–08–098–EN.PDF

Hernández–León, R. (2004) 'Restructuring at the source: high–skilled industrial migration from Mexico to the US', *Work and Occupations*, 34(4): 1–29.

—   (2005) 'The migration industry in the Mexico–U.S. migratory system', *California Center of Population Research Online Working Paper Series* 049–05, UCLA: Los Angeles.

—   (2008) *Metropolitan Migrants: The Migration of Urban Mexicans to the United States*, Berkeley: University of California Press.

—   (2012) 'L'industrie de la migration: organiser la mobilité dans le système migratoire Mexique-Etats-Unis', *Hommes et Migrations*, 1296 (mars-avril): 34–44.

Hiro, D. (1991) *Black British, White British: A History of Race Relations in Britain*, London: Grafton.

Hirschman, A. O. (1991) *The Rhetoric of Reaction*, Cambridge, MA: Harvard University Press.

Hirschman, C., Kasinitz, P. and De Wind, J. (eds) (1999) *Handbook of International Migration: The American Experience*, New York: Russell Sage.

Hix, S. (1995) 'The intergovernmental conference and the future of the third pillar', Briefing Paper no. 20. Brussels: Churches Commission for Migrants in Europe.

Hjarnø, J. (ed.) (1999) *From Metropolis to Cosmopolis*, Esbjerg: South Jutland University Press.

Hobsbawm, E. (1983) *The Invention of Tradition*, Cambridge: Cambridge University Press.

—   (1987) *The Age of Empire*, New York: Pantheon Books.

Hochschild, J. and Mollenkopf, J. (eds) (2009) *Bringing Outsiders In: Transatlantic Perspectives on Immigrant Political Incorporation*, Ithaca, NY: Cornell University Press.

Hochschild, J., Chattopadhyay, J., Gay, C. and Jones-Correa, M. (eds) (2013) *Outsiders No More? Models of Political Incorporation*, New York: Oxford University Press.

Hodagneu-Sotelo, P. (2001) *Domestica: Immigrant Workers Cleaning and Caring in the Shadow of Affluence*, Berkeley, CA: University of California Press.

Hollifield, J. (1992) *Immigrants, Markets and States: The Political Economy of Western Europe*, Cambridge, MA: Harvard University Press.

—   (2004) 'The emerging migration state', *International Migration Review*, 38(3): 885–912.

—   (2007) 'The politics of international migration: how can we "bring the state back in"?' in Brettell, C. and Hollifield, J. (eds) (2nd edn) *Migration Theory: Talking Across Disciplines*, New York: Routledge, pp. 183–238.

Hollis, M. (1994) *The Philosophy of Social Science: An Introduction*, Oxford: Oxford University Press.

Hollis, M. and Smith, S. (1990) *Explaining and Understanding International Relations*, Oxford: Clarendon Press.

Holmes, D. (2000) *Integral Europe: Fast Capitalism, Multiculturalism, Neo-Fascism*, Princeton, NJ: Princeton University Press.

Hönekopp, E. (1991) *Migratory Movements from Countries of Central and Eastern Europe: Causes and Characteristics, Present Situation and Possible Future Trends – The Cases of Germany and Austria*, Strasbourg: Council of Europe.

Honeyford, R. (1988) *Integration or Disintegration? Towards a Non-Racist Society*, London: Claridge Press.

Höpner, M. and Shäfer, A. (2012) 'Embeddedness and regional integration: waiting for Polanyi in a Hayekian setting', *International Organization*, 66: 429–455.

Horowitz, D. and Noiriel, G. (eds) (1992) *Immigrants in Two Democracies: French and American Experiences*, New York: New York University Press.

Horváth, I. (2008) 'The culture of migration of rural Romanian youth', *Journal of Ethnic and Migration Studies*, 34(5): 771–786.

Huntington, S. (1996) *The Clash of Civilizations and the Remaking of the New World Order*, Chicago: Chicago University Press.

— (2004) *Who Are We? The Challenges to American National Identity*, New York: Simon and Schuster.

Inglehart, R. (1990) *Culture Shift in Advanced Industrial Society*, Princeton, NJ: Princeton University Press.

Iredale, R. (2001) 'The migration of professionals: theories and typologies', *International Migration* 39(5): 7–26.

— (1991) 'Facing the true fortress Europe: immigrants and politics in the EU', *Journal of Common Market Studies*, 29(5): 451–480.

— (1994) *The Policy Challenge of Ethnic Diversity: Immigrant Politics in France and Switzerland*, Cambridge, MA: Harvard University Press.

Jacobs, D. (1998) *Nieuwkomers in de Politiek: Het parlementaire debat omtrent kiesrecht voor vreemdelingen in Nederland en Belgie (1970–1997)*, Ghent: Academia Press.

— (2000) 'Multinational and polyethnic politics entwined: minority representation in the region of Brussels–Capital', *Journal of Ethnic and Migration Studies*, 26(2): 289–304.

Jacobs, D. and Tillie, J. (2004) 'Introduction: social capital and political integration', *Journal of Ethnic and Migration Studies*, 30(3): 419–427.

Jacobson, D. (1996) *Rights Across Borders: Immigration and the Decline of Citizenship*, Baltimore, MD: Johns Hopkins University Press.

Janoski, T. (1998) *Citizenship and Civil Society*, Cambridge: Cambridge University Press.

Janoski, T. and Glennie, E. (1995) 'The roots of citizenship: explaining naturalisation in advanced industrial societies', in Martiniello, M. (ed.) *Migration, Citizenship and Ethno-national Identities in the European Union*, Aldershot: Avebury, pp. 11–39.

Jensen, O. and Richardson, T. (2003) *Making European Space: Mobility, Power and Territorial Identity*, London: Routledge.

Jileva, E. (2002) 'Visas and free movement of labour: the uneven imposition of the EU acquis on the accession states', *Journal of Ethnic and Migration Studies*, 28(4): 683–700.

Joly, D. (1995) *Britannia's Crescent: Making a Place for Muslims in British Society*, Aldershot: Avebury.

Joppke, C. (1996) 'Immigration and multiculturalism: a comparison of the US, Germany and Britain', *Theory and Society*, 25(4): 449–500.

— (ed.) (1998a) *Challenge to the Nation State: Immigration in Western Europe and the United States*, Oxford: OUP.

— (1998b) 'Immigration challenges the nation state', in Joppke, C. (ed.) *Challenge to the Nation State: Immigration in Western Europe and the United States*, Oxford: Oxford University Press, pp. 5–46.

— (1999) *Immigration and the Nation State: The United States, Germany and Great Britain*, Oxford: Oxford University Press.

— (2004) 'The retreat of multiculturalism in the liberal state: theory and policy', *British Journal of Sociology*, 55(2): 237–257.

— (2014) 'Europe and Islam: alarmists, victimists and integration by law', *West European Politics*, 37(6): 1314–1335.

Joppke, C. and Lukes, S. (eds) (1999) *Multicultural Questions*, Oxford: Oxford University Press.

Joppke, C. and Morawska, E. (eds) (2003) *Toward Assimilation and Citizenship: Immigrants in Liberal Nation States*, London: Palgrave Macmillan.

Joppke, C. and Torpey, J. (2013) *Legal Integration of Islam: A Transatlantic Comparison*, Cambridge, MA: Harvard University Press.

Jordan, B. and Düvell, F. (2002) *Irregular Migration: Dilemmas of Transnational Mobility*, Cheltenham: Edward Elgar.

Kaczmarczyk, P. and Okólski, M. (2005) *International Migration in Central and Eastern Europe: Current and Future Trends*, United Nations Expert Group Meeting on International Migration and Development, Report: UN/POP/PD/2005/12.

Kastoryano, R. (1993) *Etre turque en France*, Paris: L'Harmattan.

— (1997) *La France, l'Allegmagne et leurs immigrés: négocier l'identité*, Paris: Armand Colin.

— (ed.) (1998a) *Quelle identité pour l'Europe? Multiculturalisme à l'épreuve*, Paris: Presses de Sciences Po.

— (ed.) (1998b) 'Transnational participation and citizenship: immigrants in the European Union'. ESRC Transnational Communities Working Paper Series, WPTC-98-12, http://www.transcomm.ox.ac.uk/working papers/riva.pdf

Katznelson, I. (1973) *Black Men, White Cities*, Oxford: Oxford University Press.

Keane, J. (1990) 'Decade of the citizen: interview with Ralf Dahrendorf', *The Guardian*, 1 Aug.

Kepel, G. (1994) *A l'ouest d'Allah*, Paris: éditions du Seuil.

Kesler, C. (2006) 'Social policy and immigrant joblessness in Britain, Germany and Sweden', *Social Forces*, 85(2): 743–770.

— (2010) 'Immigrant wage disadvantage in Sweden and the United Kingdom: wage structure and barriers to opportunity', *International Migration Review*, 44(3): 560–592.

Kesler, C. and Safi, M. (2012) 'Immigrant/native labor market inequalities: a portrait of patterns and trends in France and the United Kingdom, 1990–2007', Paris: Sciences Po/OSC/CNRS, Notes & Documents: Working Paper 2012–01.

Kesler, C. and Schwartzman, L. (2014) 'From multi–racial subjects to multi-cultural citizens: social stratification and ethnic and racial classification among children of immigrants in the United Kingdom', *International Migration Review*, Available online, 22 May: 1–47.

Kesteloot, C. (2000) 'Brussels: Post-Fordist polarization in a Fordist spatial canvas', in Macuse, P. and van Kempen, R. (eds) *Globalizing Cities: A New Spatial Order*, Oxford: Blackwell, pp. 186–210.

King, R. (2002) 'Towards a new map of European migration', *International Journal of Population Geography*, 8(2): 89–106.

—— (2012) *'Geography and migration studies: retrospect and prospect, Population, Space and Place'*, 18(2): 134–53.

King, R. and Ruiz Gelices, E. (2003) 'International student migration and the European 'year abroad': effects on European identity and subsequent migration behaviour', *International Journal of Population Geography*, 9: 229–252.

King, R., Black, R., Collyer, M., Fielding, A., and Skeldon, R. (2010) *The Atlas of Human Migration: Global Patterns of People on the Move*, London: Routledge.

King, R., Warnes, T. and Williams, A. (2000) *Sunset Lives: British Retirement Migration to the Mediterranean*, Oxford: Berg Kiriakos, C.

—— (2010) *The World is My Workplace? The Meaning of Locality and Distance for Finnish Professionals in Silicon Valley*, European University Institute: Florence, PhD.

Klausen, J. (2005) *The Islamic Challenge: Politics and Religion in Western Europe*, Oxford: Oxford University Press.

Kloosterman, R., van der Leun, J. and Rath, J. (1998) 'Across the border: immigrants' economic opportunities, social capital and informal business activities', *Journal of Ethnic and Migration Studies*, 24(2): 249–268.

—— (1999) 'Mixed embeddedness: (in)formal economic activities and immigrant businesses in the Netherlands', *International Journal of Urban and Regional Research*, 23(2): 252–266.

Kofman, E. (2000) 'The invisibility of skilled female migrants and gender relations in studies of skilled migration in Europe', *International Journal of Population Geography*, 6: 45–59.

—— (2005) 'Figures of the cosmopolitan: privileged nationals and national outsiders', *Innovation* 18(1): 83–97.

Kofman, E., Phizacklea, A., Raghuram, P. and Sales, R. (2000) *Gender and International Migration in Europe*, London: Routledge.

Koikkalainen, S. (2013) *Making it Abroad: Experiences of Highly Skilled Finns in the European Union Labour Markets*, University of Lapland. PhD.

Koopmans, R. (2010) 'Trade-offs between equality and difference: immigrant integration, multiculturalism and the welfare state in cross–national perspective', *Journal of Ethnic and Migration Studies*, 36(1): 1–26.

— (2013) 'Multiculturalism and immigration: a contested field in cross–national comparison'. *Annual Review of Sociology*, 39: 147–169.

Koopmans, R. and Statham, P. (1999) 'Postnationalism, multiculturalism and the collective claims making of migrants and ethnic minorities in Britain and Germany', *American Journal of Sociology*, 105(3): 652–696.

— (eds) (2000) *Challenging Immigration and Ethnic Relations Politics: Comparative European Perspectives*, Oxford: Oxford University Press.

Koopmans, R., Michalowski, I. and Waibel, S. (2012) 'Citizenship rights for immigrants: national political processes and cross-national convergence in Western Europe 1980–2008', *American Journal of Sociology*, 117(4): 1202–1245.

Koopmans, R., Statham, P., Giugny, M. and Passy, F. (2005) *Contested Citizenship: Immigration and Cultural Diversity in Europe*, Minneapolis: University of Minnesota Press.

Koser, K. (2007) *International Migration*, Oxford: Oxford University Press.

Koser, K. and Lutz, H. (eds) (1998) *The New Migration in Europe*, London: Macmillan.

Krings, T., Moriarty, E., Wickham, J., Bobek, A. and Salamońska, J. (2013) *New Mobilities in Europe: Polish Migration to Ireland Post–2004*, Manchester: Manchester University Press.

Krissman, F. (2005) 'Sin coyote ni patrón: why the "migrant network" fails to explain international migration', *International Migration Review*, 39(1): 4–44.

Kupiszewski, M. (2002) 'How trustworthy are forecasts of international migration between Poland and the European Union?', *Journal of Ethnic and Migration Studies*, 28(4): 627–645.

Kyle, D. (2000) *Transnational Peasants: Migration, Networks and Ethnicity in Andean Ecuador*, Baltimore, MD: Johns Hopkins University Press.

Kymlicka, W. (1989) *Liberalism, Community and Culture*, Oxford: Oxford University Press.

— (1995) *Multicultural Citizenship: A Liberal Theory of Multicultural Rights*, Oxford: Oxford University Press.

— (1998) *Finding Our Way: Rethinking Ethno-Cultural Relations in Canada*, Oxford: Oxford University Press.

— (2000) 'Nation building and minority rights: comparing west and east', *Journal of Ethnic and Migration Studies*, 26(2): 183–212.

— (2007) *Multicultural Odysseys: Navigating the New International Politics of Diversity*, Oxford: Oxford University Press.

— (2010) 'Testing the liberal multiculturalist hypothesis: normative theories and social science evidence', *Canadian Journal of Political Science*, 43(2): 257–71.

Kymlicka, W. and Norman, W. (1994) 'Return of the citizen: a survey of recent work on citizenship theory', *Ethics* 104(2): 352–381.

Lamont, M. (1992) *Money, Morals and Manners: The Culture of the French and American Upper Middle Class*, Chicago: Chicago University Press.

— (2000) *The Dignity of Working Men: Morality and Boundaires of Race, Class and Immigration*, Cambridge, MA: Cambridge University Press.

Lapeyronnie, D. (ed.) (1992) *Immigrés en Europe: politiques locales d'intégration*, Paris: La documentation française.

— (1993) *L'Individu et les minorités: La France et la Grande Brétagne face à ses minorités*, Paris: Presses universitaires françaises.

Laurence, J. (2012) *The Emancipation of Europe's Muslims: The State's Role in Minority Integration*, Princeton, NJ: Princeton University Press.

Lavenex, S. (2005) 'Interdependence of migration research and its sociopolitical contexts: national frames in migration research: the tacit political agenda' in Bommes, M. and Morawska, E. (eds), *International Migration Research: Constructions, Omissions and the Promise of Interdisciplinarity*, London: Ashgate, pp. 243–264.

— (2006) 'The competition state and the multilateral liberalization of highly skilled migration' in Smith, M. P. and Favell, A. (eds) *The Human Face of Global Mobility: International High Skilled Migrants in Europe, North America and the Asia Pacific*, New Brunswick, NJ: Transaction Press, pp. 29–52.

Lavenex, S. and Uçarer, E. (2002) *Migration and the Externalities of European Integration*, Lanham, MD: Lexington.

Layton-Henry, Z. (1992) *The Politics of Immigration*, Oxford: Blackwell.

Le Bras, H. (1998) *Le démon des origines: démographie et extrême droite*, Paris: Éditions de l'aube.

Lesthaege, R. (ed.) (1997) *Diversiteit in sociale verandering: Turkse en Morokkaanse vrouwen in Belgïe*, Brussels: VUB Press.

— (ed.) (2000) *Communities and Generations: Turkish and Moroccan Populations in Belgium*, Brussels: VUB Press.

Levitt, P. (2001) *The Transnational Villagers*, Berkeley, CA: University of California Press.

Levitt, P. and Glick Schiller, N. (2004) 'Conceptualizing simultaneity: a transnational social field perspective on society', *International Migration Review*, 38(3): 885–912.

Lewis, P. (1994) *Islamic Britain: Religion, Politics and Identity Among British Muslims: Bradford in the 1990s*, London: Tavistock.

Ley, D. (2010) *Millionaire Migrants: Trans–Pacific Lifelines*, Malden, MA: Wiley-Blackwell.

Light, I. (2006) *Deflecting Immigration: Networks, Markets, and Regulation in Los Angeles*, New York: Russell Sage.

Light, I. and Gold, S. (2000) *Ethnic Economies*, San Diego, CA: Academic Press.

Lionnet, F. and Shi, S. -M. (eds) (2005) *Minor Transnationalism*, Durham, NC: Duke University Press.

Losada, M. (2011) *L'acceuil des étudiants étrangers entre attraction et contrôle: logiques institutionnelles et stratégies individuelles*, Sciences Po: Paris, PhD.

Loury, G., Modood, T. and Telles, S. (eds) (2005) *Ethnicity, Social Mobility and Public Policy: Comparing the USA and UK*, Cambridge: Cambridge University Press.

Lowell, L. B. (1996) 'Skilled and family-based immigration: principles and labor markets' in Duleep, H. and Wunnava, P. (eds) *Immigrants and Immigration Policy: Individual skills, Family Ties, and Group Identities*, Greenwich, CT: AIS Press, pp. 353–372.

Lucassen, L. (2005) *The Immigrant Threat: The Integration of Old and New Migrants in Western Europe since 1850*, Urbana, IL: The University of Illinois Press.

Lukes, S. (1985) *Marxism and Morality*, Oxford: Oxford University Press.

— (1993) 'Five fables about liberty', in Shute, S. and Hurley, S. (eds) *On Human Rights*, New York: Basic Books.

Maas, W. (2007) *Creating European Citizens*, Lanham: Rowman & Littlefield.

McLaughlan, G. and Salt, J. (2002) *Migration Policies Towards Highly Skilled Foreign Workers*, London: Home Office.

McNevin, A. (2014). 'Beyond territoriality: Rethinking human mobility, border security and geopolitical space from the Indonesian island of Bintan', *Security Dialogue*, 45(3): 295–310.

Majone, G. (1989) *Evidence, Argument and Persuasion in the Policy Process*, New Haven: Yale University Press.

— (1996) 'Public policy: ideas, interests and institutions' in Goodin, R. and Klingemann, D. (eds) *New Handbook of Political Science*, Oxford: Oxford University Press.

— (1996) *Governing Europe*, London: Routledge.

Malyutina, D. (2012) *Migrant Sociality in a 'Global City': Friendship, Transnational Networks, Racism and Cosmopolitanism. A Study of Russian-Speaking Migrants in London*, University College London. PhD.

Mann, M. (1988) 'Ruling class strategies and citizenship' in Mann, M. (1998) *States, Wars and Capitalism: Studies in Political Sociology*, Oxford: Blackwell, pp. 188–210.

— (1993) *The Sources of Social Power: Vol 2. The Rise of Classes and Nation-States 1760–1914*, Cambridge: Cambridge University Press.

— (2005) *The Dark Side of Democracy*, Cambridge: Cambridge University Press.

March, J. and Olsen, J. (1989) *Rediscovering Institutions: The Organizational Basis of Politics*, New York: Free Press.

Marcuse, P. (1996) 'Of walls and immigrant enclaves' in Carmon, N. (ed.) *Immigration and Integration in Post-Industrial Societies*, London: Macmillan, pp. 30–45.

Marshall, T. H. (1950; 1992) 'Citizenship and Social Class' in Marshall, H. H. and Bottomore, T. (eds) *Citizenship and Social Class*, London: Pluto.

Martin, P. (2006.) '*The trade, migration and development nexus*', Migration For Development programme, Davis: University of California Press.

—   (2011) 'Migration, trade and development: comparing Mexico-US and Turkey-Europe', Conference paper, University of California Davis.

—   (2012) 'High skilled migrants: S & E workers in the United States', *American Behavioural Scientist*, 56(8): 1058–1079.

Martiniello, M. (1992) *Leadership et pouvoir dans les communautés d'origine immigrée*, Paris: CIEMI: L'Harmattan.

—   (1995) *L'ethnicité dans les sciences sociales*, Paris: PUF.

—   (ed.) (1998) *Multicultural Policies and the State: A Comparison of Two European Societies:* Utrecht: ERCOMER.

Martiniello, M. and Rath, J. (eds) (2010) *Selected Studies in International Migration and Immigrant Incorporation*, Amsterdam: University of Amsterdam Press.

—   (eds) (2013) *An Introduction to International Migration Studies*, Amsterdam, University of Amsterdam Press.

—   (eds) (2014) *An Introduction to Immigrant Incorporation Studies: European Perspectives*, Amsterdam: University of Amsterdam Press.

Massey, D., Alarcón, R., Durand, J. and Gonzáles, H. (1987) *Return to Aztlan: The Social Process of Migration from Western Mexico*, Berkeley, CA: University of California Press.

Massey, D., Arango, J., Hugo, G., Kouaouci, A., Pellegrino, A. and Taylor, E. J. (1993) 'Theories of migration: a review and appraisal', *Population and Development Review*, 19(3): 431–466.

—   (1998) *Worlds in Motion: Understanding International Migration at the End of the Millennium*, Oxford: Clarendon Press.

Massey, D., Durand, J. and Malone, N. (2002) *Beyond Smoke and Mirrors: Mexican Migration in an Era of Economic Integration*, New York: Russell Sage.

Mattli, W. (1999) *The Logic of Regional Integration*, Cambridge: Cambridge University Press.

Mau, S. (2010) *Social Transnationalism*, London: Routledge.

Mau, S. and Verwiebe, R. (2010) *European Societies: Mapping Structure and Change*, Bristol: Policy Press.

Mau, S., Brabandt, H., Laube, L., Roos, C. (2012) *Liberal States and the Freedom of Movement: Selective Borders, Unequal Mobility*, London: Palgrave Macmillan.

Maxwell, R. (2012) *Ethnic Minority Migrants in Britain and France*, New York: Cambridge University Press.

Mazower, M. (1998) *Dark Continent: Europe's Twentieth Century*, London: Penguin.

Meardi, G. (2012) *Social Failures of EU Enlargement: A Case of Workers Voting With Their Feet*, London: Routledge.

Meehan, E. (1993) *Citizenship and the European Union*, London: Sage.

Mendus, S. (1990) 'The tigers of wrath and the horses of instruction', in Parekh, B. (ed.) *Free Speech*, London: CRE.

Menz, G. (2008) *The Political Economy of Managed Migration*, Oxford: Oxford University Press.

Merton, R. (1957) *Social Theory and Social Structure*, Glencoe: Free Press.
Messina, A. (1989) *Race and Party Competition*, Oxford: Oxford University Press.
Messina, A., Fraga, L., Rhodebeck, L. and Wright, F. (eds) (1992) *Ethnic and Racial Minorities in Advanced Industrial Democracies*, London: Greenwood Press.
Miera, F. (2008) 'Transnational strategies of Polish migrant entrepreneurs in trade and small business in Berlin', *Journal of Ethnic and Migration Studies*, 34(5): 753–770.
Migration Policy Group (1996) *The Comparative Approaches to Societal Integration Project*, Brussels: Migration Policy Group.
Miles, R. (1993) *Racism after 'Race Relations'*, London: Routledge.
Milkman, R. (2006) *L.A. Story: Immigrant Workers and the Future of the US Labor Movement*, New York: Russell Sage.
Miller, D. (1995) *On Nationality*, Oxford: Oxford University Press.
— (2000) *Citizenship and National Identity*, Oxford: Polity.
Milward, A. (1992) *The European Rescue of the Nation-State*, London: Routledge.
Mitchell, K. (2003) 'Educating the national citizen in neoliberal times: from the multicultural self to the strategic cosmopolitan', *Transactions of the Institute of British Geographers*, 28(4): 387–403.
Moch, L. P. (2003) (2nd edn) *Moving Europeans: Migration in Western Europe Since 1650*, Bloomington: Indiana University Press.
Modgil, S., Verma, G., Mallick, D. and Modgil, C. (1986) *Multiculturalism: The Interminable Debate*, London: Falmer.
Modood, T. (1992) *Not Easy Being British: Colour, Culture and Citizenship*, London: Runnymede Trust and Trentham.
— (1994) 'Establishment, multiculturalism and British citizenship', *Political Quarterly*, 65(1): 53–73.
Modood, T., Beishon, S. and Virdee, S. (1994) *Changing Ethnic Identities*, London: Policy Studies Institute.
Modood, T. with Berhoud, R., Lakey, J., Nazroo, J., Smith, P. Virdee, S. and Beishon, S. (1997) *Ethnic Minorities in Britain: Diversity and Disadvantage*, London: Policy Studies Institute.
Modood, T., Hansen, R., Bleich, E., O'Leary, B., and Carens, J. (2006) 'The Danish cartoon affair: free speech, racism, Islamism and integration', *International Migration*, 44(5): 3–62.
Modood, T., Triandafyllidou, A. and Zapata-Barrero, R. (2006) *Multiculturalism, Muslims and Citizenship: A European Approach*, London: Routledge.
Modood, T. and Werbner, P. (eds) (1997) *The Politics of Multiculturalism in the New Europe: Racism, Identity and Community*, London: Zed Books.
Money, J. (1999) *Fences and Neighbors: The Political Geography of Immigration Control*, Ithaca, NY: Cornell University Press.
Money, J. and Zartner Falstrom, D. (2006) 'Interests and institutions: comparing flows of skilled migration in the IT and nursing sectors' in Smith, M. P. and Favell, A. (eds) *The Human Face of Global Mobility: International High Skilled Migrants in Europe, North America and the Asia Pacific*, New Brunswick, NJ: Transaction Press, pp. 131–158.

Morales, L. and Giugni, M. (eds) (2011) *Social Capital, Political Participation and Migration in Europe: Making Multicultural Democracy Work*, London: Palgrave-Macmillan.

Morawska, E. (2002) 'Transnational migration in the enlarged European Union: a perspective from East and Central Europe' in Zielonka, J. (ed.) *Europe Unbound*, Oxford: Oxford University Press, pp. 161–90.

— (2011) *A Sociology of Immigration: (Re)Making Multifaceted America*, New York: Palgrave MacMillan.

Morosanu, L. (2011) *Migrant Social Networks and the Contingent Role of Ethnicity*, University of Bristol, PhD.

Mouffe, C. (2000) *The Democratic Paradox*, London: Verso.

Mulhall, S. and Swift, A. (1992) *Liberals and Communitarians*, Oxford: Blackwell.

Münch, R. (2001) *Offene Räume: Soziale Integration diesseits und jenseits des Nationalstaats*, Frankfurt: Suhrkamp.

Nauck, B. and Schönpflug, U. (eds) (1997) *Familien in verschiedenen Kulturen*, Stuttgart: Enke.

Nicholls, D. (1994) (2nd edn) *The Pluralist State*, London: Macmillan.

Nicholls, W. and Uitermark, J. (2013) 'Post-multicultural cities: a comparison of minority politics in Amsterdam and LA 1970–2000, *Journal of Ethnic and Migration Studies*, 39(10): 1555–1575.

Nohl, A.-M., Schittenhelm, K., Schmidtke, O., Weiβ, A., (2014) *Work in Transition: Cultural Capital and Highly Skilled Migrants' Passages into the Labour Market*. Toronto: University of Toronto Press.

North, D. (1990) *Institutions, Institutional Change and Economic Performance*, Cambridge: Cambridge University Press.

Odmalm, P. (2005) *Migration Policies and Political Participation: Inclusion or Intrusion in Western Europe*, London: Palgrave Macmillan.

Okólski, M. (2001) 'Incomplete migration: a new form of mobility in Central and Eastern Europe – the case of Polish and Ukrainian migrants', in Wallace, C. and Stola, D. (eds) *Patterns of Migration in Central Europe*, London: Palgrave MacMillan, pp. 105–128.

Ong, A. (1999) *Flexible Citizenship: The Cultural Logics of Transnationality*, Durham: Duke University Press.

O'Reilly, K. (2012) *International Migration and Social Theory*, London: Palgrave Macmillan.

Papastergiadis, N. (1999) *The Turbulence of Migration: Globalization, Deterritorialization and Hybridity*, Cambridge: Polity Press.

Parekh, B. (1989) 'Between holy text and moral void', *New Statesman*, 24 Mar.

— (1990a) 'The Rushdie Affair: Research Agenda for Political Philosophy', *Political Studies*, 38(4): 695–709.

— (1990b) 'The Social Logic of Pluralism' in Parekh, B. (ed.) *Britain: A Plural Society*, London: CRE.

— (2000) *Rethinking Multiculturalism: Cultural Diversity and Political Theory*, London: Macmillan.

Parekh, B. and Bhabha, H. (1989) 'Identities on parade: a conversation', *Marxism Today* (June).

Parsons, C. and Smeeding, T. (eds) (2006) *Immigration and the Transformation of Europe*, Cambridge: Cambridge University Press.

Pastor, R. A. (2001) *Toward a North American Community: Lessons from the Old World for the New*, Washington, DC: Peterson Institute.

Peach, C. (ed.) (1996) *Ethnicity in the 1991 Census* (vol.2), London: HMSO.

Peck, J. (2010) *Constructions of Neoliberal Reason*, Oxford. Oxford University Press.

Penninx, R., Berger, M. and Kraal, K. (eds) (2006) *The Dynamics of International Migration and Settlement in Europe: A State of the Art*, Amsterdam: Amsterdam University Press.

Penninx, R., Spencer, D., and Van Hear, N. (2008) (eds) *Migration and Integration in Europe: The State of Research*, Oxford: ESRC Centre on Migration, Policy and Society (COMPAS).

Peri, G. (2005) 'Skills and talent of immigrants: a comparison between the European Union and the United States', Institute of European Studies Working Paper, 050304, Berkeley: University of California.

Phalet, K. and Swyngedouw, M. (1999) 'Integratie ter discussie' in Deschouwer, K., Phalet, K. and Swyngedouw, M. (eds) *Minderheden in Brussel*, Brussels: VUB Press.

—   (2001) 'National identities and representations of citizenship: a comparison of Turks, Moroccans and working class Belgians in Brussels', *Ethnicities* 2(1) 5–30.

—   (2003) 'Measuring integration: the case of Belgium', *Studi Emigrazione* XL, 152: 773–803.

Phalet, K. and Heath, A. (2010) 'From ethnic boundaries to ethnic penalties: urban economies and the Turkish second generation', *American Behavioural Scientist*, 53(12): 1824–1850.

Phalet, K., van Lotringen, C. and Entzinger, H. (2000) *Islam in de multiculturele samenleving*, Utrecht: ERCOMER.

Phillips, A. (1993) *Democracy and Difference*, Oxford: Polity Press.

Phizacklea, A. (1998) 'Migration and globalization: a feminist perspective', in Koser, K. and Lutz, H. (eds) *The New Migration in Europe*, London: Macmillan.

Pierson, P. (2004) *Politics in Time: History, Institutions and Social Analysis*, Princeton, NJ: Princeton University Press.

Piore, M. (1979) *Birds of Passage: Migrant Labor in Industrial Societies*, Cambridge: Cambridge University Press.

Pizzorno, A. (1991) 'On the individualistic theory of social order' in Bourdieu, P. and Coleman, J. (eds) *Social Theory for a Changing Society*, Boulder, CO: Westview, pp. 209–44.

Portes, A. (ed.) (1995) *The Economic Sociology of Immigration*, New York: Russell Sage Foundation.

—   (1996) 'Transnational communities: their emergence and their significance in the contemporary world-system' in Korzeniewicz, R. and Smith, W. C. (eds) *Latin America in the World Economy*, Westport, CN: Greenwood Press, pp. 151–168.

—   (1997) 'Immigration theory for a new century: some problems and opportunities', *International Migration Review*, 31(4): 799–825.

—   (1998) 'Globalization from below: the rise of transnational communities', ESRC Transnational Communities working paper series, WPTC–98–01, Oxford: Oxford University Press.

Portes, A. and De Wind, J. (2004) 'A cross-Atlantic dialogue: the progress of research and theory in the study of international migration', *International Migration Review*, 38(3): 828–851.

—   (2007) *Rethinking Migration: New Theoretical and Empirical Perspectives*, New York: Berghahn.

Portes, A. and Landolt, P. (1996) 'The downside of social capital', *The American Prospect*, May-June (26): 18–21.

Portes, A. and Rumbaut, R. (2001) *Legacies: The Story of the Immigrant Second Generation*, Berkeley, CA: University of California Press.

Portes, A. and Walton, J. (1981) *Labor, Class and the International System*, New York: Academic Press.

Portes, A. and Zhou, M. (1993) 'The new second generation: segmented assimilation and its variants', *Annals of the American Academy of Political and Social Sciences*, 530: 74–96.

Portes, A., Aparicio, R., Haller, W. and Vickstrom, E. (2010) 'Moving ahead in Madrid: aspirations and expectations in the Spanish second generation', *International Migration Review*, 44(4): 767–801.

Portes, J. (2013) 'Benefit tourism – the facts', *The Guardian*, 14 October.

Poulter, S. (1990) *Asian Traditions and English Law*, London: Runnymede and Trentham.

Powell, W. and DiMaggio, P. (eds) (1991) *The New Institutionalism in Organizational Analysis*, Chicago: University of Chicago Press.

Pries, L. (ed.) (2001) *New Transnational Social Spaces: International Migration and Transnational Companies in the Early Twenty-First Century*, London and New York: Routledge.

Preuß, U. (1995) *Concepts, Foundations and Limits of European Citizenship*, Bremen: Centre for European Legal Policy.

Putnam, R. (1993) *Making Democracy Work: Civic Traditions in Modern Italy*, Princeton, NJ: Princeton University Press.

—   (2007) 'E Pluribus Unum: diversity and community in the twenty-first century', *Scandinavian Political Studies*, 30(2): 137–174.

Rath, J. (1991) *Minorisering: De sociale constructie van 'ethnische minderheden'*, Amsterdam: SUA.

Rath, J. and Kloosterman, R. (eds) (1998) *Rijp en Groen: Het zelfstandig ondernemerschap van immigranten in Nederland*, Amsterdam: Het Spinhuis.

Rawls, J. (1971) *A Theory of Justice*, Oxford: Oxford University Press.
— (1993) *Political Liberalism*, Princeton, NJ: Princeton University Press.
— (1995) 'Reply to Habermas', *Journal of Philosophy*, 92(3): 132–180.
Raz, J. (1986) *The Morality of Freedom*, Oxford: Clarendon Press.
Recchi, E. (2005) '*Migrants and Europeans: An Outline of the Free Movement of Persons in the EU*', AMID Working Paper Series: 38. Aalborg: Academy for Migration Studies in Denmark.
— (2006) 'From migrants to movers: citizenship and mobility in the European Union' in Smith, M. P. and Favell, A. (eds) *The Human Face of Global Mobility: International High Skilled Migrants in Europe, North America and the Asia Pacific*, New Brunswick, NJ: Transaction Press, pp. 53–77.
— (2008) 'Cross-state mobility in the EU: trends, puzzles and consequences', *European Societies*, 10: 197–224.
— (2009) 'The social mobility of mobile Europeans' in Recchi, E. and Favell, A. (eds) *Pioneers of European Integration: Citizenship and Mobility in the European Union*, Cheltenham: Edward Elgar, pp. 72–97.
— (2013) *Senza Frontiere: La Libera Circolozione delle Persone in Europa*, Bologna: Il Mulino.
— (2015) *Mobile Europe: The Theory and Practice of Free Movement in the EU*, London: Palgrave.
Reitz, J. (1998) *Warmth of the Welcome: The Social Causes of Economic Success for Immigrants in Different Nations and Cities*, Boulder, CO: Westview Press.
Rex, J. (1970) *Race Relations in Sociological Theory*, London: Weidenfeld and Nicolson.
— (1985) *The Concept of a Multi-Cultural Society*, Occasional Papers no.2. Warwick: CRER. [Republished in Guiberau, M. and Rex, J. (eds) (2nd edn) *The Ethnicity Reader: Nationalism, Multiculturalism and Migration*, Cambridge: Polity, pp. 217–229].
— (1991) *Ethnic Identity and Ethnic Mobilisation*, Monographs in Ethnic Relations no. 5, Warwick: CRER.
— (1996) *Ethnic Minorities in the Modern Nation State*, London: Macmillan.
Rex, J. and Drury, B. (eds) (1994) *Ethnic Mobilisation in a Multicultural Europe*, Aldershot: Avebury.
Rex, J. and Moore, R. (1967) *Race, Community and Conflict: A Study of Sparkbrook*, London: Oxford University Press for the Institute of Race Relations.
Riccio, B. (2001) 'From 'ethnic group' to 'transnational community': Senegalese migrants' ambivalent experiences and multiple trajectories', *Journal of Ethnic and Migration Studies*, 27(4): 583–599.
Rigby, E. and Parker, G. (2014) 'David Cameron shelves migration report amid lack of evidence', *Financial Times*, Jan 14.
Rogers, A. (2000) 'A European Space for Transnationalism?', Transnational Communities Programme Working Paper Series, WPTC-2K-07. Oxford, http://www.transcomm.ox.ac.uk/working papers/rogers.pdf

Romero, F. (1991) *Emigrazione ed integrazione europea 1945–1973*, Rome: Edizioni Lavoro.

Rose, E. J. B et al. (1969) *Colour and Citizenship: A Report on British Race Relations*, London: Oxford University Press for the Institute of Race Relations.

Rother, N. and Tina N. (2009) 'More mobile, more European? Free movement and EU identity', in Recchi, E. and Favell, A. (eds) *Pioneers of European Integration*, pp. 120–155.

Rowell J. and Penissat, É. (2012) 'Note de recherche sur la fabrique d'une nomenclature socioéconomique européenne, ESeC', *Actes de la recherche en sciences sociales*, no. 191–192: 126–135.

Ruhs, M. (2013) *The Price of Rights: Regulating International Labour Movement*, Princeton, NJ: Princeton University Press.

Rumford, C. (2006) 'Theorizing borders', *European Journal of Social Theory*, 9(2): 155–169.

Ryan, L. and Mulholland, J. (2013) '"Wives are the route to social life": an analysis of family life and networking amongst highly skilled migrants in London', *Sociology*, 48(2): 251–267.

— (2014) 'Trading places: French highly skilled migrants negotiating mobility and emplacement in London', *Journal of Ethnic and Migration Studies*, 40(4): 584–600.

Safi, M. (2009) 'The immigrant integration process in France: inequalities and segmentation', *Révue française de sociologie*, 47(1): 3–48.

— (2011) 'Penser l'intégration des immigrés: les enseignements de la sociologie américaine', *Sociologie* 2(2).

— (2013) *Les inégalités ethno-raciales*, Paris: La découverte.

Safi, M. and Simon, P. (2014) Les discriminationsx ethniques et raciales dans l'enquête Trajectoires et Origines : représentations, expériences subjectives et situations vécue, *Economie et Statistique* avril, 464–466: 245–275.

Saggar, S. (1991) *Race and Public Policy: A Study of Local Politics and Government*, Aldershot: Avebury.

— (ed.) (1996) *Race and British Electoral Politics*, London: Prentice Hall.

— (2009) *Pariah Politics: Understanding Western Radical Islam and What Should Be Done*, New York: Oxford University Press.

Salih, R. (2003) *Gender in Transnationalism: Home, Longing and Belonging Among Moroccan Migrant Women*, London: Routledge.

Salt, J. (1992) 'Migration processes among the highly skilled in Europe' *International Migration Review*, 26(2): 484–505.

Samad, Y. (1992) 'Book burning and race relations: political mobilisation of Bradford Muslims', *New Community*, 18(4): 507–519.

Samers, M. (2003) 'Invisible capitalism: political economy and the regulation of undocumented immigration in France', *Economy and Society*, 32(4): 555–583.

— (2004) 'An emerging geo–politics of "illegal" immigration in The European Union', *European Journal of Migration and Law*, 6(1): 23–41.

—   (1982) *Liberalism and the Limits of Justice*, Cambridge: Cambridge University Press.

Sapir, A., Aghion, P., Bertola, G., Hellwig, M., Pisani-Ferry, J., Rosati, D., Viñals, J. and Wallace, H. (2004) *An Agenda for a Growing Europe*, Oxford: Oxford University Press.

Sassen, S. (1996) *Losing Control? Sovereignty in an Age of Globalization*, New York: Columbia University Press.

Sassen, S. (2001) (2nd edn) *The Global City*, Princeton, NJ: Princeton University Press.

—   (2006) *Territory, Authority, Rights: From Medieval to Global Assemblages*, Princeton, NJ: Princeton University Press.

Sayer, A. (1999) 'Long live postdisciplinary studies! Sociology and the curse of disciplinary parochialism/imperialism', Dept of Sociology, Lancaster University, http://www.lancaster.ac.uk/sociology/research/publications/papers/sayer–long–live–postdisciplinary–studies.pdf

—   (2000) *Realism and Social Science*, London: Sage.

Saxenian, A. (2006) *The New Argonauts: Regional Advantage in a Global Economy*, Cambridge, MA: Harvard University Press.

Scarman, L. L. (1981) *The Brixton Disorders 10–12 April 1981: Report of an Enquiry*, London: Penguin.

Schain, M. (1988) 'Immigration and changes in the French party system', *European Journal of Political Research*, 16(6): 597–621.

—   (1999) 'Minorities and immigrant incorporation in France', in Joppke, C. and Lukes, S. (eds) *Multicultural Questions*, Oxford: Oxford University Press, pp. 199–223.

Schattschneider, E. E. (1961) *The Semi-Sovereign People: A Realist's View of Democracy in America*, New York: Free Press.

Schierup, C. -U. (1993) *På Kulturens Slagmark: Mindretal og Størretal om Danmark*, Esbjerg: Sydjysk Universitetsforlag.

Schinkel, W. (2008) *De Gedroomde Samenleving*, Amsterdam: Klement.

—   (2013) 'The imagination of "society" in measurements of immigrant integration', *Ethnic and Racial Studies*, 36(7): 1142–1161.

Schinkel, W. and van Houdt, F. (2010) 'The double helix of cultural assimilationism and neo-liberalism: citizenship in contemporary governmentality', *British Journal of Sociology*, 61(4): 696–715.

Schlesinger, A. (1992) *The Disuniting of America: Reflections on a Multicultural Society*, New York: Norton.

Schmidt, V. and Thatcher, M. (eds) (2013) *Resilient Liberalism in Europe's Political Economy*, Cambridge: Cambridge University Press.

Schmitter-Heisler, B. (2004) 'The sociology of immigration from assimilation to segmented integration: from the American experience to the global arena', in Brettell, C. and Hollifield, J. (eds) (2nd edn) *Migration Theory: Talking Across Disciplines*, New York: Routledge, pp. 77–98.

Schnapper, D. (1991) *La France de l'intégration*, Paris: Gallimard.

— (1992) *L'Europe des immigrés: essais sur les politiques de l'immigration*, Paris: Bonnin.

Scholten, P. (2011) *Framing Immigrant Integration: Dutch Research-Policy Dialogues in Comparative Perspective*, Amsterdam: Amsterdam University Press.

Scholten, P., Entzinger, H., Penninx, R. and Verbeek, S. (eds) (2014) *Research Policy Dialogues on Migrant Integration in Europe*, Amsterdam: University of Amsterdam Press.

Schuck, P. (1992) 'The politics of rapid legal change: immigration policy in the 1980s', *Studies in American Political Development*, 6(1): 37–92.

Schulz-Forberg, H. and Stråth, B. (2010) *The Political History of European Integration*, London. Routledge.

Scott, A. (ed.) (1997) *The Limits of Globalization*, London and New York: Routledge.

Scott, J. C. (1998) *Seeing Like a State: How Certain Schemes to Improve the Human Condition Have Failed*, New Haven, CT: Yale University Press.

Selbourne, D. (1994) *The Principle of Duty: An Essay on the Foundations of Civic Order*, London: Sinclair Stevenson.

Sennett, R. (1998) *The Corrosion of Character: The Consequences of Work in the New Capitalism*, New York: W. W. Norton.

Shaw, J. (2007) *The Transformation of Citizenship in the European Union*, Cambridge: Cambridge University Press.

Shepard, T. (2006) *The Invention of Decolonization: The Algerian War and the Remaking of France*, Ithaca, NY: Cornell University Press.

Silberman, R., Alba, R. and Fournier, I. (2007) 'Segmented assimilation in France? Discrimination in the labour market against the second generation', *Ethnic and Racial Studies*, 30(1): 1–27.

Simon, P. (1997) 'La statistique des origines: l'ethnicité et la 'race' dans les recensements aux Etats-Unis, Canada et Grande-Brétagne', *Sociétés Contemporaines*, 26: 11–44.

— (2005) 'The measurement of racial discrimination: the policy use of statistics', *International Journal of Social Science*, 57(183): 9–25.

— (2012) 'Collecting ethnic statistics in Europe: a review', *Ethnic and Racial Studies*, 35(8): 1366–1391.

Skinner, Q. *see* Tully (ed.).

Sklair, L. (2001) *The Transnational Capitalist Class*, Oxford: Blackwell.

Smith, D. and King, R. (eds) (2012) 'Remaking migration theory: Transitions, intersections and cross-fertilisations', *Population, Space and Place*, 18(2): 127–224.

Smith, M. P. (1999) 'The new high-tech braceros? Who is the employer? What is the problem?' in Lowell, L. B. (ed.) *Foreign Temporary Workers in America*, Westport, CT. and London: Quorum Books, pp. 119–147.

— (2001) *Transnational Urbanism: Locating Globalization*, Malden, MA and Oxford: Blackwell.

Smith, M. P. and Bakker, M. (2007) *Citizenship Across Borders: The Political Transnationalism of El Migrante*, Ithaca, NY: Cornell University Press.

Smith, M. P. and Guarnizo, L. (eds) (1998) *Transnationalism from Below*, New Brunswick, NJ: Transaction.

Smith, R. (2005) *Mexican New York: Transnational Lives of New Immigrants*, Berkeley, CA: University of California Press.

Soehl, T. (2014) *Modes of Difference and Connection: Language, Education and Religion in Migrant Families*, Ph.D. Dissertation, University of California Los Angeles, Department of Sociology.

Solomos, J. and Back, L. (1996) *Racism and Society*, London: Macmillan.

Solomos, J. and Wrench, J. (eds) (1993) *Racism and Migration in Western Europe*, Oxford: Berg.

Soysal, Y. N. (1993) 'Immigration and the emerging European polity', in Anderson, S. and Eliassen, K. (eds) *Making Policy in Europe: The Europification of National Policy*, London: Sage.

— (1994) *Limits of Citizenship: Migrants and Post-National Membership in Europe*, Chicago: Chicago University Press.

— (1997) 'Changing parameters of citizenship and claims-making: organized Islam in European public spheres', *Theory and Society*, 26(4): 509–527.

— (2012) 'Citizenship, immigration and the European social project: rights and obligations of individuality', *British Journal of Sociology*, 63(1): 1–21.

Spencer, S. (ed.) (1994) *Strangers and Citizens: A Positive Approach to Migrants and Refugees*, London: IPPR and River Oram Press.

Spencer, S., Ruhs, M., Anderson, B. and Rogaly, B. (2007) *Migrants' Lives Beyond the Workplace: The Experiences of Central and East Europeans in the UK*, Oxford: Rowntree Foundation.

Spinner-Halev, J. (1994) *The Boundaries of Citizenship: Race, Ethnicity and Culture in the Liberal State*, Baltimore, MD: Johns Hopkins University Press.

Stark, O. (2004) 'Rethinking the brain drain', *World Development*, 32(1): 15–22.

Statham, P. (1999) 'Political mobilisation by minorities in Britain: negative feedback of 'race relations'?', *Journal of Ethnic and Migration Studies*, 25(4): 597–626.

Steinmo, S., Thelen, K. and Longstreth, F. (eds) (1992) *Structuring Politics: Historical Institutionalism in Comparative Perspective*, New York: Cambridge University Press.

Strange, S. (1996) *The Retreat of the State: The Diffusion of Power in the World Economy*, Cambridge: Cambridge University Press.

Straubhaar, T. (2000) 'International mobility of the highly skilled: Brain gain, brain drain or brain exchange', HWWA Discussion Paper, 88. Hamburg: HWWA.

Streeck, W. (2011) 'The crisis of democratic capitalism', *New Left Review*, 71, Sept-Oct.

— (2013) *Gekaufte Zeit*, Berlin: Suhrkamp.

Swann, L. (1985) *Education for All*, London: House of Commons, Cmnd, 9453.

Szelenyi, K. (2006) 'Students without borders? Migratory decision making processes among international graduate students in the US?' in Smith, M. P. and Favell, A. (eds) *The Human Face of Global Mobility*, New Brunswick, NJ: Transaction Press, pp. 181–210.

Taleb, N. (2008) *The Black Swan: The Impact of the Highly Improbable*, New York: Random House.

Tarrius, A. (1992) *Les fourmis de l'Europe: migrants riches, migrants pauvres et nouvelles villes internationals*, Paris: L'Harmattan.

—— (2000) *Les nouveaux cosmopolitismes: mobilités, identités, territoires*, Paris: Éditions de l'aube.

Taylor, C. (1992) 'The politics of recognition', in Gutmann, A. (ed.) *Multiculturalism: Examining the Politics of Recognition*, Princeton, NJ: Princeton University Press, pp. 25–74.

Taylor, P. (2004) 'Material spatiality of cities and states', *ProtoSociology*, 20: 30–45.

Theodos, B. (2006) *Geographic Mobility and Geographic Labor Mobility in the United States*, Washington DC: The Urban Institute.

Thomas, E. (2011) *Immigration, Islam and the Politics of Belonging in France: A Comparative Framework*, Philadelphia, PA: University of Pennsylvania Press.

Todd, E. (1994) *Le destin des immigrés: assimilation et ségrégation dans les démocraties occidentales*, Paris: Éditions du Seuil.

Togeby, L. (1999) 'Migrants at the polls: an analysis of immigrant and refugee participation in Danish local elections', *Journal of Ethnic and Migration Studies*, 24(4): 665–684.

Torpey, J. (2000) *The Invention of the Passport*, Cambridge: Cambridge University Press.

Treiman, D. and Ganzeboom, H. (2000) 'The fourth generation of comparative stratification research', in Quah, S. and Sales, A. (eds) *The International Handbook of Sociology*, Newbury Park, CA: Sage.

Triandafyllidou, A. and Gropas, R. (eds) (2012) (2nd edn) *European Immigration: A Source Book*, Aldershot: Ashgate.

Triandafyllidou, A. (ed.) (2013) *Circular Migration between Europe and its Neighborhood: Choice or Necessity*, Oxford: Oxford University Press.

Tribalat, M. (1995) *Faire France: une enquête sur les immigrés et leurs enfants*, Paris: La découverte.

Tribalat, M. with Simon, P. and Riandey, B. (1996) *De l'immigration à l'assimilation: une enquête sur la population étrangère en France*, Paris: INED.

Tully, J. (ed.) (1989) *Meaning and Context: Quentin Skinner and his Critics*, Princeton, NJ: Princeton University Press.

Turner, B. (ed.) (1993) *Citizenship and Social Theory*, London: Sage.

Uberoi, V. (2007) *Multicultural Nation-Building: A Canadian Way to Foster Unity among British Citizens*, University of Oxford. DPhil.

Uberoi, V. and Modood, T. (2013) 'Inclusive Britishness: a multicultural advance', *Political Studies* 61(1): 23–41.

Uitermark, J. (2012) *Dynamics of Power in Dutch Integration Politics: From Accommodation to Confrontation*, Amsterdam: University of Amsterdam Press.

Unterreiner, A. and Weinar, A. (2014) '*The conceptual framework of the INTERACT project*', Interact Research Report 2014/01, Florence: European University Institute.

Urry, J. (2000) *Sociology Beyond Societies: Mobilities for the Twenty-First Century*, London: Routledge.

—   (2007) *Mobilities*, Cambridge: Polity.

Vallet, L. -A. (1996) 'L'assimilation scolaire des enfants issus de l'immigration et son interprétation: un examen sur données françaises', *Revue française de pédagogie*, 117: 7–27.

van Bochove, M. (2012) *Geographies of Belonging: The Transnational and Local Involvement of Economically Successful Migrants*, Erasmus University Rotterdam. PhD.

Vandenbrande, T., Coppin, L. and van der Hallen, P. (2006) *Mobility in Europe: Analysis of the 2005 Eurobarometer Survey on Geographical and Labour Market Mobility*, Dublin: European Foundation for the Improvement of Living and Working Conditions.

van Steenburgen, B. (ed.) (1994) *The Condition of Citizenship*, London: Sage.

Veenman, J. (1997) *Keren de kansen? De tweede generatie allochtonen in Nederland*, Rotterdam: ISEO.

—   (1998) *Buitenspel: Over langdurige werkloosheid onder ethnische minderheden*. Van Gorum: Assen.

Verma, G. (ed.) (1989) *Education for All: A Landmark in Pluralism*, London: Falmer.

Vermeulen, H. (ed.) (1997) *Immigrant Policy for a Multicultural Society: A Comparative Study of Integration, Language and Religious Policy in Five Western European Countries*, Brussels: Migration Policy Group/ IMES.

—   (2010) 'Segmented assimilation and cross national comparative research on the integration of immigrants and their children', *Ethnic and Racial Studies*, 33(7): 1214–1230.

Vertovec, S. (1997) 'Social cohesion and tolerance' in *Key Issues for Research and Policy on Migrants in Cities*, Metropolis Discussion Paper, Toronto: Metropolis.

—   (1999) 'Minority associations, networks and public policies: re-assessing relationships', *Journal of Ethnic and Migration Studies*, 25(1): 21–42.

—   (1999) 'Conceiving and researching transnationalism', *Ethnic and Racial Studies*, 22(2): 447–462.

—   (2007) 'Super-diversity and its implications', *Ethnic and Racial Studies*, 30(6): 1024–1054.

Vincenza Desiderio, M. and Weiner, A. (2014) 'Supporting immigrant integration in Europe? Developing the governance for diaspora engagement', European University Institute, Florence/Migration Policy Institute, Europe, Interact Document, May.

Wagner, A. -C. (1998) *Les nouvelles elites de la mondialisation: une immigration dorée en France*, Paris: Presses Universitaires de France.

Waldinger, R. (1996) *Still the Promised City*, Cambridge, MA: Harvard University Press.

— (2001) *Strangers at the Gates: New Immigrants in Urban America*, Berkeley, CA: University of California Press.

— (2013) 'Crossing borders: international migration in the new century', *Contemporary Sociology: A Journal of Reviews*, 42(3): 349–363.

— (2015) *The Cross-Border Connection: Immigrants, Emigrants and Their Homelands*, Cambridge, MA: Harvard University Press.

Waldinger, R. and FitzGerald, D. (2004) 'Transnationalism in question', *American Journal of Sociology*, 109(5): 1177–1195.

Waldinger, R. and Soehl, T. (2013) 'The political sociology of international migration: borders, boundaries, rights and politics' in Gold, S. J. and Nawyn, S. (eds) *The Routledge International Handbook of Migration Studies*, New York: Routledge, pp. 334–344.

Waldrauch, H. (ed.) (2001) *Die Integration von Einwanderern: Ein Index der Rechtlichen Diskriminierung*, Frankfurt: Campus.

Waldrauch, H. and Hofinger, C. (1997) 'An index to measure the legal obstacles to the integration of migrants', *New Community*, 23(2): 271–286.

Wallace, C. (2002) 'Closing and opening borders: migration and mobility in East-Central Europe', *Journal of Ethnic and Migration Studies*, 28(4): 603–625.

Wallace, C. and Stola, D. (eds) (2001) *Patterns of Migration in Central Europe*, London: Palgrave MacMillan.

Walzer, M. (1983) *Spheres of Justice*, New York: Basic Books.

— (1987) *Interpretation and Social Criticism*, Cambridge, MA: Harvard University. Press.

Watson, J. (ed.) (1977) *Between Two Cultures: Migrants and Minorities in Britain*, Oxford: Basil Blackwell.

Watson, W. (1964) 'Social mobility and social class in industrial communities', in Gluckman, M. (ed.), *Closed Systems and Open Minds: The Limits of Naivety in Social Anthropology*, Edinburgh: Oliver and Boyd, pp. 129–157.

Weber, E. (1976) *Peasants into Frenchmen: The Modernization of Rural France 1870–1914*, Palo Alto, CA: Stanford University Press.

Weil, P. (1991) *La France et ses étrangers: l'aventure d'une politique de l'immigration*, Paris: Calmann-Lévy.

— (1996) 'Nationalities and citizenships: the lessons of the French experience for Germany and Europe' in Cesarani, D. and Fulbrook, M. (eds) *Citizenship, Nationality and Migration in Europe*, London: Routledge, pp. 74–87.

Weiler, J. (1998) *The Constitution of Europe*, Cambridge: Cambridge University Press.

Weiner, M. (1996) 'Determinants of immigrant integration: an international comparative analysis' in Carmon, N. (ed.) *Immigration and Integration in Post-Industrial Societies*, London: Macmillan, pp. 46–64.

Weldon, F. (1989) *Sacred Cows*, London: Chatto & Windus.

Werbner, P. (1999) 'What colour success? Distorting value in studies of ethnic entrepreneuship', *Sociological Review*, 47(3): 548–579.

Wiener, A. (1997) *European Citizenship Practice: Building Institutions of a Non-State*, Boulder, CO: Westview.

Wieviorka, M. (ed.) (1996) *Une société fragmentée: le multi-culturalisme en débat*, Paris: La découverte.

Willis, P. (1981) *Learning to Labor: How Working Class Kids Get Working Class Jobs*, New York: Columbia University Press.

Williams, A. and Baláž, V. (2002) 'Trans-border population mobility at a European crossroads: Slovakia in the shadow of EU accession', *Journal of Ethnic and Migration Studies*, 28(4): 647–664.

Wimmer, A. (2013) *Ethnic Boundary Making: Institutions, Power, Networks*, New York: Oxford University Press.

Wimmer, A. and Glick Schiller, N. (2002) 'Methodological nationalism and beyond: nation-state building, migration and the social sciences', *Global Networks*, 2(4): 301–334.

Winant, H. (2001) *The World is a Ghetto: Race and Democracy Since World War II*, New York: Basic Books.

Worsley, P. (ed.) (1970) *Modern Sociology: Introductory Readings*, London: Penguin.

Wrench, J. (1996) *Preventing Racism at the Workplace*, Dublin: European Foundation for the Improvement of Living and Working Conditions.

Yanasmayan, Z. (2013) *Turkey Entangled with Europe? A Qualitative Exploration of Mobility and Citizenship Accounts of Highly Educated Migrants from Turkey*, University of Leuven, PhD.

Yeoh, B. and Willis, K. (2005) 'Singaporean and British transmigrants in China and the cultural politics of contact zones', *Journal of Ethnic and Migration Studies*, 31(2): 269–285.

Young, I. M. (1990) *Justice and the Politics of Difference*, Princeton, NJ: Princeton University Press.

Zaiceva, A. and Zimmermann, K. (2008) *Scale, Diversity, and Determinants of Labour Migration in Europe*, IZA DP No. 3595, Bonn: Forschungsinstitut zur Zukunft der Arbeit.

Zhou, Y. and Tseng, Y. -F. (2001) 'Regrounding the "ungrounded empires": localization as the geographic catalyst for transnationalism', *Global Networks*, 1(2): 131–153.

Zielonka, J. (2006) *Europe as Empire: The Nature of the Enlarged European Union*, Oxford: Oxford University Press.

Zolberg, A. (1989) 'The next waves: migration theory for a changing world', *International Migration Review*, 23(3): 403–430.

— (1999) 'Matters of state: theorizing immigration policy' in Hirschman, C., Kasinitz, P. and De Wind, J. (eds) *Handbook of International Migration: The American Experience*, New York: Russell Sage.

Zúniga, V. and Hernández-León, R. (eds) (2005) *New Destinations: Mexican Immigration in the United States*, New York: Russell Sage.

Index

and cultural pluralism 54–5
integration discourse/framework
76 n.1
nationalising ideology 114, 182
new institutionalist framework of
53–4, 57–9
minority rights in 94
multiculturalism in x, 22, 25, 26,
27, 31–2, 34–5, 38, 41, 46–7, 52,
58, 59–60
colonial classificatory devices,
use in 29–30, 31, 38, 39, 42
EU context of 39, 59–60
as multi-ethnic Britain 52
and Muslim groups 38, 43–9
race relations, logic of 27, 30, 31,
38, 45–6
Rushdie case analysis 34–5, 44, 47
welfare issues in 38, 52
see also under Islamic migration/
integration
Muslim community 38, 43–9
discrimination claims, use of 48
institutional context, effect on
47–9
opportunism/self-interest in 47
race relations and racism xii, 31, 39,
41, 42, 43, 49–53, 57–9, 90, 110
academic development of 80–1 n.7
English liberalism of 53
and EU legislation 49–53
as EU model 95 n.27
religious/cultural interests,
promotion of 46–7
social mobility analysis *149*, *157*
welfare state 57, 197
rights of 31
see also London
United States of America (USA) 1, 2,
15, 16–17
assimilation 63–5, 67, 84, 88 n.17,
115
dimensions of (Gordon) 63–4

downward assimilation 64, 115,
181
functionalist view of 64, 67
multiculturalist debates on 64–5
use of term in 63–5, 67, 84
African-American population 64
civic culture/democracy ideal in 85
civil rights movement 64, 84, 90
cultural identity, vision of 64–5
hyphenated identities 65
EU comparison 2, 15, 16–17, 174,
175
immigration, effects of in 2, 15–17,
141–3, 175, 193
as 'brain gain' 175
economic dependence on 15–16,
and international students 134,
141, 142
labour discrimination 131, 138–9
Mexican migrants 15, 16, 65,
142–3, 170, 174, 175, 178,
188, 210
nativism, rise of 16
9/11, influence in 142
immigration policy 16, 132, 133,
141–2, 175
global economic pressures on
141, 175
and labour market demand 188
multiple visa categories of 141,
142
and skilled migrants 133, 139,
141–2, 143, 175
security issues 136
shift from formal control 137
temporary H-1B visas 132, 134,
138
integration, use of term in 65, 84
and desegregation 84
migration research 174–5, 199,
202–3
see also Mexican Migration
Project (MMP)

www.ingramcontent.com/pod-product-compliance
Lightning Source LLC
Chambersburg PA
CBHW072057020426
42334CB00017B/1548